How Terrorism Ends

How Terrorism Ends

UNDERSTANDING THE DECLINE AND DEMISE OF TERRORIST CAMPAIGNS

Audrey Kurth Cronin

PRINCETON UNIVERSITY PRESS

PRINCETON AND OXFORD

Published by Princeton University Press, 41 William Street, Princeton, New Jersey 08540
In the United Kingdom: Princeton University Press, 6 Oxford Street, Woodstock,
Oxfordshire OX20 1TW
press.princeton.edu

Fifth printing, and first paperback printing, 2011
Paperback ISBN 978-0-691-15239-4

The Library of Congress has cataloged the cloth edition of this book as follows
Cronin, Audrey Kurth, 1958–
  How terrorism ends : understanding the decline and demise of terrorist campaigns /
Audrey Kurth Cronin.
      p.   cm.
  Includes index.
  ISBN 978-0-691-13948-7 (hbk. : alk. paper) 1. Terrorism. I. Title.
  HV6431.C766 2009
    363.325—dc22   2009004555

British Library Cataloging-in-Publication Data is available

This book has benefited from the generous support of the U.S. Institute of Peace, the
Leverhulme Trust, and the Fell Fund of Oxford University. It contains only the author's
personal views and does not necessarily reflect the position of the U.S. National War
College, the U.S. Department of Defense, or any other U.S. government agency.

This book has been composed in Sabon

Printed on acid-free paper. ∞

Printed in the United States of America

10   9   8   7

For Patrick

Contents

Acknowledgments

THIS BOOK WAS WRITTEN while I was Director of Studies at the Changing Character of War program at Oxford University, 2005–2007. Having spent breathless years in Washington, D.C., operating in the crisis atmosphere following the attacks of September 11th, it was refreshing to get away. Those who were responsible for the protection of the American people were understandably focused on the specter of another attack; but daily threat briefings were not conducive to strategic thought. Without the opportunity to be a part of the Oxford University community, I would never have been able to write this book.

The specific idea for the project first germinated in 2003, when I was the Specialist in Terrorism at the Congressional Research Service. One day a senior senator asked if I could provide a broader historical perspective of al-Qaeda's campaign, as a counterpart to the anxious picture he was getting in dozens of briefings. I responded that al-Qaeda, like its predecessors, would eventually end, and discussed some possible scenarios. Although I was soon swept up in other short-term matters, that conversation started me thinking. In a sense, then, from concept to final publication the book has taken six years. Despite its remaining flaws, the manuscript has gone through five drafts and been cut by 40 percent from its original length. My apologies, dear reader, if you think I should have done a sixth.

Many people helped me along the way. First, I am grateful to my colleagues at the Foreign Affairs, Defense and Trade Division of the Congressional Research Service. I enjoyed the stimulating intellectual environment and mentorship of the excellent analysts with whom I was privileged to work, in particular Larry Nowels, Francis Miko, Carol Migdalovitz, and Rhoda Margesson. Second, I am thankful for my students and colleagues at the National War College, particularly David Auerswald, Frank Mora, Bard O'Neill, Mark Pizzo, Harvey Rishikof, and Omer Taspinar. My friend Karen Wilhelm, Col. (ret.) USAF, slogged through the entire first draft, emailed to her from Oxford. She deserves (another) medal; I am particularly indebted to her for all the late nights and weekends that I spoiled.

In Oxford, I have had a wonderful group of colleagues in the Changing Character of War (CCW) program. The Director, Hew Strachan, Chichele Professor of the History of War at All Souls, could not have been more kind or supportive. I am deeply in his debt. I am also grateful to professors Henry Shue, Guy Goodwin-Gill, and Anne Deighton. My former

DPhil supervisor and dear friend Professor Sir Adam Roberts deserves special mention: his steady support has been crucial not only for this book, but during the ups and downs of my life since I was his student at St. Antony's College, Oxford. I am grateful also to his wife Prinkie, for her thoughtful generosity. The CCW Research Associates Alexandra Gheciu, Thomas Hippler, Patricia Owens, Sarah Percy, and Uwe Steinhoff were great intellectual resources and cherished friends. I benefited from all of the visiting fellows and other CCW senior associates who participated in Oxford seminars, many of whom provided feedback on my work. Notably among them was the late Sir Michael Quinlan, who gently but firmly corrected me more than once—always with a smile, invariably right. It was my honor to know such a brilliant, dedicated public servant. I am also greatly indebted to the Leverhulme Trust, whose financial support made the whole program possible.

The CCW program benefited from being at the Department of Politics and International Relations during my time in Oxford University. I am grateful to Professor Neil MacFarlane, chair of the department, and the support staff, especially Alison Hunt, Marga Lyall, and Maria Moreno, who made my time at Manor Road pleasant. My two superlative research assistants were John Wooding (who has gone on to study law) and Carolina Johnson (now doing a PhD in political science). This book benefited hugely from their rigor, hard work, and ample talents. The Center for International Studies at Oxford also provided valued support, both financial and intellectual. My old friend Andrew Hurrell, now Montague Burton Professor of International Relations, was a great resource for brainstorming about ideas. He and his wife, Yasmin, have been kind and generous friends to my whole family for many years. In addition, I received a grant from the University of Oxford's Fell Fund to support this research, and I am very grateful for that.

There were numerous expert readers and advisors for the manuscript. Brian Michael Jenkins, Adrian Guelke, Michael Brown, and an anonymous reviewer gave me outstanding, detailed, constructive comments. Martha Crenshaw read two different drafts of the manuscript (poor thing), and gave me generous, insightful feedback each time. I am indebted to them all. Others read portions of the book, including Rahul Roy-Chaudury, Mamoun Fandy, Bruce Jentleson, and again Sarah Percy and Alexandra Gheciu.

I have yet to read a perfect book, and I certainly have not written one. None of these people is responsible for the remaining flaws.

Ian Malcolm, my editor at Princeton University Press, believed in this project, was unswerving in his commitment, and gave me excellent advice all along the way. I also thank Director Peter Dougherty, and the editorial board members who approved the publication of this book. Terri

O'Prey was the senior production editor and guided the book through its stages with a steady hand. Other members of the Princeton team included Richard Isomaki, Jennifer Roth, Kimberley Johnson, James Curtis, and Bob Bettendorf: I am grateful to them all. Finally a special note of thanks to Matthew Foley, my wise and patient freelance editor in the UK: I learned about better writing by studying what he had done with my manuscript.

I received a substantial grant from the U.S. Institute of Peace (USIP) in Washington, D.C., to support the research for this book. I am grateful to USIP President, Richard Solomon, a visionary who has guided the institute to its current prominence. Also at USIP Carola Weil, Taylor Seybolt, and Andrew Blum deserve my sincere thanks for their support of this project. The institute does valuable work, and I have been honored to be a part of it.

The International Institute for Strategic Studies in London played a prominent role in supporting this research as well. I was a research associate there, relying heavily on the hard work and good graces of the talented staff. Director-General John Chipman enthusiastically supported this project from the outset, for which I am grateful. Also at the IISS, I am indebted to Caitlin Brannan, Michael Draeger, Katharine Fletcher, Elizabeth Hills, Raffaello Pantucci, Sally Taylor, Hanna Ucko, Adam Ward, and Peter Webb. The energy and talent bottled up in that place amazed me.

To anyone that I have failed to mention here, my apologies and thank you most sincerely.

I am also grateful to my family, including my parents, Ronald and Charlene Kurth, and my brother and sister-in-law, Steve and Lois Kurth, who supported me when I needed it and teased me when I was too dour or serious. My lively and strong-minded children, Christopher and Natalie, kept me laughing, smiling, and questioning myself as only adolescents can. I hope that in some small way this book can contribute to a more hopeful future for them both—they have certainly goaded me on to finish it! Finally, Patrick Cronin deserves his own lengthy paragraph of thanks, but that would only embarrass him. He has read each draft of each chapter, debated each dilemma, cursed each setback, and applauded each success along with me. No aspect of this book would have been possible without his advice, energy, steadfast support, brilliant feedback, and constant encouragement. It is rightfully dedicated to him.

LTTE	Liberation Tigers of Tamil Eelam
LVF	Loyalist Volunteer Force
MEK	Mujahedin-e Khalq
MILF	Moro Islamic Liberation Front
MIPT	Memorial Institute for the Prevention of Terrorism
MK	Umkhonto we Sizwe
MNLF	Moro National Liberation Front
NAP	Armed Nucleus (Nuclei Armati Proletari)
PAC	Pan Africanist Congress
PFLP	Popular Front for the Liberation of Palestine
PFLP-EO	Popular Front for the Liberation of Palestine-External Operations
PFLP-GC	Popular Front for the Liberation of Palestine-General Command
PFLP-SC	Popular Front for the Liberation of Palestine-Special Command
PIJ	Palestinian Islamic Jihad
PIRA	Provisional Irish Republican Army
PKK	Kurdistan Workers' Party (Partiya Karkaren Kurdistan)
PLO	Palestine Liberation Organization
PLOTE	People's Liberation Organisation of Tamil Eelam
RAF	Red Army Faction
RIRA	Real Irish Republican Army
SDLP	Social Democratic and Labour Party
SL	Sendero Luminoso (Shining Path)
TELO	Tamil Eelam Liberation Organisation
TNA	Tamil National Alliance
UDA	Ulster Defence Association
UDA/UFF	Ulster Defence Association/Ulster Freedom Fighters
UDF	Ulster Defence Force
UN	United Nations
UVF	Ulster Volunteer Force

How Terrorism Ends

Introduction

> There are two things that a democratic people will always
> find very difficult, to begin a war and to end it.
> —*Alexis de Tocqueville, 1840*[1]

TERRORIST CAMPAIGNS may seem endless, but they always end. Why?

There is vast historical experience with the decline and ending of terrorist campaigns over the past two centuries, yet few are familiar with it. Analysis of the lessons of that experience is vital if we are to inoculate ourselves against the psychological manipulation of terrorist violence, rise above unfounded assumptions and short-term passions in the wake of attacks, and think strategically about dealing with current and future threats. Modern terrorism draws its power from the nation-state, and the only way to avoid being drawn into a tactical dynamic of attack and counterattack is to understand how individual terrorist campaigns have ended and then drive toward that aim. Viewing this counterterrorism campaign as an endless "long war" is counterproductive and potentially self-defeating. The United States and its allies can use the lessons of how terrorism ends to avoid prior mistakes, save lives, conserve resources, and, most important of all, face their adversaries with a broader strategic perspective so as to win.

This book scrutinizes the closing phases of terrorist campaigns to lay out an intellectual framework that explains the recurrent patterns, common elements, and crucial points leading to their demise. Many people focus on the causes of terrorism, but few direct attention toward its end.[2] Yet, as we shall see, understanding the causes of terrorist campaigns tells us no more about how they actually end than understanding the causes of war explains war termination: naturally the question has some relevance, but it is overshadowed as the conflict unfolds. Objectively analyzing the historical record of how terrorism ends can clarify how best to construct a counterthrust.

Studies of terrorism are often event driven, spurred by attacks and the need to respond to a specific threat. As a result, the bulk of research is descriptive analysis focused on one group, detailing its organization, structure, tactics, leadership, and so on. True to this pattern, since the terrorist attacks of September 11, 2001, there has been an outpouring of research on al-Qaeda, but little attention to analyzing terrorism within a wider body of knowledge. To the extent that broader cross-cutting research has been done, it is largely concerned with root causes and narrow questions having to do with the weapons and methods being used. This bias reflects the strengths of the international security and defense community, which has far more expertise, for example, on nuclear weapons and proliferation than on the Arabic-speaking networks that might use them, on operational methods such as suicide attacks than on the operatives who employ them, and on the causes of wars than on their termination. Yet, just as a war's conclusion may be more portentous for the international system than its beginning, how terrorist campaigns end is vital to understanding the strategic implications of terrorism for the United States and its allies, and the shape of the new era.

In this age of pervasive popular paranoia, three crucial premises underlie the argument. First, like all other terrorist organizations, al-Qaeda *will* end.[3] Although a nebulous movement that both exploits and reflects the current international context, it is not unprecedented in all respects: some aspects are unusual, but many are not. The fear that a small organization with a loose network has metamorphosed into a protracted, monolithic, global ideological struggle without end is misguided and ahistorical. Second, ending terrorist campaigns is difficult. Terrorist movements are often at their most dangerous just before they die. But how terrorist movements end reflects, among other factors, the counterterrorist policies taken against them; it therefore makes sense to formulate those policies with a knowledge of historical precedents and a specific end in mind. Third, in counterterrorism, experience matters. We would not expect military strategists to create an effective battle plan without a solid grounding in military history and familiarity with the canon of strategic thought. This does not mean that war is unchanging, only that prior theory and experience matters. The same principle applies for counterterrorism policy. History provides centuries of practice with terrorist movements, and there are many important parallels with the current threat.

Those who argue that the past is irrelevant to Islamist terrorism are just as wrong as those who argue that al-Qaeda and its associates are little more than the IRA with long beards.[4] The truth lies somewhere in between. Current research on al-Qaeda and its associates fails to analyze them within a broad historical and political context. Yet this context sheds light on crucial assumptions and unanswered questions. What do scholars know about how terrorist movements end? What has worked in previous campaigns? Which of the lessons we can draw from them are relevant to understanding how, and under what circumstances, al-Qaeda will end? These are the questions addressed here.

Radical Islamists will pose a threat to the United States and allied interests for a long time to come. But there is a difference between sporadic and local acts of terrorism by religious extremists, and the coordinated growth of al-Qaeda, with its meticulous planning, mass casualties, and global reach. The strategy to counter this group has comprised tactics such as targeting Osama bin Laden and his top lieutenants, and denying the organization the ability, finances, and territory to regroup. Similar approaches have been employed against other groups. Carefully analyzing comparable situations can shed light on what is required to close out an epoch dominated by al-Qaeda terrorism and help us move firmly toward a post-al-Qaeda world. While studying the history of terrorism is not sufficient to explain the threat we now face, it is certainly necessary if we are to extricate ourselves from the counterproductive policies and narrow doctrinal disputes that are absorbing all of our energies.

The Evolution of Terrorism as a Strategic Threat

Terrorism's efficacy is not just a reflection of al-Qaeda's recent inventiveness, but the culmination of longer-term global trends. Over the course of recent history, terrorism has been consistently tied to the evolving politics and identity of the state, steadily gaining in its capacity to draw power from the Western nation-state and moving from a peripheral nuisance to a central strategic threat. This book does not argue that terrorism is exactly the same as it always has been. The point instead is that meeting the current threat can best be accomplished by exploiting its classic vulnerabilities, thereby diminishing its adverse impact on the evolution of the state and the international system, and reducing the longer-term threat to us all.

Over the course of the twentieth century there developed a conviction that terrorism was a promising method of popular resistance to the nation-state and a valid means of rectifying injustice. Many intellectuals admired the "propaganda of the deed" of the Russian social revolutionaries in the late nineteenth century, but that enthusiasm was swallowed up in a larger wave of uncoordinated violence at the turn of the century. A few decades later, the sweeping force of decolonization after World War II brought with it another dramatic transition in international perceptions, from seeing attacks on innocent civilians as a scourge to be condemned, to again viewing terrorism as a romanticized and promising means of pursuing a cause. The argument in defense of terrorist attacks was that they were a lesser evil than the harms visited upon oppressed peoples by the state—a comparison that in terms of body counts was undeniable. In other words, if a population were desperate enough, it could be excused for using terrorist attacks against others to attain its ends: the questionable legitimacy of the act itself was sometimes overlooked in an enthusiasm for the outcome it was meant to support.[5]

This crucial change in attitudes toward terrorism was accompanied by four other developments. First, publics were increasingly exposed to images of civilians being killed in far-flung places that previously had been thought safe and secure.[6] As media technologies expanded, terrorist operatives were able to make impressions on a wider and wider audience. The powerful psychological and emotional effects of those images became more important politically than the military or tactical benefits of the violence itself—or, indeed, the response to the violence. The strategically targeted assassinations or bombings of major figures that were popular in the latter part of the nineteenth century were replaced in the twentieth by increasingly indiscriminate, publicized attacks on ordinary citizens, who were treated as proxies for their states.[7] Terrorism in the twentieth century thus became a repugnantly voyeuristic phenomenon. Reflecting on the 1972 Munich Olympics massacre, for example, surviving gunman Abu Daoud claimed that the murder of eleven Israeli athletes before the horrified eyes of millions of viewers "force[d] our cause into the homes of 500 million people."[8] The ability to intimidate grew exponentially. If kidnappings or gruesome murders could grab the attention of a broad swath of humanity, so the reasoning went, the organization's cause could achieve international staying power.

The second development was the close connection between terrorist groups and state sponsors. Particularly during the twentieth century, terrorism was often employed as a means of exercising power and indirectly accomplishing policy aims. The formal military standoff of the Cold War resulted in a proliferation of "proxy" organizations, carrying out campaigns underwritten either by Communist or Western states. Proxy war was preferable to central war, and illicit organizations sometimes played sponsors off each other. The Soviet Union, China, East Germany, and Cuba all ran training camps and operated a formidable support network for a wide range of terrorist groups. The United States also supported groups that used terrorist tactics, including the mujahideen in Afghanistan, the contras in Nicaragua, and UNITA in Angola. With the breakup of the Soviet Union, the practice of direct state sponsorship declined internationally, although some states, notably Iran and Syria, continued to actively support terrorist groups. Yet the damage had already been done. State sponsorship not only increased the frequency of terrorism during the twentieth century, but also had a nefarious effect on its evolution: the popular sentiment that in some circumstances terrorism was acceptable was buttressed by evidence that certain state governments clearly thought so too, further degrading the legal and moral norm against targeting civilians for political ends. Condemning terrorism was seen by many as hypocrisy.

A third reason that terrorism's prospects seemed to improve after World War II was that some of its accomplishments were noteworthy. Terrorism extracted well-publicized concessions from states during the middle and late twentieth century. This was especially the case when it came to kidnappings and exchanges of prisoners. As the 1979–80 Iran hostage crisis dramatically demonstrated, helpless hostages held to blackmail elected governments exploited the link between the media, public opinion, and democratic decision-making. Many governments claimed that they would not "negotiate with terrorists." In fact, under the pressure of the publicized murder of innocents, most governments did maintain channels of communications with terrorist groups. Even when governments stood firm, the causes of those carrying out operations were disseminated by news media. The resulting distance between Western governments' public and private policies provided another point of leverage for nonstate groups.

Likewise, campaigns of suicide attacks played a role in compelling states to make territorial concessions, including the withdrawal of American and French military forces from Lebanon in 1984, the withdrawal of Israeli troops from Lebanon in 1985, the withdrawal of Israeli forces from the Gaza Strip and the West Bank in 1994 and 1995, and the recognition of at least a limited degree of autonomy for the Tamils and the Kurds by the Sri Lankan and Turkish governments in the 1990s.[9] The March 2004 train bombing in Madrid, the electoral defeat of the conservative Spanish government three days later, and the subsequent withdrawal of Spanish troops from Iraq, combined to create the impression that terrorism was an effective means of manipulating state behavior. The power of the individual to coerce a state government, especially to withdraw troops from occupied territories, seemed profound, especially in the context of increasing numbers of suicide attacks in Afghanistan and Iraq.

Finally, terrorism's perceived success was linked to greater access to more lethal means of destruction. Technological advances, particularly the increasing sophistication and potency of explosives, seemed to favor the use of terrorist violence in the twentieth century. The attacks of September 11, 2001, were a logical continuation of established trends toward mass casualty attacks using conventional weaponry. Although there were fewer attacks overall in the 1990s than there were in the 1980s, the average number of casualties per incident grew.[10] Notable mass casualty attacks included the downing of aircraft such as Pan Am Flight 103 (1988; 270 killed) and UTA Flight 772 (1989; 171 killed), the bombings of Bombay businesses (1993, 317 killed), the truck bomb that obliterated the Alfred P. Murrah Building in Oklahoma City (1995; 168 killed), and the explosion of a 500-pound bomb at the U.S. embassy in Nairobi, Kenya (1998; 213 killed, over 5,000 injured).[11] The growing death toll gave the impression of a powerful wave of increasingly effective violence—perhaps moving inexorably toward terrorism with chemical, biological, or nuclear weapons.

Over the course of the twentieth century, terrorist organizations gradually demonstrated the ability to kill more people, gain more attention, catalyze government reactions, and act as proxies for powerful sponsors. Many terrorist groups were building reputations as formidable, legitimate actors, some even acquiring sufficient strength to launch insurgent attacks on military forces, prompting states to withdraw from territory. Groups employing a seemingly weak tactic were acquiring the capacity to achieve strategic results.

In the twenty-first century, terrorism has become a threat to the fabric of the Western liberal state, thanks to its lethality and an unprecedented access to powerful weapons, its strong transnational character, its perceived legitimacy (in some quarters), its connection to other types of violence, and its potential to compel states to undermine themselves through their responses. In particular, radical Islamist terrorism is a serious threat, not just because it (and the response to it) can kill significant numbers of civilians, but also because it has the potential to evolve into a broader systemic war that can further change states and even reshape the nature of the state system. This process is well under way. Whether or not it continues on its current trajectory depends on what Western states (especially the United States) do in response, as this terrorism draws its strength, even in some senses its guidance and inspiration, from the flaws of the twentieth-century nation-state.

In facing this threat, the crucial question is not "How are we doing?" but rather "How will it end?" The United States is searching in vain for "metrics" that will provide insight into counterterrorism's progress. The only way that the United States and its allies can effectively respond to twenty-first-century terrorism is to formulate their policy with an understanding of how terrorist campaigns end and then follow a plan built on that understanding. This strategy is what the book explains, analyzes, and advocates. Unless we understand the lessons of terrorism's end, translating the conflict onto grounds where evolving state power is likely to be most effective, there is little hope of recapturing the initiative and marginalizing this threat and those that will follow it. With respect to al-Qaeda, therefore, what is important is not the *next* attack, but the very *last* attack—and probing the lessons of history to construct intelligent policies that drive toward that end.

A WORD ABOUT SCOPE AND TERMS

Terrorism is notoriously difficult to define, in part because the term has evolved and in part because it is associated with an activity that is designed to be subjective. Specialists have devoted hundreds of pages to developing an unassailable definition of the term, only to realize the fruitlessness of their efforts: Terrorism is intended to be a matter of perception and is thus seen differently by different observers and at different points in history.[12] It is a term like *war* or *sovereignty* that will never be defined in words that achieve full international consensus.

But also like *war* and *sovereignty*, the term does not require a perfect consensus. We may not agree that a particular action constitutes terrorism, but certain aspects are fundamental. First, terrorism has a political nature. It involves the commission of outrageous acts designed to precipitate political change.[13] At its root, terrorism is about justice, or at least someone's perception of it, whether man-made or divine. Second, although many other uses of violence are inherently political, including conventional war among states, terrorism is distinguished by its nonstate character—even when terrorists receive military, political, economic, and other means of support from state sources. No moral judgment is intended in this statement. States also employ force for political ends, many of which are perfidious and much worse than terrorism. When state force is used internationally, it is considered an act of war; when it is used domestically, it may be called law enforcement. But treacherous state actions are labeled crimes against humanity, a violation of the laws of war, genocide, and so on—there is an extended vocabulary to describe state uses of force. Not so for nonstate uses of force. Analysts speak of "terror from above" and "terrorism from below."[14] This book only deals with the latter: terrorism by nonstate actors. Third, state use of force is subject to international norms and conventions that may be invoked or at least consulted; terrorists do not abide by international laws or norms and, to maximize the psychological effect of an attack, their activities have a deliberately random quality that plays to an audience, either to intimidate or to inspire. Finally, terrorism has as its purpose the deliberate killing of civilians or noncombatants. It is violence intentionally directed at people who are generally considered to be defenseless, illegitimate targets.

Thus, at a minimum, the concept has the following four characteristics: a fundamentally political nature, the symbolic use of violence, purposeful targeting of noncombatants, carried out by nonstate actors. All of the cases examined in this book have these four features. For the sake of economy, entities that engage primarily in this type of violence will be called *terrorist groups* here.[15]

THE CONCEPTUAL FRAMEWORK

Most people think of terrorism as a dichotomous struggle between a group and a government. However, given their highly leveraged nature, terrorist campaigns involve *three* strategic actors—the group, the government, and the audience—arrayed in a kind of terrorist "triad." More specifically, the three dimensions are the group that uses terrorism to achieve an objective, the government representing the direct target of their attacks, and the audiences who are influenced by the violence. These three broad factors are not arranged in a neat equilateral triangle, but have different effects as circumstances vary, and thus play different parts in the termination of a terrorist campaign. Some pathways of decline are more likely to be under the control of the state, others mainly relate to a nonstate group's activity and its tendency to implode, and still others reflect the influence or opinions of observers. But the only way to understand how terrorism ends is to analyze the dynamic relationship between all three actors: group, target, and audience.

With this triad in mind, six patterns in the decline and ending of campaigns emerge from the history of terrorism: (1) capture or killing the group's leader, (2) entry of the group into a legitimate political process, (3) achievement of the group's aims, (4) implosion or loss of the group's public support, (5) defeat and elimination by brute force, and (6) transition from terrorism into other forms of violence. Each represents a dynamic intersection between government, group, and audience. Patterns of decline reflect factors that are both internal and external to the campaign itself: again, terrorist groups implode for reasons that may or may not be related to measures taken against them. They are not necessarily separate and distinct, as individual case studies of campaigns may reflect more than one dynamic for their demise. Indeed, the presence of several case studies in more than one thematic chapter in this book—for example, Russia and Chechnya, Britain and the IRA, Turkey and the PKK, and Peru and Sendero Luminoso—demonstrates that terrorist campaigns may follow multiple pathways toward decline.

This book is consciously thematic in its treatment of endings, an approach that enables the reader to move beyond the scores of detailed studies of individual terrorist campaigns toward broader conclusions drawn across the seams of current scholarship. Each pathway is defined or explained at the outset of each chapter. While analyzing them separately is in some senses artificial, these six endings—referred to here as *decapitation, negotiation, success, failure, repression,* and *reorientation*—encompass the range of patterns that emerge repeatedly in modern history. The challenge is to understand why, when, and how these pathways affect a campaign's end.

CASE SELECTION

The purpose of this book is to make sense of the most salient general patterns of how terrorist campaigns end—to determine how they work, when they work, and why. The book reflects comparative study of wide-ranging cases from throughout the globe that meet the four criteria for terrorism described, and most effectively reflect each of the patterns under examination here. Cases are thus chosen on the basis of the presence of one of the six independent variables that potentially lead to the demise of a campaign.[16]

Preparation for this study included research into hundreds of groups, from which I drew the several dozen cases that are presented herein greater depth. I have selected major cases rather than minor groups, because there is less information about the latter; and then further reduced them to their core essentials, tracing causal processes (what political scientists call "process-tracing") and presenting structured, focused comparisons of each case.[17] Hence, this is not an encyclopaedic examination of the end of every terrorist group known to exist. Neither is it a collection of complete and definitive historical case studies incorporating every detail of a campaign during its demise. That is not the purpose here. Rather, this book is a thematic analysis intended to be a springboard for further research on pathways out of terrorism, laying out questions as well as answers.

Many of the cases here are drawn from the Memorial Institute for the Prevention of Terrorism (MIPT) Terrorism Knowledge Base, a database that covers more than 800 terrorist organizations in operation after 1968.[18] Because of the temporal bias in that database, the cases in this book tend to be selected from the final years of the twentieth century and the first years of the twenty-first. This tendency was to some degree mitigated by broader historical study of primary and secondary sources on earlier terrorist organizations, but the book does not claim to present a universal analysis of the endings of all groups throughout history, especially pre-1968. While not every relevant case can be included in the descriptive chapters of the book, all are considered in the statistical analyses that underpin the overall arguments made about how terrorism ends, as is thoroughly explained in the appendix. The book considers all types of terrorism, including left-wing, right-wing, ethnonationalist-separatist, and religious or "spiritualist" terrorism, as well as all types of organizational structure, from networked to cellular to traditional hierarchical. It includes cases throughout the world, ranged against a wide array of governments, from democracies to authoritarian states. The goal is to use comparative case study analysis of terrorist campaigns in their final months so as to identify causal paths or common conditions under which terrorism ends.

OVERVIEW OF CHAPTERS

The six patterns of endings form the intellectual scaffolding for the first six chapters of this book. Chapter 1 examines the effects of decapitation in forcing the end of a campaign. It studies the unique role that leaders of terrorist groups play in building the narrative that mobilizes followers, and how that function differs from political and operational leadership in more established organizations. Leaders of groups exercise highly variable degrees of operational control, from acting as figureheads for a cause to planning and carrying out attacks themselves. Naturally, terrorist organizations function in different ways. Even when horizontally structured, however, they have required some type of symbolic head or spokesperson to justify the political change they seek. As a result, counterterrorist campaigns almost always target the top. Chapter 1 then turns to a comparative examination of major cases where the leadership was captured or killed, establishing the conditions under which decapitation has, or has not, led to the demise of campaigns. Unexpectedly, the reaction of key audiences to a leader's removal, more than the structure of the group or the availability of a successor, is the most important influence on the long-term outcome.

Shifting from targeting leaders to talking to them, chapter 2 considers the sensitive questions of whether, how, and under what conditions negotiations successfully end terrorist campaigns. Mapping the vast intellectual gulf between the rhetoric and the reality of countering terrorism, the chapter studies the reasons why governments negotiate and why terrorist leaders talk, demonstrating that idealistic platitudes are as misguided as righteous exhortations about the evils of terrorism. Examining prominent case studies, including the Northern Ireland peace process, the Israeli-Palestinian peace process, and negotiations with the Tamil Tigers, the chapter looks at the immediate effects of negotiations, from the splintering of organizations, to the stopping and starting of talks, to increases in short-term violence. Beyond individual case studies, it examines the recent record of terrorist negotiations, drawing conclusions about the general proportion of groups that talk and the degree to which the talks succeed or fail. The conclusions are surprising: after groups survive past the five- or six-year mark, it is not at all clear that refusing to "talk to terrorists" shortens their campaigns any more than entering into negotiations prolongs them. The chapter concludes by explaining seven key factors that help determine whether negotiations are likely to end terrorism.

Chapters 3 and 4 tackle the conditions under which terrorism ends when a group succeeds or fails outright. Chapter 3 first examines the rare instances where terrorism achieves a group's strategic aims, and the organization either disbands or stops engaging in violence. The goal is to determine why, how, and under what conditions terrorism succeeds and then ends. It dissects what "success" means in terrorist campaigns, particularly the crucial distinction between achievements that perpetuate violence and those that lead to its end. A wide range of statistics demonstrates that terrorist groups typically neither enjoy longevity nor achieve their desired outcome. Sometimes they are cursed with *too much* short-term success, drawing unwanted attention from the wrong con- stituency. I analyze the few cases of strategic success, including Irgun Zvai Le'umi and Umkhonto, groups that used a range of methods in addition to terrorism, scrutinizing the key question of whether terrorist tactics themselves advanced the outcome. My overall conclusion is that, except where a state overreacts or a group becomes strong enough to transition to another form of violence, killing noncombatants through terrorist at- tacks is not a promising way of achieving strategic political ends.

Dealing with failure, the other side of the coin, chapter 4 covers cases where terrorist organizations implode, lose popular support, provoke a widespread backlash, or simply burn out. It is extremely difficult to maintain the momentum of a terrorist campaign. Pressured by police or security forces, many groups make mistakes or simply cannot endure. Sce- narios for implosion covered in this chapter include failing to transition between generations, succumbing to infighting, losing operational con- trol, and accepting exit pathways offered by the government. Case studies range from the left-wing groups of the 1970s to the Colombian group M-19. Marginalization means that popular support for a group or its cause has dissipated, robbing it of a constituency and therefore of resources and recruits. Popular support may be lost for a number of reasons, including apathy, fear of government counteraction, objections to the targets and methods of the terrorists, or the offer of a better alternative. A group may lose touch with the concerns of the masses, or its guiding ideology may become outdated or irrelevant. One of the most common reasons for popular revulsion is terrorist attacks themselves, especially when a group's constituents see them as poorly targeted, ill-considered, or illegitimate. The chapter covers targeting errors committed by groups as disparate as the Italian Red Brigades and the Egyptian group al-Gama'a al-Islamiyya. In short, it focuses on specific cases where terrorism has been self-defeating and explains when, why and how it was so.

Chapters 5 and 6 deal with ending terrorism through the use of force. Chapter 5 concentrates on what the state does militarily in response to terrorist attacks, including using force at home and abroad. The most common response to terrorism, repression, by which I mean the use of overwhelming force, includes intervention, when the threat is located beyond the state's borders, and internal repression, when the threat is mainly domestic. State use of brute force has a long history: at some point in the last two centuries, countries in every part of the world— from Britain to China, Peru to Pakistan, and France to the Philippines— have tried to use force to stamp out terrorism at home or abroad, usually unsuccessfully. Indeed, it is more difficult to find cases where the state did *not* use repressive measures, especially initially. States use force to enhance power and influence others' behavior in specific ways. Most groups aim to gain a foothold by developing a popular following first, and then move toward the eventual accomplishment of their aims. Mobilization is at the heart of the tactic of terrorism, especially in the context of new web-based means of communication; repression works only when it does not catalyze either a larger countermobilization within a constituent community or a demobilization of the government's own support. In any case, a type of learning usually occurs in the use of force; the end is determined by which party learns and adapts most quickly to its failures.

Chapter 6 examines shifts in the tactics used by groups. Terrorist campaigns can end when groups reorient their violence away from a primary reliance on symbolic anticivilian attacks, toward either criminal behavior or more classic types of warfare, including guerrilla attacks, insurgency, or even major conventional war. Many groups engage in criminal behavior, including kidnappings, assassinations, bombings, drug trafficking, and other illegal enterprises to raise funds for their activities. This chapter uses the case studies of the Colombian FARC (Fuerzas Armada Revolucionarias de Colombia) and the Philippine Abu Sayyaf to explore how transitioning to criminal behavior changes the nature of violence and the means to effect its end. This chapter also explores the relationships between terrorism and insurgency: their objective characteristics (numbers, relationship to territory, targeting, etc.) and the practical real-world effects of using such labels. Finally, the chapter discusses situations where terrorist attacks led, or could have led, to a cascade of state actions that spiraled out of control, escalating to major conventional war. It is the connections between these types of violence that hold the real lessons for war in the twenty-first century. The end of "terrorism" is not necessarily the beginning of "peace."

To what extent does any of this apply to the current threat? Chapter 7 addresses that question by exploring which lessons from the decline of earlier terrorist campaigns are relevant to al-Qaeda, and which are not. Al-Qaeda is an amalgam of old and new: it is a product of our times, yet it also echoes historical predecessors, expanding on such factors as the international links and ideological drive of nineteenth-century anarchists, the open-ended aims of Aum Shinrikyo, the brilliance in public communications of the early PLO, and the taste for mass casualty attacks of twentieth-century Sikh separatists or Hezbollah. Yet most analysts miss the connections with its predecessors and are blinded by its solipsistic rhetoric. The chapter begins by tackling aspects of al-Qaeda that are considered unique, such as its fluid organization, methods of recruitment, means of support, and means of communication. Then it turns to the six scenarios for terrorism's end probed in the previous six chapters, relating each specifically to al-Qaeda. The conclusion explores the enduring implications for effective grand strategies against *any* actor that uses terrorism, as well as the broader benefits in understanding and projecting how terrorist campaigns end.

CHAPTER ONE

Decapitation

CATCHING OR KILLING THE LEADER

> [T]he cardinal responsibility of leadership is to identify the
> dominant contradiction at each point of the historical process
> and to work out a central line to resolve it.
>
> —*Mao Tse-tung*[1]

LEADERS OF TERRORIST GROUPS are often captured or killed in the final months of terrorist campaigns, dealing a death blow to the group and precipitating the demise of the movement. But the specific techniques of targeting vary, and the long-term effects of decapitation are inconsistent. While many campaigns end as a result, others barely falter and may even gain strength.[2]

The immediate effects of removing a leader vary, depending on the structure of the organization, the degree to which it fosters a cult of personality, the availability of a viable successor, the nature of its ideology, the political context, and whether the leader was killed or imprisoned. This chapter employs comparative case studies of the arrest or assassination of top leaders so as to probe the complex relationship between their removal and the ending of terrorist campaigns. A clear finding in what follows is that arresting a leader damages a campaign more than killing him does, especially when the jailed leader can be cut off from communicating with his subordinates yet also paraded in humiliation before the public. More surprising, however, a crucial consideration in determining whether the removal of a leader will succeed in ending a campaign is not the type of action a state uses against him or even his operational effectiveness, as we might logically expect, but rather the effects of his removal on potential supporters of both the terrorist campaign and the counterterrorist operation. Killing the leader of a group that has widespread popular support either has no measurable effect or is counterproductive. In this case, as in many others, the reaction of terrorism's multiple audiences proves crucial.

The "propagandist in chief" who explains the rationale for terrorism is important, even if he or she is not directing the group's operations.

Because organizations that rely on terrorist attacks typically lack the strength to employ more legitimate forms of violence, leaders must formulate a narrative that mobilizes followers and has consistent elements. First, whatever the political motivation, terrorist attacks demand a rationale that overshadows moral qualms about targeting civilians. Perception is at the core of terrorism. Without an articulated sense of political purpose, the violence is nothing more than murder and redounds against a group or its cause. Second, supporters must believe that there is no alternative to killing. This requires a carefully crafted story, infused with a sense of urgency. Grievances are a necessary but not sufficient ingredient: potential supporters must also accept that the best, in fact the only, way to remedy the injustice is by killing noncombatants. Third, followers must be convinced that civilians who are killed as a result of terrorist attacks are not really innocent, but represent "the Enemy." Finally, a compelling personality thrusts followers beyond the threshold of personal doubt. The leader convinces them that they are not only right in their actions and convictions, but innocent of the harm that they do.

All of these aspects of terrorism rely upon a carefully crafted argument. Though painful for potential victims to ponder, elements of both attraction and repulsion are essential for terrorist acts to resonate politically and to potentially be "effective." At the core of the apparent moral ambiguities, exploiting the confusing fusion between motivation and method, lies the narrative, which simplifies the complexities of life and presents terrorist attacks as a shortcut nudging history forward toward a new, more desirable reality.

Of course, not all leaders are magnetic ideologues, and not all groups require the creation of a narrative. Some pick up long-standing grievances with a built-in pedigree. Groups that pursue ethnonationalist causes have a ready means of mobilization over territory or identity, and leadership of these groups may be diffuse and discontinuous. Examples include the Basque separatist group ETA (Euskadi Ta Askatasuna) and the FLN (Front de Libération Nationale), whose campaign of violence helped to drive the French from Algeria. Others champion causes that are well-established, such as Hamas (Harakat al-Muqawammah al-Islammiyya) and the PIJ (Palestinian Islamic Jihad). Charismatic leadership is not important to all groups at all stages and at all times. However, when a leader is identifiable, states find it hard to resist targeting him.

Decapitation is an expected impulse for the military or police, but not necessarily for the right reasons. Counterterrorism policy often involves mirror-imaging: police or military organizations tend to view the enemy in their own terms, as a hierarchically structured group that is directed by a leader. Sometimes this is true, but not always. More to the point, in the aftermath of an attack, those responsible for protecting the public naturally find it difficult to take a phlegmatic approach, not least because the people demand a response. Terrorism is emblematic violence that regularly employs a human mouthpiece: it makes sense to attack the head, if only to shut him up, exact vengeance, and demonstrate resolve.

The history of terrorism yields inconsistent outcomes for this approach. Depending on the structure of the group and its evolution, the leader may exercise variable degrees of political and operational control: some are merely figureheads, others carry out attacks themselves. And the role can change: Even leaders who exercise an operational role in the early years of a group may not continue to do so as an organization and its campaign of violence (and response to violence) unfold and evolve. To silence propaganda, to deliver a form of "justice," to remove the operational role of the leader, to undercut the group, to mollify a domestic population, to raise the morale of counterterrorist forces (and the population that supports them), to disrupt impending attacks—all of these are understandable, logical motives for the use of this technique. But when has it worked? When has decapitation been a catalyst for the demise of terrorist groups and their violent campaigns?

WHAT DECAPITATION MEANS

To answer these questions, we must first clarify what we mean by "decapitation." For the purposes of this study, decapitation refers to the removal by arrest or assassination of the top leaders or operational leaders of a group. States that decide to target the leadership of a terrorist campaign must first determine whether the goal is to take the leader alive or not.[3] Decisions about whether to capture or to kill the chief may depend on local conditions; but in their effects on a campaign they embody the classic dichotomy between the so-called law enforcement paradigm and the so-called war paradigm in counterterrorism. Capturing the leader reflects the view that he is a criminal, lawfully entitled to a trial; killing him is treating him as a combatant, fair game for attack. Thus, decisions about whether and how to target leaders reflect philosophies in a state's counterterrorism approach, and historical case studies indicate that these tactical choices have significant strategic implications for the outcomes of campaigns. While this chapter does not attempt a comprehensive statistical analysis of the effects of decapitation on the endings of *all* groups analyzed in this book, it uses comparative case studies to uncover significant findings about the conditions under which decapitation ends terrorism.[4]

THE ARREST OF TOP LEADERS

Capturing a leader, putting him or her on trial and then presumably be-hind bars, emphasizes the rule of law, profiles leaders as criminals, and demonstrates the appropriate application of justice. All else being equal, it is much better to arrest and jail a terrorist leader so that his fate will be demonstrated to the public. There is nothing glamorous about lan-guishing in jail. When terrorism is primarily treated as a criminal offense, either by the state or the international system, the existing legal mecha-nisms for responding to it are reinforced. If there is a fair trial, terrorist violence carried out in the name of a political cause is labeled strictly according to the illegality and immorality of the act. The cause for which the attacks were carried out may or may not have legitimacy, but the violent acts performed in its name definitely do not, as the use of legal mechanisms clearly demonstrates. Treating terrorist leaders as "bandits" also removes the pretext that they are combatants engaged in a war, a claim that can be very useful in perpetuating a cause and establishing a degree of equivalence between states and nonstate groups. Arrest can result in a succession struggle that paralyzes a group, stymied by the fact that the leader is still alive. Most important, interrogating leaders often provides valuable intelligence on the rest of the group. In an ideal world, arresting and prosecuting terrorist operatives is the optimal solution.

Unfortunately this is not an ideal world. As many commentators have pointed out, there are numerous practical disadvantages to arresting and incarcerating terrorist leaders. Sometimes the legal system frees them on technicalities; sometimes they continue to communicate with their follow-ers from prison; sometimes, after serving short sentences, they are released to do more damage.[5] Sometimes they become more radicalized: in May 1970, Ulrike Meinhof helped to free Andreas Baader, who was imprisoned for an act of political arson, and the two then engaged in a campaign of bloody violence.[6] Jailed leaders can also be a huge liability for the citizens of the state holding them. There are scores of recent examples of hostage-taking and blackmail designed to force the release of jailed leaders.

The gloomy anecdotes abound. For example, in 1973, Black September attacked the Saudi Arabian embassy in Khartoum and took 10 hostages, among them the Saudi Arabian ambassador and chargés d'affaires from the United States, Belgium, Saudi Arabia, and Jordan. The gunmen de-manded the release of an ambitious list of prisoners, including 60 Pales-tinian guerrillas held in Jordan, all Arab women jailed in Israel, Sirhan Sirhan, killer of U.S. senator Bobby Kennedy, and members of the Red Army Faction.[7] When U.S. president Richard Nixon refused to negotiate, they shot and killed the Americans and the Belgian.[8] Terrorist kidnappings and blackmailing continued into the 1980s and 1990s. British tourists were killed in Greece and Americans were taken hostage in Beirut because leaders were jailed in their home countries.[9] Ten French citizens died in bombings in Paris because their government was unwilling to release Georges Ibrahim Abdallah, who was sentenced to life imprisonment for the 1982 murder of Lt. Col. Charles Ray, an assistant U.S. military attaché in Paris.[10] In 1994 Maulana Masood Azhar, head of a radical Pakistani group called Harkat-ul-Ansar (later renamed Harkut-ul-Mujahideen, or HuM), was captured. Five years later, he was released in exchange for 155 hostages on a hijacked Indian Airlines plane. Ansar promptly started another group, Jaish-e-Mohammad (linked to al-Qaeda), which carried out attacks in Kashmir.

Major cases of campaigns that were either destroyed or deeply wounded by the incarceration of a charismatic leader include the Peruvian group Sendero Luminoso (Shining Path), the Kurdistan Workers' Party (PKK) in Turkey, the Real Irish Republican Army (RIRA), and Japan's Aum Shinrikyo (Aum). These four cases have been selected for analysis because they represent disparate regions of the world, different motivations, have been thoroughly documented, and yield reliable data about the campaigns before and after their leaders' arrest.

Abimael Guzmán and Sendero Luminoso

Sendero Luminoso's leader Manuel Ruben Abimael Guzmán Reynoso, known as "Guzmán," a highly charismatic philosophy professor, built a powerful Marxist movement through a brutal campaign of executions of peasant leaders. The Shining Path may have been the bloodiest terrorist organization of the twentieth century; its 20-year campaign of violence resulted in the deaths of some 69,000 people.[11] Ironically, Sendero Luminoso began to engage in violence just after extensive land reform and the restoration of democracy in Peru. The earliest attacks involved burning ballot boxes in the 1980 presidential election, the first balloting to occur in Peru in 17 years and the first ever in which there was genuine universal suffrage. At just the time when Peru was emerging from a long and turbulent tradition of military government, Guzmán and Shining Path launched revolutionary operations.[12]

Beginning in the early 1960s, Guzmán had carefully built the movement from his position as a faculty member of the National University of San Cristóbal de Huamanga in Ayacucho, a remote and isolated part of Peru. Although it was an extremely poor, underdeveloped region, public access to university education had increased, enabling Guzmán, whose students were often the first members of their families to attend college, to radicalize a growing cadre of eager young supporters. He capitalized on the opportunity to gather followers among the poor, many of whom had made a precipitous leap from illiteracy to studying philosophy under his guidance.[13] Within the group, Guzmán consolidated his power partly through expelling or executing dissenters, resulting in unquestioned obedience but also a highly individualistic leadership. His goal was to institute a kind of semipermanent, quasi-Maoist Cultural Revolution in Peru. He was good at it: by the early 1990s, Sendero Luminoso had brought Peru to the brink of anarchy.

Guzmán, whose supporters also called him President Gonzalo, was a brilliant strategist and excelled at organization. His elaborate philosophy for violence, developed during 17 years of organizational planning, was known as Gonzalo Thought, a form of Marxist-Leninist theory applied to a Peruvian context, characterized by clear moral codes, rote memorization, and oversimplified ideological explanations for every act.[14] After initiating the movement, Guzmán went underground and was not seen in public. The group used tricks such as symbolically timed blackouts in the capital, Lima, and a huge light-display of a hammer and sickle on Guzmán's birthday to build up the cult of his omnipotence.[15]

During the campaign against Sendero Luminoso, some experts predicted that the organization was so well structured, with such depth of leadership, that capturing or killing Guzmán would not result in its demise.[16] Over the course of the campaign, the Peruvian government repeatedly claimed that Guzmán's key lieutenants had been captured and the organization crippled, only for them to be replaced by new militants. The organization had an elaborate, tiered membership structure, wherein members served first as sympathizers, then activists, then militants, then commanders, and finally members of the central committee.[17] But the leadership also remained highly personalized: new militants were required to write a letter of subjugation, in which they pledged their lives, not only to the cause, but to Guzmán personally.[18] Guzmán's role as the cultish, even deified intellectual leader was never in doubt; nonetheless Sendero Luminoso's organizational agility and depth seemed impenetrable and impersonal.

Guzmán's capture on September 12, 1992, dealt the group a coup de grâce. Guzmán was displayed in a cage, in a striped uniform, recanting and asking his followers to lay down their arms. Much of the top leadership was caught with Guzmán, along with computer disks that reportedly held records of the membership and financing of the movement.[19] In the year following his capture, levels of violence fell by 50 percent and continued to decline thereafter.[20] Guzmán's successor, Oscar Ramirez Duran, known as Feliciano, tried to carry on; but without Guzmán, the group factionalized and the number of active members and passive supporters sharply plummeted, further facilitated by the Peruvian government's offer of an amnesty to remaining fighters.[21] Guzmán was tried in camera

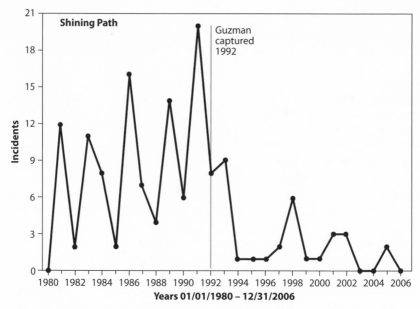

Figure 1.1: Number of Shining Path incidents by year, before and after
Guzmán's capture
Source: MIPT Terrorism Knowledge Base. This and subsequent chapter one
figures are notional graphs only. Because of the way that incidents are counted,
it is possible that the overall number is artificially low. Please see the appendix
for a full explanation.

by a military court and sentenced to life in prison; although many called
for his execution and President Alberto Fujimori urged a constitutional
amendment to allow this (the Peruvian Constitution allowed the death
penalty only in cases of treason during wartime), Guzmán survived.[22] In
subsequent years, Sendero has failed to revive itself as an ideological organization, although a blossoming connection to cocaine trafficking has
some Peruvian officials worried that the group could become a resurgent
threat, particularly if Guzmán (now 73) is allowed to reconnect with followers from his jail cell.[23] (See figure 1.1.)

Abdullah Öcalan and the Kurdistan Workers' Party

The Kurdistan Workers' Party (Partiya Karkaren Kurdistan, or PKK) also
suffered a crushing blow with the capture of its charismatic leader. The
PKK was founded in 1974 by a group of university students in Ankara, led

by Abdullah Öcalan, whose initial goal (like Guzmán's) was to provoke a rural peasant-based Maoist revolution in Turkey. Through a people's uprising against the Turkish state, Öcalan hoped to establish an independent Kurdish homeland, encompassing southeast Turkey, and probably also northern Iraq and parts of Syria and Iran. The PKK was structured as a Marxist-socialist organization, with a general secretary and party assembly.[24] Öcalan built a powerful personal following among the Kurds, many of whom affectionately referred to him as "Apo" (Uncle). He was also popular among the Kurdish diaspora in Western Europe, which represented a potent source of political and financial support.[25] Öcalan fled to Syria in 1980, just before a military coup in Turkey, and then personally directed the activities of the organization variously from Syria, Lebanon, and Europe.

Beginning in 1984, the PKK launched a campaign against the Turkish government that claimed as many as 37,000 lives, first attacking rural areas and then gradually targeting cities in the classic Maoist tradition.[26] In 1999, Öcalan was apprehended in Kenya (apparently as a result of a tip-off from U.S. intelligence).[27] Turkish secret police drugged Öcalan, bundled him onto a plane, and returned him to Istanbul. Photographs of a groggy, disoriented "Apo," slumped over with his hands tied, were broadcast around the world. Öcalan was rapidly tried and sentenced to death. On the day of the sentence, riots and demonstrations broke out among Kurdish populations throughout Europe and Central Asia. Facing his own demise, Öcalan advised his followers to refrain from violence, and the PKK essentially ceased its attacks as a result.[28] With the capture of their idol, PKK supporters transferred their main energies from terrorist attacks to a vigorous campaign to protect his life.

After Öcalan's capture, the group renamed itself KADEK and then KONGRA-GEL (KGK), and insisted that it would engage only in political activities on behalf of the Kurdish minority in Turkey. Attacks declined significantly in the months immediately after Öcalan's capture, and the group held to a cease-fire for five years. (See figure 1.2.) The invasion of Iraq in 2003 and the overthrow of Saddam Hussein provided an opportunity for them to regroup in northern Iraq, however, and in June 2004 a hard-line faction of the PKK/KGK instigated a renewed campaign of violence.[29] In addition to terrorist attacks such as car bombs in Turkish cities, PKK fighters were apparently given sanctuary by Iraqi Kurds and carried out conventional cross-border raids, including a September–October 2007 operation that killed 40 Turkish soldiers. A weeklong Turkish ground incursion into northern Iraq followed in February 2008. The decline sparked by Öcalan's capture, a masterstroke of counterterrorism, was dramatically reversed by broader destabilizing events and conventional hostilities in the region.

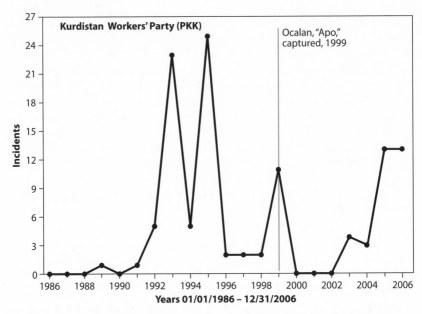

Figure 1.2: Number of PKK incidents by year, before and after Öcalan's capture
Source: MIPT Terrorism Knowledge Base. For the limitations of this database, see the appendix.

Mickey McKevitt and the Real Irish Republican Army

The Real Irish Republican Army (RIRA) split from the Provisional Irish Republican Army in 1997 because it refused to participate in the peace process with the British government. It conducted a series of attacks in 1998, including the notorious Omagh bombing, which killed 29 people (including nine children) and injured over 200. In the wake of the attack, the outrage among the Northern Irish community was so strong that the group declared a cease-fire and claimed that it had only inadvertently killed civilians. In 2000, the RIRA resumed attacks in London and Northern Ireland, focusing on government and military targets.

In March 2001, the group's leader, Michael (Mickey) McKevitt, was arrested. He was sentenced to 30 years in prison. From an Irish prison, McKevitt and 40 other imprisoned members declared that further armed resistance was futile and that the RIRA was "at an end." The group currently has between 100 and 200 active members and has continued to carry out attacks or attempted attacks; however, its activities have significantly declined since McKevitt's arrest.[30] Actions attributed to the RIRA since March 2001 include numerous small-scale attacks on police

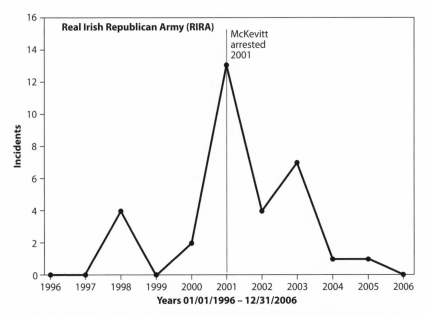

Figure 1.3: Number of RIRA incidents by year, before and after McKevitt's arrest
Source: MIPT Terrorism Knowledge Base. For the limitations of this database, see the appendix.

vehicles and facilities; large arson attacks on retail premises in Newry in August 2006; and sporadic hoaxes and threats.[31] While it is premature to take McKevitt's declaration at face value, the RIRA's decline following his capture is undeniable. (See figure 1.3.)

Shoko Asahara and Aum Shinrikyo

Aum Shinrikyo, currently also known as "Aleph," is essentially a religious cult founded in 1987 by Shoko Asahara, a half-blind Japanese mystic. Asahara (whose real name is Chizuo Matsumoto) claimed that the world was approaching apocalypse. He used an eclectic blend of Tibetan Buddhist, Hindu, Taoist, and Christian thought to attract a following, primarily in Japan but also in Australia, Germany, Russia, Sri Lanka, Taiwan, and the United States. Asahara's argument was that the United States would soon initiate Armageddon by starting World War III against Japan, necessitating extraordinary measures to prepare for the attack. By precipitating the apocalypse, Asahara argued, the group could take over Japan and the world, and hasten the emergence of a new order out of the chaos. Aum Shinrikyo is notorious for its use of sarin gas in an attack on the Tokyo subway on March 20, 1995, which killed 12 people and maimed some 6,000 others. It also tried to mill anthrax (*bacillus anthracis*) into aerosol form.

Asahara was arrested in May 1995 and sentenced to death in February 2004. The trial, which began in April 1996, was a seven-year spectacle, with 12 state-appointed defense lawyers and the defendant refusing to talk. Much of the leadership of the organization was also captured, and senior operatives likewise received death sentences. In the wake of its leader's incarceration (as well as public revelations about Aum's activities) the group shrank dramatically, from approximately 40,000 members worldwide in 1995 to about 1,650 now, mainly in Russia and Japan.[32] (Because the total number of attacks carried out by the group was small, graphical representation of activities before and after Asahara's arrest is unenlightening.)

Assassination or "Targeted Killing"

Holding terrorist leaders is difficult, and a potential liability for the state and its citizens. Should leaders of organizations that carry out terrorist attacks instead be identified, targeted, and killed? Debates over the ethics of agents of democratic states killing terrorist leaders have become increasingly public and spirited in recent years. Naming individuals and ordering their assassination is different from killing an enemy while he is engaged in an attack. It brings the fight to a different level and treads on ambiguous moral territory. It may seem a quaint consideration in these post-9/11 days, but in the wake of the 1975 Church Committee's report criticizing abuses by the U.S. intelligence community, presidents Ford, Carter, and Reagan all signed assassination bans. The most recent, Executive Order 12333, Section 2.12 states, "No person employed by or acting on behalf of the United States Government shall engage in, or conspire to engage in, assassination." Experts disagree about what exactly "assassination" is, whether it applies merely to heads of state or to other leaders killed for political purposes, and whether objections to it are superseded by the state's right to self-defense; but there is clearly something about the deliberate, covert killing of private individuals by the state that makes those who hold democratic values distinctly uncomfortable.[33]

Views differ on how to approach the ethical dilemmas in state-sponsored assassination. From a law enforcement point of view, assassination is extrajudicial killing and forbidden: executing someone without a trial or verdict is illegal. From a war-fighting perspective, the situation is more complex, not least because, in times of war, the laws of armed conflict might grant terrorists protection under the Geneva Conventions. Killing a leader is normally seen as a preemptive act—though it is permissible in "war" to kill enemy commanders.[34] The just-war tradition pushes the bar higher, prohibiting perfidious or treacherous uses of force and allowing assassination only in very restricted situations where it both prevents immediate and grave danger to noncombatants and is a last resort.[35] In practice, many argue that the legitimacy of state assassination depends upon whether a leader is engaged in active combat—that is, directing operations that are imminently dangerous to human life (the so-called ticking bomb scenario)—although very few cases meet this threshold, either because the intelligence is inadequate or because leaders feel that it is too risky to wait until an operation is actively in progress.

To those charged with ending attacks, the debate over whether to kill the leader of a terrorist group may seem a naive intellectual luxury. After all, terrorist groups themselves target not just random civilians but also specific high-profile individuals. Recent examples include former Italian prime minister Aldo Moro (Red Brigades, May 9, 1978), Egyptian president Anwar Sadat (Egyptian Islamic Jihad, October 6, 1981), Israeli prime minister Yitzhak Rabin (November 4, 1995, by Yigal Amir, a Jewish religious extremist), and Indira Gandhi (October 31, 1984, by Sikh security guards). The Liberation Tigers of Tamil Eelam (LTTE) are famous for having assassinated two heads of state, and seriously injuring a third.[36] Groups may even have elements dedicated to this purpose, such as the Sparrow Units of the New People's Army in the Philippines.[37] In the face of such an obvious threat to civilian state leaders, why should counterterrorist forces not employ the same tactics?

There are a number of reasons. Most importantly, governments are at a serious disadvantage, especially in democratic states: public figures cannot be perfectly protected; indeed, a major aspect of most elected politicians' jobs is to be visible and available, making them more vulnerable to assassination than the leaders of clandestine organizations. A policy of assassination may backfire. More to the point, adopting the tactics of terror hardly serves the interests of the state, whose long-term primary goal must be to demonstrate that terrorism is illegitimate and wrong. Engaging in terror tactics strengthens the perception that states have no more right to a monopoly on the use of force, no more legitimacy in how they employ it, than do international and substate entities. As Brian Jenkins observes, if terrorism is always wrong, how can a government's use of terror be right?[38]

In addition, unlike many who carry out terrorist attacks, those who advocate state assassination policies must think not only tactically but strategically, analyzing the second- and third-order effects of the removal of terrorist leaders. Killing a head may result in a fight for succession within a group. Who is the new leader likely to be? The original charismatic leader may indeed be irreplaceable, or he may not: the old cliché about the devil you know applies here. It is not at all guaranteed that the successor will be an improvement, from a counterterrorism perspective. For example, in 1973 Israeli agents killed Mohamed Boudia, an Algerian who had orchestrated Palestinian terrorist operations in Western Europe; he was replaced by Carlos ("the jackal"), who was much worse.[39] If, on the other hand, there is a fight for succession, will it serve the state's interests? Removing the leader may reduce a group's operational efficiency in the short term, or it may raise the stakes for members of a group to "prove" their mettle by carrying out dramatic attacks.

Will the killing of a leader result in martyrdom and more inspired recruits? One fascinating finding about the killing of leaders of Palestinian groups, for example, concludes that killing terrorist leaders increases the level of recruitment to Palestinian terrorist organizations more effectively than the deaths of ordinary Palestinian civilians killed in Israeli attacks.[40] The operational efficiency of groups is clearly reduced when a skilled operative is killed, as the number of highly skilled bomb-makers and other technicians is limited, and the number of casualties per attack apparently goes down;[41] however, in this case the deaths of leaders of groups such as Hamas and Palestinian Islamic Jihad apparently inspired more young Palestinians to join the movement. The so-called terror stock, if such a thing truly exists, is notoriously difficult to determine and measure, but if these findings are correct, then the technique is counterproductive in the long term.

A leader's effectiveness in keeping a group together may actually be useful to counterterrorist efforts. Killing a charismatic leader leaves no one individual for a state to negotiate with. Will the killing of the leader result in the fractionation of the group? This can occur because members of the group suspect each other as informers or because the lack of a firm leader results in proliferating perspectives as to how a group should carry on. Fractionation may be a good or a bad thing. Smaller factions may be weaker and less able to carry out attacks than the original group, or they may be more violent than the mother organization, and more anxious to announce their presence and prove their capacity to kill. Even if a group does not break into factions, the killing of the leader may push it to adapt, and the outcome may be a more effective, flatter, stronger, more decentralized organization that is harder to destroy. In any case, before a group is decapitated, such second- and third-order outcomes must be carefully considered.

The following three historical case studies where leadership was assassinated have been chosen because they represent different regions of the world (Southeast Asia, Europe, and the Middle East) and have accessible data adequate to analyze the policy. States that assassinate terrorist leaders do so in a clandestine manner, making it difficult to compare the situation before and after killings; but I have relied on available databases and media reports to judge the effects. In general, these cases demonstrate that groups adapt to the measures taken against them; the expected linear outcome of an end to a leaderless group may not necessarily follow.

The Philippines' Abu Sayyaf

Abu Sayyaf ("Bearer of the Sword") split from the much larger Philippine group Moro National Liberation Front in the early 1990s. Its leader, Abdurajak Abubakar Janjalani, was a charismatic Islamic scholar who had fought the Soviet Union in Afghanistan; he was killed in a clash with Philippine police in December 1998.[42] His younger brother, Khadaffy Janjalani, immediately replaced him as leader, but he lacked the magnetism and organizational skills of his sibling.[43] After the succession, Abu Sayyaf split into a loosely aligned trio of splinter groups and became essentially a criminal organization. Between 2000 and 2003, it kidnapped tourists who were held and successfully ransomed for very large sums. In 2000, for example, Libya's Mu'ammar Gadhafi publicly paid ransoms of millions of dollars to release captured foreign hostages, resulting in grateful families but irate officials, who saw the massive transfer of wealth as an indirect means of state sponsorship.[44] The Libyan payments bankrolled a dramatic increase in Abu Sayyaf assets, including a formidable fleet of high-speed boats and guns used in drug racketeering. They also made possible further kidnappings, including American missionaries Gracia Burnham and her husband Martin, who was killed in a rescue attempt.

Decapitation in this case contributed to a shift in the group's mission, as it split into smaller factions and subsumed its political agenda to criminal greed. The man most responsible for the Burnhams' kidnapping, Abu Sabaya, was killed in 2002, and another competitor for leadership, Ghalib Andang was captured in December 2003.[45] Abu Sayyaf has also developed important ties with the drug underworld in Manila. But the picture is hazy: while Abu Sayyaf mainly operates as a kind of bandit organization, there is recent involvement in bombings, which some claim reflect ties with more radical Islamist groups. For example, in February 2004, Abu Sayyaf cooperated with another small group, Rajah Solaiman Movement, to bomb a ferry (killing 116 people) and attempted to bomb the U.S. Embassy in Manilla.[46] The next year it claimed credit for attacking the Manila Metro.[47]

Critics argue that the anti–Abu Sayyaf U.S. military presence in the Philippines, beginning with the 2002 deployment of U.S. troops to support the rescue attempt, may have heightened local resentment caused by apprehension that the United States was reestablishing the foothold it had before 1992.[48] Some in the Philippine government believe that the younger Janjalani may be trying to push the group back toward its Islamist roots, but without a strong leader, the group's "ideology" still comes across as little more than clever opportunism.

Russia and Chechen Leaders

Apart from Israel, no country has been more aggressive in assassinating leaders of violent militant groups than Russia.[49] A sampling of Chechen leaders targeted by the Russians includes Ibn Khattab, allegedly poisoned in 2002;[50] former Chechen president Zelimkhan Yandarbiyev, reportedly the chief Middle East fund-raiser, killed by a car bomb in Qatar; Abue Walid (also known as Abdul Aziz Ghamdi); and an Arab militant leader who reportedly became the top Arab field commander after Khattab's death in 2002, killed in a bomb blast in April 2004.[51]

In March 2005, Russian forces killed Aslan Maskhadov, formerly the democratically elected leader of Chechnya and arguably the only Chechen rebel leader with whom Russian president Vladimir Putin might conceivably have held talks.[52] His successor, Abdul Khalim Saidullayev, was killed by Russian special forces in a raid on a Chechen village on June 17, 2006; in remarks posted on a separatist website the week before, Saidullayev had offered to negotiate, but also argued that, as long as Russian forces killed women and children in Chechnya, he could not order an end to terrorism. Lastly, Shamil Basayev, the notorious radical Islamist believed to be responsible for the 2002 Dubrovka theater siege and the 2004 Beslan school attacks, was killed on July 10, 2006.[53] Basayev's death ended his role as leader of the movement and the most visible spokesman in the service of Chechen separatism.

The brutality and comprehensiveness of the Russian assassination campaign in recent years have been unprecedented, matching the growing brutality and gruesomeness of attacks by Chechen operatives. The cycle of targeted killing and retribution seems endless. On the Russian state side, the Kremlin-sanctioned Chechen president Akhmad Kadyrov was killed by rebels in a bomb blast in Grozny on May 9, 2004, dealing a serious blow to the Putin government's plans to install a stable pro-Russia government. Colonel General Valery Baranov, the top Russian field commander in charge of Russian forces in Chechnya, was seriously wounded.[54] In a video Basayev claimed responsibility for Kadyrov's killing and also threatened his son, the current president of the Kremlin-backed government.[55] The cycle of kidnappings and killings then apparently spread to Iraq, where four Russian Embassy officials were kidnapped and killed in 2006.[56]

The conflict has shifted from a bloody separatist insurgency to an increasingly radicalized movement characterized by a grim tactical contest of terrorist attacks and assassinations. Although attacks by Chechen operatives seemed to peak in 2004 and then decline, with the spread of the conflict to the broader Caucasus, at this writing there seems to be no end to the bloodshed in sight.

Israel's "Targeted Killings"

The Israeli government also relies heavily upon the assassination of terrorist leaders, a policy that in recent years has been called "targeted killing."[57] Secret assassinations began early in Israeli's history; in the 1950s, targets included Egyptian intelligence officers, and in the 1960s, German scientists engaged in developing missiles for Nasser's Egypt. Most famously, Operation Wrath of God, personally launched by Israeli prime minister Golda Meir, was a long-term, secret program to kill those who had participated in or planned the September 1972 massacre of Israeli athletes at the Munich Olympics.[58] By avenging the eleven Olympic athletes killed at Munich, Meir sought to demonstrate that Israeli citizens could not be killed with impunity, thereby deterring future attacks. Somewhere in the neighborhood of two dozen alleged Black September operatives and Palestine Liberation Organization planners were killed in the 20-year operation.[59] The same policy of assassinations was turned on Hezbollah in the 1980s, with the killing of leaders such as Sheik Ragheb Harb and Sheik Abbas Musawi. In the mid-1990s, the Israelis targeted Hamas and Palestinian Islamic Jihad leaders, including Fathi Shqaqi and Yahya Ayyash.[60] There are many other examples of suspected or confirmed killings by Israeli agents.[61] But the total number of terrorist leaders killed by the Israeli government in all of these operations over several decades of the twentieth century probably did not exceed 50, although exact figures are not publicly known.

The new century saw a dramatic change in the pace and prominence of Israel's use of assassinations.[62] Beginning in October 2000, with the outbreak of the second, "al-Aqsa" intifada, the Israelis instituted a declared state policy of "targeted killings," with a much more widespread strategy of assassinations in the occupied territories, at first limited to the military wings of terrorist groups such as Hamas, and then against the political leadership as well. The logic was to avoid the large numbers of civilian casualties and the international condemnation that had accompanied the Israeli crackdown in the first intifada by focusing attacks on specific individuals whom the Israeli government believed were the planners and instigators of violence (especially suicide attacks) against Israeli citizens.[63] It was a form of discrimination in the use of military force, supporters argued. Using missile strikes and bombings also was seen as a means of reducing the risk to Israeli soldiers.[64]

The number of targeted killings in the short time that has elapsed since the policy was announced has been unprecedented. According to the Israeli human rights group B'Tselem, about 202 Palestinians have been killed intentionally, with a further 121 unintentionally killed in assassination operations.[65] Because of the controversial nature of the targeted killings policy and the availability of data, the Israeli-Palestinian case has been more thoroughly scrutinized than any other. The policy has been defended as an example of "active self-defense" in response to armed attacks against Israeli civilians, a deliberate application of preemptive targeting applied in responding to an existential danger to the state.[66] Whether it is justified and effective are highly contentious questions, both in Israel and internationally.[67] On the positive side, arguments for targeted killings include keeping terrorist leaders on the run, reducing their ability to carry out attacks, eliminating skilled operatives who are difficult to replace, and providing some means for Israeli political leaders to respond to domestic pressure. Some assert that the strategy also acts as a deterrent to terrorist action.[68] Targeted killings have probably prevented specific strikes and saved some Israeli lives. Many point to evidence of a drop-off in the frequency and lethality of terrorist attacks against Israeli civilians, although determining the degree to which this outcome reflects "targeted killings" as opposed to better defensive measures (such as the border fence separating Palestinian areas from Israeli areas) is impossible.

On the other hand, targeted killings have created Palestinian martyrs, drawn recruits to terrorist organizations, and resulted in retaliatory attacks against Israeli civilians. Some argue that the policy has been counterproductive, leading to an increase in the number of suicide bombers, whereas arrest and incarceration of leaders yields intelligence information and reduces the so-called terror stock.[69] Others point to an actual surge in violent attacks by Islamist groups following decapitation.[70] Deaths of civilians within the Palestinian territories have had a corrosive influence, further alienating Palestinians, undercutting moderates, and undermining the emergence of the healthy social and economic infrastructures necessary for a civil society. The means of gathering information for targeting are also highly controversial: the Israeli government's use of Palestinian collaborators to learn the whereabouts and identities of potential targets can be seen as treacherous killing and thus against international law.[71] Critics claim that targeted killings make the Israeli-Palestinian conflict "morally symmetrical," polarizing the international community and eroding the legitimacy of claims by the Israeli state to oppose terrorist attacks.[72]

Whether the tactical benefits of the policy outweigh the costs is impossible to prove, because there is no way of knowing what might have happened in its absence. Contrary to both proponents and opponents of the policy, an impressive statistical analysis of al-Aqsa uprising violence undertaken by Mohammed Hafez and Joseph Hatfield concludes that "targeted assassinations have no significant impact on rates of Palestinian violence, even when time lags associated with possible retaliations are taken into account." They argue that the military utility of the policy is therefore nil.[73] While some important domestic *political* gains may have been achieved, it is hard to show that targeted killings have made Israel any safer in the long run, and they may have contributed to a broader degeneration in the overall security situation in the region. One might just as convincingly argue that an outcome of Israel's policy of targeted killings has been the election of a Hamas government and the bloody civil strife that followed. In any case, it is difficult to see a way out of the cycle of retribution, as the election of Hamas and the degeneration of the political and economic situation in the Palestinian territories means that there is no credible negotiating partner to settle the struggle over this small area that holds both peoples, and little hope of the emergence of politically effective, moderate Palestinian forces in the near future.

These are just a few contemporary examples where the capture or killing of a leader or leaders proved to be an important element in the state policy directed against organizations that use terrorism. There are many more such cases, both current and historical, including the arrest of leaders in groups as diverse as France's Action Directe, El Salvador's Fuerzas Populares de Liberación, and the U.S. group The Covenant, the Sword and the Arm of the Lord.[74] Decapitation is virtually always irresistible for governments facing a terrorist campaign, and it may result in tactical gains; but while a well-publicized arrest may have devastating effects on a campaign, there is no evidence to support the claim that killing leaders results in strategic success.

How Decapitation Ends Terrorism

In our case studies, the effects of decapitation have varied greatly. Whether the removal of a leader results in the demise of a group or not, the event normally provides critical insight into the depth and nature of a group's popular support and is usually a turning point in its evolution. The degree to which terrorist organizations rely upon a leader, either literally or figuratively, affects the degree to which removing him is likely to devastate the group; however, the level of popular support for the cause is just as important to the outcome. Popular support is the invisible element, the third side to the terrorist "triad" that can confound efforts to kill individuals and make a group virtually immortal. If an organization's cause is well mobilized, enjoying active or passive support among widespread constituencies, then decapitation is unlikely to succeed.

On the basis of the historical record, arresting a leader is more effective in damaging a group than killing him. From a counterterrorism perspective, rather than leading to a group's demise, the killing of the leader can backfire, resulting in increased publicity for the group's cause and the creation of a martyr who attracts many new members to the organization (or even subsequent organizations). Che Guevara is the most famous example.[75] But arrest is hardly a "silver bullet": there are no shortcuts. The capture of a leader is usually the crowning event in a campaign of painstaking military and police work, keeping a leader on the run and eventually forcing him into making a mistake. Capturing a dangerous leader is arguably much harder than killing him; the results reflect the care put into the operation and the local conditions of the arrest. What happens to the leader after arrest is also crucial: a humanely treated, humbled, and deromanticized former "god" can reverse the mobilization for a cause. But even a publicized, humiliating arrest can backfire if the incarcerated leader continues to communicate with the group from prison. Sheikh Omar Abd Al-Rahman (the so-called "blind sheikh"), convicted for conspiracy in the 1993 plot to bomb the World Trade Center, is a notable example.[76] Likewise, having recently reestablished contact with his lawyer, Guzmán may be able to gather future supporters from his Peruvian jail cell.[77] As discussed here, there have also been cases where imprisoned leaders prompt additional violence on the part of remaining members of the group as they try to free them (the Red Army Faction and Al-Rahman again). In any case, if a leader is captured and jailed, it is critical to undermine his or her credibility and cut off inflammatory communications.

Terrorism depends more than other types of violence upon an audience for its symbolic power. Particularly in the twenty-first century context of instantaneous communication through globalized networks, efforts to remove leaders must be seen as complex calculations where the effects on the group can rarely be held in isolation from the effects on the audiences watching the actions of both the state and the group. Short-term gains may be achieved by decapitation, and such tactical considerations are important. Lives may be saved through the disruption of imminent operations. But lives are also saved by the effective interrogation of arrested leaders. Strategic results that undermine established terrorist campaigns demand broader scope and planning. In our case studies, popular support was more effectively reduced by the arrests of leaders than by their demise, and this is why efforts at targeted killing often backfire in the long run.

Cases where a group has halted a campaign following the killing of the leader are difficult to find, and those examined here do not support the conclusion that assassination ends terrorism. Whether or not it is justified, the Israeli government's campaign of targeted killings has certainly not undermined Hamas and other Palestinian groups, for example, and it has probably contributed to the culture of martyrdom that perversely legitimizes terrorist attacks on Israeli civilians to begin with. The Russians have killed virtually every major Chechen leader, but although Chechnya is now firmly under government control, antistate violence has spread to the wider Caucasus, especially Dagestan, Ingushetia, and North Ossetia. (More on this in chapter 5.) Perhaps key variables in whether or not decapitation succeeds are the size of the group and the depth of popular support: Abu Sayyaf, being smaller and more heavily dependent on its strong-man leaders, has also been more damaged by their demise. Of the groups presented here, it has probably also had the least amount of popular support over the years. Yet Abu Sayyaf has hardly faded away, having evolved into a criminal gang that continues to carry out attacks and pose a threat. In short, while anxious populations may want a government to show strength and crush a group, state-directed assassinations result mainly in tactical gains, because the resulting tit-for-tat equivalence between state and group over time hurts the strategic position of the government as the rightful actor.

Perhaps the most important consideration is whether the use of violence to remove the leader will further alienate supporters of both terrorism and counterterrorism, leading to a shift in position on both sides. Although terrorism is always abhorrent and wrong, it is both an ethical and a strategic error to assume that retaliatory killings by those associated with the victims' state are therefore ipso facto legitimate. Sadly, the history of political violence is written differently depending upon who does the writing: the classic defense against treacherous aggression is that the other side started it; the facts of the case may look very different depending upon when one starts the story. Typically, the most compelling justification for terrorism is the argument that the violence was carried out in self-defense, or in an extreme situation. Even when the facts clearly contradict the case made, a leader may be able to convince gullible or frustrated followers that civilian victims brought terrorist attacks upon themselves, as reprisal for some earlier, even fictional, aggression. The terrorist narrative may seem laughable or disgusting to armies or police forces charged with responding in the wake of the murder of women, children, and the elderly. But ignorance of the role that they unwittingly play in the unfolding story can lead to serious strategic mistakes in combating it.

Sometimes the hardest course for a democratic state is to demonstrate tactical restraint: there may be situations where it is best to leave a leader in place. He may be losing legitimacy within the group, a leadership struggle may be under way that will lead to the undermining of the group, or the leader may already have decided to end the campaign by pursuing negotiations or making other conciliatory gestures. He thus may be as needed by the counterterrorist forces as by his followers. Is there a chance that internal rivals will remove him themselves, leading to the fracturing of the group and the bringing of chaos to the campaign? If not, who or what will his replacement be? How will the evolution of the group change as a result of his demise? And what are the opportunity costs of devoting a large percentage of a state's military and intelligence resources to tracking him down? As argued here, unless second- and third-order effects are considered in a wise and dispassionate way, the dynamic of terrorism and counterterrorism may drive events just as easily toward escalation as de-escalation. Human nature is such that, when a cause is well established and has built a significant following, killing its mouthpiece and organizer will not end its viability. Terrorist campaigns do not end through the targeting of the leader unless the state has an accurate and sophisticated understanding of the nature of the group and the narrative that drives it, in addition to a well-thought-out and realistic exit strategy.

CHAPTER TWO

Negotiations

TRANSITION TOWARD A LEGITIMATE POLITICAL PROCESS

> If the implication of his remarks is that we should sit down
> and talk with Mr Adams and the Provisional IRA, I can say
> only that that would turn my stomach and those of most hon.
> Members; we will not do it. . . . I will not talk to people who
> murder indiscriminately.
> —*British prime minister John Major, in reply to a question*
> *from MP Dennis Skinner, November 1, 1993*[1]

DEMOCRACIES DO NOT NEGOTIATE with terrorists. At least that is what
many officials claim. The idea of negotiating with groups that deliberately
kill civilians to advance their political goals is repulsive to most people.
Who could blame them for such a view? Showing firmness in the aftermath of terrorist attacks, refusing to talk to the perpetrators or consider
their demands, could contribute to the future safety of other potential
victims, by removing incentives for future attacks and demonstrating that
terrorism "does not pay."[2] It also avoids granting recognition to a group
that uses terrorism, satisfying a righteous impulse to reject and condemn
such tactics. Holding the line against terrorism makes a great deal of sense,
especially because talks with terrorists are risky and often unsuccessful.[3]

In fact, however, democracies do negotiate with terrorists: virtually all
democratic governments facing terrorist campaigns have been forced to
negotiate at some point, and many have even made concessions, although
of course there are differences in degree.[4] As distasteful as they are, talks
of one form or another have been common. But do negotiations actually
end terrorist campaigns? In answering this question, an overview of recent efforts reveals that idealistic platitudes are as misguided as righteous
exhortations about the evils of terrorism. The data are surprising. After
groups survive past the five- or six-year mark, for example, it is not at
all clear that refusing to "talk to terrorists" shortens their campaigns any
more than entering into negotiations prolongs them. On the other hand,
negotiations can facilitate a process of decline but have rarely been the
single factor driving an outcome. While existing academic research demonstrates that civil wars that include terrorist tactics are the most difficult

to resolve, terrorist campaigns themselves are harder still.[5] As this chapter demonstrates, the record indicates that wise governments approach negotiations as a means to *manage* terrorist violence over the long term, while a group declines and ceases to exist for other reasons.

The following examination of negotiations toward the end of terrorism reveals a number of interesting patterns. First, there is a direct correlation between the age of groups and the probability of talks, but that does not mean that most groups negotiate: only about one in five groups of any age have entered into talks on strategic issues. Second, the vast majority of negotiations that do occur yield neither a clear resolution nor a cessation of the conflict. A common scenario has been for negotiations to drag on, occupying an uncertain middle ground between a stable cease-fire and high levels of violence. Third, about half of the groups that negotiated in recent years have continued to be active in their violence as the talks unfolded, usually at a lower level of intensity and frequency—a factor that governments should take into account before talks begin.

While talks frequently falter along the way, the opening of negotiations engenders a range of effects, from improved capacity for intelligence and the probing of political agendas, to the splintering of organizations on both sides of the table, to the stopping and starting of talks and even increases in short-term violence before the end of a campaign. Groups (or parts of groups) have commonly transitioned to political legitimacy and away from terrorist behavior, at least eventually, after the formal opening of a political process.[6] But the process is typically long, frustrating, painful, full of pitfalls, and even counterproductive, especially when it undermines domestic support and alienates allies.

Direct parallels between inter- or intrastate conflict and terrorism, made by academics and policymakers alike, are often incorrect or misleading when it comes to terrorism. Received wisdom about conflict resolution does not apply to campaigns primarily characterized by terrorism. Identifying and understanding the differences is important if we are to analyze how terrorist campaigns end. Thus, as with its predecessors, this chapter tackles the question of whether, how, and under what conditions negotiations successfully end terrorist campaigns, from the perspectives of both governments and challenger groups. Its conclusions will reveal surprising misconceptions about talking to terrorists.

WHY GOVERNMENTS NEGOTIATE

Whether alone or in coalitions, states negotiate with terrorist groups for reasons that may not be obvious or admitted. These motives may be intertwined, even contradictory: negotiations are not the obverse of fighting terrorism through other means. For all parties, negotiations may be a type of interaction that is seamlessly connected to more violent forms. To expect the opening of talks to mean the instant cessation of violence is naive and sets up expectations among the broader population that are counterproductive. The historical record indicates that terrorist attacks and government countermeasures typically continue to occur, usually at a lower level, into a period of negotiations, but the initiation of contact provides a possible avenue for long-term reductions in terrorist violence along a scale that ends in zero (for a given campaign). States negotiate to search for a potential exit strategy from the violence, and the journey toward an end invariably takes time and encounters setbacks.

Talks that do not get the publicity or attention of media-saturated, high-level parleys provide many potential benefits to governments. It is wrong to use the term *negotiations* as if it describes an indivisible phenomenon, as many types of talks may occur either directly or indirectly, at high (public) or low (deniable) levels, or even through third-party intermediaries. Announcements via mass media can be a mechanism for "talks" and may have dramatic results; the publication of the Unabomber's manifesto, for example, was a concession to him that yielded new intelligence information and resulted in his arrest.[7] Governments or their representatives often directly or indirectly communicate with members of terrorist organizations, even as they may deny that they are doing so: the public may find this distasteful, but in most cases the government (or its proxies) would be shirking their responsibility if they did not.

Potential tactical motivations for such talks are numerous. First, of course, negotiations hold the potential for a short-term pause in the violence, if only because it is harder to carry out effective attacks when efforts are focused elsewhere. Second, making contact with terrorist groups can provide important intelligence, particularly about the structure, hierarchy, or connections among members of a group. This is one reason why intelligence operatives are often used for making early contacts—in addition to the fact that such exchanges can be carried out covertly and disowned if they backfire. Negotiations or talks offer the prospect of disentangling the social networks that enable many terrorist groups to operate. Third, since the primary role of the terrorist leader is to appeal to his actual or potential constituency and build support (as discussed in chapter 1), the strident demands broadcast in the wake of terrorist attacks may bear little relationship to reality—or to what different elements of a group actually want or will settle for. Talking to representatives can yield insights into their motivations, as well as highlight differences among members. Fourth, and related, talks can divide followers of a cause into factions; this tendency may enable a state to hive off different parts of a movement and to turn them against each other. "Divide and conquer" works just as well in counterterrorism as it does in other types of conflict—in some respects, better. At the very least, talks can provide insights into points of divergence in philosophies, tactics, or priorities of members and make the government better able to fashion an effective response. States are mainly overt actors, terrorist groups mainly covert: anything that increases the information available to the government increases its relative strength.

But there is a broader dimension to negotiations as well. Quite apart from the effects that talks have on current members of violent groups, negotiations provide an alternative narrative for passive supporters or neutral observers of a group's activities. Often, terrorist groups assert that there is no alternative to violence, that they have been driven to terrorist attacks out of desperation and a lack of feasible alternatives. Especially if talks are patiently managed, keeping expectations of their outcome in check, negotiations undermine this claim. And supporters and sympathizers are distinct from perpetrators: providing another avenue through which to air grievances, or to appear to do so at least, in itself may undermine a group's support. Negotiations can be a way to shift public opinion within a group's constituency, even if the group itself has no genuine interest in conciliatory measures and the state has no interest in offering them. The attempt alone has appeal. Negotiations can have an impact far beyond the limited scope of their coverage, offering hope for those who might support the cause, confusing the narrative of the group, and complicating its depiction of an evil, intransigent "Enemy." Against a type of violence that thrives on symbolism, and in situations where the group draws on the sympathy of a broader public, carefully managed talks with terrorist groups can be an effective information strategy.

Many people counter that negotiations only add legitimacy to a group or to a cause, demonstrating that terrorism "wins." In this view, a government that has maintained it will not negotiate with terrorists, but is then forced to alter its position, loses credibility.[8] In the face of an inflexible government policy, subsequent talks may seem to demonstrate that groups can "bomb their way" to the negotiating table. Likewise, for a fragile government coalition, negotiations may be so controversial that continued attacks are preferable to collapsed political support or even sectarian discord among factions within the state in response to concessions. Not uncommonly, governments prefer terrorist attacks that can be blamed on others to the disintegration of their own side: as painful as they might be, riding out terrorist attacks may be the least bad alternative for a weak or faltering government. Ending terrorism is not always the top priority.

Even political leaders in strong governments, with a mandate to negotiate, may be harmed by disappointing outcomes if they undertake talks. When strong democratic forces oppose negotiations, terrorist groups may even gain the leverage to determine the fates of governments by their actions.[9] Publicly talking to terrorists can be perilous.

On the other hand, a state's refusal to engage in talks may enhance a group's position with its constituency, strengthening the argument that the only way to get the attention of the state is to commit increasingly violent acts. By refusing to talk about the issue of concern to a group (if there is one), a government is ceding the agenda to the group just as surely as if it engaged in discussion of the issue—either position represents manipulation of the behavior of the state through the killing of its civilians.[10] Martha Crenshaw points out that concessions to terrorist groups have not correlated with subsequent increases in terrorism; Argentina, Austria, Brazil, Uruguay, West Germany, and Italy all met demands, yet saw the level of terrorism decline.[11] Many simplistic assumptions about negotiations with terrorists simply do not hold.

From the government's perspective, the secret seems to be to negotiate officially only when it becomes clear that the cause is gaining popular support or legitimacy, either through the actions of the group or clumsy counteractions by the government—admittedly easier to recognize in retrospect than at the time. In those situations, negotiations may enable the status quo side to recognize select portions of the cause, or segments of the group that it wishes to highlight and strengthen. Except in popular perceptions, negotiations are almost never an all-or-nothing proposition.

WHY GROUPS NEGOTIATE

Perspective matters: the incentives and disincentives to negotiate look different depending on whether you are the sovereign power seeking the status quo (or status quo antebellum), or the challenger entity using terrorism. If the goal is to understand how negotiations end terrorism, then focusing exclusively on the calculus of the incumbent side (as most studies do) analyzes only half of the equation. The behavior of groups that use terrorism is equally important, as are the reactions of the audiences observing them.

Organizations that primarily use terrorist tactics are not the same as small or weak states, or even factions in a civil war or insurgency.[12] Relying on the assumptions and paradigms familiar from the study of negotiations between states, or even between factions in civil disputes, is a mistake. There are important differences between state-to-state coercion and bargaining, and state-to-terrorist group bargaining. For one thing, most states want a conflict to end (albeit on their own terms); it cannot be assumed that most terrorist organizations want this, and many do not. A hallmark of terrorism is confounding society's expectations, making the application of coercion theory problematic. Some groups tie their identities to the attacks they carry out and cannot exist in the absence of violent activities, orchestrating them for personal, cultural, historical, or even psychological reasons. If violence is part of the identity or livelihood of participants themselves, then the likelihood of negotiations resolving a conflict is miniscule. Nor do terrorist groups behave in the same way as factions in a civil war, being typically smaller and less likely to hold territory. Whether effected in the presence of external stabilizing powers or not, cease-fires are difficult to negotiate if one side has little else *besides* its ability to strike.[13] Terrorists signal through surprise violence. Without violence, some feel that they have no voice.

Because groups that rely on terrorism are normally small and clandestine, it can be more difficult to determine what they value, how they make decisions, what the nature of their constituency is, and the structure of their organizations. But it matters. Transferring models that apply to insurgencies or guerrilla warfare may likewise be an error, as terrorists groups may not have the broad support of a constituency. Although they engage in rational strategic behavior, groups are not unitary rational actors. Instead of affecting their cost-benefit calculations, retaliatory attacks in response to terrorism may actually increase their legitimacy, strengthening their support and weakening the state's position. It is difficult to coerce them to negotiate, at least in the same way that states are influenced or coerced. The asymmetry between the state and the group, and between the motivations driving each, may result in counterintuitive outcomes, making talks difficult. The group may have a commitment to violence for its own sake unless it proves counterproductive, usually for reasons that are beyond the state's control.[14]

Most terrorist groups choose not to negotiate at all. By carefully examining 457 groups listed in the MIPT terrorism database (covering most groups active since 1968) that clearly displayed the characteristics of terrorist behavior,[15] for example, we can estimate the proportion of terrorist groups that enter talks.[16] Data on the actions of challengers are notoriously difficult to compile, but by examining the known activities of each organization engaged in terrorist attacks (and screening out those that only carried out one attack, or only attacked economic targets, for example) we are left with the striking conclusion that only about 18 percent of recent terrorist groups have actually negotiated. In other words about 82 percent of the almost five hundred groups that by virtually any scholarly definition engaged in "terrorism" did *not* enter negotiations. (See appendix.)

Even more interesting, however, is analyzing the conditions under which negotiations *have* occurred, and the types of groups that have engaged in talks. Groups that negotiate have longer average life-spans than others, and nearly always pursue (or have in the past pursued) causes related to control of territory. This is as might be expected, since many are connected in some way to the decolonization movement of the latter twentieth century.[17] In our analysis, the mean among group life-spans that have negotiated over their fundamental aims was between 20 and 25 years, while the figure for terrorist groups overall was 5–9 years.[18] There is a strong, statistically significant relationship between participation in negotiations and longer group life-spans. (See table A.3 in the appendix.) But not all of those negotiating groups expressed tangible aims at the outset of their campaigns, often asserting Marxist or socialist claims that only later evolved into arguments over land or self-determination or current government representation that would be potentially resolvable. So popular international ideologies spur and catalyze terrorism, but they do not fully define its goals over time. In determining whether to enter negotiations, therefore, it is crucial for a government to assess what the exact goal of a group is, being sure that the leader's characterization of the aim is not just an exaggerated rallying point, that it is actually shared by those in the group, and that members perceive the violence as furthering their interests.[19] This is indeed a challenge. But the point is that stopping with the strident claims of the leader is not enough.

Nor is stopping with a snapshot of what a group wants. In longstanding groups, it is important to analyze in depth the shifts in aims that commonly occur over a group's lifetime, and to understand the relationship between the group's motivations and their connection with other groups within a broader international context. Logically enough, the data indicate that the longer a group prevails, the more incentive there is for incumbents to consider negotiations—not least because the terrorist campaign is less likely to implode of its own accord. But that incentive also applies to the members of the group, many of whom over time may press for a more tangible, negotiable expression of aims as the movement and its members age and acquire assets.

Another interesting conclusion emerging from the data is that, among those 18 percent that did negotiate, the proportion of talks that clearly failed is small: only about 1 in 10.[20] (See table A.2.) About half of the groups that negotiated continue to be active in their violence, although usually at a lower level of intensity and frequency. On the other hand, in the 9 out of 10 cases where talks have not failed outright, very few groups can be said to have fully achieved their objectives through negotiations. Most groups that negotiate either cease to exist for other reasons (discussed elsewhere in this book) or are still in periodic talks. So, unlike peace treaties at the end of interstate wars, or even some civil wars, the dramatic, publicized "eureka" moment of a negotiated accord rarely occurs. The predominant pattern is for talks to drag on, with interruptions, with setbacks, and without resolution, but also without outright failure.

The priority thus must be to understand a group thoroughly, within its own cultural and historical context, beyond the statements made by its leader or spokesman, and especially beyond a government's own ideological biases, in order to realize the group's priorities, mentality, staying power, and constituency as objectively as possible. Generalizing about the goals of a group, labeling groups "absolutist," or "contingent," or even "rational" or "irrational," may say more about an observer's superficial understanding than it does about the group's inherent logic, negotiability, or staying power. Most important, it says nothing at all about the commitment of every part of a movement to those aims. Much depends on the nature of the group, the breadth of its constituency, the cause it pursues, and the degree to which members deem violence to be advancing that cause. Factions in a civil war or insurgency normally want control over a territory. Terrorist campaigns may or may not seek that end, and often evolve in their aims so as to become either more or less coherent in expressing goals (even to themselves).[21] This is not just a matter of reaching out to moderates (though that may also help), but of disaggregating the threat and determining whether some violent elements might be neutralized. Diligent, dispassionate, apolitical analysis is the capital investment without which negotiations are bankrupt before they begin.

But how have negotiations actually fared in recent history? Under what conditions have they succeeded or failed? To answer these questions, I analyze three diverse case studies drawn from different regions of the world, with different types of groups, different motivations for the use of terrorism, and different outcomes. These are the Northern Ireland peace process, the Israeli-Palestinian peace process, and the Sri Lankan government's talks with the LTTE.

CASE STUDIES OF NEGOTIATIONS

The Northern Ireland Peace Process

The "Troubles" in Northern Ireland arguably had their roots in centuries of conflict and unrest resulting from the settlement of northern areas of Ireland by English and Scots from the sixteenth century onward.[22] The partition of the island in 1921 resulted in the southern 26 counties gaining independence from Great Britain, while the six northeastern counties, with their Protestant majority, remained an autonomous part of the United Kingdom. The twentieth century's emphasis on national self-determination contributed to ongoing tensions in Northern Ireland, where sectarian conflict was never far beneath the surface of daily life, and Northern Ireland Catholics believed that they were discriminated against in housing, welfare, education, and employment by the Protestant majority.

In the 1960s, a Catholic civil rights movement in the region led to political unrest and the introduction of British troops, which in turn enraged Irish nationalists and rejuvenated militant republicanism. The movement soon split into the Official Irish Republican Army and the Provincial Irish Republican Army (PIRA), after which the "Provisionals" quickly became the dominant faction. By early 1970, the PIRA was engaging in an active campaign of violence against the army, countered and complicated by violence by Protestant loyalist (or "unionist") militants.[23] Between 1971 and 1974, the British interned suspected paramilitaries, involving mass roundups of mainly Catholic or republican men, many of whom were beaten or otherwise ill-treated while in prison.[24] The introduction of the internment policy in August 1971 was a pivotal event: violence spiked, from 32 deaths (January–August 1971) to 154 deaths (August 1971–January 1972).[25] An undercutting of moderate political support for the Northern Ireland government, widespread Catholic anger, and an upsurge in sympathy for the PIRA also followed. Practical support manifested itself in a range of ways, from the active recruitment of militants, to the provision of safe houses, food and shelter, and smuggling and storing weapons.[26] As is often the case, the structure of family and kinship in Northern Ireland led to the development of formal and informal pro-IRA and pro-unionist networks. The situation greatly deteriorated in January 1972, when British troops fired on unarmed nationalist demonstrators, killing 13 civilians, some of whom were shot in the back as they fled, in an incident that came to be known as Bloody Sunday. A few months later, believing that the Northern Ireland government was unable to maintain order, the British abolished it and began to administer the territory from London, under a British secretary of state.

The complicated cast of characters who participated in the violence that ensued over the next two decades involved the British government (including the army, locally recruited regiments, and the police force), republican paramilitaries (especially the PIRA, the Irish National Liberation Army, or INLA, and others) and loyalist paramilitaries (including the Ulster Volunteer Force, or UVF, Ulster Defence Association/Ulster Freedom Fighters or UDA/UFF, the Loyalist Volunteer Force, or LVF, and others). More than 3,500 people had lost their lives by the mid-1990s, mainly in shootings and explosions, almost half of them (48 percent) killed by the PIRA alone.[27] The majority of the victims were nonparticipating civilians (54 percent).[28]

The first secret talks began in 1972, and there were seven attempts to reach a political settlement between 1974 and 1994, all of them initiated by the British government and all of them encompassing some version of power-sharing between Catholics and Protestants. Each was stymied by local opposition.[29] Grassroots peace efforts did emerge tentatively: Betty Williams and Mairead Corrigan, founders of the Northern Ireland Peace Movement, even shared the 1976 Nobel Peace Prize; but without an institutional framework (and tainted by charges of collaboration with the British), these efforts ran out of steam. The bloodshed, which took its heaviest toll in the 1970s, continued during subsequent decades.[30]

In 1985, unable to do more than hold the killing to what one British secretary of state for Northern Ireland termed an "acceptable level of violence" (which proved to be about 100 victims per year), the Conservative government of Margaret Thatcher took the unusual step of adjusting its apparently ironclad position on independent governance. Thatcher's government circumvented local actors and entered into an international treaty with the Irish government that, in Article 2, granted Dublin rights of consultation on all aspects of London's Northern Irish policy, through a regular Intergovernmental Conference. In return, the Irish government formally recognized the existence of the State of Northern Ireland and its right to be ruled according to the wishes of a majority of its population. The so-called Anglo-Irish Agreement of 1985 also promised that the British government would make "determined efforts" to agree with the Irish government on matters concerning the troubled territory. When unionist paramilitary forces—the UVF, UDF, and Ulster Resistance—mobilized in opposition to the agreement and began to import arms from South Africa, the British government stood them down, a crucial symbolic snub legitimating the pact.[31] While the agreement was by no means the devolution of sovereignty that Irish nationalists had sought, it did represent a watershed in institutionalizing a formal Irish government consultative role in the fate of Northern Ireland.[32]

The Anglo-Irish Agreement proved to be a foundational step for the peace process that followed during the 1990s.[33] An enhanced role for the Irish government led to a gradual reconsideration of republican strategy. In 1986, Sinn Féin, considered to be the political wing of the Irish Republican Army (IRA), ended its policy of abstention from talks; the following year the Irish government initiated contact. Meetings between Gerry Adams (head of Sinn Féin) and John Hume, leader of the more moderate nationalist Social Democratic and Labour Party (SDLP), began in 1988. Secret talks with the British government, facilitated by the Irish government through a third-party intermediary, Father Alec Reid, also commenced. Loyalists liaised with the British and Irish governments through Protestant clergy, especially Reverend Roy Magee and Archbishop Robin Eames.[34] Catholic and Protestant clergy were crucial intermediaries at this early stage, although the British government, citing the connection between Sinn Féin and the terrorist violence of the PIRA, steadfastly refused to meet openly.[35]

Northern Irish nationalists, especially supporters of the moderate SDLP, began to see potential in working toward reform of local government through political processes rather than republican violence.[36] Recognizing Ireland's interest in a settlement led to an increasingly active role for the Irish government's leader, Taoiseach Albert Reynolds, who in 1993 held talks with Adams and Hume, resulting in a series of joint statements on how the violence might end. The British and Irish governments also issued a Joint Declaration for Peace, lifting the state of emergency and declaring in December 1993 that the British government had "no selfish strategic interests in Northern Ireland."[37] Notably, 1993 was also the first year since 1968 that security forces were not responsible for any deaths in Northern Ireland.[38]

On August 31, 1994, the PIRA declared a cease-fire ("a complete cessation of military activities").[39] However, the months leading up to the cease-fire were intensely violent. The UDA and UVF increased attacks on Catholics, for the first time killing more civilians over the course of the year than the PIRA.[40] Perhaps it was a burst of violence in advance of the cease-fire, for UVF dissidents then split into the more militant Loyalist Volunteer Force (LVF) in 1996. The cease-fire lasted until February 9, 1996, when the PIRA detonated a truck bomb at Canary Wharf in London, killing two people, injuring 39, and causing damaging worth over £85 million.[41] The PIRA issued a statement accusing John Major's government of not engaging effectively enough, although paradoxically on that very day Major had been scheduled to meet Sinn Féin representatives for the first time.[42] This first attempt at a cease-fire had thus been accompanied by a sharp spike in violence beforehand, perhaps because the loyalists feared being sold out in the talks, or they wanted to settle old scores, or to enter the talks from a position of strength; it ended with a major attack on civilians in London. It was born and it died in bloodshed.

Another crucial development in Northern Ireland was a parallel secret war characterized by the gradual, persistent infiltration of the PIRA, UDA, and other groups by British army and civilian intelligence.[43] This covert activity was managed by the Tasking Coordination Group, comprising the SAS, MI5, Special Branch, and Military Intelligence. Intelligence operatives working with the British apparently infiltrated both the republican and unionist forces at the highest levels—even colluding in murders of their opponents, according to a series of inquiries later carried out by Sir John Stevens, the commissioner of the Metropolitan Police.[44] Meanwhile, the PIRA maintained what it called a Civil Administration Team, an internal security unit responsible for often brutal interrogations and killings. The dawning realization of the extent to which they were infiltrated by covert operatives undermined cohesion and operational effectiveness on all sides. In an interview with the BBC, Ulster Unionist leader David Trimble said: "We all know that the authorities try to penetrate the paramilitary organisations. . . . It is the key way in which the paramilitaries have been ground down and brought close to defeat in Northern Ireland."[45]

Meanwhile, the Americans, who had for years turned a blind eye to private Irish-American financial support for the IRA, in the early 1990s began to play an important role. In 1994, the Clinton administration granted Adams a U.S. entry visa, an act that enraged the British. The next year, Clinton visited Northern Ireland, shaking hands with Adams and addressing ecstatic crowds. He named former senator George J. Mitchell as Special Advisor to Northern Ireland, charging him to lead an international commission on arms decommissioning. The Mitchell Commission report recommended a "two track process," with decommissioning running in parallel with negotiations. The report also put forward six steps to nonviolence, later known as the Mitchell Principles. In March 1996, multiparty talks began at Stormont castle, the Belfast headquarters of the secretary of state for Northern Ireland, although Sinn Féin was excluded because of ongoing PIRA violence.

A few months later, on June 15, 1996, the northern English city of Manchester was bombed, injuring more than two hundred people and destroying the entire city center; it was the largest bomb to explode in Britain since World War II.[46] Further violence followed but did not reach the intensity of the 1970s, and the Stormont talks continued.[47] But during the same year, Sinn Féin had received 15.5 percent of the vote in elections for the Northern Ireland Forum, a strong showing that was seen as an endorsement of peace; the political emphasis seemed to be shifting to keeping the talks moving. Following a double murder in June 1997, the *Andersonstown News*, a biweekly pro-republican newspaper in Belfast, editorialized: "It is no longer good enough for the leaders of Sinn Féin to stick to the tired old mantra of refusing to indulge in the politics of condemnation . . . the IRA is fast becoming not a symptom of the problem, as they have liked to portray themselves over the part twenty-five years, but part of the problem itself."[48] On July 20, 1997, a second PIRA ceasefire was announced. The Good Friday Agreement was signed on April 10, 1998, to be overwhelmingly endorsed 12 days later by popular referenda in both Northern Ireland (71 percent support) and the Republic of Ireland (94 percent).[49]

Although the outline of the political settlement seems clear in retrospect, the long and often hesitant steps toward a negotiated solution by no means ended the sectarian violence.[50] Subsequent attacks included the August 1998 Omagh bombing by splinter group the Real IRA (more on this in chapter 5), and an upsurge in sectarian riots and killings between 2000 and 2002.[51] On the republican side, the splinter groups Continuity

IRA and Real IRA continued to threaten the peace process, with about 150 members estimated in each; the loyalist Red Hand Defenders engaged in executions of Catholics, attacks on schoolchildren, and pipe bombings against Catholic homes.[52] The change was thus more a matter of type and degree, with a diffusion of violence accompanied by clear evidence of popular support for the cease-fire through elections to the Northern Ireland Assembly.[53] Indeed, echoing this view, John Darby argued that violence after the Good Friday Agreement stemmed more from social problems, such as continued residential segregation, than the political problems that fueled conflict in past.[54] Despite reservations about the transparency of the process, in 2005 the PIRA announced an end to its armed campaign and asserted that it had decommissioned most of its weaponry.[55] Thus, while it could not be said that peace had come fully to Northern Ireland—and weapons decommissioning, policing, and prisoner releases remained sources of tension—there was a sense that the political process had replaced terrorist attacks as the focal point of popular attention and as the primary vehicle of change.[56]

ANALYSIS OF THE AGREEMENT

According to Adrian Guelke, Michael Cox, and Fiona Stephen, longstanding experts on the Northern Ireland peace process, by the early 1990s both sides of the sectarian divide seemed to sense a stalemate, with a danger that the relentless tit-for-tat violence could escalate.[57] The British shared this view, resolving not to give in to terrorism by withdrawing but also believing that the violence could not be ended by military means. Moreover, the nature of the violence was changing in the early 1990s such that the PIRA seemed to be losing the initiative to the loyalists, who were increasingly attacking working-class Catholics. The unionists, on the other hand, while deeply skeptical of the peace process and the Good Friday Agreement, reached the conclusion that they were in danger of being marginalized and that, given the British government's position, any realistic political alternatives to the settlement were likely to be worse. Thus, as the conflict ground on, militants on both sides of the sectarian divide increasingly seemed to fear losing ground. This fear was heightened on the republican side after the events of September 11 and the sharp reduction in both open and clandestine support for the PIRA from Irish Americans that resulted.

A second important element was the increasing sense of the investment that all sides had in the process. All of the parties found it increasingly difficult to return fully to an armed strategy, although splinter groups continued their armed dissent. Indeed, Darby argues that the agreement was essentially a means to regulate continued paramilitary violence.[58] In 2002, when sectarian killings indeed occurred, they were treated as criminal activity rather than breaches of the overall cease-fire. Thus, attempts by splinter factions to undermine the peace process were treated as attacks not only on unfortunate individuals but also on the peace process itself, which in turn became a means of channeling the outrage.

Third, the Good Friday Agreement was an extraordinarily complex document, containing what might be called areas of deliberate "strategic ambiguity" that enabled participants to describe the accord in terms that were palatable to their constituents. As Roger MacGinty argues, there was something in it for all participants to claim. Pro-unionist negotiators argued that the accord had maintained the union and perpetuated British sovereignty. On the other hand, Sinn Féin argued that its constitutional agenda was being advanced, and highlighted the practical security concessions made and the enhanced role for the party in governing the territory alongside the British government. The hostile reactions by some unionist factions may have made it easier for the republicans to sell the accord to their supporters.[59] Clarity would have been undermining.

Finally, the changing international context within which the negotiations occurred was crucial. Right from the outset local participants on both sides drew parallels with conflicts in other regions, particularly in South Africa and Israel/Palestine.[60] The process commenced shortly after the end of the Cold War, at a time when the postcolonial wave of national self-determination that had spawned scores of ethnonationalist-separatist terrorist movements was waning.[61] During the 1990s, parallels between the ANC and Irish republicanism were consciously drawn, and South African intermediaries intervened with the republicans at a number of points in the process.[62] A sense of a loss of global momentum for separatist causes was accompanied by a reconsideration of the role of the state within the context of ongoing European regional integration.[63] Meanwhile, an economic boom in the Irish Republic demonstrated what peace might hold for Northern Ireland. Just as terrorist movements are sparked by a sense that history is marching in a certain direction and that symbolic violence might nudge events further along, the obverse also holds: when the course of human history seems to be changing, removing a sense of timeliness from a cause and entering a period of economic, political, and ideological transition internationally, there are tangible effects on local terrorist movements. This was the case for Northern Ireland.

The Israeli-Palestinian Peace Process

The example of the Palestine Liberation Organization (and its various factions and offshoots) is often cited by those who assert the futility of negotiating with terrorist groups. As this is written, the prevailing view is that, despite the years of effort put into it, the Israeli-Palestinian peace process is dead. The evolution of international terrorist attacks in the twentieth century, especially the increasing use of suicide attacks, has been heavily influenced by the Israeli-Palestinian experience, at the heart of which have been efforts to end terrorism through negotiations. If negotiations are a time-honored means of ending terrorism, we must analyze why they do not seem to be working in this case.

The reshuffling of international relations that accompanied the end of the Cold War provided a glimmer of hope that the intractable Israeli-Palestinian conflict might be resolvable. The waning years of the bipolar contest saw a sharp increase in popular unrest in the occupied territories. The first intifada, a persistent campaign of civil resistance, strikes, and violent demonstrations, began in December 1987.[64] Young men and children threw stones at the Israelis, reasoning that using firearms would advantage the better-equipped Israeli Defense Forces and that the resulting media coverage would bring to mind David and Goliath. The PLO leadership, by this point exiled in Tunis, eventually regained limited direction of events, but the intifada was not PLO-initiated and, as a result, religiously oriented groups like Hamas and Palestinian Islamic Jihad dramatically gained support among Palestinians.

The Israelis responded ineptly. Unsure how to react to the stone-throwing and other violence of the uprising, Israeli troops initially used live ammunition, killing a large number of Palestinians; by the end of the first year, 311 had been killed by Israeli security forces, including 53 under the age of 17.[65] Approximately 60 percent of stone-throwers were between the ages of six and 14.[66] The Israeli government then instituted a policy of what defense minister Yitzhak Rabin called "might, power and beatings"—a public relations disaster that offered up global images of IDF soldiers beating adolescent rioters with clubs.[67] As a result, the Israelis switched to semilethal rubber or plastic bullets—less photogenic and politically antagonistic, but more likely to kill or injure.

As a grassroots, mass uprising, the intifada gave Palestinians a national identity that they had not had before, returning their cause to the forefront of world attention and resulting in pressure on the Israelis to negotiate over an independent Palestinian state. The intifada likewise changed the nature of Palestinian internal political dynamics, undercutting PLO/Fatah dominance and encouraging the rise of more extreme, radical factions, especially Hamas, spurring the PLO leadership to reassert its authority. The uprising demonstrated that the Palestinians, some half of whom had by now been born under Israeli rule, considered their leadership remote from the daily realities of life in the West Bank and Gaza.[68]

But it also exacted an enormous economic cost and demonstrated that a popular uprising could not, in the end, succeed in forcing the Israelis to abandon the occupied territories. By 1990, the intifada had lost direction and Palestinian groups were fighting mainly among themselves: in 1991, the Israelis killed fewer Palestinians (about 100) than did the Palestinians themselves (about 150).[69] On the Israeli side, the intifada had demonstrated the limitations of military force against popular resistance, with the role of occupier causing serious strain on values and social cohesion.[70] The IDF's killing of so many civilians, particularly children (most of whom admittedly were throwing stones), was shocking and earned worldwide condemnation.[71] Meanwhile, the increasing strength of religious groups such as Hamas made the prospect of negotiating with the PLO seem more promising than the alternatives.[72] In short, both sides found the situation untenable and had strong incentives to talk.

After the 1991 Gulf War, the United States organized a conference in Madrid, the first in a series of efforts to achieve a negotiated peace.[73] Laying the groundwork for the meeting was a delicate process, as the Israeli government refused to talk to any delegation directly linked to the PLO and insisted that Palestinian representatives at the meeting reside in the West Bank and Gaza Strip (thus excluding the exiled PLO leadership). When the parties were finally drawn together, on October 30, 1991, the atmosphere at the talks, under the joint presidency of George H. W. Bush and Mikhail Gorbachev, was cold and unfriendly. Still, initiating public bilateral contacts between the Israelis and the Palestinians was a breakthrough. The shifting international setting was pregnant with possibilities: if the Cold War could end so abruptly, then maybe Middle East peace was actually possible.

Following the conference, the Israelis and Palestinians held a series of secret meetings, initiated first by individuals and then gradually taken up by the Norwegian government. The secrecy of the talks was crucial, especially for the Israelis, who needed a way to circumvent the issue of talking to the PLO, a "terrorist" organization, and to maintain the option of dismissing the talks as unauthorized if necessary. These covert meetings eventually culminated in the Oslo Accords (formally entitled the "Declaration of Principles on Interim Self-Government Arrangements"), finalized in Oslo, Norway, on August 20, 1993, and officially signed in Washington on September 13, 1993. The Oslo Accords followed the outlines of UN Security Council Resolutions 242 and 338, particularly the guiding concept of exchanging land for peace. PLO chairman Yasir Arafat and Israeli prime minister Yitzhak Rabin also exchanged official letters, recognizing the State of Israel and the PLO as the legitimate representative of the Palestinian people. It was a dramatic achievement, a moment of high optimism with all the media buildup of a signing on the White House lawn: not long thereafter Rabin, Arafat, and Israeli Foreign Minister Shimon Peres jointly shared the 1994 Nobel Peace Prize.

Unfortunately, the Israeli polity (or its representatives) were less impressed: after a two-day Knesset debate, in late September 1993, there was a vote of no confidence that was narrowly defeated: 61 voted in favor of the accords, 50 against, with eight abstentions.[74] Similarly, in the Palestinian territories, Fatah (the largest faction of the PLO) accepted the accords, but Hamas, Palestinian Islamic Jihad (PIJ),[75] and the Popular Front for the Liberation of Palestine (PFLP) rejected them and continued to deny Israel's right to exist. The religious nature of the most extreme opposition to the agreements, characterized on the Israeli side by right-wing settler groups such as Gush Emunim (which claims a God-given right to the territory of Eretz Israel), and on the Palestinian side by Hamas and PIJ (which believe that the annihilation of Israel and liberation of all of Palestine are prerequisites for re-creating a pan-Islamic empire), severely complicated efforts to build broad acceptance of the accords.[76] Thus began a pattern that recurred throughout the peace process, with agreements painstakingly reached at the top offered to a general public that seemed to favor "peace" but had less commitment to the specific concessions needed to achieve it.

In December 1992, Palestinian militants killed eight Israeli soldiers. Israeli forces responded with a mass roundup of 1,600 Palestinians, expelling 400 from Israel and interning the rest. Meanwhile, Hamas and Islamic Jihad, newly powerful after the intifada, mounted a series of increasingly deadly suicide attacks. Periods of increased terrorist activity seemed to coincide with elections on both sides, as well as with major events in the peace negotiations. In September 1993, immediately following the announcement of the Oslo Accords, a Palestinian Islamic Jihad suicide bomber crashed an explosives-laden car into a bus carrying soldiers in Gaza, killing only himself; days later, an Israeli settler was stabbed to death by a Hamas squad.

At the top, Arafat's sincerity in pursuing peace was also suspect. A key unresolved question concerned the right of return (or compensation) for the 400,000 Palestinians who fled Israeli territory in 1967, a claim countered by the Israeli assertion that Arabs had expelled a much larger number of Jews from their countries since 1948. In various public speeches, Arafat referred to jihad, the right of return, and the Khudaybiyya armistice agreement of the seventeenth century, which historically has been seen by Islamists as a tactical compromise with the infidels rather than a true peace.[77] To some observers it seemed that the degree to which Arafat was genuinely committed to the peace process, as opposed to tactically playing to his own Palestinian supporters, depended on what language he spoke and who was listening.

Between 1994 and 1996, suicide bombings reached an unprecedented level, with operatives targeting Israeli cities, especially on Fridays and

Sundays.[78] The goal seemed to be to influence the makeup of the Israeli government and to derail the talks, though according to group statements, sometimes the attacks were merely retaliatory. Still, it was obvious that the peace process had brought with it a change in the nature of Palestinian violence, as terrorist attacks took the place of mass uprisings. Robert Pape argues that the campaign of suicide attacks was motivated by Israeli failure to meet deadlines for withdrawal of military forces from the Gaza Strip and West Bank, and that they achieved their intention of pushing Israel to withdraw from territory—an oversimplified explanation of cause and effect that ignores what groups themselves were claiming at the time.[79] In any case, robust Israeli security measures prevent confident assessments about specific timing of attacks, since there were often multiple unsuccessful efforts to stage operations.[80] And Jewish Israelis too committed terrorist attacks. On February 25, 1994, a right-wing Jewish doctor, Baruch Goldstein, turned a machine gun on Palestinian worshippers celebrating Ramadan in the Ibrahimi mosque in Hebron, killing 29 and wounding another 150 before he was overwhelmed and beaten to death by the enraged crowd.[81]

In May 1994, as a result of an Arafat-Rabin agreement reached in Cairo, Israeli forces withdrew from Jericho and most of the Gaza Strip. Arafat returned to Gaza and set up the Palestinian Authority, beginning a five-year period of interim self-rule. A year later, in September 1995, the Oslo II Interim Agreement (or Taba Accords) was signed. Among other things, Israel promised to withdraw from the West Bank six months hence, and the PLO promised to remove from its charter the articles that called for Israel's destruction. In the end, neither promise was fully carried out, but the peace process continued.[82]

Six weeks later, on November 4, 1995, Rabin and Peres were attending a peace rally in Tel Aviv with 100,000 Israeli participants when Rabin was assassinated by a 26-year-old conservative Jewish religious student named Yigal Amir. Killing Rabin dealt a huge blow to the negotiations, not least because it demonstrated extreme and passionate divisions within Israeli society about how to move the country forward.[83] Although the majority of Israelis polled supported the peace process, its specific outcomes always seemed to disappoint: there was consistent divergence between support for "peace" in general, and support for the terms of Oslo (and subsequent accords) in particular—especially in the midst of what seemed to be deteriorating personal security for Israeli citizens. When Peres assumed power in the wake of Rabin's death, he did not call elections and so had no personal mandate to institute the terms of the interim agreements. Nonetheless, in the emotional weeks following the killing, when support for violent measures on the Israeli side plunged, Peres pushed the process forward, ceding Ramallah, Nablus, Bethlehem, and several other important West Bank towns to the Palestinian Authority as called for in the Taba Accords, and ending 30 years of Israeli occupation of those areas.

Still the peace process limped on. Arafat was elected president of the Palestinian Authority in January 1996 in a landslide victory that some commentators interpreted as an indication of popular support among Palestinians for the peace process.[84] But as Kydd and Walter argue, his remarkable electoral mandate removed the argument that he was too weak politically to control Palestinian terrorist attacks.[85] Shortly thereafter, Hamas and the PIJ initiated its deadliest-ever campaign of suicide attacks against Israelis: in February 1996, four suicide bombs detonated in nine days, killing 59 Israelis including a large number of children.[86] The attacks were partly driven by the urge to retaliate for Israel's assassination of Hamas explosives expert Yehiya Ayash (known as "the engineer") in a targeted killing approved by Peres.[87] On March 3, a suicide bomber attacked a Jerusalem bus, killing 18 Israelis and wounding 10. Commenting on the February–March 1996 attacks, U.S. special envoy Dennis Ross said, "Once again terrorist violence precluded agreements, foreclosed options, and dominated the political landscape."[88] They also influenced the outcome of the Israeli elections, which were narrowly won by Benjamin Netanyahu of the right-wing Likud party. According to polls, the Israeli public believed that Likud could better protect Israel's security and interests during the negotiations.[89]

Netanyahu's election win set back the implementation of the Oslo agreements, as may have been intended. He immediately implemented a policy of "reciprocity," by which he meant that Israel would not engage in the peace process unless Arafat cracked down on Palestinian terrorism. Violence did not, however, ease. On May 13, Hamas gunmen opened fire on a bus near Beth El settlement, killing one Israeli and wounding three. In June, PFLP gunmen fired on a car near Zekharya, killing two Israelis. One of the first actions of the new government was to open a tunnel under the al-Aqsa mosque, enraging the Palestinians, who believed that the mosque's foundation was being put at risk. The result was widespread rioting, eventually put down using Israeli helicopter gunships and tanks. After three days of fighting, about 70 Palestinians had been killed and several hundred wounded, while 15 members of the IDF were killed.[90]

Following the so-called tunnel crisis, Clinton summoned Arafat and Netanyahu to Washington in another attempt to salvage the peace process. In January–February 1997, the Israelis completed their pullout from Hebron, while at the same time announcing the building of 6,500 new apartments in East Jerusalem. Nonetheless, improved Palestinian-Israeli security cooperation led to the sharing of important information, particularly about attacks planned by radical groups such as Hamas, and terrorist attacks in Israel declined.

In October 1998, Netanyahu and Arafat met at the Wye River plantation in western Maryland in the United States, to sign an agreement designed to facilitate further implementation of the Oslo Accords. It laid out the steps for a further Israeli evacuation from the West Bank, putting 40 percent of the territory under Palestinian control and specifically committing Arafat to confronting terrorist attacks on Israel. Most interesting, perhaps, the U.S. Central Intelligence Agency was given a role in monitoring Palestinian performance in preventing attacks. Although the outcome only put meat on the bones of the 1993 and 1995 accords, the fact that the talks this time included a member of Likud, not the more liberal Labour Party, raised the hope of broader Israeli popular commitment to the process. There was indeed widespread Israeli public approval for the Wye Agreement (70 percent), but also a high level of opposition among ultra-Orthodox religious parties (66 percent).[91] Israeli cabinet resignations immediately ensued, and Netanyahu's domestic political base began to evaporate. In May 1999, he lost decisively to Ehud Barak of the Labour Party.[92]

The Americans tried again to inject life into the peace process. In July 2000, Clinton invited Barak and Arafat to Camp David for a summit. What unfolded proved to be a high point in the bargaining. Barak offered Arafat virtually complete control over the West Bank and Gaza Strip (although the Palestinian areas would be broken up by Israeli roads and checkpoints), as well as Palestinian sovereignty over East Jerusalem—a meaningful and painful concession.[93] Arafat wanted full sovereignty over the West Bank and Gaza, without conditions, and a return to Israel's pre-1967 borders. Barak countered with a proposal to cede 73 percent of the land to the pre-1967 borders, to grow to 90 percent in 10–25 years, with the caveat that the West Bank would be separated by a road from Jerusalem to the Dead Sea. Arafat refused the proposal. Clinton asked for a counteroffer, but Arafat refused and walked away from the talks.

The second, or "al-Aqsa," intifada began in late September 2000, hard on the heels of a visit by Ariel Sharon (at the time head of the Likud Party) to the Temple Mount.[94] The uprising began with widespread rioting among Israeli Arabs, blocking streets, looting stores, and assaulting Jewish Israeli citizens. The police opened fire, killing 12 Israeli Arabs and one Palestinian. When two Israeli reservists entered the Palestinian city of Ramallah, they were arrested by the Palestinian Authority police. A mob rushed the police station, then brutally beat the two soldiers to death, throwing their mutilated corpses into the street. This gruesome lynching was captured by an Italian film crew; the unforgettable image of an elated young Palestinian man waving his blood-soaked hands out of the station window to a wildly cheering crowd was broadcast to the world. It seemed a symbolic point of no return: although the perpetrators were condemned by Palestinian and Israeli leaders, the event and especially its searing images had an inflammatory effect. The Israelis responded with air strikes by helicopter gunships, pummeling the police station into rubble.[95]

More people were killed in the first two weeks of the al-Aqsa intifada than had died in the first four months of the earlier intifada.[96] Within a month of the Temple Mount visit, 149 Palestinians had been killed, and the cycle of violence was escalating.[97] In February 2001, Barak called elections and lost to Sharon, whose provocative Temple Mount visit and hard-line image seemed to have boosted his popularity. A major campaign of suicide attacks and targeted killings was well under way by the next summer. The Israelis responded with massive force and a reversal of many of the withdrawals that had been achieved during the previous decade. In September 2001, Israeli tanks entered Jericho and Ramallah, and missile attacks were launched on Gaza and Rafah. By October 2001, 90 Palestinians were dead and 2,000 injured.

The failure of the Camp David summit was a watershed for both sides. Shortly thereafter Palestinian attitudes to terrorism changed dramatically. Palestinian support for suicide attacks, which had been about 25 percent throughout the 1990s, soared to 75 percent during the first two years of the al-Aqsa intifada, only falling to 60 percent shortly before the truce of June 29, 2003.[98] There was a huge corresponding increase in the total number of suicide and conventional attacks in 2001–2, well above the maximum number carried out during the 1994–96 campaign.[99] However, following the Israeli withdrawal from Lebanon in May 1999, the shift also reflected a Palestinian belief that suicide attacks by Hezbollah had "worked" and should be emulated. The Israeli Jewish public, on the other hand, believed that the breakdown was the fault of the Palestinians, and that the Israeli position had been too conciliatory anyway. Most opposed the major territorial concessions that had been offered by Barak.[100] Both sides were demoralized: in the four days following the failure of the Camp David summit, a joint Palestinian/Israeli survey of public opinion announced its findings with the following headline: "Israelis and Palestinians support the peace process and reconciliation but are less willing to pay the price than their leaders."[101]

TERRORISM AND THE TALKS

According to Ross, the foundational bargain underlying the Oslo Accords was that the Palestinians would provide security from attacks for the Israelis, and the Israelis would cede control over daily life to the Palestinians. Yet as the terrorist attacks of Hamas and Islamic Jihad continued, Israel dragged its feet, and the Palestinian economy collapsed. Neither side of the bargain was being kept. Arafat avoided taking responsibility for confronting the violence, sometimes blaming attacks on Israeli agents even as Hamas or PIJ were publicly claiming "credit," and the Rabin government imposed closures on the Palestinian territories. As early as autumn 1994, Ross argues, violence was beginning to unravel the Oslo Accords.

One of the most discouraging elements of this case is the apparent correlation between terrorist attacks and milestones in the negotiations. There were three waves of suicide attacks associated with the immediate period around the peace process: the first, a small increase from 1988 to 1990, during the first intifada, was orchestrated by Hezbollah, and happened mainly on Lebanese territory; the second, between 1994 and 1996, coincided with the implementation of the Oslo agreements and the institution of the Palestinian Authority; and the third (by far the largest), in 2001–2, followed the failure of the 2000 Camp David summit.[102] Yet the relationship between peace talks and violence must not be oversimplified: Hamas's campaign of attacks began in 1992, *before* the signing of the Oslo Accords in 1993, so the connection was one of degree, not cause and effect.

Nonetheless, the role of spoilers was important in this case, at least during the early to mid-1990s. Hamas and Palestinian Islamic Jihad increased the number of attacks at times when they believed they could drive the two sides in the peace process apart. The Israeli public was angry and increasingly insecure as a direct result of the attacks, but most demoralizing was the sense that the Palestinian Authority was unable or unwilling to halt them. One study posits that the reason why the peace process persisted in the early 1990s was that the Israelis considered Arafat too weak to stop attacks by extremist groups; but that in the second intifada Arafat's perceived greater strength ate away at the goodwill of Israeli leaders, who believed that he had the ability to stop attacks, but chose not to.[103] Interestingly, the earliest violence of the al-Aqsa intifada was not carried out by radical groups; over 80 percent of attacks were carried out by traditional secular organizations such as al-Fatah and Tanzim, factions of his own organization over which Arafat should have had the most control.[104] The argument put forth by Mia Bloom, that there was a form of competition going on between Palestinian factions for control of the insurgency, is supported by the data, which shows both conventional and suicide attacks being carried out by six different, competing Palestinian organizations—all after the peace process had already failed.[105] Terrorism during the second intifada therefore does not seem to be directly related to the peace process, but instead to internal dynamics among competing Palestinian factions.

Judging the outcome of the peace process directly according to the situation that held when each phase began is an oversimplification. The choice to enter negotiations itself changed the dynamics of the violence. The violence would probably have proceeded in its absence, and probably at higher levels. The process itself may have engendered attacks, but the absence of a process might also have done so. Thus the real question is not whether violence went up or down over the course of the negotiations, but—a much more complex assessment—whether it was higher or lower than what it *would have been* in the absence of talks.[106]

As for the peace process itself, the Israeli government and its Palestinian negotiating partners tried to disconnect the talks from the dynamic of terrorism and counterterrorism—an approach opposite to that adopted in Northern Ireland, where the popular backlash against terrorist attacks was exploited to propel the negotiations forward. The disparity in approaches was not just a matter of policy, but also reflected contrasting commitments by the two populations, their sense of gain, desirable alternatives, and willingness to make sacrifices in exchange for peace (as opposed to a competing aspiration). The Palestinians began to see terrorist attacks as complementary to the peace process instead of at odds with it, because they believed that negotiations alone would never lead to Israel's withdrawal. Polls indicate that the peace process was not perceived as at odds with the violence, but rather as another dimension for carrying it out, even as the much-desired benefits of heightened security for Israelis and better daily life for Palestinians continued to elude them both. As Luca Ricolfi points out, throughout 2000, Hamas was inactive and there was no sign of terrorist attacks until *after* the failure of the Camp David summit during the summer and the outbreak of the al-Aqsa intifada in the fall.[107] Thus, the usual conclusions about this case do not stand up: although the peace process at times contributed to short-term increases and decreases in violence, terrorism did not directly destroy it.

The LTTE (Liberation Tigers of Tamil Eelam, or Tamil Tigers)

Alternating talking and fighting has characterized the conflict in Sri Lanka from the outset. This is a classic example of repeated attempts at negotiations that have stopped and started, interrupted by shocking large-scale violence and high-profile assassinations, and characterized mainly by their apparent futility. Framing this case only as terrorism is not accurate, as the conflict is as much a large insurgency against the Sri Lankan military as it is a classic terrorist campaign targeting civilians. The LTTE itself likes to claim that it attacks only military targets, but even the most casual review of the group's history shows this claim to be false. The case is included in this chapter because of the LTTE's extensive and notorious use of terrorist tactics, especially suicide attacks by their elite Black Tigers unit, perhaps the most advanced practitioners of this gruesome art in the world.[108] And for good or ill, it is also a case that was strongly affected by the international counterterrorism initiatives put in place after 2001. Whatever else it may be, the LTTE's long-standing, deliberate, and extensive targeting of civilians earns it the label of a terrorist group.

In 2001, the Tamil Tigers and the Sri Lankan government entered into a cease-fire, raising hopes of an end to the longest armed conflict in South Asia and one of the bloodiest separatist campaigns of the late twentieth century. Over the course of the conflict, approximately 70,000 people had been killed (about two-thirds of whom were civilians) and two million displaced.[109] While talks and cease-fires had been tried on four earlier occasions, this time negotiations were initiated by the Tamil Tigers themselves. They were brokered by the Norwegian government, adding to the optimism about their prospects. The Sri Lankan government was almost a passive partner in the initial phases.[110] But in tandem with unprecedented movements toward peace, what gradually unfolded over the next four years was intense political in-fighting on the Sri Lankan government's side, defections from the LTTE, and eventually large-scale military conflict, with more than 4,000 people killed during 2006 alone, many of them civilians, as well as at least 200,000 internally displaced.

Like Northern Ireland, this is a classic case of a majority group showing too little regard for the minority. The origins of the LTTE lie in the 1972 redefinition of Sri Lanka (formerly Ceylon). Sinhalese Buddhists dominated the new country, slighting the Tamil Hindu minority in the North and East, not least by designating Sinhala as the official language. The Tamils wanted devolution of power in their regions, but for fear of breaking up the country, this request was refused. Charismatic Tamil leader Velupillai Prabhakaran founded the Tamil New Tigers (TNT) in the same year, renaming the group the Liberation Tigers of Tamil Eelam (LTTE) four years later. The LTTE's first act was to assassinate Alfred Duriappal, the mayor of Jaffna, in revenge for the death of nine civilians at the hands of the police during the 1974 World Tamil Conference in Jaffna.[111]

In July 1983, Tamils murdered 13 Sinhalese soldiers, sparking widespread pogroms—"Black July"—in which about 3,000 Tamils were killed.[112] Instead of reconciliation, the government responded by enacting another amendment to the constitution in which all members of parliament were required to disavow separatism and declare their allegiance to the Sri Lankan state. Outraged, the 16 Tamil MPs vacated their seats. Over 30 militant Tamil groups sprang up to fill the political vacuum, though the field of competitors soon narrowed to five major players.[113] Internecine warfare among those groups began in 1986. Through ruthless purges and cold-blooded murders, Prabhakaran prevailed, and the LTTE were dominant by 1987. As if to announce their status, the Black Tigers carried out their first suicide attack that year, when an LTTE truck bomb killed 110 civilians in Colombo.

The first talks with the government took place in July 1985, but quickly failed. With the conflict between the LTTE and the government escalating, neighboring India, in sympathy for its fellow Hindus, provided an air drop to starving Tamils in the besieged town of Jaffna. An accord between India and Sri Lanka followed on July 29, 1987, calling for Indian intervention between the two parties. Responding to Indian pressure, Sri Lanka granted official status to the Tamil language, and the Indians agreed to provide a peacekeeping force to enforce LTTE disarmament. The accord was a disaster for both governments: the Indian force (which withdrew in 1990) failed to subdue the LTTE, and the group used the hiatus to eliminate dissent among the Tamils and consolidate its position. Thus began the LTTE's pattern of periodically using talks and agreements to buy time, kill off rivals, and enhance itself.

A second round of talks in 1989 resulted in a tentative cease-fire.[114] Hostilities between the government and the LTTE resumed in 1990, and there were blood-baths on both sides. The LTTE forced over six hundred Sri Lankan policemen in the North to surrender, and then murdered them.[115] The Sri Lankan Air Force bombed the Naguleswaram temple, one of the holiest Hindu Shiva temples in Sri Lanka, killing 180 Tamil civilians, including five infants.[116] The killing became astonishingly brutal. The largest battle of the conflict occurred in July 1991, when the Sri Lankan army's base at Elephant Pass, which controls access to the Jaffna peninsula, was surrounded by 5,000 LTTE troops. Two thousand died on both sides in a monthlong siege. The Sri Lankan government responded with an embargo on food and medicine in the North and East, punishing the Tamil people even as the fighting continued and casualties mounted.

In 1994, the Sri Lankan governing party, the UNP (United National Party), was defeated by the Sri Lanka Freedom Party.[117] The party had run on a peace platform, and new president Chandrika Kumaratunga immediately extended an offer of peace talks. The result was a third cease-fire, in 1995, monitored by international peace committees comprising government and LTTE representatives, and chaired by representatives of the governments of Canada, Norway, and the Netherlands. These efforts also failed. After four rounds of talks and 35 letters exchanged, the LTTE again broke the cease-fire in April 1995.[118] The killing gathered pace as the year continued, including a stepped-up terrorist campaign.[119] In January 1996, the LTTE's deadliest suicide bombing ever was launched against the Central Bank in Colombo: 90 were killed and 1,400 injured. A second bombing six months later killed more than 70 people. Further government offers to negotiate were rejected.

The LTTE's hit-and-run tactics continued, alternating peace talks and bouts of terrorist violence, interspersed with conventional clashes between Sri Lankan and LTTE forces. On the last day of her campaign for reelection in 2000, Kumaratunga herself was almost killed by an LTTE suicide bomber; she lost an eye in the attack, while the explosion killed 26 others and injured more than one hundred.[120] The LTTE unilaterally declared another cease-fire in December 2000, which lasted until April 2001, when the army launched a major, but unsuccessful, offensive code-named Rod of Fire, whose aim was to recapture Elephant Pass.

Finally, in December 2001, in an apparent breakthrough, the Tamil Tigers announced their willingness to explore political devolution measures that safeguarded Tamil rights as part of a united Sri Lanka.[121] This seemed a watershed, indicating a willingness to consider an arrangement short of full independence for the Tamil regions. The Tamil Tigers declared another unilateral cease-fire in December 2001, and this act was reciprocated by the government. Both parties signed a memorandum of understanding stating mutual respect for existing frontiers. Norway agreed to mediate the process, and about seventy representatives from Nordic countries arrived to monitor the cease-fire.[122] The situation seemed more promising than ever before, especially as the financial support for the LTTE that had always flowed from the Tamil diaspora in North America and Europe had begun to dry up, pushing the group to negotiate. The government lifted the ban on the LTTE, commercial air flights to Jaffna began, roads were opened through Tamil territory, and civilian traffic began to flow again for the first time in many years.

Meanwhile, crucial developments occurred on the Sri Lankan government side that would essentially decide the fate of the talks. Kumaratunga's Sri Lanka Freedom Party (SLFP) government was defeated in an election that brought Ranil Wickremasinghe's United National Front to power. Under a so-called cohabitation agreement, Kumarantunga retained the presidency and Wickremasinghe became prime minister. This split in power meant disarray and dissent when key decisions about political devolution needed to be made.[123]

Peace talks began in 2002, and both sides agreed to "explore a solution grounded on the principle of internal self-determination in areas of historical habitation of the Tamil speaking peoples, based on a federal structure within a united Sri Lanka." Again, this seemed a breakthrough, as the LTTE was apparently dropping its demand for independence. Unfortunately, however, Kumarantunga had been excluded from the meeting, cooling her support for the government's efforts and setting off a power struggle that continued throughout the negotiations.[124] In April 2003, the LTTE unexpectedly walked out of the talks. However, the group continued to honor the cease-fire, and issued its own detailed peace proposals. These called for a devolved "Interim Self-Governing Authority" or ISGA, with broad powers in the North and East, to be controlled by the LTTE. According to the scheme, the ISGA would hold power for five years, after which independence would be granted if no other solution for the governance of the regions had been found.

This was a step too far. Sinhalese nationalists recoiled at the mention of Tamil independence. Kumaratunga declared a state of emergency and formed an alliance with two other parties to oppose the ISGA. She also took over three vital ministries—defense, interior, and the media—to prevent Wickremasinghe from granting further concessions. In November 2003, the Norwegians temporarily withdrew from the process, arguing that the power struggle in Colombo rendered further progress impossible. Kumaratunga called elections. In a result that reflected public anxiety about the negotiations, Wickremasinghe's government was voted out, while Kumaratunga's coalition also failed to secure a majority, resulting in an even more fractious government with no mandate for peace.

By this time there were signs of disarray on the Tamil side as well. In March 2004, Colonel Karuna of the LTTE defected with thousands of Prabhakarian's best troops. Karuna emerged on the government's side two years later—a huge coup for Sri Lankan intelligence and a serious blow for the LTTE, whose ironclad unity seemed newly challenged. There was also growing evidence that the Tamil Tigers were facing problems recruiting new personnel, forcing them to turn increasingly to women and children, some of them as young as nine years old.[125]

LTTE assassinations continued in 2005, including Foreign Minister Lakshman Kadirgamar (killed in August 2005), like many of the victims, a Tamil. When presidential elections were held in 2005, the LTTE tried to use violence to enforce a Tamil voter boycott. This polarized the electorate even more, effectively delivering to power Mahina Rajapakse, a staunch opponent of the talks. All hope for an agreement evaporated. The Norwegians made a last-ditch effort to salvage an accord, sponsoring a series of fruitless meetings in Geneva in February and March 2006, but the LTTE pulled out of the peace talks on April 20, 2006.

ANALYSIS OF THE FAILURE

Like most such talks most of the time, this negotiation did not lead to the end of terrorist violence. Nonetheless, the peace process had important short-term salutary effects on the country, including increased aid pledges from the international community, a small boom in construction in the north of the country, and the emergence of important additional information about the LTTE. The Tamil Tigers' increasing resort to smuggling, gunrunning, and drug trafficking to replace lost revenue hurt its political support base, as did its reputation for coercing women and children into becoming fighters and suicide operatives. Talks also helped to undercut the unity of the Tamil Tigers, an organization where brutally enforced, blind obedience to the leader had previously ensured a unified approach to the conflict. All of these factors may have damaged its support.

The government suffered politically from the breakdown of the talks. Split into acrimonious factions, it was unable to transcend the ethnic polarization that had been one of the sparks of the conflict in the first place. The willingness of the Sinhalese majority to share power with minorities within the country remained the sticking point, particularly if any agreement looked likely to result in secession and the breakup of the country.

The talks, and their associated provisions, led to a hiatus in LTTE terrorist attacks, diverting the violence into another channel that for the first time held out hope of a long-term agreement.[126] Both sides had reasons to want a pause in the violence. LTTE needed a break, not least because the heavy casualties suffered in their 2000 and 2001 campaigns had made it difficult for them to continue their military campaign. The Tamil Tigers probably believed that the military and political situation was moving against them in 2001, and during the cease-fire attempted to arrest that trend. After 9/11, the Sri Lankan military began to improve its training and capacity to fight a counterinsurgency war, turning, for example, to the Israelis for weapons and military training.[127] The government also used the cease-fire to recruit, modernize, and build up its fighting forces. Indeed, the failure of the talks was followed by an invigorated Sri Lankan military campaign against the LTTE, whose outcome at this writing is undecided. Thus, while there was a reduction in violence and apparently genuine hope of peace during the negotiation period, neither side saw the military and political situation as a stalemate. Both sides emerged from the talks militarily stronger, but politically weakened.

PROMISING AND UNPROMISING CIRCUMSTANCES FOR NEGOTIATIONS

A wide range of variables can determine the efficacy of negotiations to end terrorism, including the nature of the organization of the group (hierarchical groups having an advantage over groups that cannot control their members' actions), the nature of the leadership of the group (groups with a strong leader having an advantage over those that are decentralized), and the nature of public support for the cause (groups with constituencies who support peace being more likely to compromise). There must also be negotiable aims, which are more likely to exist with territorially based groups than with those that primarily espouse left-wing, right-wing or religious/spiritualist ideologies—although a careful study of the record indicates that over time groups evolve in their goals, or their dedication to them, invalidating superficial assumptions on this score.[128]

The degree to which opening a political dialogue with a terrorist group is a likely avenue for the decline of the group and a reduction in violence is a highly differentiated calculation, but the experience of terrorist groups and governments gives us some useful indicators as to whether or not talks will be promising. The overall quantitative analysis of groups, in combination with the three case studies examined in more depth here, indicate that whether negotiations are likely to succeed or not hinges on seven key factors: a political stalemate, strong leadership on both sides, whether or not there are third-party sponsors, the presence of suicide attacks, the splintering of groups (and government coalitions), the role of spoilers, and the international setting. Each will be discussed in turn.

Stalemate

Negotiations are most likely to be initiated when both sides sense that they have achieved a situation where additional violence is counterproductive. William Zartman coined the phrase "hurting stalemate" to refer to the most promising circumstances for talks in internal conflicts; from the perspective of a challenger group that mainly uses terrorism (rather than more conventional types of force), "hurting" reflects a political, more than a military, status.[129] Governments may employ military strategies of attrition; terrorist groups largely cannot. In his work Zartman also detailed four stages of insurgency—articulation, mobilization, insurgency, and warfare. It is because terrorist groups remain essentially in the phase of *mobilization* that they are particularly difficult to negotiate with: the level of political mobilization determines the incentives of the group. If a group perceives that the domestic constituency of a state is shifting in directions that serve its interests and go against those of the government, it will wait to negotiate. Or if the constituency that a group aims to activate is responding to its violence in ways that serve its interests, then it will wait.[130] Putting in place extensive preconditions for talks is simply another part of a group's negotiating strategy and a means to manipulate the political context.

But it is important to remember that only about one in five terrorist groups choose to negotiate at all, and thus terrorist campaigns are even harder to resolve in this way than are civil wars, of which Zartman argues about a quarter to a third involve talks.[131] Zartman also predicts that the greater the structural imbalance between parties the more likely it is that elements other than negotiations will determine the outcome.[132] As terrorist campaigns are above all characterized by sharp imbalances that drive groups to target civilians, negotiations are least of all likely to resolve them alone.

Negotiations with terrorist groups occur most easily in situations where the group perceives itself to be losing ground in the conflict, because of competition with other groups (as the PLO with the rise of competitors in the intifada), infiltration by government agents (as the PIRA), an undercutting of support (as the LTTE after 9/11), a backlash by its own constituency (see chapter 5), or a host of other reasons. Like other actors, terrorist groups are loss averse, even as they are eager to gamble on future gains.[133] A common impetus for talks is actual or prospective increases in civilian casualties in the group's constituency that are directly the result of the activities of the group (not the government). Intelligent counterterrorism strategy aims to manipulate these political conditions, taking advantage of circumstances before, during, and after negotiations. Central to this strategy is ensuring that a focus on the efficacy of military means is not at odds with the broader political realm. Contrary to popular perception, the political context within which talks occur is more important than the substance of the talks.

Governments must be mindful that there is no guarantee that the *military* situation will be improved by negotiations, especially in the short term. Groups sometimes enter talks disingenuously, so as to lessen the pressure of counterterrorist measures and rearm. The Provisional IRA continued to rearm following the 1998 Good Friday Agreement, buying guns in Florida and importing AN-94 rifles from Russia.[134] The Tamil Tigers, having repeatedly entered into peace talks and cease-fires with the Sri Lankan government, have regularly built up their military capabilities during reprieves. There are other cases not specifically discussed in this chapter: for example, the Basque group ETA announced a cease-fire in 1998, following a public backlash in response to the murder of a popular young councillor, and then renounced it in 1999, claiming that the group had wanted a reprieve from government pressure in order to rearm.[135] Obviously, responsible governments also use talks as a breathing space. Because of the risky nature of negotiations for both sides, it is naive to expect groups to halt their usual preparations. Talks are best seen as a redirection of the competition into another forum; unless they contain specific provisions about disarmament—indeed, even in some cases if they do—groups often continue to arm themselves. This is why entering into a negotiation process should be seen (by governments that are strong enough to consider it) as just another form of competitive interaction, to be decided upon according to its merits, approached as a process, and accompanied by low expectations that behavior will change, especially in the short run.

Strong Leadership

Some sources on conflict resolution argue that a change of leadership can increase the likelihood of succeeding in negotiations. Charles King, for example, argues that, in civil wars, leadership changes often offer promising opportunities for negotiations, especially in situations where the presence of a key leader is the primary obstacle to peace, and his successors all want peace.[136] It is not at all clear that this dynamic operates in the same way with campaigns that are characterized mainly by terrorism, however.[137]

As seen in chapter 1, the role of a leader who advocates terrorism is distinctive. Terrorism is a type of violence employed most often in situations where the population is not sufficiently activated for a cause; civilians are targeted as a means of mobilization and to garner support, partly by inducing the adversary to use indiscriminate force. When groups that originally employed terrorism transition into (or out of) ethnic violence and civil war, the conflict shifts with the degree of popular mobilization.[138] But for negotiations to succeed, there must be some sort of organization to negotiate with, as well as a spokesman or leader.[139] Although negotiations may serve other purposes, such as determining the priorities of the disaggregated parts and exploring the potential to buy them off, groups that persist often become more difficult following a leadership change. If the group survives the transition, a change of leadership may result in a more diffuse organization that is more difficult to parley with, because its different parts chase different aims. Because it targets civilians, the size of a terrorist group is not necessarily directly correlated with its motivation or ability to kill, so fractionation might make the problem worse, at least in the short term.

On the government side, the importance of strong leadership is commonly recognized and highly valued, as is strong bipartisan consensus in favor of a peace process.[140] Negotiations by democratic states are virtually impossible without both. But as reviled as he is likely to be, a strong, charismatic terrorist leader who pursues talks and can at least pretend to be relatively untainted by the violence can be equally crucial.

Sponsors

The role of third-party states is crucial, as are mediators, outside guarantors, and other external actors willing to push along or support negotiations. The Israeli-Palestinian peace process could not have begun without the Israeli government's realization that it could not circumvent the PLO by talking to Jordan, Syria, or non-PLO Palestinians within the occupied territories.[141] But the failure of key Arab states such as Syria to demonstrate a commitment to the peace process also helped to undermine it. The signing of the Anglo-Irish Agreement, and the Republic of Ireland's subsequent efforts to influence and support Northern Ireland republicans, provided an international framework and safety net, and was arguably a key turning point in the early moves toward peace. The

Norwegian government's impressive commitment in Sri Lanka was probably the main reason why violence was modulated there at all.

Likewise, early facilitators for talks are especially important in negotiations, both because terrorist groups are normally clandestine and hard to reach, and because the domestic political cost to a government that engages with a terrorist group is potentially high. Figures who are considered legitimate by both sides are crucial. Early contacts may be made by religious leaders or other private citizens (as with the PIRA), the United Nations (as in Cyprus, among others), or other nongovernmental organizations (as in South Africa and the Israeli-Palestinian conflict). Governments may also use third-party government intermediaries: the Reagan administration used Swedish foreign minister Sten Andersson to pass messages to Arafat.[142] States also regularly use intelligence officers. Uninvolved third-party states may insert themselves voluntarily: Norwegian politician Erik Solheim's efforts to assist the LTTE / Sri Lankan peace process are a notable example.[143] Early contacts may evolve from confidential interactions among private citizens to public dialogues involving organized lectures, panels, and discussions, and onto more formal "prenegotiations," such as seminars between influential individuals in closed, neutral environments, and secret meetings aimed at hammering out agreements.[144]

This being said, however, having carefully orchestrated, carefully worded agreements can be counterproductive in some circumstances. As we saw in the case of Northern Ireland, good negotiated agreements in conflicts as complicated as terrorist campaigns often have an element of ambiguity that actors can interpret in ways that suit their particular constituents. Ensuring continued interaction of the parties, providing a potential avenue out of terrorism, offering the elusive hope of a peace dividend may be the best that can be expected for a while. For this reason, international lawyers may not be the best agents for change in terrorist conflicts: good agreements may heighten the hopes of beleaguered constituencies by avoiding the brittleness of legal contracts between states. Clarity in the negotiations is not necessarily a desirable goal, and can indeed undermine long-term prospects for peace.

Suicide Campaigns

The inclusion of suicide attacks in a terrorist campaign seems to make resolution through negotiation even more problematic, as it reduces the willingness or ability of the factions to live side by side. Negotiations occurring in the aftermath (or midst) of suicide campaigns are especially difficult to conclude successfully, for a number of reasons. The constituencies involved are more than ever driven to be separated from each other territorially; intermingling among different ethnic, religious, or national groups becomes virtually impossible when civilian counterparts might be human bombs. Suicide terrorism is a problem not only for security forces manning checkpoints, but also for ordinary people going about their daily activities in the fear that other ordinary human beings among them might want to destroy them all. Almost nowhere is safe. In addition, the attention given to attacks that involve suicide is higher than for normal attacks.[145] The operatives' deaths that are so publicly part of such attacks are a kind of communal "sacrifice investment" that in itself raises the stakes, as it is very difficult for communities to admit that human life has been purposely discarded in vain.[146] Suicide attacks both engender and reflect an arguably unique level of ideological commitment by the operative. It is therefore especially difficult to remove the negotiations from the angry passions that surround them. The level of personal distrust imbued by suicide attacks may also be uniquely high, thus undercutting talks that, at least at some level, must depend on a modicum of trust and mutual commitment to proceed.

Thus, suicide attacks force a cultural and sociological change in societies that use them and are targeted by them, an alienation that is difficult to overcome. They inhibit the free movement and intermingling of peoples, only a small proportion of whom may be either engaged in or targeted by them.[147] The construction by Israeli of the fence, for example, was the outward manifestation of a separation catalyzed by an increase in suicide terrorism, although such barriers are by no means uncommon.[148] Similar barriers have been constructed by the United States in Iraq, for example, so as to reduce the incidence of sectarian suicide attacks.

Given that widespread popular support for a peace process is a crucial variable in negotiations with groups that use terrorism, the increasing prevalence of suicide attacks internationally is a sobering development. It is no coincidence that the two terrorist conflicts with some of the most frustrating negotiations are over the two plots of land where more than 80 percent of recent suicide attacks have occurred: Sri Lanka and the Israel-Palestine region.

Splintering

Despite the successful negotiated outcomes that can result between the major parties, a common effect of political processes is the splintering of groups into factions that support the negotiations (or their outcome) and those that do not. For example, the Real Irish Republican Army split off from the IRA;[149] and the Popular Front for the Liberation of Palestine

(PFLP), Democratic Front for the Liberation of Palestine (DFLP), and the Popular Front for the Liberation of Palestine–General Command (PFLP-GC) split with the PLO over the Israeli-Palestinian peace process. Efforts to negotiate with ETA likewise resulted in the group splintering, with Basque radicals continuing urban violence and extortion as the political wing, Batasuna, seemed to be moving toward normalization. From a counterterrorist perspective, dividing groups can be a purpose of the negotiations, as it isolates and potentially strangles the most radical factions.[150] But such splintering can also occur on the "status quo" (or, usually, progovernment) side, as happened in South Africa (with the Afrikaner white power group Farmer's Force, or "Boermag") and in Northern Ireland (with the Ulster Volunteer Force). As in traditional war, governments confront huge difficulties negotiating with organizations with which they are still fighting.[151]

The most extreme case of counterproductive splintering is Colombia, where the signing of peace accords between the Colombian government and the Ejercito Popular de Liberacion (EPL) in 1984 resulted in the formation of right-wing paramilitary groups that opposed the granting of political status to the EPL.[152] Before long, leftist groups, paramilitary groups, and the Colombian army had all stepped up their attacks, unraveling the peace, increasing the violence, and further polarizing the political actors. Splinter groups are often more violent than the "mother" organization, as they respond to the imperative to demonstrate their existence and signal their dissent. They can be seen as engaging in a new "layer" of terrorism with respect to the original group or their own government, as, for example, when groups such as Hamas and Hezbollah enter elections and take on a governing role while maintaining active terrorist activities.

Splintering may be advantageous and strategic. It is foolish to think of negotiations strictly in the formalized, around-the-table, publicized meeting sense. Intelligent, targeted concessions made openly or clandestinely by a government can chip away at the challenger side—which should be one of their purposes. Weak governments are likewise threatened by conciliatory approaches by terrorist groups. Often, in early stages, negotiations are occurring with one part of a group, even as another part of a group is engaging in violence. This is not the ideal situation, but it is how the process typically unfolds. If a group is growing in size or strength, negotiations may be seen by the state as a means of disaggregating the threat by splitting off factions with whom the government can work, whose demands can be appeased, or whose interests do not fully comport with the goals of the overall campaign being fought in their name—although, of course, the splinter group must be weighty enough to have a credible constituency.[153] Again, for negotiations to hold promise, thorough knowledge of the movement and its constituent parts is crucial. In all these cases, however, the long-term goal (a viable political outcome) and the short-term goal (a reduction in violence) may be at odds.

Spoilers

Related to the formation of splinter groups, additional terrorist attacks have often been used to derail or destroy peace negotiations, and they have been remarkably successful in doing so. The common term used to describe those who do this is spoilers, although there are important differences between those who use terrorism to undermine peace talks in wars or civil wars, and those groups for whom terrorism was the primary *modus vivendi* that led to the talks. According to one study of the efficacy of terrorist attacks in the context of negotiations, between 1988 and 1998, 14 peace agreements were signed between parties to civil wars. If terrorist attacks occurred in association with the talks, only one in four peace treaties were put into effect. If they did not occur, 60 percent took effect.[154] The record for accords where the principal type of violence is terrorism is likely worse.

The most thoroughly examined case of the interaction between terrorist attacks and talks is the Israeli-Palestinian peace negotiations, a case that, for the reasons described above, may not be fully representative. Not all terrorist campaigns involve territory; talks may also be about such things as minority representation or rights in existing states, changes in governments, rights to religious freedom or practice, and so on. In the Israeli-Palestinian peace process, furthermore, the role of spoilers has been thoroughly analyzed only with respect to one group (Hamas) rather than the many actors involved directly or indirectly in the genesis, operation, and outcome of the talks. Modeling negotiations between terrorist groups and governments as a dichotomous "game," as in the study of Hamas, distorts as much as it clarifies: because of the inherent asymmetry of the violence involved and the parties engaging in it, peace processes with terrorist organizations are never a simple matter of two parties interacting as if they were at war, for example.

Terrorist attacks in Northern Ireland were likewise frequently timed to coincide with developments in the peace process. But that case demonstrates that in the presence of a foundation of popular support for the talks, strong outside guarantors, and identification of the negotiators with the process itself, terrorist "spoiler" attacks actually strengthened the commitment to the negotiations rather than undermined it. Having a peace process itself became not only a source of vulnerability (to spoilers and terrorist attacks) but also a source of strength, as attacks could now be described as hurting not only the victims but also the process. This helped deflect hatred from the opposing side as a whole, to the faction that was undermining the peace process, making the negotiators *more* resilient, not less. In Northern Ireland, spoiler attacks actually strengthened the commitment to peace, rather than undermining it.

Thus, one conclusion from academic studies of civil wars that directly applies to ending terrorist campaigns is that, when spoiler violence occurs, it matters whether or not outside parties label it illegitimate.[155] Whether states support the cause of the incumbent or challenger side, absent or ambiguous responses to terrorist attacks carried out by spoilers augment their effectiveness and undermine negotiations. When the response is outrage at the attackers themselves, on the other hand, spoilers may not spoil the talks at all.

Setting and Story

An important element in determining whether negotiations end terrorist attacks is whether terrorist groups have correctly understood the broader historical context within which they are operating, and have responded correctly to it. To explain why negotiations end terrorist attacks (or not), the tactical, proximate matters discussed above must be viewed in the context of broader ideological developments in the public sphere. Of particular concern are the relationships between terrorist groups who share sources of inspiration across regions, and may have actual or imagined connections to other groups that are either gaining or losing momentum. Terrorism has been an international phenomenon throughout the modern era, even when the globalized ties that currently exist were more ideological than practical.

Every group whose campaign has recently ended in a negotiated agreement espoused a cause that was no longer in the ascendancy on the international stage. The most successful negotiations occurred with groups that were part of the wave of decolonization that occurred in the middle to late twentieth century, which confronted colonial powers that were on the defensive for other reasons.[156] The international context directly affects the degree to which terrorist campaigns are "ripe" for resolution. This can be seen in a very practical way in Northern Ireland, where the angry moral overtones of the Northern Irish peace process were replaced by a kind of pragmatism, especially on the part of the British.[157] In turn, events in Northern Ireland have been important in driving ETA to negotiate, though talks have as yet been unsuccessful. Likewise, the LTTE was heavily influenced by the international environment that followed 9/11. For good or ill, the international environment had shifted, as states such as the United

States, the United Kingdom, Israel, and India moved toward greater sympathy with the Sri Lankan government's counterterrorism efforts in the context of the so-called war on terror. The problem there was that neither side perceived a military and political stalemate locally, so the conflict continued. International conditions did not surpass local dynamics.

A changing international context may be a necessary but not sufficient condition for negotiations to end terrorism. Popular ideas about the state, economics, and human aspirations do matter in the resolution of local conflicts that employ symbolic violence aimed at broader audiences, and those ideas in turn are influenced by the fate of local actors, especially in the context of increasingly globalized communications that project the narratives of terrorist campaigns far beyond their usual constituencies.[158]

How Negotiations End Terrorism

The answer is, very rarely in the short term. Negotiations are best thought of as an essential elements in a broader range of policies to marginalize a group, as conciliatory gestures or proposals change the dynamics of support; to exploit differences, hive off factions, and enable members to leave or constituencies to turn elsewhere; to provide crucial information about how a group functions; and to reduce the degree and intensity of attacks over time, as groups lose momentum or make errors. Negotiations carry with them many benefits; however, instantaneously ending the violence is not one of them. Given the small number of operatives needed for terrorist attacks to continue, negotiations do not typically end the violence alone, and it is foolish to promote expectations that they will.

The relevant question for a government is whether the situation following the opening of negotiations has become better or worse than it might have been without the negotiations. Being a counterfactual, the question cannot be answered. But it is important to avoid the fallacious belief that the alternative to negotiation would be a return to the situation that existed at the moment talks began—that is, that time has essentially stood still while talks proceeded. It is equally likely that the situation would have *worsened* in the absence of talks. Judging the efficacy of negotiations is thus not simply a matter of whether or not they result in the end of violence in the short term. The most likely result for a government that chooses to negotiate and can withstand domestic pressure is long-term management of the threat over a lengthy period of gradual demise of the terrorist campaign, while other factors lead to its end.

Unlike civil wars and interstate conflicts, when it comes to ending terrorism, negotiations are most effective if they are consciously employed to redirect the contest into a less violent channel as talks proceed and the campaign also winds down for other reasons. They carry risks and can be a serious challenge to the democratic state that enters into them without a firm domestic mandate, managed expectations, and a backup plan if or when terrorism recurs. From the state's perspective, negotiations are not a promising tactical means to end terrorist campaigns, but if well handled, they are nonetheless a wise and durable strategic tool for managing the violence, splintering the opposition, and facilitating its longer-term decline.

CHAPTER THREE

Success

ACHIEVING THE OBJECTIVE

> A victory, immediate, splendid, and decisive, such as that
> obtained by an insurrection, is utterly impossible by means
> of terrorism. But another victory is more probable, that of
> the weak against the strong, that of the "beggars" of Holland
> against the Spaniards. In a struggle against an invisible,
> impalpable, omnipresent enemy, the strong is vanquished not
> by the arms of his adversary, but by the continuous tension of
> his own strength, which exhausts him, at last, more than he
> would be exhausted by defeats.
> —*Sergei Stepniak-Kravshinski, 1883*[1]

SOMETIMES TERRORISM ENDS because it succeeds. Terrorist groups achieve
their political aims and either disband or stop engaging in violence. This
is an awkward reality that can be difficult to analyze objectively, not
least because history is written by the "winners." Leaders of groups that
were engaged in terrorist attacks sometimes become revered statesmen,
and their organizations become respected political parties or even ruling
governments. Terrorism has periodically been used as a means to pursue
admirable ends, such as the freedom and self-determination of an oppressed or displaced people, and the groups that engaged in those means
have occasionally gained legitimacy over time. Recognizing that terrorism sometimes succeeds does not legitimize the tactic and may even be
a necessary step toward reducing and eliminating it. Denying it, on the
other hand, is wishful thinking and an impediment to objective analysis.

Most Europeans begin the study of terrorism with the assumption that
the tactic always fails in the long run, and work from there. Americans,
traumatized by 9/11 and lacking the phlegmatic attitude common in Europe, tend to argue that it is uniquely dangerous and usually succeeds.
The reality, of course, is somewhere in between. In any case, a comprehensive investigation of how terrorism ends must analyze why, how, and
under what conditions terrorism succeeds. First, however, we must decide
what "success" means in terrorist campaigns.

What Does "Success" Mean?

When it comes to evaluating the effectiveness of terrorism, success is a nebulous concept, often loosely employed and reflecting the intellectual biases of the observer more than the priorities of the group itself (or its constituents). Most commonly, success is evaluated according to the perceptions of the targeted state, especially its sense of the level of threat. This analytical narcissism is a mistake, however, since the perspectives of those in the terrorist group, and especially their active and passive supporters, are more important than other viewpoints in determining whether or not the violence ends.

Whether terrorist groups succeed is not a question answered merely by evaluating the statements of terrorist leaders—although, of course, that is a good start: leaders are often the most accessible source of insight into the outcome a group aims to achieve. Terrorist leaders are frequently familiar with the history of previous failed campaigns. Their sense of the likelihood of accomplishing their aims must be affected by the belief that they can avoid the mistakes of their predecessors.[2] The decision to engage in terrorism is, as Samuel Johnson said of remarriage, typically the triumph of hope over experience.[3] It is precisely because terrorism so often fails that leaders must vigorously propagandize and overstate their ability to win. The most effective terrorist leaders are always, first and foremost, sophisticated manipulators of information.[4] Naturally they highlight those aspects of their campaigns that appear to make gains. It is in the interests of leaders of terrorist movements to publicize a sense of momentum in the direction of the political change they desire, but even in those cases it is difficult to demonstrate that terrorism itself is the reason for success.

Thus terrorism's success cannot be judged merely by studying the statements of leaders; we must also consider the population on whose behalf terrorism is claimed to be undertaken. At its heart, terrorism is intended to be an altruistic act, aimed toward a political end that represents a better fate for those on whose behalf attacks are carried out. Terrorism without the pursuit of justice (at least as someone sees it) is nothing but mass murder and lacks the legitimacy necessary to attract a political following. When terrorism succeeds, as it rarely does, it yields benefits for those on whose behalf it is undertaken. Leaving them out of the equation is to be duped by the claims and ambitions of leaders whose main task is, after all, to manipulate perceptions.

Terrorism is seen as the violence of the underdog. The harder the odds, the more some see a perverse romance in the campaign. And terrorism's apparent successes, in terms of attacks and influence, are more storied than its failures. An added complication is that terrorism can sometimes be used in support of something that was going to happen anyway. In perpetuating terrorism, the key variable is not how many groups actually achieved their objectives, but how many successor groups *believed* that they had.[5] How many people hear about groups that fizzled out after a year, had their operations disrupted before they were carried out, or gave up on their ideological notions in the face of the state's formidable obstacles? When a terrorist campaign succeeds, it takes time.[6] The celebrated terrorists are those who persist, and they are the ones who get all the attention. To examine the phenomenon more objectively, terrorism's "success" might be analyzed using apolitical metrics, ranging from the viability of groups over time to the demonstrated achievement of their political aims, both tactical and strategic. These criteria will be dealt with here in turn.

Survival

Popular impressions of the efficacy of terrorism are overblown.[7] If the survival of the group—like the Weberian imperative for the state—is itself a fundamental goal of terrorism, then it is a dubious tactic. Political scientists tend to apply models derived from the strategic behavior of states to terrorist organizations, despite the fact that terrorist groups cannot count on the most basic of state characteristics, namely survival.[8] Political actors cannot be effective if they cannot endure.

More detailed, long-term analysis of terrorism's viability in recent years reveals that it is not a very promising way to make a living. A careful study of the life spans of the hundreds of groups listed by the MIPT database demonstrates that the average length of time a terrorist group has survived is approximately eight years. (See figure A.1. See the appendix for detailed explanations of all of these estimates.) Groups on the State Department's Foreign Terrorist Organizations list have a longer life-span of about 19 years, but the list only includes groups that the U.S. government considers currently the most notorious, and against whom U.S. economic sanctions are to be applied.[9] (See figure A.3.) The so-called FTO list is not a fully representative sampling of terrorist groups, either across regions or across time, representing at most 5 percent of the total number of groups in the MIPT database (43, compared to 860), albeit a larger proportion of *durable* international groups.[10]

Longevity in the twentieth century was associated with the ideological motivation of a group: the longest-lived groups were those linked with decolonization and nationalism. Their greater average longevity seemed to result, at least in part, from support among the local populace of the same ethnicity for the group's political or territorial objectives. In discussing the longevity of terrorist groups in 1991, Martha Crenshaw noted only three significant groups with ethnonationalist ideologies that had ceased to exist within 10 years of their formation (one of which, EOKA [Ethniki Organosis Kyprion Agoniston], disbanded because the goal of removing the British from Cyprus was attained). By contrast, a majority of the terrorist groups Crenshaw listed as having existed for 10 years or longer had recognizable ethnonationalist ideologies, including the IRA (in its many forms), Sikh separatist groups, ETA, the various Palestinian nationalist groups, and the Corsican National Liberation Front.[11] This correlation was understood by the leaderships of terrorist organizations at the time: often, groups that started with other ideological goals endeavored to connect themselves to an anticolonial, nationalist cause in order to increase their following and enhance their chances of success.[12] Groups with ethnic constituencies could often rely on sympathetic diaspora communities and foreign sanctuaries. In the twentieth century, a connection with territory and national self-determination was the key to survival—and a shot at success.

It is difficult to be sure whether there will be a comparable variable for the longevity of terrorist groups in the twenty-first century. Some experts argued in the late 1990s that the key to future staying power would be terrorist groups' connections with religious or open-ended causes. As the third millennium approached, analyses of the "new" religious terrorism emphasized the connection between the growing numbers of casualties per attack, the increasing availability of more lethal technologies, and the increasing proportion of attacks carried out by groups motivated by religion.[13] Religious groups have had the most staying power in earlier centuries, so there is some historical foundation for this belief. It is too soon to compile good data on the average life-span of contemporary groups motivated by religion (or at least groups that appeal to religious concepts as a mobilizing force); however, the remarkable staying power of early religious terrorist groups such as the Hindu Thugs, in existence for at least 600 years, would seem to indicate the inherent durability of sacred or spiritually based motivations.[14] Another argument holds that religion is unimportant, and that the connection to territory will persist: an association with a piece of land will continue to be the most important factor for longevity. There is evidence to support this view, as some groups are displaying both religious and ethnonationalist traits.[15] In any case, after 9/11, the prevailing sentiment in the West has been that terrorist groups in general, and al-Qaeda in particular, will last for many decades. Yet careful study of the full empirical record, across regions and types of groups, and over time, indicates that for terrorist groups, longevity is the exception, not the rule.

Achievement of Objectives

While terrorist attacks have killed increasing numbers of people, terrorist groups continue to have difficulty translating that violence into the political ends they seek. But that is not to say that terrorism is an astrategic tool. Although terrorists may not "win," their campaigns always involve assessment of their progress toward an end.[16] The standard way of describing progress toward such goals is to look at tactical and strategic aims.[17] Most organizations have used terrorism as a means to achieve either short-term, tactical (proximate) aims or long-term, strategic (ultimate) goals—or some dynamic mixture of the two.

The classic argument made in the latter twentieth century was that terrorism often succeeds tactically but is virtually nowhere a strategic success. However, this seductive mental framework can mask the essential interactive nature of terrorism: as many in the U.S. military like to say, in terrorism as in war, the "enemy gets a vote." Some tactical achievements have strategic consequences for progress toward overall goals, and the strategic objectives themselves normally evolve in the course of a terrorist campaign, making it very difficult to judge exactly what "success" means in a given case. Borrowing from economics, another way to think about the distinction is to distinguish between "process goals" and "outcome goals."[18] The central question here is: what kinds of successes have perpetuated terrorism, and what kinds have led to its end?

PERPETUATING TERRORISM: TACTICAL OR "PROCESS" GOALS

Terrorist attacks serve many narrow or immediate tactical goals. The purposes of such attacks can be internal or external, aimed at a large number of different audiences. Short-term "process" aims are directed not just at the perceived enemy (usually the state) and those related to or sympathetic to the victims; terrorist attacks are just as frequently aimed at a wide range of other audiences, including competitors for control of a cause, current members of the group, potential recruits, active supporters, passive supporters, and even neutral bystanders. Terrorist attacks can serve internal organizational goals, such as enhancing one individual's status at the expense of another, or external organizational goals, such as enhancing the position of one group with respect to another competing group. Process goals are regularly achieved and can lead those within a terrorist organization to enter into a kind of bounded rationality, where the campaign continues to follow its own logic even though the accomplishment of broader outcome goals is becoming increasingly distant and unlikely. Tactical or process goals tend to perpetuate terrorist campaigns, not lead to their end.

Terrorist organizations do not construct strategies as if they were states. States generally go to war over disagreements about the relative distribution of international power. There is no disagreement over the distribution of power between a state and a terrorist organization: the latter has little and exploits its absence. Indeed, terrorist groups are compelled to consciously draw their power from states. They are not sovereign entities, having neither the strengths nor the weaknesses of states: they do not have the responsibilities and constraints implied in governing—indeed, they cannot even count on their own survival. The common assumption (especially among political scientists) that strategic theories developed on the basis of state behavior are directly comparable to terrorist group activities glosses over vital differences in their decision-making processes, as will be seen below in the study of outcomes. In their behavior, terrorist groups do not behave as if they were the equivalent of weak little states, and efforts to analyze them as if they were are misguided.[19]

Some analysts argue that terrorists engage in attacks as a costly means of signaling resolve to a state; while that is sometimes true, it is just as often the case that the signal is not aimed at a government at all, but rather at other observers in a wide range of other potential audiences.[20] To conceptualize the strategies of a terrorist group, it is useful to think of a set of concentric circles. A thorough analysis of the strategies of a terrorist campaign includes, at a minimum, a dissection of the motivations, goals, and incentives of individual members (leaders, powerful deputies); factions within the group (individuals from one tribe, family, social group, or nationality competing with others); rivalries between groups (competition to represent a cause or constituency); attracting new followers (by showing strength or viability); satisfying external donors (demonstrating organizational effectiveness so as to attract support or resources); and swaying potential supporters (e.g., attracting new allies, again by showing strength). All of these are proximate goals, not strategic accomplishments, and they may not necessarily be designed to directly engage any state at all. They are aimed at tactical or operational means, not longer-term political ends—unless, of course, the "end" is merely the perpetuation of the campaign itself.[21]

There are countless illustrations of these kinds of "process" or tactical goals sought by terrorist groups.[22] Sometimes groups or individuals use terrorist attacks to show strength or ruthlessness, or to lionize a leader. The videotaped, ritualistic beheadings of journalists, backpackers, and contractors by the late Abu Musab al-Zarqawi and his associates in Iraq were an obvious example.[23] To demonstrate continued viability, groups may step up attacks after a major blow to their campaigns, including the capture of a leader or the arrest of members. There are many examples of this behavior, including a short spike in attacks by the Real IRA immediately following Mickey McKevitt's arrest in April 2001, and a step-up in violence by the Abu Sayyaf following the killing of Abdurajak Janjalani in a gun battle December 1998. Suicide attacks against Israeli citizens have at times been used to increase the strength of one Palestinian faction against another, a process sometimes called "outbidding."[24] Or terrorists may simply be carrying out revenge for the sake of revenge: on April 19, 1995, Timothy McVeigh drove a truck bomb into the Alfred P. Murrah Building in Oklahoma City, killing 168 civilians (including 19 children), an attack meant to avenge the siege of the Branch Davidian compound in Waco, Texas, exactly two years earlier. All of these are reasons why attacks are carried out that do not seem to make sense from the perspective of a group's longer-term, end-state goals.

Other short-term actions have been employed to shore up support, such as increasing the number of recruits (for example, videos of attacks released by the Mujahideen Army in Iraq), preventing interference in recruitment efforts (as in the FARC's 2004 attack on a church that opposed recruitment of local youth), or the flow of money and other resources (for example, the Tamil Tigers, the Sikhs, the Basques, and the IRA holding the attention of far-flung diaspora sympathizers).[25] Satisfying the demands of a state sponsor is another classic short-term motivation for groups, even though the strategic aims of the group may or may not align over time with those of the state involved. Yasir Arafat's Fatah faction and its relationship with Syria is a good example of tactical accommodation but strategic ambivalence.[26] Finally, terrorism is quite often used as a spoiler, especially when states or nonstate actors are involved in negotiations that might be derailed by renewed violence, as discussed in chapter 2.

Some short-term, process goals can also relate to manipulating the actions of a state or undermining state governance. Terrorist attacks can be designed to provoke overreaction and thereby gain adherents to the cause, who are repulsed by the state's response. Terrorism has been commonly used as a means of coercion to earn the release of prisoners (for example, Hezbollah's capture of two Israeli soldiers in 2005). Or groups may simply want to demonstrate the inability of a state to protect its own citizens, as was the case with the IRA, who frequently claimed that their aim was to make Northern Ireland ungovernable. It can be a means of bringing down a government, even though many terrorist organizations are not strong enough or politically agile enough to replace it. Examples include the Russian social revolutionaries and the Tupamaros of Uruguay, both of whom played a role in destroying the governments they opposed, but were unable to replace them with their desired alternative, resulting in far more repressive regimes and their own elimination. Terrorism can be used when state governance is already weak and its perpetrators have a sense of opportunity: attacks on civilians are meant to provoke ethnic or civil unrest. Examples include violence between blacks in the closing days of apartheid South Africa and the sectarian violence that occurred in Iraq. In these cases, terrorism may be a precursor (or companion) to civil war.

Often organizational survival overshadows the cause, in the short term. Jerrold Post argues that a group must be "successful enough in its terrorist acts and rhetoric of legitimation to attract members and perpetuate itself, but it must not be so successful that it will succeed itself out of business."[27] In other words, enjoying too much success or having too high a profile can lead to an overpowering counterreaction by the state or, at the other extreme, the collapse of state governing structures that a terrorist group may need. Not all groups want to bring down a government, especially if it provides useful services and if the group has no interest in replacing it.[28] The short-term goal of terrorism may simply be to attract members, publicize the cause, and survive, so as to pursue a long-term ideological change.

A comprehensive listing of short-term tactics would be ludicrous; the point is that they are numerous, common, and often fruitful in perpetuating a conflict.[29] Terrorism can be a short-term tactic in a campaign that has many other tactics. Of course, sometimes it backfires and undermines a group; but, unfortunately for its victims and for the international community as a whole, in the short run terrorism regularly succeeds in perpetuating a campaign. However, that does not mean that it "wins." All of these forms of success offer no insight into the effectiveness of the tactic in achieving its political ends—and into how and why terrorism ends.

ENDING TERRORISM: STRATEGIC OR "OUTCOME" GOALS

Strategic goals are the end states or "outcomes" that a terrorist organization attempts to achieve through violence targeted at civilians. Strategic goals may be political (relating to the state—its regime, organization, boundaries, population), economic (redistributing resources or wealth), social (racial or ethnic identity, modernization), or religious (relating to spiritualist identity, values, strictures, virtues), or some combination of these aims. Groups operating in the twentieth century tended to fall into four categories, sorted according to their motivations: left wing, right wing, ethnonationalist-separatist, and spiritualist. The first three categories oriented themselves toward political organization and ideology—a pressing source of conflict throughout the modern age, spawning waves of fascism, communism, and nationalism that led to the outbreaks of both world wars, the Cold War, and the wave of decolonization that followed.[30]

Strategic goals typically relate either to the nature or behavior of the state, or to the identity of its population. Groups may wish to bring down a specific government in order to replace it with a more "just" form of organization or governance. Maoist groups, such as the Shining Path of

Peru, the Naxalites of India, and the New People's Army of the Philippines, sought a new society with power residing in the peasants; the Russian social revolutionaries and their aspiring descendants, including the Italian Red Brigades, Action Directe in France, the Baader-Meinhof gang in Germany, and the Weathermen in the United States, sought to overthrow the capitalist system and replace it with a communist society. Fascist groups sought to wipe out a race and ensure the dominance of the white majority. Neo-Nazi groups in the United States and Europe fit this description.

National self-determination was the most important goal of terrorism in the twentieth century. There are many examples of groups motivated by the sense of opportunity that the end of the colonial era brought, such as the Viet Cong, the Algerian FLN, the Cypriot EOKA, and numerous other groups that fought for control over the nature and identity of a successor state. Groups have also wished to gain independence or autonomy within an established state, including the Tamil Tigers, the Kurdistan Workers' Party, and Basque separatists. Other long-term aims may be less clearly visualized: the goal may be to bring on the apocalypse (as with Aum Shinrikyo) or to glorify the actions of the "fighter" (some Italian right-wing groups in the 1970s) or to act as a catalyst for the forces of history (again the Russian social revolutionaries). Sometimes religious groups may seek to please a god or spiritual force, such as the Hindu Thugs, who sought to placate the goddess of suffering, Kali.

If few terrorist groups enjoy longevity, even fewer appear to achieve their strategic political objectives. Taking into account the stated goals of groups leads to the unavoidable conclusion that, whatever its narrower gains, terrorism is not a promising avenue for change. Of the more than four hundred terrorist groups that I analyzed from MIPT database, for example, only a small minority, less than 5 percent, have by their own standards succeeded in fully achieving their aims.[31] (See appendix, table A.4.) In the midst of campaigns, terrorist leaders appear to enter a kind of bounded rationality, where tactical objectives that keep a terrorist campaign going are readily achieved, but strategic gains that advance its ultimate triumph almost never are.

Terrorism often fails in its aims because its shocking nature provokes popular revulsion and sweeping retaliatory force. At times, this reaction has resulted in the undermining of democratic institutions and the ascent of military or authoritarian rule, for example in countries such as Peru, Uruguay, Algeria, and Turkey.[32] In Argentina the result of a terrorist campaign was a bloody war and thousands of "disappearances."[33] Yet even these brutal government reactions and moves toward repression must be put into perspective when analyzing the viability of terrorism: states may be gravely weakened by terrorist violence over the long run, but terrorist groups are weakened even more. States often move toward their primal natures, particularly the use of force and, all else being equal, are far more effective at it than terrorists. When the objectives of terrorist groups are achieved, it is often not from the use of terrorist attacks (an inherently weak tactic) but as the result of a transition into more traditional means of political coercion, such as insurgent attacks on military forces. (See chapter 6.) Even in such cases, campaigns employing terrorism succeed more despite the use of violence against innocent civilians than because of it; there is far more evidence supporting the efficacy of insurgent attacks on armed forces, for example, than of terrorist attacks on civilian targets.[34] Yet attacks on military targets by virtually any commonly accepted rigorous definition do not constitute terrorism.

In killing noncombatants, terrorism can attract attention, provoke tactical responses, lead a state to undermine itself, and create a cause celebre; but it almost never installs new rulers, inspires ideological change, takes over territory, or constructs new institutions of governance (as terrorist leaders typically claim). Historically, by virtually any standard of measurement, terrorist success stories, that is, campaigns that achieve their long-term objectives and then end their attacks on civilians, are the exception, rather than the rule.

CASES OF SUCCESS

Writing about success as the reason for the end of a terrorist campaign drives us to examine a small proportion of cases where groups have achieved their overall aims, enabling their leaders to declare victory and disband (or rule). Often, the "success" of terrorism is a sidebar in a movement also characterized by other methods of pursuing political change, and to the extent that terrorist attacks were employed, they were engaged in by a minority and may actually have set back the broader cause. Case studies of success are nonetheless vital in understanding how terrorism ends, not only because they show one pattern of completion and the conditions under which it occurred, but much more importantly because the political and psychological effects of these campaigns have had a disproportionate impact upon the evolution of both international terrorism and counterterrorism. The following are two well-known cases of strategic success that have been influential in the recent evolution of global terrorism.

Irgun Zvai Le'umi (Irgun or IZL)

Irgun Zvai Le'umi (National Military Organization, also known either by its Hebrew acronym Etzel, IZL, or Irgun) was founded in 1931 in the British Mandate of Palestine to protect Jews and ultimately advance the cause of an independent Jewish state. It was a radical offshoot of Haganah, which was essentially the military arm of the Jewish Agency, the defensive militia for the Yishuv (Hebrew for the Jewish community), and the precursor of the Israeli army. Before World War II, the Arabs, not the British, were Irgun's primary target; the latter were for the most part treated as allies. The organization engaged in reprisal attacks against Arabs hostile to the growing Jewish presence in Palestine, including sporadic attacks on Arab urban centers, buses, and marketplaces. Irgun's rivals within Eretz Israel, including the Haganah, the trade unions, and the Jewish Agency, bitterly opposed these activities and claimed that the violence threatened the Jewish community and undermined its long-term security in Palestine. The Haganah condemned Irgun's attacks on civilians, calling them "terror" and urging a policy of restraint toward the Arabs.[35]

With the outbreak of World War II, Irgun shrank to a group of only a few hundred people, without arms and resources and in danger of extinction. Many of its members joined the Allied cause, enlisting in the British army to fight the Nazis, including in the Jewish Brigade Group, a unit that served admirably in the 1944 Italian campaign. Lehi,[36] another offshoot organization headed by Avraham Stern (thus also known by the British as the "Stern Gang"), was founded in 1940 in the belief that collaboration with the British was the wrong approach, even in a time of war. Although the Germans were a serious threat, Stern believed the more direct obstacle to independence in Palestine was the British, not the Germans. Lehi fought the British between 1940 and 1942, including carrying out bank robberies and assassinations. Stern died in British custody in February 1942, but the group continued into the postwar years.

These three organizations—Irgun, Lehi, and Haganah—jockeyed for position within the Yishuv during the years of struggle for an independent Jewish state. From October 1945 until July 1946, under the banner of the Jewish Resistance movement, Irgun and Lehi joined with Haganah, in order to fight British restrictions on Jewish immigration; but it was a short-lived alliance. Historical accounts of their activities are hampered by lingering controversy and argument, not least because rival figures in all three organizations later went on to political prominence, including Menachem Begin (head of Irgun), Yitzhak Shamir (a leading figure in the Stern gang), and Yitzhak Rabin and Ariel Sharon (both in Haganah), all of whom later became prime ministers of Israel. With most relevant documents having been destroyed for security reasons long ago, differing personal accounts of the nature and significance of Irgun's activities are subject to passionate dispute in Israeli politics.

Members of the Irgun believed that British authority over Palestine under the League of Nations Mandate was wrong, not least because

of Britain's refusal to allow mass immigration of Jews fleeing Nazi oppression from such places as Romania, Germany, Poland, and Hungary.
Angered by what they saw as Britain's failure to rescue millions from
Nazi gas chambers, prevention of Jewish immigration to Palestine, and
indirect contribution to the Holocaust, members of Irgun demanded the
immediate transfer of sovereignty to a provisional Jewish government.
In January 1944, Begin wrote a declaration of armed revolt, which was
widely publicized and for the first time expressed the clear and unequiv-
ocal goal of establishing a Jewish state in Palestine. A few weeks later, in
February 1944, Irgun resumed violent operations, this time homing in
on the British. Its targets were symbols of British authority in Palestine,
including police headquarters, immigration offices, income tax offices,
the Acre prison, and the railway system. The goal was to make the territory ungovernable, raise the costs of control, and undermine Britain's
authority in the region.

Irgun was never a strong military organization, making many mistakes
and at least on the surface lacking sufficient grassroots popular support,
membership, and resources to pose a serious military threat to the British. But at the heart of Irgun's efforts was its popular propaganda war,
what one prominent member labeled the "campaign of enlightenment."
In the Mandate this included ubiquitous posters on shop windows and
walls, communiqués regarding operations, explanations of political positions, radio broadcasts, and pleas for support. Members of Irgun also consciously and deliberately courted international media attention for their
statements, broadcasts, and operations, particularly newspapers in the
United States. International publicity effectively lionized Irgun members,
drew additional support for the Jewish population, and increased the political pressure on the British government, particularly in the wake of horrifying evidence of the widespread extermination of Jews by the Nazis.[37]

But condemnation of the tactics of violence by both Irgun and Lehi
was also widespread. For example, when two members of Lehi assassinated Lord Moyne, the British minister resident in Cairo, on November 6, 1944, the killing was universally condemned, including by David
Ben-Gurion and other Jewish Agency leaders in Palestine. Attempting to
distinguish itself from Lehi, Irgun adopted a strategy designed to minimize civilian casualties by attacking buildings, rather than people, and
providing warnings of operations; but many civilians, both Jewish and
non-Jewish, died in Irgun operations nonetheless. Much of the sharpest
opposition to the violence came from official Jewish organizations, which
denounced Irgun members as "terrorists."[38]

One of the largest attacks took place on July 22, 1946, when the King
David Hotel, headquarters of British rule in Palestine, was bombed.[39] The
attack, ordered by Begin, killed 91 people, mostly civilians: 41 Arabs, 28

Britons, 17 Jews, and five others.[40] Public reactions to the bombing were universally critical, including among the Jewish population in Palestine, and the backlash nearly led to the destruction of Irgun. In response, the British on July 25, 1946, launched Operation Shark, a huge search-and-seizure exercise involving 15,000 troops; it was the largest exercise of its kind ever carried out by the British army and police force in Palestine, and it dramatically set back Irgun operations. Operations nonetheless continued, including the bombing of a police station in Haifa, killing 13 and injuring 28. Seventeen British officers were killed and 27 wounded when Irgun drove a truck loaded with explosives into Goldsmith House, the officers' club in Jerusalem, an attack that prompted the institution of martial law.[41] On July 30, 1947, in one of the most notorious incidents of Irgun's campaign, two British soldiers were strangled and hanged, prompting widespread revulsion and increasing pressure for withdrawal in the United Kingdom. The way that the soldiers were killed and their bodies mutilated outraged domestic opinion in Britain: one of the hanging corpses was booby-trapped, and exploded when approached, injuring a British officer and blowing the body to bits. Widespread, detailed publicity in Britain about the episode, in the context of overwhelming anger about the costs of the occupation at a time of overstretched budgets and deprivation at home, catalyzed the decision to return the Mandate to the United Nations and withdraw British troops from Palestine.[42]

It would be specious to argue that the British left Palestine strictly as a result of Irgun; however, within a highly politicized international context, including widespread concern about the plight of the Jewish people, the British decision to quit was already ripe for implementation. Irgun disbanded with the creation of the state of Israel in May 1948. At Ben-Gurion's insistence, its members integrated into the newly formed Israeli army.[43]

The African National Congress and Umkhonto

The African National Congress (ANC) engaged in passive resistance for almost five decades but turned to armed struggle in 1961, in response to the Sharpeville massacre of March 1960. Antiapartheid demonstrators had gathered in Sharpeville to protest new government "pass laws" that limited where blacks were allowed to go. The police opened fire on the crowd, killing 69 people, many of them shot in the back as they fled.[44] The South African government declared a state of emergency and banned the ANC.[45] In December 1961, key ANC members, including Nelson Mandela, Walter Sisulu, and Oliver Tambo, established Umkhonto we Sizwe (meaning "Spear of the Nation" and shortened to Umkhonto, or

MK), which was also co-founded by the South African Communist Party. Essentially the ANC's armed wing, MK was dedicated to the overthrow of the regime and the ending of apartheid.[46] The MK's initial purpose was to engage in symbolic acts of sabotage and thus channel the growing frustrations of the Africans into a form of violence *other than* terrorism, targeted against Africans as well as whites, violence that Mandela feared would get out of control and destroy any hope of a multiracial state. According to Mandela's courtroom testimony at his 1963–64 trial, MK was meant to attack only political, military, and economic targets, with minimal loss of life, in an effort to change government policy.[47] Whatever the initial design, however, the MK's tactics later included targeting civilians, implicating the ANC in terrorist violence.[48]

The ANC's emphasis on racial inclusion distinguished it from the rival Pan Africanist Congress (PAC), created in 1959 under the leadership of Robert Sobukwe. The PAC, which adopted a Maoist doctrine and argued that South Africa was above all an African country that should belong to black Africans, later inspired the formation of the Black Consciousness Movement under the leadership of Steve Biko.[49] Compared to the PAC, the racially inclusive ANC seemed moderate, even as it increasingly engaged in armed attacks and competed with the PAC for popular support. ANC members were motivated by the writings of Che Guevara, Regis Debray, and Frantz Fanon, as well as by armed uprisings in Algeria and Cuba—although the ANC never developed the classic characteristics of a guerrilla movement, especially widespread support within the indigenous population and a strong internal underground movement.[50] According to Mandela, the organizational structure was actually fashioned after Irgun.[51] MK attacks were intended as "armed propaganda," catalysts for broader action, while avoiding large-scale war between the races in South Africa.[52] However, the failure to build a widespread underground network inside South Africa meant that the government was able to capture MK operatives relatively easily, and the relationship with the Communist Party also made it a focus of wider Western hostility. The first 15 years of the MK's campaign had symbolic effects on the government and on mass opinion by demonstrating continued resistance to apartheid, but they by no means gained the kind of momentum necessary to overthrow the regime.

The Soweto riots of 1976 were a crucial turning point in the campaign. The riots were sparked not by armed ANC-MK activity, but by popular anger toward the government's education policy, which required schoolchildren to learn and be taught in Afrikaans. The response was a truly mass uprising, with schoolchildren going on strike to protest learning "the language of the oppressor" (as Archbishop Desmond Tutu later put it). The Soweto Students' Representative Council's Action Committee organized a mass rally on June 16, 1976, involving between 3,000 and

10,000 children. They were met by police with tear gas and eventually fired upon. Between 200 and 600 people died, and more than 1,000 were injured, many of them children.

The Soweto riots were a watershed in the evolution of South African resistance to apartheid, representing the broad radicalization of young people and the passing of the cause to a new generation. Following the riots, several thousand young people reportedly joined MK camps in states around South Africa, including Angola, then-Rhodesia, Mozambique, and what later became Namibia.[53] Many white South Africans were outraged by the violence and withdrew their support for the regime. The riots also internationalized the antiapartheid movement. Photographs of dying children were transmitted around the world, broadening political support for the antiapartheid cause and leading to increased international sanctions against the South African government. The MK did not initiate this growing popular resistance, although it, and the cause of the ANC as a whole, clearly benefited from it.[54]

The ANC's disjuncture in political and military strategies and lack of broad organizational scope within South Africa continued to dog the group throughout the subsequent decade, however. Mandela's initial intention to confine MK violence to sabotage against "hard" targets, avoiding terrorist attacks against civilians, was not sustained during his years of imprisonment. The ANC had inadequate command and control structures, making the management of targeting effectively impossible. Notable MK attacks included the January 8, 1982, attack on the Koeberg nuclear power plant near Cape Town, the 1983 bombing of a street near the South African Air Force Headquarters in Pretoria (21 killed, 217 injured—both military and civilians), and the June 14, 1986, car-bombing of Magoo's Bar in Durban (three killed, 73 injured). As the decade unfolded, many more civilian targets were bombed, including "Wimpy Bar" fast food outlets and grocery stores, a rugby stadium in Johannesburg, and a bank in Roodepoort. The MK's professed focus on "hard targets" had by the end of the 1980s fully descended into a muddle, although growing Afrikaner government paramilitary activities admittedly made MK attacks seem minor by comparison.

Yet the disarray and lack of targeting discipline arguably had certain advantages for the ANC, by appearing to demonstrate strength. An MK attack on a bank in 1982, in which hostages were taken, illustrates how the ANC was able to straddle a difficult moral dilemma: the organization responded to conservatives within its ranks by denying responsibility for the incident, while benefiting from the widespread support for the attack when 10,000 young people attended the funeral of the three militants involved, whose caskets were draped in an ANC flag.[55] The organization was thus able to build support from as broad a spectrum as possible while maintaining a flexible and utilitarian relationship with the MK—a hazy moral connection that arguably later facilitated the ANC's transition from opposition movement to mass party of government in the early 1990s.

But the broader unrest in South Africa and the counterproductive government response to it played a far greater role in undermining the apartheid regime than did the activities of the MK. In 1984, protests against Tricameral Parliament elections ended in pitched battles between youth "comrades" and police. Two years later, in November 1984, inhabitants of townships in the Vaal Triangle rioted in response to rent rises implemented by black local councillors appointed by the apartheid regime.[56] In March 1985, a crowd of 4,000 was fired upon at Port Elizabeth, killing 20. Black councillors who were considered government collaborators were beaten and burned. From October 1984 to March 1985, 680,000 workers were on strike, and 400,000 were boycotting schools in the Johannesburg area alone. Between 1987 and 1990, clashes in the townships around Pietermaritzburg resulted in the deaths of 40,000, most of whom were young people.[57] Political violence erupted between urban and rural dwellers and between young and old residents, not necessarily between black and white or the government and the movement.

The ANC formally renounced violence in August 1990 and declared that its campaign had ended. On the heels of the announcement, an unprecedented wave of killing erupted, with 500 people dying in the next 10 days, apparently as a result of Zulu Inkatha Freedom Party (IFP) attacks sponsored by a government-linked paramilitary force.[58] Between 1990 and 1994, 14,000 people died in attacks, including random shootings on commuter trains and massacres at shanty towns—a much higher level of violence than at any time in the history of the antiapartheid conflict.[59] There was also a series of vicious attacks on trains by armed gangs that were probably members of the IFP, in which 600 people died and 1,400 were injured. Even as the ANC renounced its armed wing and began to share the center ground with the ruling National Party, South Africa was erupting in ethnic violence that was uncontrolled and perhaps uncontrollable.

The ANC became a legal political actor in 1990, having achieved its objective of ending the apartheid regime, and Nelson Mandela, imprisoned for terrorist acts from 1964 to 1990, was elected first president of postapartheid South Africa. The armed struggle was an important element in this success, but it was not the only factor. It may not even have been the most important. The extensive pressures that led to the end of apartheid, including economic, sporting, and cultural sanctions by the international community, a revolt among white English- and Afrikaner-speaking youth, a political revolt among members of the South African National Party, widespread, grassroots frustration and violence within the black community, and overreaction and violence by the Afrikaner regime, all undermined the legitimacy of the policy of apartheid and were more important than terrorist attacks.[60] Also crucial was the ending of the Cold War, a key development that rendered long-standing cooperation between the ANC-MK and the Communist Party instantly irrelevant. Indeed, while it is never possible to prove the counterfactual, in the broad context of the ending of the bipolar contest, the decaying political legitimacy of the Afrikaner regime, and the eruption of widespread ethnic violence, it is just as easy to argue that MK attacks on civilian targets *held back* the ANC's cause as it is to find evidence that they advanced it.

Other Notable Cases

A handful of other cases are regularly cited as successes for terrorism. The Zealots and Sicarii succeeded in provoking a mass insurrection in the first century of the Common Era, although it is debatable whether that was their true objective: insurrection was important mainly as a sign of messianic intervention.[61] Installed by the Nazis, the Croat Ustasa succeeded in obtaining their own state during World War II, but their "victory" was short-lived and their postwar terrorist acts accomplished nothing.[62] In 1998, the Colombian government conceded a "liberated zone" south of Bogota to the left-wing FARC, a move that some labeled a success for terrorism, but the territory was effectively retaken in 2002 and is therefore clearly not an example of strategic success.[63] The IRA is often said to have been rewarded for its terrorism by the power-sharing agreement in Northern Ireland, but the long-term purpose of the IRA campaign was to bring about a united Ireland, and in this it clearly failed. None of these is a serious example of terrorism's success.

Many groups that arose amid the mid-twentieth-century wave of national self-determination engaged in terrorist attacks that hastened the departure of colonial powers. In Algeria, the FLN used a combination of intimidation, terrorism, and information operations to influence and co-opt the population, both European and indigenous. The French often responded with overwhelming reprisals, leading to a spiral of violence. Although the FLN was weak militarily within Algeria, radicalization in metropolitan France and the strength of regional and international support overwhelmed the tactical successes of the French army's counterinsurgency campaign. In the end, the French concluded that, as long as the FLN could rely on support from outside Algeria, they would never stop fighting. Terrorism drew international attention to the cause and undermined the national political consensus that saw Algeria as an integral part of France, but the process of independence might well have occurred without it.[64]

EOKA is another example of a postcolonial-era struggle for national self-determination, in this case with respect to the British, but the organization's goal was not "independence" per se. The EOKA (Ethniki Organosis Kyprion Agoniston, or National Organization of Cypriot Fighters) fought to expel the British from Cyprus and unify the island with Greece. Launched with a series of bomb explosions across Cyprus on April 1, 1955, the EOKA campaign targeted British civilian installations and pro-British Cypriots, members of the Communist Party, pro-Turkish Cypriots, and members of the British military. The population was approximately 80 percent Greek Cypriot (Greek-speaking Greek Orthodox communicants) and 18 percent Turkish Cypriot (Turkish-speaking Muslims).[65] While the two groups had lived together reasonably peacefully, the struggle for Cypriot independence awakened the interest of the two mother countries in the fate of the island. EOKA was secretly aided by the Greek government, which sent arms and money, and broadcast propaganda supportive of the movement.[66] EOKA disbanded with the signing of the Zurich agreement in February 1959, paving the way for British withdrawal (although not unification of the island with Greece) and the eventual transfer of sovereignty to the independent republic of Cyprus in 1960.[67] The group had succeeded in its primary aim of British withdrawal, but the underlying problem of Greek and Turkish nationalism remained, resulting in the establishment of the EOKA-B in 1971 and, ultimately, the de facto division of the island.[68] This case can therefore be seen as a partial strategic success.

Palestinian terrorism against Israel likewise deserves mention here. Many argue that terrorism has been a demonstrated success for the Palestinians because it has attracted attention to their cause, fostered a national identity, earned them a seat at the negotiating table, and forced the Israeli government to concede the need for a Palestinian state.[69] There is no question that terrorism has given Palestinian groups more media coverage and more short-term leverage than might otherwise have been the case. But apart from notoriety and short-term leverage, has it advanced Palestinian national aspirations or quality of life? The emphasis on success in tactical terms takes away from the strategic perspective. The Palestinians may have kept their cause more prominently on the international agenda, but it is impossible to demonstrate that they have materially advanced it through terrorism.

There are many aspects of the Israeli-Palestinian case, media coverage being one, that are unique and do not transfer well to other cases. As Walter Laqueur points out, most generalizations about terrorism are made on the basis of the Palestinian example, and this has led to widespread and mistaken conclusions.[70] While it is impossible to prove a counterfactual (i.e., to assert the situation as it would be if the Palestinians had never turned to terrorism), it would be just as easy to argue that terrorism has delayed Palestinian national aspirations as it would be to argue that it has advanced them. The hyperbole associated with this case has distorted the reality: in the long run, despite widespread international interest in and focus on their plight, there is no convincing evidence that the Palestinians have benefited from the terrorist campaigns launched on their behalf.

How Success Ends Terrorism

Some campaigns eventually succeed and then end. This examination of case studies of success demonstrates a number of conditions under which campaigns that employed terrorism have achieved their strategic ends. First, they have succeeded when the goals of the group involved were well-defined and attainable.[71] Groups differ in the degree to which they project a specific, realistic vision of the future. Those that project vague or conflicting aims have difficulty attracting support. They struggle to exploit political opportunities when they arise, and find it hard to pass the cause on to the next generation of activists (a common problem examined in more detail in chapter 4). Territory is probably the most tangible and easily described goal, followed closely by support for kinfolk of a common religious or ethnic identity. These primal motivators are more effectively passed down through generations and perpetuated among a group's constituency, enabling the cause to spread and the group to endure.

Second, campaigns tend to succeed when their goals comport with broader historical, economic, and political changes that are occurring anyway in the international system. The popularization of the concept of national self-determination, the weakening of the colonial empires in the two world wars, and the wave of decolonization that followed in the mid-twentieth century led to a sense of opportunity for people living under foreign rule. It is no accident that the most successful cases of terrorism in the twentieth century were those in which a colonial power was no longer able to hold onto its territories. The Palestine Mandate, Ireland, Cyprus, Vietnam, and Algeria were all territories where national movements were eventually successful in their aim of achieving independence. Many of the terrorist organizations still carrying out attacks look admiringly at these "wars of national liberation" and rightly or wrongly engage in an enduring search for national self-determination, for example in such hot spots as the Basque region, Sri Lanka, and Sudan. The relationship between local movements and broader historical events can be crucial: the ending of South African apartheid aligned with the ending of the Cold War, not least because the links between the ANC and the South African Communist Party ceased to be an obstacle to the transition.

Third, campaigns succeed when terrorism is one part of a broader effort, soon supplemented or replaced by more legitimate uses of force. Terrorism is the *weak* tactic of the weak: attacks on civilians, by themselves, almost never lead to long-standing political results. In Palestine,

South Africa, and Algeria, terrorist attacks gained attention and resulted in short-term intimidation, but they were not the key element in the achievement of success. In the Palestine Mandate, the attacks of Irgun and Lehi almost resulted in war between Jewish groups as much as between the Jews in Palestine and the British. Well-known attacks such as the bombing of the King David Hotel resulted in repressive measures on the part of the British that lost them popular support; however, these attacks also undercut the legitimacy of the groups conducting them among their constituency and thus damaged their capacity to govern. In South Africa, the victory of the ANC was not achieved through the terrorist attacks engaged in by the MK, but was more a result of the popular uprising that occurred in the townships and the overreaction of the apartheid government in its response. In Algeria, terrorism was soon replaced by more traditional guerrilla warfare against the French, who were much more effective militarily even as their legitimacy was undercut by torture and atrocities that became known in mainland France. In short, despite popular perceptions, terrorism itself did not achieve the strategic objective in any of these cases, and may not even have advanced it.

Fourth, terrorist campaigns succeed when groups can convince more powerful actors of the legitimacy of their cause, especially if it means external funding, arms, and other support—as well as external political pressure, sanctions, and moral opprobrium against the targeted state. In the Irgun case study, strong postwar anger and guilt with respect to victims of the Nazi Holocaust led to widespread sympathy for the Jews in Palestine and support for the establishment of a Jewish homeland. This was a particularly powerful sentiment in the United States, which pressed the British to make concessions. Algerian nationalists gained legitimacy after political independence was granted to neighboring Tunisia and Morocco in 1956, and both states provided support and sanctuary. In South Africa, international sanctions helped to undermine the South African economy; decolonization combined with the civil rights movement in the United States put powerful pressure on the South African government and helped advance the antiapartheid cause. Terrorism was a relatively minor element in the final triumph of the ANC, which benefited from an internationally supported popular uprising in South Africa and arguably took power despite the activities of the MK, not because of them.

Conclusions

Terrorism is not a very promising vocation. The research detailed here demonstrates that the average life-span of a group is only about eight years, and the vast majority of campaigns fail. Only a small minority, less than 5 percent, have by their own standards fully succeeded in achieving their aims. Killing civilians in terrorist attacks is not a promising means of achieving political ends.

Terrorist attacks are as often retrogressive and undermining of a political cause as they are a successful means of achieving it. Rarely do terrorist assaults guide the world along the novel path the terrorists seek—be it the surrender of control over territory, the establishment of a new form of government, or the institution of a new social or religious system. They are most often successful when their cause comports with what is happening anyway in the broader international context. Terrorist leaders seldom choose to conclude a campaign on the grounds that their fundamental long-term political objectives have been achieved, because they very rarely are.

Yet sometimes terrorist attacks do play a role in bringing about political change. This is particularly the case when terrorist campaigns are in the service of very well-defined aims and complement the broader flow of history. Even then, however, groups that kill noncombatants must either transition to other more legitimate forms of violence, such as insurgency or conventional war, or acquire state sponsors, who often have their own political motivations for supporting them, or both. In 1977, Laqueur claimed that there was no historical case of a small terrorist group successfully taking power in a state. This still holds.[72] When a campaign is well under way, two further conditions improve the odds for success: first, the state has to overreact in its response; second, the terrorist group has to capture the imagination of a broader audience, mobilize popular support, and gain strength.

The only cases in the modern era where terrorism and its cause have truly triumphed are those in which a group has taken over the functions and governance of a state. All other "successes" are tactical advances—like the intrawar accomplishments of bombing campaigns, blitzkriegs, or invasions—satisfying to observers who appreciate the tactile and tangible, but wanting in terms of the struggles for legitimacy that these movements ultimately represent. And targeting civilians goes against that attempt to acquire legitimacy, so it must ultimately be disowned for a group to truly "win." Thus, it is impossible for terrorism *alone* to lead to success. It succeeds only in combination with other tools of political coercion and military force. There are countless short-term aims that keep a terrorist campaign under way, but terrorist campaigns in the modern era only succeed and end when they achieve the legitimacy of a state—or prod a state to concede legitimacy on its own.

damn good argument

CHAPTER FOUR

Failure

IMPLODING, PROVOKING A BACKLASH, OR BECOMING MARGINALIZED

> There is a point at which methods devour themselves.
> —*Frantz Fanon*[1]

TERRORISM CAN BE SELF-DEFEATING. Most terrorism ends because the group employing the tactic fails and eventually disintegrates. The short life-span and limited success of most groups that use terrorism demonstrate that violence deliberately targeted against civilians repels rather than attracts popular support. Indiscriminate killing creates a backlash and undermines political staying power. Terrorism creates havoc, murders innocent people, draws morbid fascination; but it is insufficient to achieve political or social change. Even when it is combined with more traditional methods of securing power, historical case studies indicate that the tactic most often works *against* the desired outcome and eventually has to be disavowed. As was demonstrated in the last chapter, terrorism succeeds strategically only when the state overplays or bungles its response and hands the group derivative power, or when the group has gained sufficient popular strength to transition to another form of violence.

But *why* does terrorism usually fail? What happens in the closing months of a doomed campaign? Since terrorism research tends to be subsidized by governments and affected by policy imperatives, the role of counterterrorism is often overemphasized in answering this question. The degree to which groups evolve independently of government action is seldom fully appreciated. Government data are what analysts know, what they can acquire, what they can most easily quantify and verify. Even with the best of intentions, they can be biased toward linking decline to specific government policies, especially after the fact, although the relationship between cause and effect may be unclear and unverifiable. Frequently the most powerful forces of decay operate within the group itself and are only indirectly affected by the policies of governments.

It is extraordinarily difficult to maintain the momentum of a terrorist campaign. More often than not, terrorism ends because the group implodes or loses its constituency, nudged along by pressure from the police or security services. Implosion happens when there is in-fighting over the mission, operations, competition for dominance, differences of ideology, loss of interest among members—even simple exhaustion or burnout. Groups that do not implode may be cut off from their supporters. Marginalization occurs when there is a diminution of active or passive public support, or even a popular backlash against the violence. This chapter examines patterns of failure that lead to the endings of groups, particularly the numerous ways that terrorism defeats *itself*.

IMPLOSION: MISTAKES, BURNOUT, AND COLLAPSE

As we have seen, most terrorist groups do not last long. Four typical scenarios for group implosion are failing to navigate the transition between generations, succumbing to in-fighting among members, losing operational control, and accepting amnesties or other exit pathways offered by the government. Each of these will be dealt with in turn.

Failure to Pass the Cause to the Next Generation

Groups that use terrorism face vulnerable passages, milestones that, if not reached and passed, quicken their demise. A particularly sensitive time is the point when an organization is transitioning from one generation to the next. Some groups have more staying power than others; certain characteristics may affect whether or not a group persists over numerous generations. As has been demonstrated here (and discussed in the last chapter) appealing to issues of identity such as religion or nationality, particularly when attached to a piece of territory, helps to lock in a connection to a constituency and promote the longevity of a group. But in general, terrorist organizations appear to be at their most susceptible when they are handing authority from one leader or cadre to another—a reason why governments may be attracted to the targeted killing tactics examined in chapter 1.

One way to judge where a group is in its life span is to look for developmental stages, especially psychological stages of growing alienation or moral disengagement.[2] Leonard Weinberg and Louise Richardson have argued that conflict theory applies to the life cycles of terrorist groups, including stages of emergence, escalation, and de-escalation. Unfortunately, they conclude that the framework is only useful in examining terrorist groups originating or operating in Western Europe in the late twentieth century (arguably the most overanalyzed period of terrorist violence);

its direct applicability to other places and periods is open to question.[3] Others suggest that there may be developmental stages for specific types of groups wherever they operate. The late Ehud Sprinzak, for example, argued that right-wing groups exhibit a unique cyclical pattern. Being driven by grievances that are specific to a cultural group, members are directed against "enemy" segments of the population defined by who they are—by race, religion, sexual preference, ethnicity, and other traits—not by what they do. A government that defends the target population also becomes a legitimate target. But the cycle of violence reflects underlying factors that may continue to exist, and experiences periods of flare-up and remission, depending on the degree to which the government is able to bring campaigns of violence under control.[4]

Some researchers, the intellectual descendants of Ted Robert Gurr, study the evolution of terrorist groups as types of social movements.[5] The more highly developed literature on social movements posits, for example, that terrorism may appear at the end of a cycle of the rise and fall of movements of mass protest.[6] From this perspective, the best way to understand the life span of a particular group is to study the broader movement of which it is a part. But social movements are rarely oriented mainly toward violence, and may just as easily be drawn toward more idealistic means. Understanding the pattern of mobilization may be important for dissecting the origins of an established group, but may not be as revealing of its likely end. While it is important, research into social movements on the whole gives more insight into the origins of terrorist groups than it does into their decline.

Finally, David Rapoport poses the broadest, historically based hypothesis on the life cycles of terrorist groups. He argues that over the course of modern history waves of international terrorist activity last about a generation (by which he means approximately 40 years). These waves are characterized by expansion and contraction and have an international character, with similar activities in several countries driven by a common ideology. Two factors are critical to Rapoport's waves: a transformation in communication or transportation patterns, and a new doctrine or culture. Using this perspective, the best way to predict or understand a group's demise is to study its relationship to broader generational patterns. When a wave of international terrorism reaches its peak and then declines, individual groups will find it more difficult to persist.[7]

All of these hypotheses provide insight into the phenomenon of terrorism overall, but they lack explanatory power when applied to specific cases and groups. While there are patterns, the story of each group's demise differs from the others—both the general and the particular are important. To truly understand this intergenerational process, we must examine case studies of particular groups or movements.

GENERATIONAL PATTERNS: LEFT-WING GROUPS IN THE 1970S

The nature of a group's ideology seems to affect its cross-generational staying power. The left-wing and anarchistic groups of the 1970s, for example, were notorious for their inability to articulate a clear vision of their goals that could be handed down to successive generations after the first group of radical leaders departed or were destroyed. The Second of June Movement, the Weather Underground Organization / Weathermen, and the Symbionese Liberation Army are examples of extremely dangerous, violent groups in which a leftist or anarchist ideology became bankrupt, undermining effective transition to a second or third generation.[8]

One of the most prominent and intensively-studied groups of the so-called New Left was the Rote Armee Fraktion (Red Army Faction), better known in the media as the Baader-Meinhof group. To say that they had an ideology would be an overstatement, as their guiding principles seemed to be a kind of cafeteria-style reference to ideas from Marxist-Leninism (especially anti-imperialism), anarchism, and the philosopher Frantz Fanon's theories about the beneficial, cleansing role of violence. They emerged in the late 1960s in the context of student unrest in Germany, channeling anger at the Vietnam War and the fate of Palestinians, and directing their rage at the U.S. military and the West German state. Andreas Baader, who founded the group along with his partner Gudrun Ensslin in 1968, was convicted as an arsonist following the bombing of a pair of department stores in Frankfurt. He escaped from jail with the help of a well-known left-wing journalist named Ulrike Meinhof, who gained access to the prisoner because she was allegedly helping him to write a book.

The fates of the convict and his intrepid rescuer quickly became a source of popular intrigue, especially as the image of daring countercultural revolutionaries had broad appeal among disaffected students. Baader, Meinhof, and compatriots went on another bombing spree, publicized by Meinhof, and were captured again in 1972. While they languished in jail, a second generation arose, reworked the tactics and mission of the group (particularly when the Vietnam War ended), and became a pale echo of their forebears, oriented toward gaining their leaders' freedom.[9] This new generation was on average five years younger than the original members, and many were younger brothers and sisters of older members, or friends, spouses, employees, lovers. The second generation's efforts peaked with the hijacking (in conjunction with the Popular Front for the Liberation of Palestine) of a Lufthansa aircraft in October 1977. The German tourists aboard were held as ransom for the release of 11 group members, including their leaders. When a German counterterrorist unit stormed the plane, killing three of the four hijackers and rescuing the hostages, the tide of history seemed clearly to have turned against them. Baader and Ensslin apparently shot themselves in their cells when they heard the news.[10]

As the group transitioned between generations, it became increasingly introspective, and its capacity to inspire a durable following declined. Although the RAF (as it was now generally known) continued into the 1980s, it also became increasingly isolated and irrelevant, arguably bearing little relation to its founders.[11] With the fall of the Berlin Wall, all of the Western European left-wing groups—in Belgium (the Fighting Communist Cells, or CCC), France (Action Directe), Portugal (the Popular Forces of April 25, or FP-25), Germany (RAF, Second of June Movement), and Italy (Brigatte Rossa and others)—recognized the end of an era of Marxist-Leninist revolutionary action.[12] After years of inactivity, the Red Army Faction succumbed to the obvious and announced its dissolution in 1998 with the words, "I was, I am, I will be again."[13]

GENERATIONAL PATTERNS: RIGHT-WING GROUPS IN THE 1990S

Right-wing groups, which draw their inspiration from fascist or racist concepts, can also have difficulty persisting over generations, though, as Martha Crenshaw observes, this phenomenon may reflect the challenges of tracking them rather than the actual disintegration of the group.[14] Examples include the numerous neo-Nazi groups in the United States and elsewhere.[15] Still, the racist causes of many of these groups can persist long after the vanishing of the group itself; their disappearance underground,[16] or their reemergence under a different name or structure is common.[17]

Extensive examinations by academic experts and the FBI of right-wing groups in the United States during the 1990s, especially after the 1995 Oklahoma City bombing, revealed a tendency to operate according to a common modus operandi, ideology, or intent, especially so-called leaderless resistance, which involves individual operatives or small cells functioning independently in pursuit of an understood purpose.[18] Such organizational decentralization complicates conclusions about beginnings and endings of right-wing groups; but it also may militate against truly effective generational transition. Furthermore, to support their activities, some right-wing groups engage in criminal behavior, such as bank robberies, racketeering, and counterfeiting, which, in the United States, have undermined group longevity by providing telltale evidence for the police.

Numerous right-wing groups in Europe demonstrate similar decentralized structures and episodic violence. The British neo-Nazi group Combat 18, for example, was originally formed to provide security at British National Party events, but in 1992 it split off to engage in violence.[19] The group reportedly also had connections with the Northern Irish Ulster Defence Association and the Ulster Volunteer Force, as well as sympathizers within the British army and among English soccer hooligans.[20] In 1996, apparently inspired by the Oklahoma City bombing, Combat 18 launched a campaign of letter bombs, while a neo-Nazi called David Copeland set off a series of nail bombs in ethnic minority areas of London and in Soho, a center of the city's gay culture: three people were killed and more than 140 injured.[21] Copeland, just the sort of so-called lone wolf that a horizontal, networked structure encourages, had learned how to construct the bombs from an Internet site. The lone-wolf style has its drawbacks, however: just as with Oklahoma bomber Timothy McVeigh, Copeland's mistakes and clumsy evidence trail eventually led to his arrest and conviction. On the one hand, operatives may be hard to preempt or catch when they operate according to individual initiative; on the other, they are difficult to control, lack staying power and are unlikely to groom successors.

Admittedly, staying power may not be their primary interest. Their objective may not be mobilization but provocation: right-wing groups in Britain have neither the strength nor the desire to develop a broad-based movement, aiming instead to prompt a backlash among ethnic minorities. Along with its splinter group White Wolves, Combat 18 urged members to kill nonwhites (so-called "aliens") so as to provoke a race war. "If this is done regularly, effectively and brutally, the aliens will respond by attacking the whites at random, forcing them off the fence and into self-defence," their declarative document read.[22] Combat 18 and other right-wing groups remain dangerous because of their capacity to provoke reactions among minority communities: they played an important role in the race riots in northern England in May 2001, for example. But as is the case with right-wing extremists in the United States, they are heavily infiltrated by informers and government agents, and the violence tends to be peripatetic. Without a broad social base, coordinating activities and perpetuating the cause between generations is a challenge.[23]

It is very risky to join an underground group that engages in violence; participation exacts a high cost from members, who may at any time be killed or arrested. Sometimes, individuals drift away because they simply do not see the promised goals materializing—either the organization's aims or the person's ambitions—or because they no longer find the goals compelling. In the absence of evidence of success or progress, operatives commonly experience burnout.[24] Revolutionary action is a young person's game. If there is no way to transition to a younger generation as members age, then the group may die of inertia. Failure to pass the legacy to a new generation is a common historical explanation for a group's decline or end.

Infighting and Fractionalization

Outside observers, especially those unwilling or unable to analyze individual groups in depth, often miss evidence of infighting and fractionalization among members. This is hardly surprising: the public image of a terrorist group is crafted so as to be a clear and uncomplicated expression of the group's ideological aims. An image of unity is essential. But it is a mistake to accept such a picture whole and uncritically, as it often papers over serious divergences of view that can lead to a group's end.

Terrorist attacks are designed to satisfy the requirements of a broader campaign; however, individuals or constituencies within that campaign may have different philosophies about the level and type of violence that occurs. Sometimes radicalized members want an attack so as to maintain morale at just a time when the broader population of active or passive supporters may be alienated by one. This happened, for example, in Italian and German left-wing groups, who engaged in much higher levels of violence than their public constituencies could withstand, in an effort to hold their membership together.[25] Alienation may occur within a group; Sean O'Callaghan, who joined the PIRA at the age of 15, later recounted his disgust when fellow members wanted a murder victim to be pregnant so as to get "two for the price of one." Feelings of growing disaffection catalyzed his decision to become a police informant.[26] At other times, individual members may be anxious to carry out attacks simply because they have a compulsive need for action, want to impress their colleagues, or are personally wedded to the idea of acting violently. Although individuals who join terrorist organizations are psychologically comparable to the general population, their socialization in the group may bring out a lust for violence that gets out of control, becomes counterproductive, and harms the cause of the group.

The internal dynamics of organizations that use terrorism can be counterproductive and self-defeating, either with respect to members or their sympathizers. Ambitious individuals may struggle for predominance within a group hierarchy, as was the case with the GIA (Groupe Islamique Armé) in Algeria in the mid-1990s, where the government actively encouraged factions within the group to proliferate.[27] Or factions may compete for favor with a particular constituency, as we saw in chapter 4 with Fatah and Hamas during the second intifada. Or individuals may be at the mercy of outside actors, intervening and manipulating factions of a movement for their own purposes; state sponsors and groups often follow that pattern, as did Libya's Mu'ammar Gadhafi and Abu Nidal. All of these behaviors may undermine the viability of the group as a whole, particularly if the leadership is in hiding or on the run, less able to control members and out of contact with the real world.

Members of organizations may also disagree about their operations, style, assets, or pace of escalation. Bickering within a group can have deadly consequences, not only for individual members but also for the viability of the group, especially if revenge killings are used to maintain operational control. According to interviews with prisoners, members of left-wing groups in Italy began to be disgusted by the growing brutality of operations, particularly after the assassination of a very young member of the group who was suspected of being a traitor.[28] Members of the West German Second of June Movement (an ally of the Baader-Meinhof group) shot their colleague Ulrich Schmucker because they believed that he had botched a bombing and become a police informant. A few weeks later Gotz Tilgener, a member who had refused to murder his colleague, was also murdered.[29] In February 1997, Paul Sargent, a former Combat 18 leader, and Martin Cross, a fellow member, killed Christopher Castle over control of the lucrative "white power" music scene.[30] His killing led other members to inform on the group and try to get out. Likewise, the FLQ (Le Front de Libération du Québec) essentially self-destructed as a result of bitter disputes over operations.[31]

Another source of internal dissent may be the general purpose of the violence, rather than its nature: historically, one of the most common sources of factional in-fighting is the interpretation of the group's ideology. Because of their relative weakness, terrorist groups are almost uniquely depending on their driving narrative or vision and may turn their violence on one another: in February 1969, for example, 14 members of the Japanese Red Army were tortured and killed by their compatriots because they disagreed over ideological issues.[32] Relations with "the people" are likewise a typical source of contention. Members of the RAF sometimes criticized the leadership for its elitist attitude, placing the "commando" at the forefront of the movement, making decisions without consulting others, and ignoring the views of followers.[33]

Groups may also decline because they lose a competition for members or support with other groups. Intergroup competition occurs quite apart from the counterterrorism activities of states. At the end of a social movement, groups often find themselves vying for the same potential followers and begin to jockey with each other for position. This competition took place between Palestinian groups in the second intifada. Another example is the competitive spiral of left-wing group competition in Italy during the 1970s, with fighting between the Red Brigades, Lotta Continua, and Prima Linea.[34] Groups may be more focused on competing with one another than they are on determining the effects of their attacks upon their desired audiences.

Another classic scenario for internecine violence is when disaffected members try to leave the group. Much seems to depend upon the degree to which the surrounding population supports or expects the violence: according to a former operative, members of the Red Brigades moved in and out of the group with relative ease, probably because left-wing violence in Italy was almost endemic.[35] Groups operating in more hostile contexts or with more bizarre ideologies may demand unquestioning fealty from their members. Aum Shinrikyo, for instance, was notorious for tracking down and killing former members or their relatives; indeed, the torture and death of one member's older brother (Kiyoshi Kariya) was what tipped off police about the group's activities.[36] Departures of the faithful can lead to ruthless internal violence and can easily destroy a group, especially if it is operating clandestinely and under pressure from the police: such struggles expose the group to potential betrayal by former insiders, cast doubt on those who were close to the dissident, and undercut its ideology by demonstrating that some adherents have turned against it. Maintaining the loyalty of members becomes a top priority, since a clash of legitimacies may be hindered by any evidence of loss of faith.

Loss of Operational Control

Control over operations is another classic problem for groups. There is a reverse correlation between the nature of an organization and the nature of its planning of operations. Networked organizations may more easily carry out attacks, compartmentalize information, and keep themselves safe from detection, but whether they actually work toward the achievement of the cause is another question. Security and efficiency are always at odds, a dilemma that has been recognized by terrorist groups since the nineteenth century. Under pressure from state counterterrorism, targeting becomes more difficult and groups often progressively lose control over their operatives, resulting in a widening of acceptable targets to include more easy-to-hit "soft" targets. Meanwhile, the security imperative that leads to the compartmentalization of information and the limiting of communications among cells increases inefficiencies and mistakes.[37] Amateurish operations may become counterproductive as a lack of discrimination prompts a backlash among potential constituents. Even with the best of training and intentions, groups may find that heightened police pressure reduces their ability to reconnoiter potential targets, leading to more haphazard targeting and greater potential for a popular backlash, mistakes, and unintended consequences.

Sometimes individuals are recruited because of their skills but they then become unmanageable. A lack of operational control can lead different parts of an organization to work against each other, carrying out activities that are counterproductive to their strategic aims. This happened with the Northern Ireland protestant paramilitary groups the Ulster Volunteer Force (UVF) and the Ulster Defense Alliance (UDA) in their closing days, when their leaders were unable to control rogue killings.[38] Another example is the Weather Underground, which in 1970 split into three components, lacking central direction: one each in San Francisco, Chicago-Detroit, and New York. Without the knowledge of the others, the latter accidentally blew up a bomb factory in a townhouse, killing three members, drawing the attention of law enforcement, and changing the trajectory of the group toward its ultimate demise.[39]

Accepting an Exit

We have already examined the dynamics of groups that are considering negotiations with a government. Sometimes a form of negotiation occurs with individual members of the group, drawing them away from their colleagues either through personal incentives or threats. The state from time to time offers its enemies a way out. In Italy, laws passed in December 1979 and May 1982 offered leniency if operatives separated themselves from their groups, helped to solve old crimes, or assisted the authorities in preventing attacks. Although the amnesty guidelines were hard to apply, the program drew scores of participants: shortly after the enactment of the 1982 law, there were 130 *pentiti* informing on their former comrades. Numerous operations were foiled and lives were undoubtedly saved.[40] As a result of the work of informants, the Red Brigades (as well as all their smaller rivals) were in retreat everywhere by the end of 1982.

Sometimes groups simply come to the conclusion that their goals are not being achieved through terrorist violence. Whole groups have been amnestied by the state, even without a formal negotiation process, in exchange for an agreement to contribute productively to a political process. In Colombia, the group M-19 was given a blanket amnesty, renounced violence, and became a political party called the M-19 Democratic Alliance (Alianza Democrática M-19, or AD/M-19), fielding candidates in 1990.[41] In October 1973, U.S. federal attorneys sought to lift indictments against members of the Weather Underground going back to 1970. Militants turned themselves in, and the group had collapsed by 1976.

Amnesty offers cause internal dissension that extends well beyond the individuals who accept an exit. "Supergrasses" in Northern Ireland, recruited to inform on compatriots in return for personal amnesties and other rewards, were a major factor in unraveling the republican movement.[42] Internal informers are particularly devastating to groups that have organized into cells and are difficult to track otherwise.[43] But apart from their intelligence value, the specter of betrayal can lead to fratricide. ETA members accepted a 1981 amnesty offer from the Spanish government; the group was diminished, although in this case the violence persisted.[44] Members of the ETA who decided to accept the amnesty were harassed, injured, and killed by younger recruits who thought their elders had gone soft or were betraying the movement.[45] Their murders elicited outrage among the Basque population, further undermining the organization's ability to recruit. Still, groups that are in their final phases may not necessarily be more peaceful: the ETA carried out a series of bomb attacks in 2004 while it was again engaged in talks about amnesty with the Spanish government.[46]

While this chapter treats the reasons for group implosion, it does not review the full range of reasons why *individuals* voluntarily leave terrorist groups: motivations to quit terrorism may reflect proclivities or experiences that differ from person to person. These may include developing social bonds with individuals outside a group (romantic attachments, marriage, having a child, becoming devoted to family), deciding to join a competing group, being demoted within a group, or simply getting too old to keep up with one's compatriots. Expectations about the life of a revolutionary may be disappointed, individuals may lose interest or enthusiasm, they may fall out with comrades, or they may simply get tired of life on the run. They may also be caught and imprisoned, obviously changing the nature of a person's involvement (though disengagement is by no means foreordained).[47] The question of individual disengagement from terrorism has been explored by psychiatrists and psychologists, particularly through interviews with prisoners in Italy, Germany, Israel, and Northern Ireland, as well as more recent work in South and Southeast Asia. Psychological research on individuals, though important and deserving of further development, is beyond the scope of this study.[48]

Marginalization: Diminishing Popular Support

Terrorist groups are strategic actors that usually deliberate about their targets and calculate the effects of attacks on their constituent populations. However, they can undermine their cause if they miscalculate, resulting in plummeting popular support and even the demise of the group. They generally cannot survive without either active or passive support from a surrounding population. Active support includes hiding members, raising money, providing other sustenance, and, especially, joining the organization. Passive support, as the phrase implies, is more diffuse and includes ignoring obvious signs of terrorist group activity, declining to cooperate with police investigations, sending money to organizations that act as fronts for the group, and expressing support for the group's objectives.

Popular support for a terrorist group can dissipate for a number of reasons. First, people who are not especially interested in the political aims of a group may fear government counteraction. Apathy is a powerful force; all else being equal, most people naturally prefer to live their daily lives without the threat of being targeted by counterterrorism laws, regulations, sanctions, raids, and threats. Sometimes even highly radicalized populations can pull back from active or passive support for a group, especially if the government engages in strong repressive measures and people simply become exhausted. The apparent loss of local popular support for Chechen terrorist groups is a good example.

Second, the government may offer supporters of a terrorist group a better alternative. Reforms, increased spending, and job creation in underserved areas can all erode sources of terrorist violence. But this approach is not a panacea: it can also result in heightened instability and a sense of political opportunity, situations that have sometimes led to *more* terrorist acts. Evidence suggests that the extent to which societal conditions lead to a sense of "indignation" or frustrated ambition during a period of transition might be crucial in the decision to turn to terrorist violence.[49] Reforms must be carefully calibrated to local conditions. Sometimes terrorist attacks are seen as an effort to nudge the flow of history further in one's direction. If history is moving along the right way (and at the right pace), then the incentives for violent behavior decrease.

Third, populations can lose interest in the ideology or objectives of a terrorist group; events can evolve independently such that the group's aims become outdated or irrelevant. A sense of historical ripeness or opportunity may have been lost. Examples include many of the Marxist groups inspired by communist ideology and supported by the Soviet Union. This is perhaps a major reason why the nature of international terrorism has evolved beyond primary reliance upon state sponsorship toward a broader range of entrepreneurial behaviors. Case studies of decline will be explored in greater depth below.

The Ideology Becomes Irrelevant

To inspire a following, a group's ideology must have achievable goals, some evidence of progress toward those goals, some degree of organization, and relevance to broader historical circumstances. While members may actually be inspired by overwhelming odds, a truly lost cause eventually becomes obvious even to the faithful. Terrorist leaders are all amateur historians: historical irrelevance is the death knell of any group.

There are many examples of groups that were essentially left behind by history. Members of the Weather Underground were surprisingly effective at evading arrest, for example, but the end of the Vietnam War, for reasons that had nothing to do with their activities, spelled its demise.[50] Many groups that had been supported, directly or indirectly, by states such as Cuba, East Germany, or the Soviet Union found themselves fading through the 1990s. The Red Army Faction, the official IRA, and the ETA all received indirect support from the Soviet Union through East Germany and what was then South Yemen; likewise, the PFLP was given arms by the Soviet Union.[51] Sudan had largely ended its support for terrorism by the end of the decade, and Libya expelled Abu Nidal and cut off support to Palestinian groups such as the PIJ and the PFLP-GC.[52] The fall of the Soviet Union and the demonstrated irrelevance of Leninist ideology seriously undercut many leftist groups.

The ultraleftist Greek group Revolutionary Organization 17 November is an example of an organization whose ideology gradually lost touch with reality even as the group itself lost touch with the people on whose behalf it claimed to act. Born in anger at the U.S.-supported military junta that ruled Greece from 1967 to 1974, 17 November first gained attention with the murder of CIA station chief Richard Welch in 1975. Over the next 27 years, it conducted more than 100 bombings and assassinations, killing a total of 23 people.[53] However, by the time it was dismantled by the police the group had no known support base, and the public mood had turned sharply against it. The June 8, 2000, killing of British military attaché Brigadier Stephen Saunders led to widespread revulsion, especially after the moving public appearance of his widow Heather Saunders, pleading for help in tracking down her husband's killers. The Greek Orthodox Church held a prayer service for the victims of terrorism, politicians spoke out against the killing, and attitudes toward the violence shifted dramatically. Greece had signed all 12 of the U.N. counterterrorism conventions by the end of 2000.[54]

Over most of the group's lifetime Greek authorities seemed to have little knowledge of (and some say, little interest in) how big 17N was or who was in it, until a botched 2004 operation enabled them to work out the connections between members. Savvas Xiros, a religious icon painter, was standing near the ticket office of Hellas Flying Dophins in the port city of Piraeus when a bomb he was carrying blew up, apparently prematurely. His face, hands, and chest seriously injured, Xiros was rushed to a local hospital where police were able to interrogate him.[55] He informed on the organization's operations, revealed the location of weapons caches, and named other members. They turned out to be surprisingly ordinary folk, including schoolteachers, shopkeepers, a telephone operator—all of whom led otherwise mundane lives. Three of the terrorists were brothers, two others were cousins, and another was godfather to the others' children.[56] As is so often the case with terrorist groups that endure, members of 17N were drawn from family and kin—blood ties that both strengthened bonds of trust and also made the group susceptible to collapse.[57]

17 November lacked the organizational capacity or even inclination to be either a broad-based guerrilla force or an effective mass movement. Its leftist revolutionary ideology was a relic of the past. The group's strategy had been to provoke the people into action against the regime; however, by the time its campaign unraveled in the wake of a minor mistake, 17N was the subject of popular revulsion, isolated from mainstream political thought, and unable to rely on the kind of broad-based support that lends staying power.

Loss of Contact with "the People"

Because of the role of ideology and popular mobilization, a common point of contention concerns the degree to which a group represents the "people" or is actually a small elite. This is not just a Marxist theme, framed in terms of class conflict; it is also evident among groups that describe themselves as nationalist, right-wing, even anarchist. Not all groups have as their goal reaching out to the people; but at some point virtually all speak of catalyzing or inspiring the masses and gaining a base. Humans are by nature social creatures, and true political transformation eventually requires a following.

One of the biggest problems for many groups in the twentieth century was trying to remain in touch with a constituency even as they operated underground. The more groups drew in upon themselves, because of state repression, police successes, or the revulsion of the public, the more they tended to operate according to their own internal dynamics and become further removed from the public, thereby undermining both their raison d'être and their ability to operate.[58]

One of the main effects of police pressure is to prevent groups from being able to communicate well with their public. Life underground was catastrophic for the Red Brigades, for example, as the group became more and more detached from its grassroots sympathizers.[59] As militants engaged in increasingly self-perpetuating violence, they hardly noticed their supporters deserting them, making their activities counterproductive and irrelevant.[60] The secrecy and organizational dispersion necessary to evade the police worked against their central purpose of communicating with the masses. One of the ways that they tried to deal with this problem was by creating what they called "double militance" (*doppia militanza*), where members took part in underground work and also engaged in public political work. Following extensive arrests in May 1972, however, the group reverted to "clandestinity."[61]

Some groups have tried to compensate for their isolation from the public by building international connections with other groups. For example, the Red Army Faction was connected to the Spanish Group GRAPO (First of October Antifascist Resistance Group), the Belgian CCC (Communist Combatant Cells), and France's Action Directe (Direct Action). Likewise, the Japanese Red Army formed connections with Palestinian groups, especially the Popular Front for the Liberation of Palestine, but also had contact with M-19 in Colombia and Islamists in Syria, Libya, Thailand, and Malaysia.[62]

Targeting Errors and Backlash

Terrorist attacks can cause backlash among the group's actual or potential public constituency. This is a common strategic error and can easily cause the group to implode. Independent of the specific counterterrorist policies of a government, a terrorist group may choose a target that a wide range of its constituents considers illegitimate, undercutting the group and transferring popular support to the government's response. As we have seen, for example, the Omagh bombings resulted in deep shock and fury in Northern Ireland. Despite hasty statements by RIRA leaders that they did not intend to kill civilians, the group never recovered.[63] Following the bombings, the RIRA was plagued by in-fighting; morale was so low that in 2002 some members reportedly sought a separate cease-fire deal with the Irish government.[64] Other examples of tactical miscalculation abound. In February 1970 the Popular Front for the Liberation of Palestine–General Command sabotaged a Swissair plane en route to Tel Aviv, resulting in the death of all 47 passengers, 15 of whom were Israelis. The PFLP-GC first claimed responsibility for the event, but tried to retract its claim when the scale of public revulsion became clear. In Canada, the FLQ's 1970 killing of Pierre Laporte sharply drove Québecois public opinion away from the group and toward more conventional political participation.[65] Public revulsion was a factor in the undermining of support for Sikh separatism in India,[66] while the Beslan school seizure destroyed sympathy for Chechen separatism in Western Europe.[67]

The Basque case is interesting in this context. In 1978, in an effort to provoke public anger against the government, ETA bombed the construction site of a nuclear power plant. Two people were killed in the operation, and 14 were injured. The organization had badly misjudged the effects of its actions, however. Instead of being inspired by the symbolic violence and empowered against the government, tens of thousands of

Basque residents took to the streets to demonstrate against the group.[68] The next year the group made a similar mistake when it planted bombs in tourist areas and in Madrid, killing 10 people and injuring around one hundred, again leading to outrage and large popular demonstrations. Since then popular support has continued to erode as ETA has become increasingly indiscriminate in its targeting.[69] In 1997, a survey indicated that almost half of all Basques had participated in at least one demonstration against the group.[70]

Another famous Western European example of an operation that seriously hurt the cause was the killing of Aldo Moro by the Italian Red Brigades (Brigatte Rossa, or BR) in 1978. Twice prime minister and a leading candidate for president, Moro may have been the most important political figure in postwar Italy. Fifty-five days after seizing him (killing his chauffeur and five bodyguards in the process), the BR left his bullet-riddled body in the trunk of a red Renault, parked exactly halfway between the Communist Party headquarters and the Christian Democratic Party headquarters in Rome (an allusion to Moro's attempts to form a coalition government with the Communists).[71] The ability of the group to evade a huge manhunt made them appear strong and earned them respect: recruitment increased and resources grew.[72] The PFLP (Popular Front for the Liberation of Palestine) in particular took the Moro operation as evidence that BR was a serious and like-minded group, and began to supply it with arms.[73]

But Moro had been a popular politician, and even his enemies found his killing deeply repulsive. During his days in captivity, he had written numerous well-publicized letters to his family and colleagues in government, begging them to make the concessions necessary to earn his release.[74] Following the killing, thousands of people took to the streets in Rome, holding signs reading "Moro Lives," and vowing a united front against terrorism. Political leaders and the pope denounced the murder, and the Italian parliament passed a tough new antiterrorism law. Even jailed members of the BR later said they could not fathom why Moro had been chosen as a target, and began to cooperate with police in the effort to hunt down their compatriots. Dissent grew within the organization, with BR members such as Adriana Faranda and Valerio Morucci declaring their opposition to the killing and eventually openly breaking with the group.[75]

The Moro killing reversed the upward trajectory of the Red Brigades. The state began a harsh and widely applauded counterterrorism campaign, popular support for the group dried up, the Red Brigades began to crumble from within, and by 1982 it had effectively faded. The end was formally declared by the group itself: in April 1984, four of the Red Brigades' key leaders wrote a communiqué from their jail cells, ending the campaign and claiming that "the international conditions that made this struggle possible no longer exist."[76]

Another notorious targeting debacle concerns the November 1997 killing of 62 people in the town of Luxor in southern Egypt by the Islamist group al-Gama'a al-Islamiyya, or GAI. The attack arose out of a split between those who believed that accommodation with the Egyptian government was unavoidable, and those who bitterly opposed it.[77] GAI's first plan was to strike the opening performance of Verdi's opera *Aida*, which was to be attended by Suzanne Mubarak. Killing the president's wife would be a symbolic strike against the state, as well as an outrageous provocation, demanding an overreaction by the government. On the night, however, the performance venue—in front of Queen Hatshepsut's temple—was swarming with 3,000 security officers. The attackers shifted to a softer target: the archaeological sites at Luxor. On the morning of November 17, 1997, six men wearing military fatigues and red headbands killed 58 foreigners and four Egyptians. Among the dead were a five-year-old British child and four young Japanese couples on their honeymoon. Thirty-five of the dead were Swiss, with other victims including Germans, French, Bulgarians, and Colombians. One Swiss woman saw her father's head cut off in front of her. One of the assailants died at the scene, and the other five died under circumstances that are still debated: local villagers may have lynched them, but it is more likely that the security services killed them or they took their own lives.[78] Egyptians were revolted by the attacks, both because of their brutality and because they targeted the tourist economy upon which many depended. The incident mobilized public opinion against terrorism, and imprisoned Islamists claimed themselves shocked by the killings. Islamist terrorism in Egypt all but disappeared.[79] According to Lawrence Wright, in the five years before Luxor, Islamist groups in Egypt had killed more than 1,200 people, many of them foreigners; after Luxor, attacks abruptly stopped.[80] (See table 4.1.)

How Failure Ends Terrorism

The core of a terrorist organization's viability is its claim to be acting altruistically, on behalf of a larger cause. This claim of legitimacy is the source of its strength, but also its vulnerability: if a group miscalculates and targets poorly, the blunder is potentially more damaging than a comparable error by the state. States have a degree of immortality in the international system; groups do not. Governments are expected to be hypocritical; terrorist organizations cannot afford it. States that fail to publicize and exploit targeting errors by terrorist groups are missing a time-honored opportunity to facilitate the end of a campaign.

TABLE 4.1
Historical Cases of Group Failure

Implosion: Mistakes, Burnout, and Collapse	
Failed generational transition	Second of June Movement
	Weather Underground
	Red Army Faction (RAF)
	National Warriors of South Africa
	Christian Patriots
	Aryan Nations / the Order
	Hammerskin Nation
	The Anti-Zionist Movement
	Combat 18 / White Wolves
	German People's Union
	National Front in Europe
Infighting and fractionalization	FLQ (Front de Libération du Québec)
	PIRA
	Second of June Movement
	Combat 18
	Japanese Red Army
	Aum Shinrikyo
Loss of operational control	Ulster Volunteer Force (UVF)
	Ulster Defence Alliance (UDA)
	Weather Underground
Amnesties / accepting an exit	Red Brigades
	M-19
Marginalization: Diminution of Popular Support	
The ideology becomes irrelevant	Revolutionary Organization 17 November
	Weather Underground
	Abu Nidal Organization
Loss of contact with "the people"	Red Brigades
	Red Army Faction
	Japanese Red Army
Targeting errors and backlash	Real Irish Republican Army (RIRA)
	PFLP-GC
	FLQ
	Sikh separatists
	Chechen separatists
	ETA
	Red Brigades
	al-Gama'a al-Islamiyya (GAI)

Operational errors are the most well-established method of rapid self-defeat. Groups of many types and motivations know that tactical errors can be devastating to their cause. According to Phil Andrews, a member of the right-wing National Front in Britain who served time in jail for attacking a police sergeant, "There were always elements from the grass roots who wanted us to move toward terrorism, but these demands were always resisted by the leadership. It wasn't that they necessarily had any moral problems with it, more that they were worried the tactics would backfire."[81] As we have seen, mistakes can happen when a group chooses its tactics poorly, or even when its members begin to operate independently and counterproductively without central control. For all the popular enthusiasm about networked operations, their downside is the encouragement of rogue or amateur operatives, unconvinced and uncontrolled by a strategic plan. Knowledge of the "commander's intent" only goes so far when circumstances change, particularly when there are numerous self-appointed "commanders" jockeying for predominance. Because of the symbolic, leveraged nature of terrorist violence, popular repulsion in the wake of stupid attacks is more perilous to groups than is state repression; best of all for hastening terrorism's end are state actions that spotlight repulsive killings and exploit mistakes, amplifying their resulting backlash among a group's constituency so as to wipe out any residual romanticism about the cause.

Other causes of organizational "suicide" include failing to excite the interest of a second or third generation, experiencing burnout, succumbing to individual members' departures or betrayals, and breaking into competing splinters. All of these may result in the group turning its violence against itself instead of the state. All can be promoted by steady pressure against a group applied by either the military or security services; however, there is no substitute for understanding the unique dynamics of individual groups within their local cultural, historical, and political contexts, and then tailoring precise policies to exploit their specific individual and organizational vulnerabilities. State policies formed through vague sweeping generalizations, ignorance of cultural tendencies, ideological blinders, and unawareness of the nature of ties among members only offer incentives for groups to pull together and unite against the "other." They are a gift to the group.

Of course, not all groups are dependent on mass support, and many deliberately try to provoke government repression so as to increase the likelihood that they will attract recruits. They may also be able to cause a great deal of damage and suffering in the short run. Yet in the absence of some minimal level of public sympathy, there is nowhere for members to hide, and it is difficult to operate effectively over time. A group may endure, but without demonstrated progress toward its goal, the weight of history is against it: a group's ideology may be overtaken by events, its supporters may be cowed by government counteraction, or it may find another solution to the problem that originally catalyzed the movement.

Crucial developments in the twenty-first century have altered the relationship between groups and their constituencies in ways that both add to and detract from their potential vulnerability. On the plus side, the decline of state-sponsored terrorism has meant that the relationship between a group and its constituents is more important than ever. State support had to some extent insulated groups from the effects of backlash or erosion of public support by providing a separate source of income and protection. State-sponsored groups were as a result more lethal than those without government benefactors.[82] Now, however, most groups have diversified their resources, acquiring support from a broader range of sources, including charities, criminal activity, and diasporas. The Internet and associated technologies have greatly enhanced the ability of groups to communicate directly with individuals, targeting their message to potential recruits anywhere in the world. Easy access to a broader public enables groups to maintain contact through relatively anonymous channels that may seem impervious to interference.

But this seeming invulnerability is deceptive. The flip side of diversification of terrorist assets and channels of communication is the relative sensitivity of their assorted sources of support to targeting errors or changes in the public mood. If terrorist groups have been forced to become more "populist" by increasing their appeal and widening their reach to potential constituencies, they are likewise increasingly subject to the changing whims of their putative constituencies. States may not now be able to pressure other states to end support for groups through the usual diplomatic or military channels, or to control media or borders or resource flows as effectively or as easily as they might have done in the past; but they can certainly produce counteracting messages, appealing to targeted constituencies and gathering intelligence through the sophisticated use of the Internet. Every link, however brief, between an individual and a group is both a conduit for violence and a window into the organization's structure and operations. Groups can cause a lot of damage even in the absence of widespread support, but they are unlikely to perpetuate political change or attract the resources necessary to be most effective.

The point of understanding these masochistic aspects of terrorist campaigns is decidedly *not* that states can simply sit back and wait for a movement to end in failure. Terrorist groups can do a great deal of damage even as they hobble along, especially in the context of enhanced access to increasingly destructive weapons. But comparative study demonstrates that some policies are synergistic with the natural tendency of groups to implode, while others increase their ability to prolong themselves, or even gather momentum. Waiting passively for failure is insufficient; but under-standing these self-defeating dynamics and nudging them along through carefully targeted, synergistic counterterrorism is indispensable. A major purpose of terrorism is to use shock and outrage to mobilize a popula-tion. To the extent that that population does indeed become mobilized, however, terrorism may become counterproductive, because terrorist vio-lence contains within itself the seeds of repulsion and revulsion. Violence has an international language, but so does decency.

CHAPTER FIVE

Repression

CRUSHING TERRORISM WITH FORCE

> We have scored a success in Chechnya. The problem has been solved.
> —*Russian defense minister Sergei Ivanov, February 2007*[1]

ANSWERING THE THREAT of terrorism with repression, a state's strongest means of defending itself, is natural—even instinctive. Terrorism is meant to frighten and provoke, and state leaders are among those who get scared and angry. It is a basic human instinct to fight fire with fire, force with force, and terror with terrifying responses. The state's response takes the form of intervention, when the threat is based beyond the borders of the target state (as with Israel's 1982 involvement in Lebanon); or internal repression, when the threat is mainly domestic (as in Turkey with the PKK); or, as is typically the case, some combination of the two (as in Colombia).[2] The nation-state was forged as a unique composite of law and strategy, the internal and external realms of authority; terrorism assaults both.[3] We should hardly be surprised that states respond in the way that they were designed to respond.

Sanctimonious statements about the foolishness of force reveal an ignorance of history, or at least a selective memory. From the French Revolution to the present, repression—meaning the state's use of overwhelming, indiscriminate, or disproportionate force, internally or externally (or both)[4]—has been a common answer to terrorism, frequently bringing with it enormous costs. The Western nation-state was consolidated through terrorism: we are often reminded that the earliest modern use of the term dates to the Jacobin reign of terror between March 1793 and July 1794.[5] History demonstrates that extremism and terrorism are birth pangs of the state, particularly during periods of broader global transition. At some point in the last two centuries, states in every part of the world have used oppressive force to stamp out terrorism at home or abroad.[6] In fact, it is much harder to think of states that did *not* use repression than those that did. By comparison, the United States, notwithstanding the current wars in Afghanistan and Iraq, has rarely used military force—not because it has been uniquely restrained, but because terrorist attacks on U.S. interests have been comparatively distant or un-threatening.[7] It has not been comparably tested.

Pundits who argue that the reflexive use of force against terrorism today is abnormal or unusual are either being hypocritical or absent-minded—or both. Europeans invented modern terrorism and then used it extensively. European leaders who have happily passed their period of greatest anxiety during the nineteenth and twentieth centuries—when terrorist attacks by anarchists, social revolutionaries, fascists, leftists, and nationalist/separatists threatened the stability of regimes, the continent, and arguably the rest of the world—can hardly claim to be ignorant of the challenge terrorism can pose to the state. Nor can they deny a long history of responding to challengers with brute force. New regimes in other regions have likewise tended to use overwhelming force in answer-ing terrorist attacks, perhaps because the challenge is keenly threaten-ing in the early phases of a regime—and also because more restrained, phlegmatic counterterrorism policies grow from experience, even trial and error. Notable examples of brutal crackdowns include postcolonial governments in Algeria, Sri Lanka, Egypt, and India.

Terrorism slashes at the very fabric of the modern nation-state, picking at a vulnerable seam between domestic law and foreign war, the inter-nal and external realms of authority. Arguing over which paradigm best suits the threat—war or crime—says more about the rigid intellectual and bureaucratic structures of the state than it does about the nature of terrorism, which is opportunistic. If looked at as a form of war, terrorists use irregular violence because they are unable or unwilling to meet a gov-ernment on the battlefield.[8] If looked at as a form of crime, terrorists cir-cumvent the law by using political motivations to excuse their actions.[9] From the state's perspective, force offers a readily available rejoinder to both that is firmly under its control. Seams are easily ripped open. Trying to shift the violence to a form that is familiar and more advantageous is an understandable response; this is exactly what is happening when a government declares martial law or sends forth the troops.

From a position of disadvantage, terrorist violence seeks to challenge the state on two levels: among its citizens, by creating doubt about the state's ability to protect them from harm; and internationally, by under-mining traditional notions of national sovereignty. Random, politically motivated attacks against noncombatants undermine the state's credibil-ity at home. Attacks abroad project an image of impotence and diminish state power, or so many leaders believe, and their perceptions enhance the strategic impact of the incidents themselves. Regardless of the strength of the state, terrorism may be perceived as a threat to its power and the na-tional interest. Before 9/11, for example, it is no accident that the United States retaliated militarily only in the wake of attacks on targets that were directly connected to the state itself, including U.S. service personnel, a former U.S. president, and two U.S. embassies.[10] Terrorism is symbolic violence, and that symbolism is not lost on political leaders.

ANALYZING THE STRATEGIES OF TERRORISM

In the wake of major attacks, officials tend to respond (very humanly) to popular passions and anxiety, resulting in policy made primarily on tactical grounds and undermining their long-term interests. Yet this is not an effective way to gain the upper hand against nonstate groups. Terrorism has been most effective as a strategy that draws its power from state action, and when governments acquiesce to it, it is almost impossible to win.
    In framing their counterterrorism strategies, many Western leaders, especially in the United States, have been heavily influenced by the apparent successes of strategic bombing during World War II. Especially in the closing phases of the war, strategic bombing seemed to work remarkably well in the end (at least for the Allies), helping to win the war and destroy the fascist powers. As such, it is the archetypal lesson of twentieth-century warfare and a seductive paradigm for counterterrorism: terrorist attacks usually involve bombings, may kill large numbers of civilians, and challenge the public will. The answer is to retaliate massively. Coming from abroad, the September 11 attacks in particular looked exactly like strategic bombing, both in their physical effects and in their psychological impact—a surprise attack in a war of annihilation, fitting right into the elaborate strategic thinking perfected over the twentieth century. Rightly or wrongly, is it any wonder that terrorist attacks on U.S. civilians elicited the same state-centered response?
    But this thinking leaves out half of the strategic equation. It is a remnant left over from a war between peer competitors, a relic that needs updating and may bear little relation to the continuing evolution of international terrorism. Lacking a significant military structure, terrorist groups evade the state's military apparatus and seek to pull it deeper and deeper into an unwinnable, irregular war. A better approach is to consider strategies from the perspective of a group aiming to influence state action for its own purposes. For nonstate challenger groups, wars of attrition and annihilation are parallel to operations that undermine the state's contract with its citizens (attrition) and operations that elicit action counterproductive to the interests of the state (annihilation). In other words, today's terrorism assaults the state by either threatening its purpose or influencing its behavior. Both are strategies of *leverage*, used by the weak against the strong. Both coerce the state either to change its policies or defeat itself.[11]

Terrorism is used for several reasons, but the most common assumption of government leaders is that groups are attempting compellence—the use of threats to manipulate or influence another actor to stop doing an unwanted behavior or to start doing something a group wants it to do.[12] Compellence may try to force states to withdraw from foreign commitments, or to make those commitments so painful that the government abandons them.[13] Sometimes this approach has been thought successful, as in the oft-cited U.S. and French withdrawals from Lebanon in 1983, the U.S. withdrawal from Somalia in 1993, and the Israeli withdrawal from Lebanon in 2000.[14] Many also argue that it succeeded in the 2004 bombings in Madrid, leading to a change of government in Spain and the withdrawal of troops from Iraq. While that is an oversimplification of what actually happened in each case, terrorism is meant to oversimplify complex situations: the interpretation is persuasive to many audiences, not least those in the West. Others see terrorism in Iraq as a foreign-inspired plan to bleed America out of Mesopotamia. Compellence tries to change a state's policy. Given their twentieth-century experience with air power and nuclear deterrence theory, Western policymakers and strategic thinkers find the logic of terrorism as punishment or attrition comfortably familiar. Terrorism resembles a kind of countervalue targeting engaged in by nonstate actors.[15] What could be more inherently coercive than a tactic that uses symbolic violence against noncombatants in pursuit of political objectives? As a result, they tend to focus exclusively on compellence, while being blind to the other typical strategies of terrorism. Yet compellence emphasizes only two parts of the dynamic of terrorism—the state and the objective—saying very little about the role and nature of the audience. Much about the strategies of terrorism is left out or ignored in this retreat to comfortable paradigms.

Provocation, polarization, and mobilization are strategies of leverage that have been used repeatedly in the modern era and for which terrorism is uniquely well suited.[16] Like compellence, these strategies have their roots in the political and historical context within which they arise. The first, provocation, tries to force a state to *do* something—not a specific policy but a vigorous action of some kind, that undercuts its legitimacy. It was firmly established as a purpose for terrorism during the nineteenth century and was at the heart of the strategy of the Russian group Narodnaya Volya, for example. As we shall see later in this chapter, Narodnaya Volya's goal was to attack representatives of the tsarist regime so as to provoke a brutal state response and inspire a peasant uprising. Other cases of provocation include ETA's early strategy in Spain, the Sandinista National Liberation Front's strategy in Nicaragua, and the FLN's strategy in Algeria.[17] Provocation is a difficult strategy to apply effectively, since terrorist groups often cause a state to behave in unforeseen ways;

but its design is to present a campaign as defensive in nature and thereby win support for a cause.

The second strategy, polarization, tries to divide and delegitimize the state. This strategy directs itself at the effects of terrorist attacks on the domestic politics of a state, driving regimes sharply to the right and ultimately forcing populations to choose between the terrorist cause and brutal state repression. The goal is to force divided populations further apart, fragmenting societies to the extent that it is impossible to maintain a stable, moderate middle within a functioning state. This is a particularly attractive strategy against democracies and has appeared regularly during the twentieth century. Examples of groups that have deliberately acted to polarize societies include the LTTE in Sri Lanka and the PIRA in Northern Ireland. Terrorist activities in Germany and Austria-Hungary after World War I were also meant to polarize.[18] Likewise, the Armed Islamic Group engaged in an extreme strategy of polarization during Algeria's civil war of the 1990s, slaughtering as many as 100,000 people.[19]

The last strategy, mobilization, is meant to recruit and rally the masses. Terrorist attacks may be intended to inspire current and potential supporters of a group, again using the reaction of the state as a means, not an end. This is what the campaign of bombings and assassinations in the late nineteenth century did for the anarchist movement, and the 1972 Munich Olympics massacre did for Palestinian nationalism. When terrorist attacks are used to mobilize, they are not necessarily directed toward changing the behavior of a state at all; they aim instead to invigorate and energize those who would support a group or its cause and to raise its profile internationally, attracting resources, sympathizers, and allies. If a group is successful in mobilizing large numbers, this strategy can prolong the fight and enable the threat to transition to other forms, including insurgency and conventional war. A mobilization strategy is focused primarily on the audience; the target and even the political objective may change to suit the needs of the audience. This strategy is uniquely well suited to the twenty-first century's globalized international community, which allows movements to mobilize on a scale and at a speed never before seen; and it also gets to the heart of why so many see the struggle with religiously inspired militancy led by al-Qaida as a multigenerational "long war."

These four strategies are not mutually exclusive, and we have already mentioned a fifth: to erode a state's legitimacy at home and abroad. A group may use a combination of several, even all, of these strategies; but what a state does in response is at the core of their efficacy. Reactions by a state in the narrow framework of one may be counterproductive with respect to the others. Thus, counterterrorism strategies that are designed to prevent a state from being compelled by a group founder if the goal is to provoke a state, polarize a population, or mobilize a constituency. And terrorist organizations may shift their approach to adjust to the demands of a fluid situation. Just as there is no evidence that terrorism is less likely to occur in democratic states (indeed, the data point the other way), there is likewise no evidence that democratic states are adept at handling these multifaceted strategies, especially in the short term. Autocratic regimes, because of their rigidity, lack of concern for human rights, and questionable legitimacy, tend to crush their challengers. Their mistakes and follies are well known. But the pressures on democratic states to respond to major attacks with indiscriminate force are arguably just as strong. Yet as is apparent in the research presented here, there are far more examples historically of strategies of *leverage* used by terrorist groups than any other type, including compellence. By concentrating on the lessons of how campaigns actually end, this book places strategies of leverage in sharper relief. Understanding the strategies of terrorism is the only way to avoid being manipulated by them.

Yet striking back with force immediately following a terrorist attack is reflexive, and it occurs for a plethora of reasons. First, overt military retaliation is a kind of strategic catharsis. Sending air strikes or military invasions seems fitting.[20] Second, military retaliation responds to domestic pressure, the need to "do something." In the aftermath of major terrorist incidents, there is often a wave of public opinion supporting military retaliation.[21] Elites respond to that pressure—or leaders' *perception* of pressure. Using military force sustains national morale and prestige, all the more so in retaliation to terrorism, a brazen and defiant act. There is much focus on the natural brakes on democratic war-making, but these may be accelerators in counterterrorism.[22] Third, obliterating the perpetrators can be seen as appropriate "justice," especially when attacks originate from outside a state's territory (as is increasingly likely to be the case). With no reliable international enforcement of laws or norms, states must use their own military power to punish those who harm their citizens, or so the logic goes. Military force extracts Old Testament justice.

The use of military force against terrorist groups may or may not deter other potential attackers, however. Those who argue that deterrence cannot affect terrorism are thinking in superficial terms.[23] Terrorist operatives are strategic actors who consider the costs, benefits, and consequences of their actions just as other actors do—albeit using different processes and reaching distinct conclusions. The best way to deter terrorism is to convince operatives (or their handlers) that their collective and individual goals cannot be achieved through terrorist attacks—that is, not deterrence by punishment, but deterrence by denial. There are many individual cases of successful deterrence, even the undercutting of groups themselves: for example, Mu'ammar Gadhafi dismantled the Arab Nationalist Youth for the Liberation of Palestine in the late 1970s, for fear that direct ties to Libya would be discovered and invite retaliation.[24] The key is to gain knowledge of the organizations, their supporters, and their members: to understand what their political goals are and to ensure that state responses do not advance them. Again, military force may or may not have the desired effect.

But contrary to conventional wisdom, there is a cost to doing nothing. Impressive shows of military force can shore up allies and alliances, by demonstrating a government's strength and resolve. Throughout the twentieth century, power was based not only on military capability but also on the perceived likelihood that it would be employed readily and effectively. The entire thrust of the complicated theology of Western nuclear strategy was that perceptions and reality are both pertinent. A state's prestige and credibility were considered part of its arsenal. In this strategic context, a humiliating bloodying by a terrorist group could have effects far greater than the short-term impact of the attacks themselves.[25]

States retaliate in an attempt to replace fear with resolve, to reverse the psychological tussle between a terror group hoping to sap public will and a state needing to regain the upper hand. At the heart of the logic of retaliation is the need to mitigate the psychological impact of terrorism by demonstrating that attempts to intimidate the state and its citizens are counterproductive. Rather than frightening the target into compliance, terrorist attacks reinforce the government's resolve to resist and respond.[26] State military responses are also calculated to destroy the enemy's ability to act. They may be designed to retaliate after an incident, preempt an imminent operation, or prevent the *possibility* of an incident in the future.[27] Showing strength in the aftermath of attacks may also influence the decision-making of other potential enemies, demonstrating that a state is impervious to blackmail. According to this logic, terrorist attacks are a threat to national security, so they should be answered with the best and most vigorous military response.

A type of learning occurs in terrorism and counterterrorism, involving both states and their challengers; it nearly always includes indiscriminate state retaliation in its early stages.[28] This use of retaliatory force then sets up a dynamic of attack and counterattack, and a familiar kind of pattern emerges. While democracies may be better able and willing to adjust their policies over time, how states use force in their initial response is more reflective of their culture and history than their acumen or type of government. The question at the heart of how that dynamic ends is which party learns and adapts most quickly to its own failures—and gains or maintains popular legitimacy in the process.

For all of these reasons, repression is the dominant initial response of the nation-state, with adaptation often prompting the government to seek the other responses described in this book. Distinctions between police and military responses are challenging to discern: although Brazil, Uruguay, and Argentina all had military governments involved in the brutal repression of terrorist groups in the late 1960s and early 1970s, for example, repression in each case involved "disappearances," arbitrary arrests, and the routine use of torture—classic tools of a police state.[29] Well before today's globalized terrorist movements, these categories were fraught with difficulty. But when does repression succeed? When is it counterproductive? What are the costs and benefits? What are the long-term political effects? The history of modern terrorism provides a rich body of data about past campaigns, yielding numerous insights into how and when repression works in ending terrorism.

CASE STUDIES OF REPRESSION

What follows is a representative sampling of a wide range of campaigns conducted by a wide range of states against a wide range of terrorist groups. Six in-depth case studies are included here: Russia and Narodnaya Volya, Peru and Sendero Luminoso, Turkey and the Kurdistan Workers' Party (PKK), Uruguay and the Tupamaros, Russia and Chechnya, and finally Egypt and the Muslim Brotherhood. These six have been chosen for four reasons. First, they are drawn from a range of modern time periods, from the late nineteenth century to the present, as well as across different regional settings including Europe, Latin America, and the Middle East. The goal is to minimize the West-centric "tyranny of the now" by casting a wider regional and historical net. Second, the cases chosen have ample, reliable documentary material available. Governments often do not want repressive counterterrorist policies publicized; this book includes only cases where the documentary evidence is reasonably complete and objective. Third, the cases encompass groups with a range of motivations, including separatist, leftist-revolutionary, and Islamist; and a range of types of terrorist organizations, from cellular to hierarchical. Fourth, they provide the opportunity to study state behavior across different types of regimes: authoritarian (Egypt, tsarist Russia), new or fragile democracies (Peru, post–Cold War Russia, Turkey), and established democracies (Uruguay). The argument is often made that democratic states are unable to end terrorism through repression, because democratic states find it difficult to maintain such campaigns over time. This set of six cases will test whether repression works in nondemocratic states as well.

Thus, drawing on a diverse collection of case studies selected to represent disparate regions of the world, types of groups, and ideological motivations, the following addresses whether or not, how, and under what conditions repression ends terrorism.

Russia and Narodnaya Volya

The intellectual origins of today's terrorism date to the nineteenth century, and understanding how aging autocratic regimes repressed these "threats from below" pertains to the threat today—not because today's groups are the same as their predecessors (certainly not), but because the state's impulsive responses to them often are. The most celebrated and well-known terrorist organization of the late nineteenth century was Narodnaya Volya (People's Will).[30] No group better demonstrates the potential leverage of terrorism against the state, and the state's foolish inclination to enhance that leverage.

Narodnaya Volya arose within the social revolutionary movement in nineteenth-century Russia, excited by a reaction to progressive European philosophy, particularly the twin influences of German idealism and scientific positivism.[31] Young Russian intellectuals, living in a relatively backward country yet cosmopolitan enough to be exposed to these ideas, were riveted by them. University students in particular came to believe that the forces of science and intellect could create a new man and a new, more perfect society.[32] Meanwhile, the broader economic and political pressures of industrialization were making themselves felt, and Russia was seized by a crisis of self-confidence following its defeat in the Crimean war. It was clear that something had to change. Tsar Alexander II (who became known as Tsar Liberator) instituted a number of dramatic reforms to tamp down growing popular unease and modernize Russian society. Beginning in 1855, he reorganized the court system, introduced compulsory military service, granted limited self-government, and, most important of all, emancipated the serfs. For the intelligentsia, the emancipated peasant became an irresistible target for enlightenment and uplift to the status of fully activated citizen. This process would then naturally bring down the state, the church, and all social institutions—irrelevant, dysfunctional anachronisms for the new man, in any case.

But how should this be done? One group, the *narodniki*, essentially went native, believing that the peasant must know best, that intellectuals should live in the villages, stop preaching, and try to learn from the people. A second faction turned its attention to the West, giving up the idea of a near-term revolution, moderating its rhetoric and gravitating toward social democracy. But a third group, frustrated by the slow pace of change and propelled by Alfred Nobel's invention of dynamite in 1866, turned to terrorism in order to provoke the government and shock the masses into action.

Narodnaya Volya's first act was to issue an ultimatum: if the government did not call a constituent assembly, it would engage in a campaign of violence.[33] When the demand went unnoticed, Narodnaya Volya devoted its short life to assassinating the tsar so as to demonstrate his vulnerability, and through him the vulnerability of the Russian state. Over the course of eight months, beginning in autumn 1879, Narodnaya Volya launched six carefully planned but unsuccessful attempts on the life of the tsar.[34] These failures drew the group into the limelight, resulting in both a police crackdown and a flood of young recruits. By spring 1880 members were on the run.[35]

A year later, under the direction of Sophia Perovskaya, daughter of the governor general of St. Petersburg, the group executed a seventh attempt.[36] On March 1, 1881, Narodnaya Volya member Nikolai Rysakov threw a bomb under the tsar's carriage as it drove through St. Petersburg, injuring one of his Cossack escorts and a small boy, who lay on the road screaming in agony.[37] (He died a few days later.) Alexander II climbed down from the carriage and approached his attacker. Meanwhile, a second operative, Kotik Grinevitski, threw another bomb directly at Alexander's feet. The tsar's legs were shattered. Some twenty other people were also hurt, most of them badly, including Grinevitski, who died later that day. Alexander was whisked off to the Winter Palace, where he died about an hour later.[38]

Killing the tsar also killed the group. One hundred and fifty people were arrested. Conspirators informed on one another, allowing the police to capture virtually all of the members of the leadership. Six, including Andrei Zhelyabov (mastermind of the group, arrested a few days before the attack), and Sophia Perovskaya, were executed. Narodnaya Volya had failed miserably in its aim to mobilize the masses to agitate for a new, more just and representative government; yet as events unfolded, their goal of provoking the state had wildly succeeded. From the assassination of Alexander II until the October Revolution of 1905, the Russian government grew increasingly rigid and unresponsive to the economic, social, and political changes under way in the country. The tsar's murder set off a brutal domestic crackdown and prompted a sharp turn away from reform.[39] Under his son, Alexander III, the regime veered back toward autocracy, conservatism, Orthodox clericism, xenophobia, and narrow Russian nationalism.[40] Emergency measures were introduced forbidding all social, public, and private gatherings, and the power of the police was considerably enhanced. Alexander III, who had seen his father, the liberator and reformer, literally shattered by terrorism, believed that a strong state was the only rational response. In this very human reaction to terrorism, however, he prolonged a decaying autocracy, alienated the public, and resisted the incremental changes that might have held off the forces of rebellion.

There were many other contributing factors in the demise of the tsarist regime; but the assassination was a watershed. A deep chasm opened between an evolving socialist ideology and a government unable or un-willing to meet the challenges of modernization and industrialization except by repression, with its legitimacy increasingly shaky. There was no room for a stabilizing, moderate middle among the cognoscenti and thus no hope of gradual reform. And while the state was not learning, its challengers were. The Bolsheviks carefully studied the experience of Narodnaya Volya, concluding that while individual acts of terrorism merely provoked the regime and led nowhere, a broader campaign of terror could incite and then protect a revolution. For the Russian intel-ligentsia, the lessons of Narodnaya Volya were twofold: the regime was irredeemable, and well-planned acts of violence could radically divert the flow of history.

Narodnaya Volya spawned dozens of followers and imitators, including a new organization calling itself the Terrorist Section of the People's Will, dedicated to the killing of Tsar Alexander III. In 1886, a failed assassination attempt led again to trials and executions. One of those executed was Alex-ander Ulyanov. On learning of his death, Ulyanov's 17-year-old brother Vladimir (later known to the world as Vladimir Ilyitch Lenin), declared: "I swear I will revenge myself on them." Thirty years later, he did.[41]

Peru and Sendero Luminoso

As in Russia, in Peru terrorism accompanied a time of dramatic social, economic, and political transition. In May 1980, just as the country was transitioning out of a tumultuous history of military government to-ward modernization and democracy, Shining Path launched the opening salvos of its Maoist revolutionary war. The inept use of military force by the democratic Peruvian government in turn boosted Shining Path's campaign.

As discussed in chapter 1, Sendero Luminoso was a hierarchical, cultish organization led by Abimael Guzmán Reynoso (known as "Guzmán"), a violent, narcissistic philosophy professor whose capture in 1992 was a catalyst for the ending of the organization. The image of a humiliated Guzmán, wearing striped pajamas, cowering in a cage, begging his fol-lowers to lay down their arms, had a devastating effect on the morale of his fighters, many of whom worshipped him as a god. But the Maoist movement he had spawned was astonishingly violent, with comparisons drawn to the Khmer Rouge of Cambodia in its murderous toll on the population.[42] Shining Path's 20-year campaign of violence resulted in the killing of more than 69,000 people, many murdered by the Shining Path (54 percent) but a sizable proportion of whom died at the hands of the Peruvian armed forces (28 percent).[43] Peru's response, particularly its notorious campaign of violence in the countryside, led to a horrifying cycle of violence begetting violence, resulting in one of the bloodiest terrorist and counterterrorist campaigns ever seen.[44]

Peru's modernization carried with it a series of economic and political measures put in place by the military government of the 1960s and 1970s. Not least among them were agrarian land reforms designed to expropriate land from large private estates (haciendas) and cut it up into smaller parcels within state-controlled cooperatives. The prospect of having their own land raised peasants' expectations but unfortunately not their circumstances: their overall condition worsened, as hacienda owners fled and poorly managed government cooperative programs faltered. The result was deepening frustration. Wanting to institute their own changes, rural dwellers in 1974 organized a grassroots demonstration of 15,000, agitating for land and against state reforms. When firmly put down by the police, they moved underground. There was no room for compromise and no outlet for dissent. The peasant was presented with a choice between the cooperatives, resented for taking away their historic right to land; and the state, hated for a legacy of allying with the landlords and for its bungled reform. The third way was to cooperate with the Shining Path.

Guzmán had spent 17 years building up a support base for his Maoist revolution in Ayacucho, an out-of-the-way region of Peru, mobilizing the peasants within a carefully structured hierarchy. His Shining Path had a solid, ideologically charged base of rural followers in place before it confronted the central government. When the Shining Path carried out its first attacks, the government was caught flat-footed and was slow to respond.[45] When the government finally woke up to the threat, in December 1982, it grossly overreacted, declaring a state of emergency in the Ayacucho area and giving state forces virtually free rein. The military was granted the right to detain anyone and engaged in almost unimaginable abuses. Over the course of the campaign, there were more than 7,300 cases of extrajudicial executions carried out by government forces, over 45 percent of which occurred in the first two years (1983–85).[46] The racist attitudes of the police and military, who were largely Spanish-descendants from central Peru, toward the seemingly backward, dark-skinned peasants also contributed to a cycle of alienation, revolution, and violence. During that period, 39 civilians (peasants or Shining Path members) perished for every police or military death.[47] When Alan García Pérez entered office in 1985, he began by emphasizing respect for human rights and conflict resolution, but his ideals soon evaporated when the Shining Path sharply increased its violence, attempted to assassinate him, and orchestrated a major prison revolt. By mid-1986, the García administration had likewise hunkered down and turned to repression. By 1987, the Peruvian government had the worst human rights record in the world.[48]

The violence peaked in 1990.[49] Through the indiscriminate use of force, the government had lost legitimacy and, with 90 provinces under a state of emergency, seemed unable to contain what was by now a major insurgency. The group had also successfully prevented elections by a campaign of assassination and intimidation. Peru was in the clutches of its worst economic crisis of the twentieth century when Alberto Fujimori came to the presidency. Fujimori suspended congress and the judiciary on April 5, 1992, in an *autogolpe* (or self-coup). These strongman moves gained him short-term popular support in a country desperate for an end to the violence; but they also undermined democratic processes and led to the suspension of economic assistance from the World Bank and the International Monetary Fund, further damaging the economy. The situation was dire.

Fortunately, however, the military had begun to learn from its operational mistakes.[50] It instituted a new program of counterinsurgency, including more discriminate targeting, efforts to avoid human rights abuses, and various hearts-and-minds programs in areas susceptible to Sendero influence. The government even began to arm local peasant groups for civil defense, giving them a fair shot at resisting the well-armed Shining Path. It also gradually improved its intelligence gathering. Guzmán and most of his top leadership were captured, and by 1994 it was clear that the organization was doomed. But the damage done by the many years of revolutionary war and the government's incompetent response were difficult to reverse. In addition to the thousands killed, two million Peruvians had fled from their homes, with many of the most educated and talented emigrating abroad. The domestic population was polarized, driven apart both by the intimidation of Shining Path and the abuses of the military. Casualties of the struggle included Peruvian democracy itself, delegitimized by its hapless response and damaged virtually beyond repair by Fujimori's *autogolpe*. The use of force against this vicious group was essential to protect the state, particularly after the government missed early opportunities to snuff it out; but using force the way it did, indiscriminately, with thousands of extrajudicial killings and human rights abuses, the government perpetuated a dynamic of violence that was profoundly counterproductive.[51]

In the end, the government learned from its mistakes and successfully crushed the Shining Path. But by this point tens of thousands had died needlessly and the problem had become far worse than it might have been. By the time the government understood the challenge, the Shining Path was a serious, well-mobilized threat that could *only* to be met with military force. Repression worked in the end; but the government's bungled military response and widespread abuses prolonged the Shining Path before the capture of Guzmán and the more effective use of force succeeded in taming it.

Turkey and the Kurdistan Workers' Party

The main years of struggle between the Turkish government and the Kurdistan Workers' Party (PKK) were from 1984 to 1999, with indiscriminate repression by the Turkish military, including widespread human rights abuses. Of course, the PKK were hardly innocent victims: over the years of violence, this Marxist-cum-ethnonationalist group fought Turkish military and security forces and carried out terrorist operations such as suicide bombings, car bombings, kidnappings of foreign tourists, and attacks against Turkish diplomats in Europe. The group was particularly well known for being among the first to use women as suicide attackers, openly arguing that the female sex was weaker and thus more expendable; but women were also prominent among its fighters. The PKK attacked what they considered to be symbols of the Turkish state in the Southeast, meaning anyone sent from the central government, particularly teachers. At its height (1988–91) the group probably had about 11,000 active operatives.[52]

In the earliest years of the campaign, the Turkish government, like the Peruvian government, did not take the troubles in the Kurdish region very seriously. There had always been unrest there, going back to the founding of the republic in 1923. Like Peru, Turkey has an authoritarian tradition. While after three military coups (1960, 1971, and 1980) Turkey had eventually seen the return of civilian governments, the military retained a strong role. So we see here another case of a fragile democracy facing a terrorist challenge from below, eventually succumbing to pressure from the military, which then launched a vicious campaign that killed thousands of noncombatants. The familiar pattern of indiscriminate military force included village evacuations, forcibly conscripted village guards, extrajudicial killings, and massacres of whole villages suspected of collaboration.[53] Over 15 years of violence, approximately 30,000 people died—a mix of PKK members, civilians, and security forces.[54]

Again as in Peru, the armed forces eventually improved their tactics, gradually containing the PKK through more discriminate targeting, reliance on small mobile units, and better intelligence, not to mention the deployment of as many as 250,000 personnel to the southeast. But human rights abuses continued, with regular reports of torture, killing, disappearances, forced evacuations, and the burning of homes. Displaced people flooded in from the countryside to the cities, where the military presence was stronger and they were thus better controlled. A draconian antiterrorism law came into force, placing the accused within the jurisdiction of specially empowered state security courts and employing such a broad and vague definition of terrorism that thousands were imprisoned on dubious grounds. Meanwhile, the economic condition of southeast

Turkey went from bad to worse, as the military carried out a scorched-earth policy, burning crops, killing livestock, and refusing villagers the right to harvest so as to prevent the PKK from living off the land.[55]

Turkey's hypersensitivity to the PKK arose not just from its concern about the group's immediate threat but also the historical pattern of external powers trying to exploit cleavages in the state. The nightmare of internal disintegration secretly orchestrated by its neighbors was ever-present. While the PKK was by no means an external creation, it enjoyed impressive international support, from Lebanon, Syria, Iran, and Iraq, at a minimum—as well as Armenia, Cyprus, Greece, and Russia, if government accusations are to be believed. For example, in the 1980s the PKK received training in Lebanon's Syria-controlled Beka'a Valley, and Öcalan ran his operations from Damascus.[56] The group has also repeatedly launched operations from territory in Northern Iraq.[57] Long-standing concerns about direct and indirect state sponsorship help to explain (though not excuse) the military's overreaction. On the other hand, from the perspective of the PKK, external state involvement proved to be a vulnerability: in 1998, with Öcalan holed up in neighboring Syria, and Turkey threatening to attack, Hafez al-Asad finally evicted him, sending Apo into the nomadic life that ended with his capture in Kenya a year later.

Eventually the military won their campaign in southeast Turkey and sent the PKK toward a sharp decline, catalyzed by Öcalan's capture in 1999. The case proves that, whether or not it is a democracy, if a state is willing to employ its full force, without scruples, it can crush a terrorist campaign. Turkish elites believed there was a serious threat to the state, gave the military virtually carte blanche to crush it, and had the support of the broader population as they did so.[58] Their anxiety helped to fuel the military campaign. But the cost to civilians in the Kurdish regions, victims of slaughter, displacement, human rights abuses, and sheer exhaustion, as well as to the international standing of Turkey, whose aspirations to join the European Union were damaged partly as a result, was enormous. And the threat did not completely disappear, as it spread to the broader region. Subsequent international events, especially the second war in Iraq and the apparent sanctuary given to fighters by Iraqi Kurds in northern Iraq, later led to a resurgence of the PKK, with implications that at this writing have yet to play out.

Uruguay and the Tupamaros

It would be easy to conclude from this survey thus far that only authoritarian regimes, or fragile recent democracies with authoritarian regimes standing in the wings, clumsily try to end terrorism through brutal repression. By this logic, the story of the Tupamaros should be a parable about the resilience of democracy in the face of terrorism, since the ultraleftist group attacked Uruguay, the most progressive and stable democracy in Latin America. But that is not what happened.

Uruguay had room for dissent, a robust party system, a relatively educated, urban population, and an established democratic tradition. It was the first Latin American country to adopt the characteristics of a liberal welfare state, including progressive rights for women, labor unions, and minorities, as well as welfare benefits for the poor and state intervention in the economy. Unlike Peru, the country had almost no peasantry, and 88 percent of the population was concentrated in rural towns and the capital. A strong two-party system grew out of the nineteenth century, with the urban, progressive Colorado Party dominating the traditional, rural Blanco Party for most of the twentieth. Although there was a brief period of authoritarian rule during the 1930s, democratic values and civil society seemed intrinsic to the country, as was its position as a model of liberal governance for neighboring authoritarian states. The two-party system worked well, and the state seemed stable and able to satisfy the needs of its citizens, including providing avenues for productive opposition. If democracy were an antidote to terrorism, Uruguay should have been immune.

As was the case throughout Latin America, however, the mid-twentieth century was a time of political ferment and economic distress. The economy began to stagnate in the 1950s. By the 1960s, economic distress along with the inspiration of the Cuban revolution led to the rise of a radical Left, with legal political parties as well as an ultraleftist urban guerrilla movement known as the Tupamaros.[59] The Tupamaros targeted symbols of the "imperialist regime," including businesses, airports, and diplomatic facilities of Brazil and the United States. Gradually the Tupamaros increased the audacity of their attacks, leading to a sense of paranoia in the business community and the landed elite, prompting the government to suspend constitutional rights.[60] The police were unable to restore calm, and in 1971 the government called in the army to establish order. The Tupamaros saw military intervention as evidence of the collapse of corrupt institutions and proof of their effectiveness in provoking a response. In fact, by the end of 1972, the army had crushed them. A coup followed in June 1973, and the army ruled the country for the next 12 years.

The army defended its rule on the grounds that Uruguayan sovereignty no longer rested in the people but in the necessity to protect the state. This philosophy was used to justify extensive, brutal repression, including restrictions on freedom of the press and assembly, torture, killings, disappearances, and the jailing of thousands for political crimes. Ten percent of the Uruguayan population fled the country. In 1976, Amnesty International reported that there were more people in jail per capita in Uruguay than anywhere else on earth.[61] By the early 1980s, as economic problems grew and civil resistance increased, the military began to negotiate with political parties, and democratic government was reinstated in 1985. In their short preeminence, the Tupamaros had executed one hostage and assassinated eight counterinsurgency personnel. The military regime that came to power in 1973 "disappeared," tortured, or killed thousands.[62] Although democracy was ultimately restored, the outcome of Uruguay's counterterrorism was the slaughter of its own people and the undermining of its liberal political system. Repression had worked, but at enormous cost.

Russia and Chechnya

Russia used repression to deal with Chechen terrorism and separatism in ways that could not help but echo the pattern of the nineteenth-century tsarist regime, not least the enhanced power of the police and secret services, the erosion of individual rights, the retreat from liberal reforms, and the increasing centralization of power. In Chechnya, Russian repression once again "ended" terrorism; but the broader implications for the region and for the Russian state were worrisome indeed.[63]

Of course, Russia's conflict in Chechnya was not just about terrorism but also about a separatist insurgency and civil war. In the chaos following the breakup of the Soviet Union, the Chechen people seized upon the opportunity to elect a leader, Dzokhar Dudayev, whose first decree was to declare Chechnya an independent state. President Boris Yeltsin pronounced the elections illegal, declared a state of emergency, and dispatched 2,500 Interior Ministry (MVD) troops to the region. The Russian parliament rescinded Yeltsin's order to use force, the interior troops withdrew, and Dudayev gained stature as a Chechen hero who had successfully taken on the Russian empire.[64] Yeltsin and his followers did not forget the humiliation. The decision to intervene militarily three years later was said to be in response to a series of bus hijackings and kidnappings in the region; whatever the reason, by 1994 Russia was at war.[65]

The first war in Chechnya was not, strictly speaking, a counterterrorist operation, but a poorly planned Russian counterinsurgency operation largely conducted on the streets of Grozny. There is evidence that those in the Russian military who supported the intervention believed it would be a simple show of force that would meet with little or no resistance—comparable, perhaps, to the driving of Soviet tanks into Prague in August 1968.[66] Contrary to expectations, however, the military operation, which began on December 11, 1994, met widespread and determined resistance from both Chechen guerrilla fighters and Chechen civilians.

The Russian forces' tactics in the urban combat that was at the core of the first war in Chechnya were appalling by nearly any standard. The idea was to move to Grozny and surround the rebel forces that were presumed to be concentrated in the city center. But the Russian troops were not prepared for urban warfare.[67] Casualty figures are disputed, but anywhere from 5,500 to 14,000 Russian troops died in the first war.[68] Chechen civilians fared worse than either Russian soldiers or their own fighters; although estimates vary, upwards of 50,000, including ethnic Russians living in Chechnya, died, and about a third of the Chechen population was displaced.[69] One reason for the huge losses among Chechen civilians was that Chechen guerrilla tactics made it extremely difficult for the Russians to distinguish between combatants and noncombatants. This helps to explain why the Russians fared poorly on the public opinion front in the first war. But Russian forces also bore conscious responsibility for civilian casualties. Undisciplined troops engaged in looting, raping, and assaults on the population. They carried out *zachiskti*, or cleansing operations, ostensibly to search for rebel fighters and arms but in effect as a means of rounding up the male population, and then looting and burning civilian residences.[70] They set up "filtration camps" to screen and hold civilians, especially Chechen males but also sometimes ethnic Russians. In the camps, people were murdered, tortured, and held in the most primitive conditions.[71] Alienated civilians fled Chechnya, joined the Chechen forces, or hunkered down in their homes. Many provided active or passive support to Chechen fighters.

One part of the Russian forces' problem was that they had collected virtually no intelligence. Troops did not even have reliable maps.[72] Russian forces moved in armored columns, intending, for example, to capture major buildings and the railroad station in Grozny; but the Chechens did not put up a fixed defense and instead presented a shifting and elusive target. Eventually the Russians learned from their mistakes. Employing small unit tactics and bringing in more experienced fighters, they more or less controlled Grozny through the spring of 1995, and Chechen fighters regrouped in the mountainous highlands.

Just as Russia seemed to be prevailing, however, the Chechens upped the ante. In June 1995 rebel leader Shamil Basayev took 1,200 civilians hostage in Budennovsk, a town in southern Russia about 100 miles from Chechnya. The Budennovsk hostage crisis continued for five days, and as many people died in Russian government attempts to storm the hospital as had died in the initial Chechen raid on the town.[73] It ended when the Russian government agreed to negotiate and gave Basayev and his fighters safe passage back to Chechnya, where they were greeted as conquering heroes. The Budennovsk episode was a watershed event, demonstrating the Chechens' willingness to use terrorist tactics to pursue their cause, strengthening the separatist cause just at a time when it was flagging, and forcing the Russian government into negotiations under the auspices of the Organization for Security Cooperation in Europe.[74] Still, the Budennovsk seizure initiated an increasing trend toward terrorist tactics in Chechnya, as well as in neighboring Ingushetia, Dagestan, North Ossetia, and Russia proper.[75]

This shift of focus toward the use of high-profile terrorist tactics was an important element in pushing the Yeltsin government to negotiate and withdraw its troops. Combined with the embarrassing performance of the military in the counterinsurgency campaign, the Budennovsk incident led Moscow to sign the Kasavyurt Accords. According to the terms of the agreement, troops were to be withdrawn from Chechnya in return for economic aid and a referendum on the future of Chechnya to be held five years hence (in 2001). The peace treaty was referred to in the Russian press and parliament as "Great Russia's humiliation by small Chechnya." Indeed, Yeltsin referred to Chechnya as the biggest mistake of his presidency.[76] There was widespread domestic opposition to the war, while the international community stridently condemned violations of human rights committed by the Russian army in its efforts to defeat an enemy that employed the local population as a shield.

The second war in Chechnya started after incursions by Chechen fighters led by Basayev into neighboring Dagestan in August 1999, ostensibly to establish an Islamic republic there. In addition, a series of bombings of apartment houses in Moscow and Vologodonsk were blamed on Chechen terrorists, although there is controversy about whether Russian security forces were involved.[77] The bombs killed nearly 300 people, offering both a need and an opportunity for a strong Russian riposte. The apartment bombings, whatever their genesis, seemed to galvanize Russian public opinion against the Chechens. The second war was seen as an opportunity to exact revenge, restore Russian morale, and erase the national humiliation of the first conflict. Responding to the public mood, Putin was elected in part on his promises to "flush the Chechens down the toilet"[78] and "strangle the vermin at the root."[79] In the first war in Chechnya, the Russian leadership referred to the enemy as "bandits" and "rebels"; after the Moscow bombings, they were "terrorists."[80] Long before al-Qaeda's attacks on the United States and the widespread international attention to the issue, Putin framed the second conflict as a war against terrorism, and used that motif to justify brutal repression.

For the Russians, the military tactics of the second war differed markedly from the first. There was more elaborate preparation and planning for the storming of Grozny, as well as reconnaissance and intelligence. The fighting remained slow, bloody, and difficult, with high casualties on both sides; but by early 2000 the Russians had occupied most of Chechnya and Chechen forces had been pushed into the mountainous highlands and over the border with Georgia, into the Pankisi Gorge. According to Russian reports, Chechen leaders had established a network of training camps employing some 100 foreign instructors, largely Arab Afghans but also Pakistani-based militants.[81] Disguised in Russian uniforms, the Chechens engaged in night raids on Russian positions. Chechen treatment of Russian prisoners was so appalling that Russian soldiers and airmen were terrified of capture—this may have worked against the Chechens, as it resulted in increased determination by the Russians to fight. Efforts to ambush Russian tanks were not as successful as they had been in the first conflict, because of the use of infantry escorts and reactive armor. Both sides relied heavily on the use of snipers, and the tallest building in Grozny, with its targeting advantage, was one of the most hotly contested. Although they were somewhat better equipped, the Chechens' guerrilla tactics had not changed dramatically between the first conflict and the second; however, the Russians had adapted and prepared more effectively to counter them.[82]

As they found themselves at a disadvantage, the Chechens again diverted the war into terrorist attacks away from the battlefields in Chechnya. As in the first conflict, a crucial turning point was a major terrorist event: the seizure of the Dubrovka theater in Moscow on October 23, 2002, in which 800 civilians were held hostage for three days by Chechen militant terrorists led by Movsar Baraev. In Operation Groza, the storming of the theater by Russian special forces, an unidentified anesthetic gas was used to incapacitate the operatives.[83] All 49 Chechen operatives were shot as they lay unconscious, apparently to prevent them from detonating their explosives. A further 129 civilians died of asphyxiation during or shortly after the raid. The Dubrovka theater episode marked a watershed in the gradual transition of the Chechens toward terrorist violence outside of Chechen territory. It was followed by a quickening pace of terrorist attacks on Russian territory, culminating in the killing of more than 300 people, most of them schoolchildren, in Beslan, North Ossetia on September 3, 2004.

Tactics with respect to the media differed markedly during the second war, with strict government control over the press.[84] The Russian government made a concerted effort to manage the image of the second war and to restrict access by the Russian and international media.[85] Critical television coverage was essentially shut down. The semantics changed: where the press had previously referred to the conflict as a "war" they were now increasingly accepting the official description of it as a "counterterrorist operation." Restricted access and conscious attempts by the Russian government to "spin" the information emerging from the conflict seemed to have a clear effect upon domestic public opinion, which was far more supportive of the second war, of "counterterrorism," than it had been of the first.

The Putin government's two-pronged policy of limiting the public's awareness of casualty rates, human rights abuses, and the economic costs of the war through control of the media, and emphasizing the national security aspects of the war, was effective—as Putin's overwhelming and essentially unopposed reelection in March 2004 confirmed.[86] But it certainly did not encourage the flowering of what most Westerners would consider a pluralistic civil society. The war in Chechnya, including the counterterrorist campaign by the government, had a corrosive effect on the democratization of post-Soviet Russia.

Despite the complexity of this conflict and the long history of its origins, making it a matter of terrorism and counterterrorism came to suit both sides. For the Chechens, it served three purposes. First, terrorism was used as a mechanism of shock. Having suffered brutally at the hands of Russian forces, the Chechens employed terrorism increasingly to jolt the Russian people, especially in Moscow but also elsewhere in Russia. This shock also seemed to have been intended to mobilize both international and domestic public opinion, in order to drive the Putin government to make concessions. Second, terrorist attacks were used during sensitive political periods as provocations. For example, in 1995 the Budenovsk hostage crisis helped to end the first war. The 1999 Moscow apartment bombings, whoever the perpetrators were, apparently precipitated the outbreak of the second. The October 2002 Dubrovka theater siege ended the search for a semblance of political legitimacy, if not actual peace, and effectively destroyed the moderate Chechen presidency of Aslan Maskhadov. All of these events were triggers to dramatic changes in the course of the conflict. Third, terrorism was an attempt to level the playing field, to improve a losing position by enlarging the battlefield and expanding the range of potential targets. In both wars, the Chechens used terrorism when they were at a disadvantage, when the Russian counterinsurgency seemed to be prevailing. All three strategies failed in the face of increasing Russian repression.

Terrorism was counterproductive for the Chechens and for the Russian people, but in some respects it served the interests of the Putin government. In the face of terrorist attacks, Putin's position was strengthened domestically, and his hold on executive power increased, enabling him to do almost whatever he liked in Chechnya. In short, terrorism exacted a cost from the Russians, but the Chechens paid a much greater price. Responding to terrorism provided the perfect leitmotif for the Russian state's familiar pattern of repression, and in this sense it worked.

Repression resulted in polarization, both within Russia and within the Chechen republic: on the one hand, following each terrorist attack blamed on Chechen operatives there was an outflow of passionate Russian hatred of the Chechens; this seemed to have a palpable influence on the evolution of the Russian state toward more executive power, more restriction of civil liberties, and greater willingness to use force. Terrorist attacks succeeded in mobilizing the Russian population *against* the Chechens, even as they failed to stir the Chechen people. On the other hand, there was a fractionizing occurring within Chechnya itself, as the Kremlin-supported government seemed to engage in criminal behavior against its own people and increasing numbers of Chechens seemed to be swayed by militant Islamic groups. There was no going back from this repression, as the regime deliberately made negotiations impossible: in March 2005, the Russian security forces assassinated Aslan Maskhadov, elected president of the separatist government of Chechnya and the only person with whom the state might possibly have talked.[87]

By 2007, the situation in Chechnya began to stabilize. The pace of fighting had slowed, not least as a result of several high-profile killings by the Russian government, including the July 2006 killing of Shamil Basayev, alleged mastermind of the Beslan school siege.[88] The Kremlin put large amounts of money into rebuilding the Chechen economy, including building schools, hospitals, and houses, and had good reason to argue that the war in Chechnya was over. The Chechen people were exhausted, and there was no one left to lead the fight.[89] On the other hand, Russian repression of Chechen separatists promoted the spread of the conflict to neighboring areas in the North Caucasus, especially Ingushetia, Dagestan, Karbardino-Balkariya, and North Ossetia.[90] In Ingushetia, for example, death squads reportedly carried out summary executions of those appearing on "Wahhabi lists."[91] In Chechnya, military repression ended terrorism; but it remained to be seen whether the cyclical historical pattern of harsh repression followed by resurgent rebellion would eventually repeat itself.

It is easy to make the usual argument about the importance of good tactics and discriminate targeting in responding to terrorism with military force. But in discussing how terrorism ends, there is a matter of degree here: it is one thing to kill tens of thousands of innocent people, in an incompetent effort to root out terrorist operatives. It is another thing to use so much conventional military force that you bomb a city essentially back to the Stone Age, as they say, and drive virtually the entire population out of its homeland, which was what the Russians did to Grozny in the second Chechen war. This was akin to the bombing of Dresden in World War II—brutal and effective at driving toward an end. There is a point at which military force, particularly when used internally against a threat within one's territory, succeeds in destroying terrorism because it destroys *everything*. That was what the Russians did in Chechnya. In other words, if all you want to do is end terrorism, at whatever cost, you can certainly do so through military repression.

Egypt and the Muslim Brotherhood, 1928–1966

The Muslim Brotherhood (al-Ikhwan al-Muslimeen) is associated with a range of Islamist groups whose doctrines, variously interpreted or distorted, justify today's most threatening terrorism.[92] Experts argue bitterly about the degree to which the original Brotherhood organization is responsible for the violence committed by its progeny, some of them connected to al-Qaeda.[93] A detailed discussion of the Brotherhood's origins, evolution, beliefs, contemporary role, and abundant offshoots is beyond the scope of this study. It is a group "whose historic unfolding has been accompanied by an inordinate measure of both positive and negative hysteria," as the well-respected historian Richard Mitchell wrote; and these dueling hysterias will not be resolved here.[94] Nonetheless, its early history, about which there is general agreement, continues to resonate today and provides insight into the effects of state repression upon the evolution of groups that resort to terrorism, as well as on the development of the states that confront them.

The Muslim Brotherhood was founded in Egypt in 1928 by Hasan al-Banna.[95] Banna's first job had been as a schoolteacher in the Suez Canal Zone city of Isma'iliyya, a city occupied by the British military and filled with foreigners living in luxurious houses overlooking the squalid dwellings of their Egyptian workers.[96] Banna was deeply concerned about the degree to which Egyptian Muslim youth, subject to foreign influence and overwhelmed with materialism and self-doubt, had departed from the goals of their faith. Gradually he gathered admirers, opposed to the British occupation and the foreign domination of Egyptian politics, economy, and culture, and anxious to find a meaningful direction for themselves and their communities. The concept of civic obligation was at the core of Banna's philosophy, placing an individual's obligation toward the community above self-interest or material gain. Always the goal was to move toward the creation of an Islamic order (*al-nizam al-islami*), grounded in sharia, or Islamic law.[97] The Muslim Brotherhood's charter reads, "God is our objective, the Quran is our Constitution, the Prophet is our leader, jihad is our method, and death for the Sake of God is the highest of our aspirations."

Banna soon moved to Cairo, where he gained access to more influential circles. He was a gifted organizer and preacher and quickly gathered a diverse membership, including civil servants, students, urban laborers, and peasants. During the late 1930s, the society also became more involved in politics, collecting funds for the Arabs of Palestine, for example. The crucial issue soon arose of whether or not Egypt's salvation through Islam should be sought through violence. Banna rejected the use of force, arguing that reason, persuasion, and a gradual approach was better; but others argued that abominations against Islam must be corrected immediately, with "the force of the hand." In 1939, this debate led to the first defection, the "Youth of Our Lord Mohammad" group. The departure had little immediate effect on the movement but foreshadowed a key philosophical rift.

During World War II, the Brotherhood's antipathy to the British led Banna to make contact with Anwar el-Sādāt, a member of a revolutionary group of Egyptian army officers, for discussions about how to free Egypt from foreign domination. These conspiracies resulted in Banna being banished by the British to Upper Egypt in 1941. Also during the war, Banna formally established the Brotherhood's "Secret Apparatus," an armed wing. The Brotherhood's antipathy to foreign domination, burgeoning secret activities, and early connections with the army likewise proved to be important later.

The postwar years, with their realignment of power in the Middle East, were tumultuous in Egypt. The Muslim Brothers were by this point a very well mobilized, grassroots organization, a powerful presence in Egyptian politics and seen as a potential threat to the government. The society itself lacked a clear idea of the number of members it had; from 1946 to 1948, membership seems to have fluctuated between about 300,000 and 600,000.[98] Following the 1947 UN decision to partition Palestine, some Muslim Brothers obtained weapons. A series of attacks within Egypt followed, including the bombing of the King George Hotel in Isma'iliyya and arson attacks across the country. Not long thereafter, the Secret Apparatus assassinated a judge, Ahmad al-Khazindar Bey, who had sentenced a Brother to life imprisonment. Hasan al-Banna expressed revulsion at the killing, later claiming that he feared that the Secret Apparatus had escaped his control, but the tenor of the group had clearly changed. In December 1948, the Brotherhood was dissolved on charges of "attempts to overthrow the existing order, terrorism, and murder."

Soon there was no doubt about the violent tendencies of at least some members of the group. On December 28, 1948, Prime Minister Nuqrashi was assassinated by 'Abd al-Majid Ahmad Hasan, a member of the Brotherhood's Secret Apparatus. At Nuqrashi's funeral, people shouted, "Death to Hasan al-Banna."[99] For his part, Banna was seized with worry about the Brotherhood's future; he saw real tactical errors in the conduct of the Secret Apparatus and contemplated dissolving the organization. The monarchy also asserted itself in response to the violence: 'Abd al-Hadi, chief of the royal cabinet and head of the Sa'dist party, began a campaign of official state terror against virtually all sectors of Egyptian politics and society, causing widespread resentment and hatred, especially among officers in the army. Meanwhile, Banna engaged in negotiations with the government and asked young members of the Brotherhood to refrain from violence, arguing that perpetrators "are neither Brothers, nor are they Muslims." Banna said that he would interpret any further violence as being directed against his own person, and told the government he would bear full legal responsibility for any further attacks, to discourage members of his organization from additional violence. The government was unconvinced, and in late January 1949 the organization was dissolved by decree.

The full legal and illegal power of the state came crashing down on the Brotherhood, especially the Secret Apparatus. Members were imprisoned, tortured, and abused. Banna wrote a small pamphlet, *Qawl fasl*, denouncing the decree of dissolution. In it he denied all charges, insisting that the Brotherhood's arms were legally sanctioned by the government as part of an arrangement between the Brotherhood and the Arab League for the Palestinian cause. This pamphlet enumerated grievances: torture in the prisons, loss of jobs and property, unwarranted searches, and press censorship. Banna argued that the real reason for the dissolution was pressure from foreign governments, preparations for negotiations with the British and the Zionists, and the government's wish to divert attention from failures in Palestine, the "hidden fingers of international Zionism, communism, and the partisans of atheism and depravity."[100] On February 12, 1949, almost certainly on the orders of the government, Banna was assassinated by the political police. Hasan al-Hudaybi, a respected judge and compromise candidate, was chosen as Banna's successor.

On July 23, 1952, a group of young army officers, supported by the Muslim Brotherhood, overthrew the constitutional monarchy established in Egypt by the departing British and installed a new military regime under Colonel Gamal Abdel Nasser. As he consolidated his power, Nasser established what he called Arab or Islamic socialism and made a well-publicized pilgrimage to Mecca to burnish his religious credentials.[101] There were promises of dramatic new political, economic, and social opportunities. Many concluded that the new government would institute the Brotherhood's Islamic program, but to their deep disappointment, this did not happen. On October 26, 1954, a member of the Secret Apparatus tried to assassinate Nasser before a huge throng in Alexandria. Having been fired at eight times, Nasser paused briefly in his speech while the bullets whizzed by him, then coolly delivered a rousing oration while virtually the entire country listened.

The assassination attempt seemed to give Nasser the excuse he needed to rid himself of the Brotherhood for good. At least 3,000 members, most of whom had no knowledge of the foolhardy operation, found themselves in prison.[102] Most were released after a "profession of faith" in the regime was extracted from them under torture. Two thousand were imprisoned for longer, and about 1,000 Muslim Brothers were eventually tried for complicity in the assassination attempt. Over half were acquitted or given suspended sentences, but 15 death sentences were meted out, and six prominent members were hanged.[103] This crackdown caused the organization to atrophy, in part because of the huge risk of joining it; but also because the Nasser regime launched a media blitz to discredit it. But those who languished in prison—tortured by fellow Muslims, betrayed by the regime—developed an even stronger bond among themselves, were radicalized and permanently alienated from the secular, nationalist government.

One of those imprisoned was a bookish, idealistic young man named Sayyid Qutb, an intellectual who had joined the Muslim Brotherhood relatively late, some time around 1950.[104] His writings, initially grounded in progressive beliefs in social justice, gradually evolved toward Islamist tenets. While in jail he continued writing, but, enduring harsh conditions and torture, he became more and more radically Islamist. Qutb's most strident work appears after 1957, when more than 20 Brothers were brutally killed by the camp guards.[105] His philosophy then shifted from evolution to revolution. In particular, his book *Milestones* (also translated as *Signposts*), published in 1964, accused regimes in all countries, including majority Muslim ones, of being anti-Islamic, and their members apostates (*kafireen*). Qutb called on his coreligionists to overthrow the present *jahiliyya* (i.e., barbaric and ignorant) order and defined jihad as an armed rebellion against the secular system. He also wrote very influential commentary on the Quran that continues to be cited today. Qutb was hanged in 1966, but his work remains a source of inspiration and mobilization within the current Islamist revival.

At the heart of the question of the Brotherhood's role in the Islamist movement is the question of the degree to which the organization is dominated by the thinking of Banna or Qutb. Banna promoted working gradually through the system, a nonviolent return to the foundations of Islam and the service of the Muslim community that would eventually lead to a better order.[106] Beginning with that altruistic community-oriented philosophy, the doctrines of Qutb go further, diagnosing social problems, shunning some coreligionists, and urging the ending of apostasy through violence. This kind of ideological framing and mobilization is uniquely well-suited for the use of terrorist tactics. Terrorism is always justified altruistically, always about the primacy of the public good over the pursuit of individual self-interest. It is always purported to further a broader cause. Lacking a veneer of selflessness, terrorism is meaningless criminal violence and motivates no one.

While in prison himself, leader Hudaybi disputed Qutb's arguments, particularly the practice of judging another Muslim as apostate *(takfir)*. Many argue that Hudaybi's more tolerant interpretation, in keeping with Banna's original philosophy, prevails in the Brotherhood today.[107] Others insist that all Islamists, including mainstream Muslim Brothers, crave political power and the imposition of sharia law, which is inherently authoritarian and undemocratic.[108] This argument will not be resolved here. Meanwhile, the Egyptian government has continued to keep a lid on the group, alternating accommodationist and repressive strategies, though never as extreme as under Nasser.[109]

Whatever the true intentions of the Muslim Brotherhood today, as a result of its early treatment by the Egyptian regime and the extremist doctrines that emerged then, the original organization threw off numerous radical and dangerous offspring both inside and outside Egypt. After they were driven out, many of the Egyptian Brothers found refuge in Saudi Arabia, where Sayyid Qutb's writings gained a growing contingent of followers after they were edited and published by his brother, Muhammad Qutb.[110] In the Palestinian territories, Hamas, alias the Islamic Resistance Movement, was founded in 1988 as the local branch of the Muslim Brotherhood. Between 1976 and 1982, the Brotherhood organized in Syria to violently oppose the secular Ba'athist regime of Hafez el Assad and were brutally crushed, a strategic failure that is a principal case study in the analyses of al-Qaeda strategist Abu Mus'ab Al-Suri.[111] Splinter organizations include Egyptian al-Gama'a al-Islamiyyah (EIG) and al-Jihad, two violent groups at the core of al-Qaeda whose leaders, especially Ayman Zawahiri, have been the intellectuals behind the al-Qaeda movement.[112] Indeed, Zawahiri's great uncle was Sayyid Qutb's lawyer[113]—another intergeneration connection to a simmering anger and ideology. In 1954, Nasser's repression worked: the terrorism of the Egyptian Muslim Brotherhood ended; but the most extreme Islamist ideas, perversely nurtured by a totalitarian state, gained credibility and spawned the dangerous progeny we confront decades later.

How Repression Ends Terrorism

Repression alone seldom ends terrorism because terrorist groups resort to strategies designed to turn a state's strength against itself. Indiscriminate, retaliatory police or military force used in a frontal assault, at home or abroad, may set back a movement. Overwhelming—and unscrupulous—use of force may even obliterate groups using terror tactics. But it may be a pyrrhic victory. If the ideas that are the source of popular mobilization persist, repression will be temporary, even counterproductive—as was the case with Nasser's policies toward the Muslim Brotherhood and the tsar's policies toward Narodnaya Volya and its social revolutionary successors. More important, if the nature of the state engaged in repression changes, then the victory is a hollow one. Repression, often brutal, wiped out terrorist groups in Brazil, Uruguay, Argentina, Peru, and tsarist Russia; however, the response itself undermined the legitimacy of the state.

The central questions in determining whether repression will end terrorism are: how well mobilized is a group's support; who is the audience—that is, what specific constituency are they trying to reach with their actions; how likely are they to further influence that constituency through violence; and how will a state's actions affect their ability to do so? In other words, the key variables for whether repression ends terrorism are how mobilized the population is for a cause and how despised a regime makes itself in its response. It comes down to perception and identity, a social-political tug-of-war for support that the state or regime usually wins, but at great cost.

Terrorism is not a threat to be analyzed using the kind of unitary actor theories that are the foundation of twentieth-century strategic thought in the West. States operate in a world where they benefit from a constituent population and the right to use force. Groups that use terrorism have neither; they are premodern and postmodern, subnational and transnational, and transcend our Westphalian state system. There are no existential terrorist organizations; instead, terrorist groups are really political, religious, ethnic, and ideological communities. When a state treats such a community like another state, it suffers from a fundamental misreading of the challenge. States use force to enhance power and influence others' behavior in specific ways. Most groups are concerned with gaining a foothold by developing a broader constituency and a degree of popular legitimacy first, so as to move toward the eventual accomplishment of their aims. There is much more similarity between the actions of various states (difficult enough to generalize about) than there is between the actions of various groups that use terrorism (almost always reactive and distinctive). It is foolish to treat the latter as a monolith. Instead we must disaggregate the individual groups, review their mobilizing systems of belief, find the similarities and differences in their philosophies, and dissect their strategic thinking very carefully—then calculate how particular state actions will advance or frustrate them.

Repression is more than simply state use of brute force against challenges from below. That dichotomous framework misses an entire dimension of strategic effectiveness over the longer term, which is the various audiences that are witnessing the violence—sympathetic to the state or to the group. Allusions to "nonstate actors" testify to the intellectual rigidity with which academics and policymakers approach these threats. This thinking leads to errors of analysis, in particular a glossing over and lack of appreciation of the source of strength for a revolutionary movement, and a mistaken focus on its weapons and tactics. Instead the struggle is between states and violent subnational or transnational communities for loyalty and identity. Repression succeeds when it mobilizes the rightful forces of the state effectively against the violent perpetrators (and their supporters) within a community, without either catalyzing a larger countermobilization by that community or a demobilization of the government's own support.

The use of repression against terrorism can shift the threat to another place, almost like pushing the disease to where it is no longer a threat to vital organs. The cases that we have reviewed demonstrate that force used in an indiscriminate way against groups that have grassroots support for their ideas shoves the threat either underground or to other regions. The PKK in southeast Turkey was crushed by the Turkish government, for example, but many of the fighters were simply banished to sanctuaries in northern Iraq. Narodnaya Volya disintegrated under tsarist repression, but its philosophies went underground, survived its demise, and contributed to the coming Russian Revolution. The Egyptian Islamists' reactionary and extreme ideology actually grew out of repression and now powers a violent international movement. The state suffers from all the advantages and disadvantages of being the incumbent actor. Especially in our age of globalized communications, no amount of force can kill an infectious inspiration—a potential source of countermobilization, especially when it is spread through informal networks operating below the radar of state bureaucracy.

In determining the likelihood of demobilizing a state's active *internal* support, on the other hand, the key variable is the degree to which the state and its actions are considered to be legitimate. The terrorism that occurred in Peru, Russia, and Egypt came at a time of change and opportunity in the political system. Transitions in power within a state provide an opening for rebel activity. And in the process of repressing terrorism, states often change their own natures, leading to their own delegitimation. By the time it realized the scale of the threat, the government of Peru had no choice but to respond militarily to the Shining Path. But as it did so, it unleashed an unrestrained bloodbath that resulted in the slaughter of tens of thousands of its own people and, with Fujimori's *autogolpe*, the elimination of its democratic institutions. The Turkish government also failed to respond quickly to the PKK, resulting in a problem that was then turned over to the military, which dealt with it in a brutal and indiscriminate way. The Tupamaros had weak community support for their cause, as their quick collapse following the use of force confirmed: this was all the more reason why the Uruguayan military's subsequent power grab was so appalling. Whether or not democracies outlast terrorism may depend on whether competing factions in the country see themselves as better alternatives, as well as whether the domestic population is terrified and just wants the problem *dealt with*. But over time the key variable is the degree to which the state and its actions are considered by its people to be legitimate, rather than the type of government it has.

On the whole, democracies have been the most legitimate governments in the modern world, and thus they have had the most staying power against terrorism. That said, democracies or liberal governments face particular short-term difficulties in repressing terrorist groups. Because military or police action requires a target, the use of force against operatives works best in situations where members of the organization can be separated from the general population. This essentially forces "profiling" or some method of distinguishing members from nonmembers—always a sensitive issue, particularly when the only available means of discrimination relates to how members are defined (race, age, religion, nationality, etc.) rather than what they do (or are planning to do). Excellent intelligence is essential for the latter, especially in advance of an attack, but even in the best of situations it is typically scarce. Repressive measures also carry high resource and opportunity costs. Long-term repressive measures against suspected operatives may challenge civil liberties and human rights, undermine domestic support, polarize political parties, and strain the fabric of the state itself, thus further undercutting its ability to respond effectively to future terrorist attacks. Mistakes and abuses by governments, including democracies, are endemic in counterterrorism, but usually democracies have the stamina to maintain internal support as they learn and adapt their methods over time.

It is true that terrorism is the tactic of desperation, but not for the reasons usually cited (e.g., poverty, humiliation, frustration, oppression). Instead, the desperation of terrorism results from the need to use this attention-getting violence to mobilize support for an idea or cause. Terrorism kills innocent civilians in a way that is repulsive to most people. Groups that have well-mobilized support generally do not have to resort to such a risky and potentially counterproductive tactic to gain attention to their cause. States are blind to this logic, because they are the status quo actors and generally do not concern themselves with establishing their fundamental legitimacy. Not so revolutionary organizations, which, if they had sufficient mobilized support, would not be likely to employ the tactic of terrorism. As we have seen, there are far more effective ways to use force.

Of greatest importance in understanding the use of terrorism today—indeed, the use of force in any form in the twenty-first century—is the unique, revolutionary effects of globalized communications upon the ability to animate and legitimate violence. Terrorism, like other forms of political violence, arises out of the beliefs and aspirations of communities and must be analyzed within a social and political context. The strategic dynamic is not between states and "nonstate actors"—an anachronistic phrase that is a negation, not a concept. The core of the relationship is between states and communities that are competing over the capacity to mobilize support, and it is success or failure in that dimension which ultimately determines whether or not repression ends terrorism.

CHAPTER SIX

Reorientation

TRANSITIONING TO ANOTHER MODUS OPERANDI

> Because I do it with a petty ship, I am called a robber, whilst
> thou who dost it with a great fleet art styled emperor.
> —*A pirate, in St. Augustine's* City of God[1]

TERRORISM CAN "END" when the violence continues but takes another form. Groups may transition out of a primary reliance on terrorist tactics toward either criminal behavior or more classic types of regular or irregular warfare. This transformation may be good or bad news for the state. It is good news when a violent group stops killing civilians and turns to petty criminality, as occurred with elements of the PIRA following the Good Friday Accords.[2] The state is better designed to deal with this kind of criminal behavior, which falls squarely within a legal framework and usually does not intimidate its citizens to the same degree. Or the transformation can be bad news when the group gains enough strength that it no longer relies primarily upon terrorism (an inherently weak tactic, as we have seen) because it has developed more effective means, such as guerrilla warfare, insurgency, or even major conventional war. This has happened at various times over the history of the Tamil Tigers, for example.[3] Terrorism can instigate or escalate into other forms of violence; the end of terrorism is not necessarily the beginning of "peace."

Transition to criminal behavior implies shifting away from collecting resources as a means of pursuing political ends toward acquiring goods and profits that are ends in themselves. Groups that have undertaken such transitions in recent years include Abu Sayyaf in the Philippines and the so-called narco-terrorist groups in Colombia.[4] Of course, international terrorist and criminal networks overlap, confounding facile generalizations; but when a group shifts toward criminal behavior, it diverts its energies from a political goal that challenges the status quo toward personal or collective material gain within the current order. The driving purpose becomes personal profit. This changes both its ability and incentive to attract a popular following, and it has implications for the type and degree of threat posed to the state and to the international system.

Terrorist groups can also escalate to insurgency or even conventional war in order to achieve their political ends. Notable examples include the LTTE, Kashmiri separatist groups, the Khmer Rouge, and the Communist Party of Nepal–Maoists. During the twentieth century, transitions in and out of insurgency have been common among ethnonationalist-separatist groups, whose connection to a territory and grounding in an ethnic population provide a natural base to maintain or mobilize further support. In these situations, the evolution in the form of violence involves changes in size or type of operations (do they operate as a military unit and attack mainly other military targets?), and whether or not the organization holds territory (even temporarily). Terrorism and insurgency are not the same thing; but they are cousins, distinguishable by the strength of the movement and differences in targeting. Very weak territorially based movements use terrorist attacks and transition to insurgency when they gain strength, especially when (as was the case for most groups in the twentieth century) their enemy is a single state government. Concepts overlap, as insurgencies typically use terrorist tactics alongside irregular guerrilla warfare; but during the last century, the key in understanding the relationship between the two has been to analyze the group's motivation, attraction to a constituency, size, strength, targeting, and degree to which its goals are associated with control of a piece of territory.

Transitions to full-blown conventional war can occur when the group is able to use terrorist attacks to influence the behavior of a state according to its own interests, or even when an act of terrorism has unintended consequences. The outbreak of World War I is the classic example: as Adam Roberts points out, the assassination of Archduke Franz Ferdinand in July 1914 was not intended to set off an international cataclysm.[5] Terrorism can be so provocative that it results in a cascade of state actions that culminate in systemic war, especially if the initial attack is perceived to have been sponsored by a state. In this circumstance, the original political purpose of terrorist attacks may bear no relationship to the outcome of the major interstate conflict they catalyze.

These concepts—terrorism, crime, insurgency, war—have different emphases and purposes. They have always been ambiguous in relation to one another and are only becoming *more* confused in the twenty-first century. The haziness in terminology reflects the changing nature of the nation-state as it interacts with emerging state and nonstate variants in mission, structure, and organization, as well as a mix of new and old ways of using force. Projecting a false clarity between them only lays bare the limitations in the language we use. Yet how we use these terms *does* matter, because the language has practical effects upon what governments do and the subsequent evolution of the violence. When we declare a "war on terrorism," for example, or label the al-Qaeda movement an "insurgency," we tap into language that is evocative. The phrase affects the way we frame conflicts, how we fight them, the narratives that emerge out of them, and, most important of all, the degree to which the parties involved are able to mobilize support for or opposition to the campaigns at the heart of them—all of which affect a group's viability.

CRIMINALITY AND TERRORISM

Criminal groups and terrorist groups often engage in similar behavior, including kidnappings, assassinations, and bombings, but their purposes are different. Many, if not most, terrorist groups engage in criminal activity in order to fund their operations. Particularly in the wake of the end of the Cold War and the withdrawal of much clandestine state funding, terrorist organizations diversified their sources of income, branching out into both legal and illegal enterprises. To raise funds, Hezbollah carried out an elaborate cigarette-smuggling operation in the United States, for example, one of many sources of illicit revenue for the group.[6] But their core mission continues to be the pursuit of a political cause, served by symbolic violence.[7] As one commentator put it, "It could be said that criminals use violence to enable them to acquire resources, whereas terrorists acquire resources to enable them to practice violence."[8] Criminal syndicates aim toward personal gain, and their activities are normally hidden from view. Indeed, whether or not a group wants publicity can indicate whether it is engaged in terrorism, which is symbolic violence intended to have a psychological impact upon an audience, or criminality, which results in personal, material gain and is not helped by exposure.

Another easy way of distinguishing between criminality and terrorism is to consider whether the group wants the perpetuation of the current political order. The criminal group is a status quo actor, content to operate within the current order, from which illicit gains are siphoned off. Domestically, criminal groups circumvent the legal structure but do not directly threaten the political foundation of the state or the nature of its government. They can be brutally violent but rarely want to run governments themselves. The terrorist group is a revisionist actor, having as its ultimate goal altering the national or international political system in accordance with some concept of justice, piety, fulfillment, or popular welfare. The group may or may not be able to transition to political leadership—and as we saw in chapter 3, few actually do; but they certainly want to determine what that political structure is and who controls it. It is because criminal groups are status quo actors rather than revisionists that they are less directly threatening to the current global order.[9]

As is the case with terrorism, insurgency, and war, however, the concepts of criminality and terrorism are imperfect and overlapping. The evolution of the nation-state is affecting them as well: as the internal (legal) and external (strategic) faces of nation-state authority have become increasingly indistinct, terrorism and criminal behavior have likewise become further intertwined. Groups that are transitioning away from a political aim may fall back on established competencies, such as kidnapping, robbery, racketeering, drug trafficking, and assaults on competitors. This is what occurred with the demobilization of paramilitaries in South Africa and Northern Ireland, for example.[10] As groups sample the astonishing profits made by meeting the demand for illicit substances (especially in the wealthy West), their political motivations can be eclipsed by greed.[11] The international drug trade is becoming increasingly integrated with local conflicts in many parts of the world.[12] But while the drug trade can strengthen nonstate actors and weaken the state, it is not aimed at overthrowing the state and replacing its government with another political system. Criminal behavior is by no means good news, but it may be more easily confronted than terrorism within existing legal frameworks.

Let us now examine two groups that have reoriented themselves away from ideological motivations toward criminal behavior: the Colombian FARC and the Philippine Abu Sayyaf.

Colombia and the FARC

Colombia, with a long-established record of violence going back well into the nineteenth century, is a state whose identity seems almost uniquely tied up with internecine warfare. Having historically failed to consolidate either a monopoly over the use of force or control over its population and territory, much less a well-functioning state judiciary, Colombia never really became a modern nation-state. The continuing factions within its territory grow out of that unusual predicament, which has yielded a weak central government and endemic corruption, lawlessness, and fighting. In such a muddled political context, labeling the violence presents special difficulty, with pundits variously calling it terrorism, narco-terrorism, insurgency, criminality, and civil war. Arguably it is all of these things. However, the integral connections between the international drug trade and the factionalized conflict within Colombia give it an almost unique status as a criminal ecosystem. Some writers even use the noun *Colombianization* to describe a process of descent into generalized criminality.[13] This strange marriage of political violence and criminal motivations is seen in the activities of one of the main nonstate actors, the Revolutionary Armed Forces of Colombia (Fuerzas Armadas Revolucionarias de Colombia, or FARC).

The FARC was established in 1964 following yet another bloody period known as La Violencia (1948–58). It is the oldest of many substate groups in Colombia and has engaged in the longest continuous campaign of armed violence in Latin America. Initially the FARC was made up of landless rebels who formed the military wing of the Colombian Communist Party. Its stated goal was (and technically continues to be) the establishment of a Marxist state in Colombia. The legendary founder, Manuel Marulanda, a diminutive man also known as *Tirofijo* (or "Sureshot"), led the group for 44 years. In 1982, the FARC added the words "people's army" (*ejército del pueblo*) to its name, giving it the awkward acronym "FARC-EP," but we will opt for the simpler form, not least because the purported parallel with a classic people's revolutionary war is increasingly inaccurate.

The very complex relationship between political and drug activity by the FARC defies generalization. It controls one of the world's richest and most powerful insurgent armies, holding territory and behaving as a military organization. In 2007, the International Institute for Strategic Studies estimated that the group had about 12,000 armed combatants.[14] The FARC has engaged in activity that threatens the stability of the Colombian government, attacking political and military installations, targeting candidates for election, and even firing a mortar at the presidential palace. But the FARC's political roots as a Maoist insurgency have been overshadowed by its connections to narcotics and its desire to make a profit. Perhaps the eclipse of left-wing causes following the end of the Cold War explains the FARC's transition to an armed organization whose activity mainly revolves around organized crime and the drug trade. It has been the premier producer and global exporter of cocaine; according to a U.S. federal indictment, the 50 senior leaders of the FARC control 50 percent of the cocaine traffic in the world.[15] While such things are difficult to measure, academic studies estimate that the vast majority of the FARC's murders, anywhere from 75 percent to 88 percent of the total number of killings, have been related to apolitical, economic goals, particularly protecting the routes and assets of the narcotics trade.[16] The group mostly targets competitors, rural outposts, and public infrastructure, as a way of maintaining control and predominance. The primary attraction of the group to its members, many of whom are poor and uneducated rural dwellers, has increasingly been the livelihood they earn rather than the political ideology of the group.[17]

While it continued to kill and kidnap, the FARC drifted away from its original Marxist political goals and become more interested in perpetuating an alternative "government" in the territory it held, powered by its drug empire and protected by its conventional military strength.[18] The level of profit the FARC earned from the production and commercialization of drugs evolved into a stable system that served the interests of the group. In 2003 alone, the FARC earned something in the neighborhood of $1 billion from drugs, kidnapping, and extortion.[19] The FARC exercised a pseudo-sovereignty over its territory, using violence in an authoritarian way to control the population.[20] It also built an elaborate, self-sustaining economic infrastructure, collecting taxes from coca growers, and additional revenue from extortion, ransoms, and protection money paid by landowners and businesses.

The relationship between Colombia and the United States is an important element in the evolution of conflict between the Colombian state and the FARC and other substate groups.[21] Colombia receives the third largest amount of aid from the United States, behind Israel and Egypt, having been given $4 billion between 2000 and 2004 alone. Under the Clinton administration, the U.S. distinguished between counternarcotics and the civil war, allowing U.S. aid in the "Plan Colombia" program to be used for the former but not the latter.[22] U.S. State Department officials even met with FARC representatives in December 1998, to discuss possible recognition of the FARC as a "belligerent force," an important goal of the group.[23] Following September 11, however, the Bush administration merged the war on terrorism and the war on drugs; in 2002 the U.S. Congress loosened restrictions on aid, freeing the Colombian government to use U.S. aid money to battle the FARC and other groups directly. Also since September 11, Colombian state authorities have regularly alleged that al-Qaeda or other radical Islamists have infiltrated Colombia, claims that U.S. authorities within the country have greeted with surprise. There is currently no reliable evidence of collaboration between the FARC and al-Qaeda.[24]

The FARC's fortunes took a sharp turn for the worse in 2008. Driven by Colombia's popular president, Álvaro Uribe, steady pressure from Colombian police and army forces put the FARC on the defensive, driving it into remote jungles near the country's borders and loosening its grip on the drug trade and its profits. Buoyed by American money, Uribe bolstered the number of government troops by 40 percent, cracked down on exchange houses used for money laundering, and dramatically improved surveillance with U.S. eavesdropping equipment. In March 2008, the FARC's second-in-command, Raul Reyes, was killed in a raid in Ecuador, which also yielded a huge cache of intelligence that revealed the names and activities of dozens of other senior leaders.[25] There were reports of internecine witch-hunts, with FARC members distrustful of each other and with executions of betrayers. These measures contributed to the dramatic rescue of 15 hostages from an enclave in southern Colombia, including Ingrid Betancourt, French Colombian presidential candidate and *cause célèbre* whose release without so much as a shot fired was a symbolic blow to the reputation of the group. After their release, the hostages spoke of the horrors of their imprisonment, revelations that heightened popular revulsion at the FARC.[26]

As the FARC's base of popular support disintegrated, numerous commentators spoke of the imminent collapse of the group. A key point in the group's loss of legitimacy was its reorientation from a political organization with legitimate grievances, to an organized crime syndicate whose local supporters abandoned it when the FARC was no longer able either to buy them off or protect them. At this writing, it is not clear what the outcome of these events will be; but the future looks dim for the FARC.[27]

The Philippines and Abu Sayyaf

Another group more interested in crime than converts is Abu Sayyaf. It operates in a rectangular patch of the Pacific Ocean known as the Sulu Sea, reaching northeast from the coastline of Borneo to the main body of the Philippine islands, bounded on the other two sides by the long, thin island of Palawan and a chain of a thousand small islands called the Sulu Archipelago. Abu Sayyaf's traditional headquarters has been Jolo Island, one of the southern islands in the Philippine archipelago. For centuries, this part of the world between the Philippines and Malaysia has been a playground of pirates, avoided by Western warships and beyond the reach of state law enforcement.

Abu Sayyaf's proclaimed goal, which dates to the centuries-old friction between the Philippines' Muslim minority and its Christian majority, is the establishment of a separate Islamic state. In the early 1990s, it broke off from the Moro National Liberation Front, which had waged war against the Philippine government in the 1970s and 1980s and then reached a negotiated accord in 1996.[28] Relatively small (it has about 200 members) Abu Sayyaf draws young men directly from colleges and universities.[29] Following the death of its founder, Abdurajak Abubakar Janjalani, in 1998 the group splintered into several factions[30] and transitioned mainly to criminal activities, especially kidnapping for ransom.

One leader who came to prominence after Janjanlani's death was Aldam Tilao (also called Abu Sabaya, or "Bearer of Captives"). Tilao, a flamboyant former student of criminology, held the dubious distinction of having been tossed out of both Zamboanga College in Mindanao and an al-Qaeda training camp in Libya. He loved the limelight. After capturing several dozen tourists and dragging them through the jungle, he regularly offered boastful interviews from his satellite phone, broadcast over the radio in Mindanao. Even as he oversaw the rape and murder of hostages, Tilao developed a following of sorts among young people in the Philippines fascinated by the concept of a hip revolutionary. And he nourished the image: Tilao wore a black do-rag on his head, a hoop earring, and Oakley sunglasses—a kind of pirate-*cum*-hip-hop artist look. He even nicknamed himself "DJ." Among his victims were U.S. Christian missionaries Gracia and Martin Burnham. Seized in May 2001, the Burnhams were virtually ignored until 9/11, when the United States began to see Abu Sayyaf within the broader context of an Islamist movement, and committed troops and intelligence aid to the Philippine government.[31]

Whether Abu Sayyaf is genuinely connected to an ideology is the subject of vigorous debate. Philippine president Gloria Macapagal Arroyo describes the group as a "money-crazed gang of criminals."[32] It has collected millions of dollars in ransom from the governments of Malaysia, Libya, Germany, and France, which it has used to develop a formidable fleet of quick, state-of-the-art vessels. The group is increasingly connected to the growing drug trade in Manila.[33] Both the Moro Islamic Liberation Front (MILF) and the Moro National Liberation Front (MNLF) have condemned Abu Sayyaf's criminal activities and tried to distance themselves from the group. Others argue that Abu Sayyaf is still a radical terrorist organization closely intertwined with al-Qaeda.[34] Before 1996, Abu Sayyaf had a close working relationship with al-Qaeda (it is alleged to have been funded by bin Laden's brother-in-law, Mohammed Jamal Khalifa, in the early 1990s). It continues to have connections with Jemaah Islamiya, an Islamist group active in Southeast Asia. And since 2003, its connections to bombings in the Philippines may indicate a resurgence of its original Islamist tenets.

Still, concrete evidence of its ideological mission remains thin. According to Gracia Burnham, her captors had a shallow, even adolescent understanding of Islam, with no knowledge of the Quran and only a vague sense of the religion as a set of behavioral rules that could be broken at will.[35] Abu Sayyaf can hardly be described as a seamless extension of the Islamist movement. Though it is clearly dangerous, at this writing Abu Sayyaf's mission, a kind of murderous opportunism, is more reminiscent of Blackbeard than bin Laden. The desire to make money seems the primary source of attraction to its followers and is an important indicator of the group's local origins, its sources of vulnerability, and its distinctiveness.

INSURGENCY AND TERRORISM

The terms *insurgency* and *terrorism* overlap. Insurgencies often use terrorism as one of many tactics; to assert that terrorist organizations and insurgencies can be neatly distinguished would be foolish: neither term is fully satisfactory. However, degrees of difference and emphasis are important in analyzing what a group is trying to achieve, how great a threat it poses, and how best to respond to it.

From the perspective of state military forces, transitioning to insurgency can put a terrorist group onto more familiar ground. Best thought of as military rebellions against indigenous governments or foreign occupiers, insurgencies present themselves as alternatives to the current regime, hold a type of sovereignty over people and territory, and use force as pseudo-armies or guerrilla forces. For this reason, they primarily target the opposing military forces of the state, often using guerrilla-style hit-and-run tactics.[36] Insurgents may use terrorism, particularly when they target "noncombatants" such as government officials, police forces, or noncompliant civilian leaders; but unlike terrorist organizations, they can hold territory and engage the military.[37] Summing up the differences between the two, Bruce Hoffman argues that, compared to terrorist groups, insurgencies are numerically larger organizations of armed individuals who operate as military units, target military forces, and seize and held territory (at least temporarily).[38]

Which label we use has practical effects.[39] One imparts a kind of legitimacy to a cause: *terrorism* is a pejorative term; *insurgency* is not. But again the touch point is the modern state: insurgencies are driven by grievances against a nation-state, suggest a connection with national self-determination, and are considered to have more serious combatants. Military officers prefer to describe their opposites as insurgents rather than terrorists: the term *insurgents* makes them worthy opponents, imparts a degree of professionalism to the foe, and creates a military framework for engagements with them. Members of organizations that use terrorism likewise prefer the term *insurgents*, for the same reasons. But the language used then frames the response. Insurgents feed on grievances and are best met with classic counterinsurgency techniques to answer those grievances, for example by providing other avenues for improved security, poverty abatement, better opportunities, more equal treatment—in short, better ways to live in the present, within a defined territory. Terrorists also take advantage of grievances but, lacking sufficient military capacity, they draw their ability to threaten the nation-state from leveraging the political and military actions of the state itself. Their goal is to use symbolic violence to demonize a government and inspire potential constituents, to grab their attention and shift it from the present to a vision of the future, so as to justify the extraordinary, gruesome, and illegitimate measures they take against ordinary people as they seek to get there.

In short, most terrorist groups *aspire* to become insurgencies—though they may not foresee the escalation of violence that their attacks spark. In the next section we will consider a group that transitioned out of a primary reliance on terrorist attacks into insurgency, and eventually ignited widescale atrocities and civil war.

Algeria and the GIA

In 1991, Algeria seemed to be on the verge of becoming the most democratized state in the Arab world. Having emerged from its bloody war of liberation from France, Algeria had a stable authoritarian government that gave signs of passing from a postcolonial regime of elite control and patronage into a mature and well-operating pluralistic state.[40] The FLN (Front de Libération Nationale), the victorious party in the struggle against France, was joined in the 1980s by a proliferation of other parties and actors who seemed poised to share power on the national stage. The most important of these was the Front Islamique de Salut (Islamic Salvation Front, or FIS). As with many other cases in this book, the bloody outburst of terrorism and tragedy that followed in the 1990s found its impetus in a moment of hope and political opportunity gone terribly wrong.

The roots of Algeria's unrest are a subject of contention. Some argue that the problem was mainly economic: Algeria's economy is heavily dependent upon revenues from oil and gas; in 1986, the price of oil dropped by a third, from $30 per barrel to $10, undermining the basis of a carefully balanced system.[41] Others point to the aged FLN revolutionaries who had been in power since 1962 and still acted as if the state were their own personal property, living well, driving expensive cars, and making no room for successors.[42] Still others blame the mismanagement of the government, whose 28 years of authoritarian rule had yielded high inflation, high unemployment, housing shortages, poor education, and widespread privation.[43] What is undisputed is that, in October 1988, 5,000 young people went on a rampage, prompting the rattled regime to declare a state of siege and empower state security forces to shoot on sight. On October 4, at least 500 were killed and 3,500 arrested, including large numbers of youths and children. The unrest had not been instigated or controlled by any one group, being, as one writer describes it, a "straightforward explosion of protest against the regime."[44] But Islamists seized the chance to channel popular passions into mass marches.

Following what became known as "Black October," President Chadli Benjedid concluded that political liberalization was required. In February 1989, he pushed through a new constitution, increased freedom of the press, and opened the field for participation by other political parties. Scores of new little parties emerged, clustered around social issues or prominent individuals. Fashioning itself after the populist FLN of the 1950s, the FIS was founded and legalized in September 1989, quickly becoming Algeria's best-organized and most popular movement.[45] In parliamentary elections in 1991 the FIS received more than twice as many votes as the FLN—approximately 3.3 million (47 percent) to 1.6 million (23 percent)—and a large plurality of seats.[46] This was a shock for the government, and even more of a shock for the armed forces. The army executed a bloodless coup, compelled the resignation of Chadli, and installed its own man.[47] The new regime declared a state of emergency, dissolved the 400 local councils controlled by the FIS, and threw the party's two founders into jail.[48] The party was officially dissolved by decree in March 1992. Calling the dissolution "a return to rule by the sword," the FIS began small-scale terrorist violence, targeting government officials.[49]

Disagreements over the right way to carry out the struggle against the government soon led to splits and factionalization. In September 1992, unity talks in Tamesguida were attacked by government security forces, killing several leaders and leading followers to conclude that their opposites were infiltrated by state security agents.[50] Out of anger and frustration a new entity arose, which was initially a loosely aligned group of smaller gangs that had little effective coordination but soon became known as the Armed Islamic Group (Groupe Islamique Armé, or GIA). Most cells of the GIA began as small bands of young men clustered around an "emir" operating in poor suburban areas and slums. The membership reportedly included numerous criminals, as well as a significant number of what were called Algerian "Afghans," driven by a Salafist dogma. Decentralized, undisciplined, and without a consistent strategy, the GIA made atrocious violence its trademark. To the extent that there was a discernable rationale, the priority was a radical re-Islamization of society *first*, then a change of regime.[51] The GIA was opposed to elections, democratization, coalitions with other groups, and anything that implied compromise, expressing a hyperviolent pseudo-religious nihilism.

On the government side there were also moderates and extremists, the latter especially in the army, who wanted the total eradication of the Islamists and the establishment of a fully secular state. In 1994, President Zeroual tried to engage in dialogue so as to reach a compromise solution, but was held back by military leaders. Peace initiatives and talks followed, but they were undermined by extremists on both sides. Following elections in November 1995, the GIA declared the entire country to be "apostate."[52] The GIA declared war on the FIS, the military launched a huge conventional offensive against all the armed Islamists, and by 1995 the situation had degenerated beyond isolated acts of terrorism into full-scale civil war.[53]

Catalyzed by the GIA, the scale of the carnage ratcheted up astonishingly, reaching a peak in 1997. The group's violence was directed against those who opposed Islamist demands or defied Islamist principles such as a conservative dress code. Members of the GIA dragged 16-year-old girls out of classrooms and slaughtered them because they had the temerity to attend school. Whole villages were massacred because they refused to contribute money or support (or discontinued prior support), usually in isolated rural areas that had supported the FIS in the 1991 elections. Old people and newborn babies were disemboweled or hacked to death, the throats of women and children slit like animals.[54] Journalists and clerics were killed by the dozen. But there was a sinister side to the military's behavior as well: villages close to security force barracks and posts were massacred; the security forces neither stopped the attacks nor pursued the perpetrators, leading to suspicions that the security services were complicit in the killings.[55] Extremists had apparently so infiltrated each other's organizations that at times no one was certain who was responsible for the crimes, with some alleging that military forces were instigating or encouraging atrocities to demonize the GIA. Whatever the truth, the GIA's communiqués became increasingly extreme; one newsletter read: "blood and corpses create glory . . . and death creates life."[56] These words were certainly not aimed at mobilizing the public, the vast majority of whom supported no one and cowered in fear and exhaustion.

In 1999, newly elected president Abdelaziz Bouteflika offered an amnesty to GIA guerrillas, many of whom chose to "repent"; others were hunted down and killed by the army. A few years later, a blanket amnesty was provided for security forces "for actions conducted for the purpose of protecting persons and property, safeguarding the nation or preserving the institutions" of Algeria, and the country entered a period of uneasy calm.[57] But at least 120,000 people had died, and violence remained close to the surface. In 2006, the GSPC (Groupe Salafiste pour la Prédication et le Combat, or Salafist Group for Call and Combat), comprising GIA members that refused the amnesty, announced an alliance with al-Qaeda and initiated a campaign of kidnappings and terrorist attacks in Algiers a year later.[58] Thus, in this case, acts of terrorism had devolved into a full-scale conventional war.

Terrorism as a Catalyst for Major War

Compared to conventional war, terrorism is an unimportant tactic. But it is a powerful means of leverage, and therein lies its menace. There are two ways in which terrorism can be so powerful that it kills millions and destabilizes the international system. The first, use of a "weapon of mass destruction" (especially nuclear) by a nonstate actor, represents a looming threat of which many are aware. The proliferation of nuclear technology and materials following the breakup of the Soviet Union and the end of the Cold War holds greater potential and opportunity for groups such as al-Qaeda (and associates) to buy or steal a small nuclear device. The international community is right to focus on this problem; in particular, a large number of academics and policymakers who dealt with nuclear weapons and the complicated theology of nuclear strategy during the Cold War have turned their attention to the breakdown of the international nonproliferation regime, and are coming up with new means of controlling or tracing nuclear substances (especially highly enriched uranium). This is an outstanding use of their skills that may well lead to a reduction in this threat.[59] One only hopes that extensive knowledge of the supply side of nuclear weapons technology is eventually matched by equal sophistication regarding the demand side, especially the motivations and opportunities of nonstate actors (about which there is relatively little good research). In any case, if a terrorist group were to use a nonconventional weapon, there is no doubt that the result would almost immediately be major war.

The second, much less discussed or well-known threat is the use of conventional terrorism as a catalyst for interstate war. As we have seen, terrorism feeds both hope and insecurity. Attacks by nonstate actors can set off a pernicious process, where attempts to increase security by one state lead to increasing insecurity for another state, and so on, setting off a negative spiral of state actions that results in catastrophic war. This outcome is most likely to happen when there are a number of other factors present. First, the target government must be unable or unwilling to put in place measures to defuse the inflammatory potential of terrorism. These may range from confidence-building measures to a sophisticated understanding of the threat. In other words, the state must be vulnerable to being manipulated or provoked into unwise or emotional action in the wake of a terrorist attack, particularly in a context where its population supports the use of military force in response to terrorism. Second, the terrorist attack must be perceived as sponsored by another state. This provides a target for retaliatory military action that may then escalate out of control, destabilizing local or regional power balances and leading to the perception that other states must arm to protect themselves from their neighbors. Third, the international system must be in a state of flux, with shifting military relationships and alliance systems providing a sense of both danger and opportunity.

This constellation of circumstances and events has happened at least once before in history, notably with the outbreak of World War I. The assassination of Archduke Franz Ferdinand, heir to the throne of Austria-Hungary, in Sarajevo on June 28, 1914, was in itself a relatively unimportant act. Assassination had been endemic for decades. Apparently no country was immune: as we have seen, Tsar Alexander II was assassinated in 1881; other victims included French president Sadi Carnot (killed in 1894), Spanish prime minister Antonio Cánovas Del Castillo (1897), King Humbert of Italy (1900), and U.S. president William McKinley (1901). But because of other factors in place in 1914, that assassination in Sarajevo became the catalyst for cataclysmic systemic war.

The origins of the war are complex and the subject of voluminous histories. For present purposes, it is enough to recognize that all three of the factors we have mentioned were present.[60] First, Austria-Hungary, an unstable dynastic state composed of 11 nationalities, was led by Emperor Franz Josef, uncle of the assassinated man and single-handedly responsible for declaring war. According to accounts at the time, the 84-year-old was personally shaken by the assassination of his heir and worried about the broader implications for the future of the monarchy.[61] Second, the government in Vienna was convinced that the assassination had been orchestrated by Serbia.[62] Finally, Europe was in a state of flux, completing a transition from imperial order to states based on nationhood and popular representation in the West and communist authoritarianism in the East. Thus, a symbolic act of individual terrorism triggered war.

The murder of the archduke set off a series of seemingly irreversible policy decisions, beginning with Austria-Hungary's ultimatum to Serbia on July 23 and then declaration of war exactly a month after the killing, leading to Russian mobilization, Germany's declaration of war on Russia on August 1, and French and British declarations of war against Germany on August 3 and 4, 1914.[63] By early August, the entire continent was engulfed in a war that would, over the next four years, kill millions. Nothing about terrorism and its toll is worth mentioning beside such an unimaginable calamity—except the key fact that it was a terrorist act that set it all in motion and that, under the right international conditions, another such act could do so again.

India, Pakistan, and the Kashmiri Separatist Groups

If any region demonstrates the potential for terrorism to have huge strategic consequences it is South Asia, and particularly its flashpoint, Kashmir, over which India and Pakistan have fought three major conventional wars, in 1947–48, 1965, and 1971. Kashmir-associated terrorism is a critical destabilizing factor in the India-Pakistan relationship, a rivalry that has all the potential for major catastrophic state uses of force up to and including nuclear strikes.

Jammu and Kashmir consists of five regions, three of which are under Indian administration (the Valley of Kashmir, Jammu, and Ladakh). The other two are under Pakistani administration ("Azad (Free) Kashmir" and the "Northern Areas"), divided along a Line of Control (LOC).[64] As India controls the majority of the contested territory, the status quo most closely serves its interests. In order to challenge this position, the Pakistani government has to varying degrees clandestinely supported or sponsored a number of insurgent and terrorist groups, providing training, arms, material assistance, and help in crossing the Line of Control. The largest and best trained are Lashkar-e-Taiba (LT), Hizb-ul Mujahideen (HM), Jaish-e-Mohammed (JeM), and Harakat ul-Mujahidin (HuM).[65] The wars in Afghanistan have yielded a bountiful supply of weapons for Kashmiri separatists.[66] Further complicating matters, the line of demarcation between Indian- and Pakistani-controlled territory runs through rough and unpopulated terrain linked by primitive roads, making it very difficult to monitor.[67] Crossings (or suspected crossings) are commonplace—a factor conducive to indirect and irregular types of warfare.

India and Pakistan last clashed directly over Kashmir in 1999, following an incursion by militants and Pakistani regular forces across the Line of Control at Kargil.[68] The Indian army responded with air strikes on May 26, as well as heavy artillery barrages and a massive buildup of conventional forces. Over the next six weeks of fighting about 1,000 people were killed on both sides and thousands of civilians displaced. A kind of hysteria gripped both countries.[69] The significance of the crisis was radically enhanced by the fact that both powers had conducted nuclear tests exactly one year earlier. There were real fears of nuclear use. In the end, the crisis was defused with U.S. help, including direct intervention by President Bill Clinton, pressuring the Pakistani government to withdraw back behind the Line of Control. But the lesson of the Kargil conflict was that local events in remote Kashmir held the potential for major catastrophe.

Two years later, in late 2001, two serious terrorist attacks again brought the region to the brink of major war. In October, a suicide attack on the Srinagar assembly in Kashmir killed 38 people.[70] Then in December 2001, militants stormed the Indian Parliament building in New Delhi and opened fire, killing 14. Lashkar-e-Taiba and Jaish-e-Mohammed were blamed for the attack, and the Indian government ordered the mobilization of half a million troops along the Line of Control and the international border with Pakistan—the largest conventional mobilization in Indian history.[71] India also demanded that Pakistan turn over 20 key terrorism suspects, shut down terrorist training camps on its territory, choke off their finances and weapons supplies, and stop infiltrating militants into Jammu and Kashmir.[72] Flights between India and Pakistan were suspended, the border was closed, and tempers flared. Pakistan military spokesman Major General Rashid Qureshi argued that the whole incident was a propaganda stunt. "The attack on parliament is a drama staged by Indian intelligence agencies to defame the freedom struggle in occupied Kashmir," he claimed.[73]

On January 1, 2002, Pakistan also mobilized its forces along the border. A ten-month standoff ensued, with a million Indian and Pakistani troops eyeballing each other and the U.S. government publicly stating that it was "deeply concerned . . . that a conventional war . . . could escalate into a nuclear confrontation."[74]

This time the crisis was not set off by military operations near the border but by terrorist groups that had infiltrated well into Indian territory to carry out a provocative attack on the legislature. This was symbolic, leveraged violence. Again the United States and Britain intervened. Pakistan's president, Pervez Musharraf, promised the United States that he would end support for militancy in Kashmir, and Pakistan outlawed the two groups blamed for the attack. Shortly thereafter, on December 24, 2001, the United States also added Lashkar-e-Taiba and Jaish-e-Mohammed to the list of "Foreign Terrorist Organizations," a legal action that carries extensive economic and political sanctions. A number of high-profile meetings between Pakistan and India followed, yielding some encouraging results, including a cease-fire along the Line of Control, a new bus service between the Indian- and Pakistani-controlled parts of Kashmir, and other conciliatory measures. While the level of violence has gone down, infiltrations continue, and India still stations a large number of troops in Kashmir (250,000 regular soldiers and more than 100,000 paramilitaries).[75] The larger territorial questions remain unresolved, and the situation remains ripe for violence and instability: for example, there are reports that the Indian army has prepared retaliatory attacks against targets in Pakistan should there be another major terrorist attack thought to emanate from Islamabad.[76]

The Pakistani military government practices an opaque policy of co-opting religious extremists apparently so as to offset domestic secular pressure for liberalization.[77] The result is a highly schizophrenic relationship with militant organizations that are involved, directly or indirectly, in carrying out terrorist attacks in Kashmir, Afghanistan, India, and even Pakistan itself. Two assassination attempts on President Musharraf in December 2003 alone were proof of the perils of the policy. A successful terrorist attack against a Pakistani president carried out by disgruntled extremists who have turned against the regime could easily upset the delicate balance of the region. Just as alarming, however, would be the prospect of a successful assassination by a jihadist terrorist group of an Indian prime minister or other senior official, or another major terrorist operation on Indian soil. Whatever the reality, such an event would be seen to be sponsored by the Pakistani government. The outcome could be a cascade of actions by both sides that might easily become unstoppable.

With the discovery of the A. Q. Kahn network and its dissemination of nuclear technology, attention has focused on the prospect of proliferation to nonstate actors, including terrorist groups. While this concern is justified, recent events in the India-Pakistan-Kashmir triangle demonstrate that a more urgent, short-term possibility is that nonstate actors may, wittingly or unwittingly, use terrorism to catalyze actions by nuclear states. The absence of robust confidence-building measures between the two sides, the culture of mistrust and miscommunication, the lack of experience with regional nuclear deterrence, and the destabilizing wild card of jihadist groups provide an ideal setting for disaster.[78] It is conceivable that a terrorist attack in South Asia could end in nuclear war.

OUTDATED PARADIGMS, PRACTICAL IMPLICATIONS

Terrorism, insurgency, and *war* are all terms that describe the use of force by or against the modern nation-state as it emerged and was consolidated during the nineteenth and twentieth centuries. They have meaning today in reference to the organizational and intellectual structures of that kind of state, especially its legal and strategic communities. The early twenty-first century is another period of transition—but not toward the dissolution of the state itself and its replacement by nonstate actors, a false and ahistorical dichotomy drawn by short-sighted pundits. Instead, in keeping with a long-standing pattern, today's familiar nation-state is evolving to become a range of other types of states. For good or ill, we are witnessing the natural evolution of the nineteenth-century European-style nation-state toward new, more flexible structures better suited to the challenges of the global, information-based context of the twenty-first century, with virtual communities overshadowing parliaments, international corporations displacing government bureaucracies, and private contractors supplanting national armies.

How states and nonstate actors use force is naturally evolving as well, dragging our descriptive concepts along behind them. Terrorism continues to embody certain core ideas, including a fundamentally political nature, the surprise use of symbolic violence against seemingly random targets, and the targeting of civilians. But there are crucial areas of ambiguity as well. These hazy aspects are not the result of our inability to be intellectually rigorous, or our hypocrisy or deceit in describing the violence—though terrorism is, admittedly, designed to be a matter of perception and always has been. Our uncertainty is a reflection of our limited understanding of the changes under way for nation-states and their use of force.

These changes are casting new light on old ideas that drew their meaning from structures of the state. Most notably: what is a civilian? In a world where borders are increasingly permeable, where the organization of state armed forces is becoming more diffuse, and where the use of armed contractors is increasingly taking the place of traditional military members, this concept (always difficult) becomes still more tricky. Historical, cross-cultural norms derived from secular and religious traditions insist that civilians are by definition illegitimate targets, to be avoided through the discriminate use of force. States may have described them as "collateral damage," unavoidable victims sacrificed in the cause of ending a war (self-conscious excuses that are revealing in themselves). But rightly or wrongly, the international community had accorded nation-states the authority under certain circumstances to use force, and those states gained or lost legitimacy on the basis of their efforts to do so discriminately. Indeed, this norm is at the heart of what makes terrorism wrong: its *deliberate* targeting of civilians.[79] But how do we isolate civilians from attack when we are no longer clear exactly where the boundaries of "civilian" lie? To our discomfort, even the reliable reference to "innocent women and children" fails in a world where child soldiers are coerced into becoming combatants and women are suicide bombers.[80] For good or ill, we are moving backward, into the prenational era—risking something akin to the chaos of the civil and religious wars of the sixteenth and seventeenth centuries. For reasons that are partly of our own making and partly reflective of broader historical forces, it is becoming increasingly difficult for the nation-state to use force legitimately.

The concept of civilian is imperfect and in need of updating because, as the nation-state evolves, its boundaries (both physical and political) are more and more difficult to discern. Whether or not one wears a uniform or receives a paycheck from a state does not give us as much to go on in identifying "civilians" as it once did, and therefore in clarifying the legitimacy or illegitimacy of the force that is used against them. We will resolve this issue only through agreement on the sources of legitimacy for the future state—the question that is, after all, at the core of the problem.[81] Some have argued that the new state should draw its legitimacy from being "democratic," for example. In response, some terrorist groups counter that, with universal suffrage at the heart of democracies, all citizens share responsibility for the actions of their governments and are legitimate targets of attack. This interpretation makes a mockery of the norm of the discriminate use of force—reflecting the confusing status of the twenty-first-century state.

Likewise, what is the difference between a state and a nonstate actor? In a world with a proliferation of warlords, contractors, networks, and private security firms—or even nongovernmental organizations, web-based movements, regional networks, and global corporations—what is a nonstate actor? State terror means the illegitimate state use of force, employed against citizens of that state and (historically, at least), carried out with impunity. The repression described in chapter 5 can also be labeled "state terror," or terror from above. In the modern era, the state use of force has been subject to norms that are long-standing and reasonably well developed (though not well enforced). On the other hand, terrorism from below has been identified as surprise attacks by nonstate actors against innocent citizens of states. But is everything that is *not* a state a nonstate actor? No wonder we have difficulty distinguishing between, and naming, the uses of force that those widely disparate, proliferating nonstate actors employ. Yet we know that, when they deliberately target innocents, without shame—indeed with self-righteous claims about moving forward the course of history or rectifying past injustice—that behavior is wrong and must be eliminated. And that behavior is "terrorism."

As we have seen, insurgency is likewise a tricky and evolving concept. One wise commentator defined an insurgency as "a popular movement that seeks to overthrow the *status quo* through subversion, political activity, insurrection, armed conflict and terrorism."[82] But what is the status quo? Of course, the status quo has been the twentieth-century nation-state. So, again, an insurgency is defined in reference to its opposition to a structure that is evolving. By emphasizing that they operate as military units, target military force, and seize and hold territory, we have defined them as challenging and mimicking the behavior of the armed forces of the nation-state. Insurgents engage state armed forces and assert themselves as alternatives to them. There is no wonder that *insurgency* is a more favored term than *terrorism* to the military mind: for a movement to be a worthy opponent, it must be more than just a terrorist group—it must target the military. The nonstate group benefits from the concept as well: insurgencies typically resist occupation and benefit from a long historical tradition of partisan resistance. But again we face ambiguity. Does targeting private contractors make the act insurgency or terrorism? There is no agreement on whether contractors are military or civilian, because the degree to which they carry the imprimatur of the state itself is disputed. No wonder we are struggling to analyze and counter these behaviors! Existing paradigms are increasingly inadequate and outdated.

In struggling with these paradigms and their imperfect, overlapping, and sometimes incoherent language and definitions, the only way forward is through reference to the phenomenon that has been at the core of the modern state: the capacity to mobilize popular support. In the era of the nation-state, that mobilization occurred in the furtherance of national aims. The European powers demonstrated the height of such intellectual and physical mobilization through the industrial era, culminating in two bloody world wars and later perfected by major powers as disparate as the United States, USSR, and People's Republic of China. Since the eclipse of the artificial stasis of the Cold War, we have been witnessing shifts in the purpose or focal point of the use of force that reflect changes in the character of the nation-state, especially its internal and external realms of authority. The most important element in the concurrent shift in tactics by *nonstate* groups is their ability to mobilize people and resources to use force against the state, or to provoke states to take actions themselves. Only through popular mobilization do such groups gain resources, legitimacy, numbers, and the military capacity to be a serious threat to the state.

As we have seen, national or international periods of transition are uniquely vulnerable to the catalytic use of force that terrorism represents. Especially in the context of twenty-first-century globalized communications, terrorist groups are nonstate actors that target the most vulnerable members of society as a means of provoking outrage, garnering attention, and, most importantly, gaining adherents to their cause—as a means of mobilizing a popular movement. Guerrillas and insurgents are actors who have successfully mobilized enough popular support, in both physical and ideological terms, to be strong enough to take on the power of the state by targeting its representatives and seeking military gains for the cause. Both of these tactics are distinctive and defined only in relation to the mass movements they aim to catalyze. Insurgencies are larger, more mobilized groups that have the strength and popular constituency to take on the military forces of the state using irregular warfare tactics. They primarily target military or government forces instead of ordinary civilians because they realize the risk of backlash and implosion in targeting illegitimates (see chapter 4). Both terrorism and insurgency are more dangerous now than they have been in the past because, again in the context of proliferating globalized communications, their means of popular mobilization have multiplied, while those of the state have comparatively diminished, resulting in increased leverage for the nonstate actor and an undercutting of the legitimacy of the nation-state, well beyond the outcome of individual engagements.

Thus, during this time of transition, as the traditional structure of the modern nation-state begins to seem less clear, even less legitimate, other types of human organization have been asserting themselves. Tribal groups, sects, crime syndicates, families, social networks all existed long before, but were generally subsumed in the overarching identity and purpose of the nation-state, and their ways of using force were overshadowed or controlled by the industrial nation-state's unprecedented ability to mobilize its people and monopolize power at home and abroad.[83] But this is changing. While the state retains unprecedented power, it is losing its capacity to mobilize as it once did. With the aid of globalized communications, other actors are gaining a competitive edge not just in how they use force, but much more importantly in how they mobilize and inspire people to support, participate in, and legitimate their use of force. Nonstate groups that use terrorism are emerging from these age-old human networks and connections to use twenty-first-century means that empower them in unprecedented ways to mobilize and inspire others. Whatever we name them or however we respond to them, their ability to inspire and mobilize popular movements is the real source of their threat to the current order. Until we realize this, we will continue to throw twentieth-century solutions (and language) at a twenty-first-century phenomenon, and history will leave us behind.

How War Ends Terrorism

Terrorism can "end" by evolving into or sparking other types of violence, ranging from criminal behavior to nuclear war. Today, the language we use to describe that violence is anachronistic. More relevant to understanding the role of political violence in the twenty-first century is to examine two dimensions: the ability of a group to mobilize and to shape state behavior. Terrorism as a means of mobilization is a long-established phenomenon, as old as the tactic itself; but today its power to mobilize is enhanced by uniquely favorable international circumstances, especially new means of communication, the breakdown of economic barriers, and increasingly porous borders between states. No matter what we name it, success or failure in mobilizing a following determines the form the violence will take, be it terrorism, insurgency, guerrilla warfare, or civil war.

Far more serious, a terrorist act may provoke a state to take actions that are against its own interests. Under conditions of global transition, where an act of terrorism is perceived to threaten a state's stability or to be sponsored by a rival state, it may be especially dangerous. In addition to Kashmir, examined in this chapter, other hot spots are highly vulnerable to the provocation of a terrorist attack, notably including Iran or North Korea. Simply the belief (correct or not) that these states were involved in a terrorist attack could be destabilizing, prompting massive retaliation by another state (even the United States) before the source of the initial attack could be confirmed. In an age of anxiety, terrorist attacks are a catalyst for instability. Use of a so-called weapon of mass destruction is not necessary to create what many call an "existential threat" (although, of course, such use is a serious worry). It is the *connections* between these paradigms—terrorism, insurgency, war, often artificially divided in our lexicons, doctrines, and theories, but not in practice—that should worry us. Well short of nuclear, chemical, or biological weapons use, a terrorist attack that dramatically changes the policy or perception of a major power can result in a negative cascade of reactions, triggering far more serious forms of interstate violence, up to and including nuclear war.

CHAPTER SEVEN

How Al-Qaeda Ends

THE RELEVANCE AND IRRELEVANCE OF HISTORY

> All we have to do is send two mujahedin . . . [and] raise a
> piece of cloth on which is written "Al Qaeda" in order to
> make the generals race there, to cause America to suffer
> human, economic and political losses.
> —*Osama bin Laden, videotaped message, 2004*[1]

HOW DOES one put an end to al-Qaeda when Western analysts cannot
even agree upon what precisely al-Qaeda is? Al-Qaeda began in the
1980s as a computer database with the names of foreign fighters in Afghanistan so that a wealthy Saudi dilettante would have a way to inform
their next of kin if they were killed, and over the course of the next two
decades it became a global entity capable of bloodying a superpower on
its own soil and frightening millions of people into supporting a "war on
terror." Following the September 11, 2001, attacks, the United States and
its allies threw everything they had at this group, including major wars in
Afghanistan and Iraq, a worldwide campaign of counterterrorism, new
United Nations' measures against terrorist financing, a dramatic shift in
U.S. foreign and defense policies, new U.S. legal practices at home and
abroad, and billions of dollars of American expenditure, only to find several years later that they were mired in a civil war in Iraq, losing ground
in Afghanistan, and, according to prevailing expert opinion, *worse off*
with respect to the threat of terrorism overall.[2] For its part, al-Qaeda
absorbed the impact of Western military force, including the death or
capture of 75 percent of its original leadership, and transformed itself
from a small hierarchical organization into a global presence facilitated
by twenty-first-century communications that made its reach seem ubiquitous and its radicalization of young Muslims seem unstoppable.[3] At a
time when a plethora of other long-term, pressing priorities in economic,
military, and foreign policy deserved U.S. attention, this elusive group
presented a persistent challenge, with high stakes for the future of the
Muslim world, the security of the West, and indirectly even the stability
of the international system. Yet we and our allies seemed unable to defeat

it. Why? Does all of this history yield specific insights into how to extract ourselves from this conundrum?

Above all, calm reason needs to prevail, and the challenge must be put in perspective: al-Qaeda will end. *All* movements that use terrorism as a tactic end, and although they can cause appalling damage both to their targets and their own constituencies, they rarely achieve their strategic aims. In addition to their ethical drawbacks, experience clearly demonstrates that terrorist attacks on civilians are not a particularly *effective* means of realizing political change.

This books explores a framework of six broad explanations for, or critical elements in, the decline and ending of terrorist groups in the modern era: (1) capturing or killing the leader; (2) entering a legitimate political process; (3) achieving strategic goals; (4) marginalization and implosion; (5) crushing with military force; and (6) transitioning to another modus operandi. These factors have been consistent across different types of groups in modern history, in many regions of the world, with various motivations; and we have drawn upon a wide range of cases to analyze each one. Any given group's decline might demonstrate more than one dynamic at play, as the relevant factors are not necessarily separate and distinct; but usually one explanation is dominant and the reasons for a group's decline become self-evident. Broad study of the historical record has also enabled us to identify typical situations, even in some cases specific conditions, where scenarios such as decapitation, negotiations, and repression were more or less likely to bring a group successfully to its end. But to what extent does any of this apply to al-Qaeda and its associates, or for that matter to a broader so-called jihadist movement adhering to violent extremism and mimicking al-Qaeda's rhetoric? The task now is to determine which lessons from the historical experience with terrorism's decline are relevant to al-Qaeda, and which are not.

Is Al-Qaeda Unique?

Al-Qaeda combines elements of continuity and discontinuity with other terrorist groups, and lessons to be learned from the successes and failures of past and present counterterrorist responses are applicable to it.[4] Senior members of the al-Qaeda movement know all too well that history applies to them, as they assiduously examine historical case studies so as to draw lessons for their own campaigns. These studies range from broad historical treatments of comparative case studies, to focused examinations of individual groups in the Islamic world, in the West, and elsewhere.[5] Yet, to determine where the patterns of demise for other groups are relevant and where they are not, we must clarify what is actually unique to al-Qaeda and its associates (or imitators) and what is not. Four vital characteristics, in nature or degree, distinguish al-Qaeda from its predecessors: its resilient structure, its methods of radicalization, its means of support, and its means of communication. Each will be examined here in turn.

Resilient Structure

It is partly because there is so much vague use of the name *al-Qaeda* that it seems superhuman and ubiquitous, but it is not. In examining al-Qaeda's remarkable ability to change its form, therefore, we must be precise as to what exactly al-Qaeda is. The purpose of the founders of al-Qaeda has always been to spark a broader rebellion among the Muslim masses, initially by attacking governments in the Middle East and then turning to the West, to provoke the masses into seeking revenge and eventually rising up against corrupt regimes. Theirs is a time-honored terrorist tactic, to leverage power through provocation and mobilization. When we employ the term *al-Qaeda* loosely, we enhance the capacity of its propagandists to construct and perpetuate their desired image and to mobilize that support. We also put in place a mental framework for counterterrorism policy that cannot be effective against it.

This entity was never intended to be called *al-Qaeda* by the original leaders of the group. The name can be traced to Abdullah Azzam, the leading ideologue for Sunni Muslim radicals, who in 1987 called for *al-qaeda al-sulbah* (a vanguard of the strong) to act as an example and a mobilizer of the Islamic world against its oppressors.[6] While bin Laden's followers were engaged in militant activities throughout the 1990s, the particular alliance of groups that became known as al-Qaeda was born 10 years later, in the backlash against the 1997 slaughter of tourists in Luxor, Egypt, described in chapter 4. After it became clear that public opinion in Egypt was shifting against the Islamist militants, Ayman Zawahiri announced the formation of a coalition calling itself the Islamic Front for Jihad Against Jews and Crusaders, in a fatwa published on February 23, 1998, by *Al-Quds al-Arabi*. Signatories included Osama bin Laden, Zawahiri, Rifai Ahmed Taha (former leader of the GAI), Sheikh Mir Hamza (secretary of Jamiat-ul Ulema of Pakistan), and Fazlul Rahman (leader of the Jihad Movement in Bangladesh). But there was discord and disagreement from the beginning: in particular, Taha's Islamic Group did not welcome the fatwa; GAI cadres were appalled at being roped into this coalition without their consent, and Taha was soon forced to withdraw from it and resign his leadership. The name was still not favored by the signatories at this point.[7] It was the West that first relied upon it to describe bin Laden's front: as it needed a named entity for legal reasons, the

FBI labeled the group "al-Qaeda" when the agency was investigating the 1998 U.S. Embassy bombings in Kenya and Tanzania.[8] This is one reason why analysts argue over the shape, status, form, and nature of al-Qaeda.

Since September 11, al-Qaeda has consistently been a melding of three main elements: a core central group of leaders and strategists who are bin Laden and Zawahiri's direct associates; a nebula of more traditional groups that are formally or informally aligned with the core and sometimes respond to central guidance (often called the "network"); and localized factions (even individuals) that have no physical contact with the center but strive to associate themselves with the worldview and vaunted label *al-Qaeda*.[9] This last element is particularly troublesome: some militants who are called al-Qaeda, either because they trumpet the name or skittish politicians do, are *not* formally aligned.[10] Western leaders calling every localized plot by this name only perpetuate the myth. And this outcome is fully intended by members: one training videotape specifically instructs sympathizers to make false claims of responsibility in the wake of actions throughout the world, so as to further the movement.[11] (Again, it is no wonder that understanding of al-Qaeda in the West is generally so poor.) The balance among these three elements has shifted since 9/11, with the core hollowed out by military operations, a decrease and then increase in the number of organizations formally attaching themselves to al-Qaeda, and an increase in amateurs stepping forward to take part in the "legend"; yet the tripartite array persists. Often those who argue about the nature of al-Qaeda are referring to different parts of this nebula and thus reaching different conclusions about its status and viability.

Unfortunately, all three aspects of al-Qaeda—its core leadership, network, and followers—have adapted. The hierarchy in place on September 11, 2001, was dismantled with the invasion of Afghanistan and the dispersal of the center; many of those original leaders have been killed and replaced by new players.[12] The gutting of the original apex forced the group to evolve and to rely more heavily on the Internet and other means of communication to carry on the message and purpose of al-Qaeda, which is above all to mobilize the Islamic masses.[13] The invasion of Iraq helped greatly in that process, as well as providing practical training to a large and growing number of fighters who then returned to their local origins.[14] The original front, which included groups from Algeria, Bangladesh, Egypt, and Pakistan, was joined by a growing number of established organizations that were connected in some way. These included the Moro Islamic Liberation Front (Philippines), Jemaah Islamiah (Southeast Asia), Egyptian Islamic Jihad (merged with al-Qaeda in 2001), al-Ansar Mujahidin (Chechnya), al-Gamaa al-Islamiya (Egypt, and a worldwide presence), Abu Sayyaf (Philippines), the Islamic Movement of Uzbekistan, the Salafist Group for Call and Combat (Algeria), Harakat ul-Mujahidin

(Pakistan/Kashmir), and many others.[15] With increased connections to established groups, the leaders began to achieve their ambition of sparking a "global jihad movement," consisting of web-directed and cyberlinked groups, as well as ad hoc cells driven by the worldview that al-Qaeda represents.

Al-Qaeda is today both a virtual movement and once again a traditional hierarchical organization as well, exercising varying degrees of operational control over entities that were formally or informally aligned. Starting in late 2004, the core began to reconstitute itself in the tribal region between Pakistan and Afghanistan, especially North Waziristan, rebuilding the ability to direct operations.[16] Arab, Pakistani, and Afghan operatives reestablished a base in that mountainous region, functioning under the general guidance of Zawahiri. These included a band of training camps in the tribal regions near the Afghan border. In addition to preparing groups of 10 to 20 men, this training infrastructure provided a fresh operational hub for connections to al-Qaeda affiliates in the Middle East, North Africa, and Europe. Thus, the central leadership once again exerted a capacity for command and control, sometimes facilitating operations from the center, as well as inspiring and enabling local groups to carry out attacks independently.[17] By 2007, al-Qaeda again had a core, a decentralized network of associates, and a following of amateurs and admirers who sometimes tapped the core as a resource.

In its evolution, al-Qaeda has demonstrated an unusual resilience and international reach. Al-Qaeda is a wealthy resource center, sometimes an operational facilitator and a now-legendary ideological and propaganda focal point for a wider movement. It remains a tripartite threat because of its reconstituted core, its capacity to enable operations both centrally controlled and independently instigated through its broader network of groups, and, most important of all, its brilliant media campaign perpetuating an image attractive to a diverse range of followers. No previous terrorist organization has exhibited quite the elasticity, agility, and global reach of al-Qaeda, with its fluid operational style based increasingly on a common mission statement and brilliant media campaign, rather than standard operating procedures and a pervasive organizational structure.[18]

Methods of Radicalization and Recruitment

The staying power of al-Qaeda is related secondly to the way it has perpetuated itself by radicalizing followers, who then provide operatives and support. With its tripartite structure of core, network, and periphery, al-Qaeda behaves more like a social movement than a classic terrorist group. Involvement in the movement's periphery has come not from pressure by senior al-Qaeda members, but from local groups or individual volunteers competing to win a chance to train or participate.[19] The process is a matter of "joining" more than one of being recruited, so the traditional organizational approach to analyzing this group is incomplete. But the inspirational draw of al-Qaeda should also not be exaggerated: in the evolving pattern of associations, attraction to the mission or ideology is a necessary but not sufficient condition. Exposure to its ideas is not enough, as reflected in the initial failure to recruit in Afghanistan and the Sudan, where bin Laden was located from 1991 to 1996, and 1996 to 2001, respectively.[20] Concepts of ideological "contagion" are misguided, since preexisting social bonds play a crucial role in al-Qaeda's patterns of development.[21] So it is not quite correct to say either that al-Qaeda is simply an "organization" or an "ideology," as it has characteristics of both, overlaid with the cohesiveness of a dynamic social movement with a clear narrative at its heart.

While it is not the only important Islamist social movement, al-Qaeda is uniquely able to use existing social networks to mobilize global supporters and transform sympathizers into violent activists. Marc Sageman's seminal study of established links among al-Qaeda operatives who had engaged in attacks indicates that they joined the organization mainly because of ties of kinship and friendship, enabled by what he calls a bridging person or entry point, perpetuated in a series of local clusters in the Maghreb and Southeast Asia, for example. Other scholarship demonstrates that the group relies on and exploits existing transnational networks of Muslims in the Middle East, many of whom have deeply embedded economic and political links constructed in response to years of Arab state repression.[22] This is one reason why some scholars argue that calling lower-level al-Qaeda activists "members" may itself be misleading.[23] Al-Qaeda is not *creating* these bonds; random individuals are almost never tapped. Social movement theory argues that the best predictor for involvement in a movement is knowing someone who is already involved; and that pattern is borne out for al-Qaeda.[24]

Al-Qaeda likewise taps social bonds among Muslims in the West, using established networks there to inspire, radicalize, and draw them into combat. Clear links between al-Qaeda's core and local operatives in Europe can be difficult to determine, particularly since 2004.[25] Some operatives have been connected to al-Qaeda and its agenda in an indirect or informal way, having neither gone to al-Qaeda camps nor had much formal training: examples include the June 29 and 30, 2007, plots in Glasgow and London, the March 11, 2004, Madrid bombings, and the May 16, 2003, Casablanca attacks.[26] Although many claim a connection to al-Qaeda's radical ideology, there are often no logistical trails and thus no link for traditional intelligence methods to examine.[27] This explains, for example, the tremendous difficulty in retracing connections after an attack (not to mention beforehand) and the ambiguity that may hang over the question of whether or not it is truly "al-Qaeda." Ties specifically between the Pakistani diaspora community in Britain and al-Qaeda have been easier to trace: the July 7, 2005, London bomber Mohammad Sidique Khan refers to the al-Qaeda leadership in his taped message, a relationship he apparently pursued by traveling to Pakistan—but even here the other three London bombers were not directly connected.[28] Others leave to fight Western forces in Iraq, a pipeline that goes in two directions: it is a magnet for young men wanting to develop their skills and gain experience fighting "the infidels" (especially the British and Americans) and also a conduit back to Western communities in which to radicalize, recruit, and carry out operations.[29]

A hefty proportion of those drawn to the al-Qaeda movement have connected or heightened their commitment after receiving a Salafist message disseminated over the Internet, which then links in some way to action in the physical world. Online resources like the Saudi jihadist strategist Muhammad bin Ahmad as-Salim's article "You Don't Need to Go to Iraq for Jihad" and his 2003 book *39 Ways to Serve and Participate in Jihad* have been wildly popular, and are translated from the original Arabic into numerous other languages. The process of joining al-Qaeda, or aligning oneself with its activities and its worldview, is different in the West than it is in majority Muslim states where there is an established Salafist network. In Europe, for example, the impulse to join the movement may arise from a desire to belong or take action in a context where the prospective recruit is excluded from, repulsed by, or incapable of successful integration into a Western community.[30]

European counterterrorism officials are observing the radicalization of members of an alienated diaspora—sometimes second- and third-generation immigrants—who are vulnerable to al-Qaeda's vitriol because they are not thoroughly trained in fundamental concepts of Islam, are alienated from their parents, and feel betrayed by the communities in which they find themselves. Internet messages do not pass through the traditional process of vetting by an imam. Many in Britain, for example, find imams in their neighborhood mosques old-fashioned and irrelevant: they have been trained in traditional South Asian seminaries, preach only in Urdu (and may not even speak English), and are able to provide little meaningful help to young Internet-savvy Muslims. The allure of al-Qaeda's worldview, presented through sophisticated images over the web that enrage and excite the viewer, may be irresistible—especially when images of attacks in places like Chechnya, Bosnia, Israel, and Iraq are marketed to vulnerable young men as a Western assault on Islam that can only be beaten back by the brave mujahideen. The result can be the radicalization of ordinary, formerly law-abiding young Europeans, accomplished in the privacy of their homes, gyms, or community centers.

Al-Qaeda defies twentieth-century thinking about organizational structure and function. The process of radicalization and recruitment is highly complex and different in different parts of the world. Tracing the command-and-control relationships in a changing movement is difficult, and focusing exclusively on the core, the nebula, or local radicalized individuals does not reveal the whole story.[31] These innovations make comparisons with earlier, more traditional terrorist groups harder but by no means impossible: there are parallels, for example, between al-Qaeda and the global terrorist movements that developed in the late nineteenth century, including the wave of anarchists and social revolutionaries, as discussed in chapter 5.[32]

Means of Support

Financial support for al-Qaeda is likewise robust, ranging from money channeled through charitable organizations to grants given to local terrorist groups that present promising plans for attacks that serve al-Qaeda's general goals. Unprecedented international efforts to choke off those finances have not succeeded. Most of its operations have relied on a small amount of "seed money" provided by bin Laden's organization, supplemented by operatives engaged in petty crime and fraud. Indeed, some experts argue that al-Qaeda can best be described as a franchise organization with a marketable "brand," rather than a traditional, top-down organization that plans attacks, provides the resources for them, and puts people in place to carry them out.[33] Indeed, as time has gone by since September 11, al-Qaeda has often behaved more often as a facilitator than an organizer. Relatively little money has been required for most al-Qaeda-associated attacks.[34]

Another element of support has been the autonomous businesses owned or controlled by al-Qaeda; at one point, bin Laden was reputed to direct approximately 80 companies around the world. Many of these continue to earn a profit, providing a self-sustaining source for the movement. International counterterrorism efforts to control al-Qaeda financing have been robust, including important initiatives under U.N. Security Council Resolution 1373, efforts that have frozen at least $147 million in assets.[35] Still, cutting the financial lifeline of an agile and low-cost movement that has reportedly amassed billions of dollars and needs few resources to carry out attacks remains a formidable, and possibly unrealizable, challenge. Many wonder about the degree to which these efforts have had practical, operational effects, since they may simply increase the incentives to engage in untraceable, illegal channels that circumvent the West's ability to gather intelligence.[36]

Choking off funds destined for al-Qaeda through regulatory oversight confronts numerous obstacles. Formal banking channels are not necessary for many transfers, which instead can occur through informal channels known as "alternative remittance systems," "informal value transfer systems," "parallel banking," or "underground banking." Examples include the much-discussed *hawala* or *hundi* transfer networks and the Black Market Peso Exchange, which operate through family ties or unofficial reciprocal arrangements. Value can be stored in commodities such as diamonds and gold that are moved through areas with partial or problematical state sovereignty. Al-Qaeda has also used charities to raise and move funds, with a relatively small proportion of gifts being siphoned off for illegitimate purposes, often without the knowledge of donors.[37] Efforts to cut off charitable flows to impoverished areas harm many genuinely needy recipients and heighten resentment, which in turn generates additional political support for the movement.[38] Recently there has also been worrisome evidence of a reverse flow of funding out of Iraq toward al-Qaeda's reconstituted headquarters in northern Pakistan, from donations to the anti-American insurgency and criminal activities there.[39]

Al-Qaeda's deep pockets make it more autonomous than many of the late-twentieth-century state-sponsored groups, but it is not completely without peers or precedents: the Tamil Tigers' formidable financial connection to diaspora communities in Canada and Scandinavia, the PKK's funding from displaced Kurds, and the Provisional Irish Republican Army's connections to Irish expatriates in the United States immediately spring to mind. There are many other organizations that generate their own resources through international business networks, both legal and illegal; Hezbollah, ETA, and, again, the PIRA are good examples—not to mention the so-called narco-terrorist groups such as the FARC. The difference is one of degree, not nature.

Means of Communication

The most important new aspect of al-Qaeda is its means of communication. Related to its effective recruitment and radicalization, the al-Qaeda movement has used the tools of globalization to connect with multiple audiences, including potential new members, new recruits, active supporters, passive sympathizers, neutral observers, enemy governments, and potential victims. These tools include mobile phones, text messaging, instant messaging, and especially websites, email, blogs, chat rooms, and other tools of the Internet, used for everything from administrative tasks and fund-raising to research and logistical coordination of attacks.[40] Although al-Qaeda is by no means the only terrorist group to exploit these means, it has been especially adept at doing so. The close connection between burgeoning methods of communication and the rapid dissemination of al-Qaeda's message of radicalization marks this movement as a new stage in the evolution of terrorism. And the leadership knows it. In a captured letter written to Mullah Muhammad 'Omar, Osama bin Laden wrote, "It is obvious that the media war in this century is one of the strongest methods; in fact, its ratio may reach 90% of the total preparation for the battles."[41]

A crucial facilitator for the perpetuation of the movement, for example, is the use of websites to convey messages, fatwas, claims of attacks, and warnings to the American public, as well as educate future participants, give instructions to operatives, and rally sympathizers to the cause. The Internet is an important factor in building and perpetuating the image of al-Qaeda, and maintaining its reputation. It provides easy access to other forms of media, facilitating al-Qaeda's efforts to both mobilize Muslims and engage in psychological warfare against the West. Indoctrinating and teaching new "recruits" is expedited by the Internet, notably through the dissemination of al-Qaeda's widely publicized training manual (nicknamed "The Encyclopedia of Jihad") that explains how to organize and run a cell and carry out attacks.[42] Suicide bombers have been recruited through cyberspace, as well as fighters who are conveyed through informal networks to Iraq, Afghanistan, Chechnya, and elsewhere. Websites and chat rooms are used to offer practical advice and build the fraternal bonds that are crucial to al-Qaeda. In a sense, members of the movement no longer need to "join" an organization at all, for the individual participates at the stroke of a few keys. The debate over the size, structure, and membership of al-Qaeda is a quaint relic of the twentieth century, displaced by the leveling effects of twenty-first-century technology.

Al-Qaeda is a creature of the web. This movement may evoke the seventh century in its propaganda, but it is in every sense a brilliant exploiter of twenty-first-century communications.[43] In addition to being a means of mobilization, the new tools also offer practical advantages. Members of al-Qaeda use the web as a vast source of research and data mining, to assess future attack sites or develop new weapons technology, at a low cost and a high level of sophistication. An al-Qaeda training manual retrieved by American troops in Afghanistan advised trainees that at least 80 percent of the information needed about the enemy could be collected from open, legal sources.[44] But members also know when *not* to use electronic means: human couriers are used to pass important information from al-Qaeda's new physical infrastructure in Pakistan's tribal areas. Al-Qaeda is not unique in using the web—virtually every major terrorist organization now has a website and uses the Internet for fund-raising and propaganda—but it is among the most advanced.[45] The global, nonterritorial nature of the information age is having a transformative effect on the evolution of all types of conflict, not least al-Qaeda's terrorism; but bin Laden and Zawahiri were among the first to understand the implications of the vast changes being wrought and to take full advantage of them to perpetuate their time-honored aim of mobilization through terrorism.[46]

Thus, al-Qaeda's fluid organization, methods of recruitment, funding patterns, and means of communication distinguish it as an advancement in twenty-first-century terrorist groups. It is a product of our times, but it also builds upon historical predecessors with which we have a long record of experience. Most analysts are snowed by al-Qaeda's rhetoric. It is easy to forget that this movement perpetuates itself by deliberately constructing an image of unity and uniqueness, tailoring its propaganda to different audiences, not least those in the West. Al-Qaeda is indeed dangerous; but it is not immortal. It is an amalgam of old and new, reflecting twenty-first-century advances in means or matters of degree rather than true originality. So, reviewing our framework of six patterns of demise, what do we know about how al-Qaeda will end?

The Relevance and Irrelevance of History for Al-Qaeda: Applying the Framework

Decapitation: Capturing or Killing the Leaders

Past experience with terrorism indicates that al-Qaeda will not end if Osama bin Laden is killed.[47] There are many other reasons to pursue him, including serving justice, removing his leadership and expertise, and increasing esprit de corps on the Western side (whose credibility is sapped because of bin Laden's enduring elusiveness). Bin Laden has been an important symbol. Removing him and his Egyptian partner, Ayman Zawahiri, in the years before the attacks of September 11 might have been effective; their role in catalyzing the movement at that point was essential.[48] They were also irreplaceable in their decision to refocus the movement toward attacking the so-called "far enemy," away from nationalist governments closer at hand. Had they been killed in the late 1990s, that fateful reorientation might never have happened.

But that is foolish hindsight. The argument that their demise will end the al-Qaeda movement now is tinged with emotion, not dispassionate analysis. Organizations that have been crippled by the killing of their leader have been hierarchically structured, reflecting to some degree a cult of personality, and lacking a viable successor. Al-Qaeda currently meets none of these criteria: it has a mutable structure, with both elements of hierarchy and a strong emphasis on individual cells and local initiative. It is not the first organization to operate in this way; comparable cell-based terrorist networks have included the socialist revolutionary and anarchist movements of the late nineteenth century.[49] The demise of those historical predecessors required much more than the death of one or two people. This movement has gone well beyond the point where decapitation might have led to its end.

Despite his astonishing popularity, bin Laden has deliberately avoided allowing the movement to revolve around his own persona, preferring instead to keep his personal habits private, talk of the insignificance of his own fate, and project the image of a humble man, eager to die for his beliefs. Al-Qaeda is certainly not a cult of personality, as were the PKK and Sendero Luminoso. Even considering the potential benefits of the capture or killing of senior al-Qaeda operatives, the United States needs to think very carefully about what the likely outcome of successful operations would be. For example, bin Laden's capture or killing would produce its own countervailing ill-effects, including (most likely) the creation of a powerful symbolic martyr, which could actually enhance his stature, in practical terms. To the extent that centralized planning for al-Qaeda continues, it may be done by Zawahiri in any case. As for viable replacements for them both, bin Laden has often spoken openly of a succession plan, and that plan has to a large degree already taken effect.[50] Removing them both would have important potential benefits; but to believe that decapitation would kill al-Qaeda at this point is ahistorical and naive.

The West may be paying more attention to these leaders' fates than are al-Qaeda's followers. Bin Laden and Zawahiri no longer have a formative impact upon the intellectual development of the next generation of jihadists. In the wake of the dismantlement of the physical infrastructure that existed on September 11, 2001, al-Qaeda's online library, the Tawhed, has become more important in influencing the faithful. There are at least 4,500 other jihadi websites that disseminate various forms of this ideology, and debates about tactics and strategy.[51] Careful analysis of the lively and rich discourses occurring within the thousands of tracts on the web indicates that other thinkers have become at least as important in the evolution of the movement.[52] Al-Qaeda on the web will certainly persist in its ability to instruct and inspire in the absence of bin Laden—who is in any case rarely mentioned in these discourses now.

The spread and fractionization of the movement that have occurred in the years since September 11 hold within them both opportunity and danger for Western strategy. The opportunity is the potential to drive a wedge between the different factions, many of whom sharply disagree about strategy. There are fundamental areas of contention. For reasons of language, ignorance, and myopia, the West is years behind in understanding the debates and differences among these al-Qaeda subgroups; our shortcomings and the anonymity of the Internet mean that some are not even known to us. Before we kill leaders who represent different factions, we must be absolutely sure that their successors will not be even more extreme and more numerous. Well beyond its operational impact, the primary aim of decapitation should be to discredit the engines of popular mobilization that drive this movement. At least one thing is clear: these motors are no longer just bin Laden and Zawahiri.

Beyond historical and theoretical arguments, our focus on killing the al-Qaeda leadership has proven strategically ineffective. The U.S. leadership has devoted a large number of intelligence agents and special operations forces to a focused campaign to capture or kill those who built al-Qaeda before 9/11, including sending a "surge" of CIA agents into Pakistan in early 2006; but good information remains frustratingly sparse. While many operatives have been killed, experts argue that little progress has been made there.[53] More important, as mentioned above, a new reinvigorated leadership has emerged in the mountainous border region between Afghanistan and Pakistan.[54] These are younger men in their mid-30s with battlefield experience fighting in places such as Chechnya, Iraq, and Afghanistan. In contrast to what many counterterrorism officials had believed, these new leaders in Pakistan are exercising a degree of operational control: for example, an Egyptian named Abu Ubaidah al-Masri, located in Pakistan, orchestrated a plot to destroy multiple commercial airlines departing from London. Al-Masri emerged following the death of another Egyptian, Abu Hamza Rabia, killed by a missile strike in 2005. We seem to be faced with an organization that has both local initiative and important regional planning hubs, including Pakistan and Iraq; counterterrorism officials say that they do not know the degree to which there is clear communication with bin Laden and Zawahiri.[55] We need a broader and more well-informed political strategy: decapitation may be irrelevant.

In short, while there have been vital tactical and operational gains as a result of taking out al-Qaeda operatives, decapitation of the top leadership is not a promising avenue for al-Qaeda's demise. If the goal is to end this movement, it would be far more strategically effective to publicly discredit bin Laden and Zawahiri and divide their followers.

Negotiations: Talking to Al-Qaeda or Its Associates

As the historical record indicates, negotiations or a transition to a legitimate political process have first required negotiable terms and a sense of deadlock. Negotiations are most likely when both sides reach a stalemate, especially a "political" stalemate from the perspective of the terrorist group, that is, members sense that they are no longer able to mobilize a constituency and move forward. Terrorist groups seeking negotiations often have an incentive to find a way out of what they consider a losing cause. This does not describe al-Qaeda, which may have increased its ability to mobilize a constituency in recent years.

But what of al-Qaeda's terms? This is not as easy a question as it might seem. The leadership has altered its specific goals repeatedly, and it targets messages to particular audiences. It is no accident that the discourse of bin Laden and Zawahiri contains elements of many other countercultural ideologies, including anti-imperialism, antiglobalization, anti-Americanism, anti-Westernization, and antimodernization.[56] They tap into a wellspring of anger, frustration, humiliation, and resentment that has built over the decades of failure for political Islam, especially in states such as Saudi Arabia, Egypt, and Pakistan.[57] This anger is brilliantly channeled by al-Qaeda through its discourse about the overthrow of un-Islamic governments, the Israeli-Palestinian conflict, the war in Iraq, the war in Afghanistan, the presence of Western troops in the holy territories, and so forth. The group points to a conspiracy between Christendom and Judaism to destroy Islam, setting up a Manichaean struggle between the United States and its allies, on the one hand, and the Muslim people, or *umma*, on the other.[58]

Apart from negative messages, however, the specific picture of what al-Qaeda would *replace* these international circumstances with is deliberately vague. There is a lot of evocative language, general references to restoring peace, instituting Islamic law, and installing a modern Caliphate—a hazy dream of a better, more just future to be achieved through a defensive jihad. But what exactly would that new Islamic "state" (or entity) look like? This is not specified, as doing so would undermine the movement itself. Al-Qaeda's strength—its increasing decentralization—is also its vulnerability. The broader al-Qaeda's appeal, the more the weaknesses in its ideology appear. There is, after all, little commonality in the vision pursued by Kashmiri, Chechen, Uighur, Indonesian, Filipino, and Palestinian Muslims, all of whom have been drawn into al-Qaeda's wide tent. Muslim or not, local groups have different specific grievances and want different things. This is even more the case with the European and American Muslims who are attracted to al-Qaeda's message. The goals of al-Qaeda's periphery differ, and the core does not have the resources to control far-flung "members" in any case.[59] In addition to being distasteful, negotiating with the core al-Qaeda leadership would be pointless.

What then of the periphery? As al-Qaeda has become a diverse hybrid of virtual local members and more hierarchical hubs, it is a mistake to believe its propaganda and treat it as a unified whole. It is possible that bin Laden and his lieutenants have attempted to cobble together such disparate entities (or those entities have opportunistically attached themselves) that they have moved beyond the point at which their interests can be represented in this movement. Some of the local groups and individuals that have recently claimed an association with al-Qaeda have in the past borne more resemblance to ethnonationalist-separatist groups such as the PLO, the IRA, and the LTTE than does al-Qaeda. Examples include local affiliates in Indonesia, Morocco, Tunisia, and Turkey. Successful negotiations with local groups such as the MILF or the more moderate of the Kashmiri separatist groups, for example, would demonstrate a willingness to consider the grievances of Muslim organizations on their own local terms and undermine the message of a dichotomous struggle. This is not to argue that these groups' aims are necessarily rightful or that their tactics are legitimate; only that the extensive local variation in groups and goals is being glossed over by the United States' obsession with the monolithic "al- Qaeda," that they do have important points of divergence with al-Qaeda's agenda (or "ideology"), and that the United States does no one (except perhaps al-Qaeda) any favors by failing to analyze and exploit those local differences.

The aim must be to enlarge the movement's internal inconsistencies and differences, to suggest a path toward a promising future that may be reached without engaging in Islamist violence. There is more hope of ending such groups through traditional methods if they are dealt with using traditional tools, even including, on a case-by-case basis, concessions or negotiations with specific local elements that may have negotiable terms (albeit pursued through an illegitimate tactic). The key is to emphasize the differences with al-Qaeda's agenda, and to drive a wedge between the movement and its recent adherents. The historical record of experience with terrorism indicates that it is a mistake to treat al-Qaeda as a monolith, to lionize it as if it were a completely unprecedented phenomenon with all elements equally committed to its open-ended aims, for such an approach increases anxiety, heightens the incentives to align with it, and eliminates a range of proven counterterrorist tools and techniques for ending it. It is also a mistake to accelerate al-Qaeda's current rallying point, a hatred of the West and a resentment of U.S. and allied policies (especially in Iraq and between Israel and the Palestinian Authority), facilitating the papering over of serious differences within.

At the end of chapter 2, we examined promising and unpromising circumstances for negotiations with terrorist groups. The most promising included a political stalemate between the parties, strong leadership on all sides, third-party mediators or sponsors, the absence of suicide attacks, effective government handling of splinter groups and spoilers, and an auspicious international context. As we have seen, these negotiating conditions do not apply to al-Qaeda's nucleus; however, many groups are only loosely connected with the movement, being mainly concerned about local, long-standing nationalist aims. In these cases, the conditions for negotiation should be carefully evaluated on a case-by-case basis. The nihilistic goals of the al-Qaeda movement are distinct from the aspirations of many of the groups that are now to some degree aligning with it. Our overall strategic interest is to make distinctions among them and hive them off.

Condemning the use of terrorism is imperative. But as events have unfolded since 9/11, there is a strange and paradoxical shared interest between the central propagandists of al-Qaeda and the leaders of some states fighting local groups, in emphasizing the importance of al-Qaeda links and central direction. Whether or not there are actual links between these groups is not the question—indeed, in the wake of the war in Iraq, the links are proliferating.[60] The real question is whether or not it makes strategic sense for us to recast long-standing local struggles as "al-Qaeda" strictly on the basis of those links. Doing so draws U.S. resources into murky political struggles, implies that all fights are equally of interest to the United States, and lionizes al-Qaeda as a global movement. What we should be doing is the opposite: targeting our resources to areas of national interest, disaggregating competing groups and local political agendas, and undercutting the symbolic image and attraction of "al-Qaeda."

Success: Achieving Al-Qaeda's Objectives

The likelihood of the al-Qaeda movement achieving its strategic objectives is nil. It is hard to conceive of al-Qaeda fully realizing its aims, in part because they have evolved over time, variably including achievement of a pan-Islamic caliphate, the overthrow of non-Islamic regimes, and the expulsion of all infidels from Muslim countries, not to mention support for the Palestinian cause, and the killing of Americans and other so-called infidels. Historically, terrorist groups that have achieved their ends have done so by articulating a clear and limited aim. Al-Qaeda is more interested in the so-called Islamic world than in the West; its primary aim is to remove Western influence so as to put in place a political system that governs according to Islamist principles. Yet the world of the twenty-first century is increasingly interdependent and intertwined. Al-Qaeda's goals, at least as articulated over recent years, could not be achieved without overturning an international political and economic system characterized by globalization and predominant U.S. power. With our continued assistance, this group may indeed continue to change the world—but not in the way it intends. Success is not a likely scenario for al-Qaeda's end.

Failure through Implosion

The pattern of mistakes and failures that leads to the end of many terrorist groups is amply demonstrated in the actions of al-Qaeda. Whether or not this becomes the means of al-Qaeda's demise in the future will depend upon actions by its leadership, as well as the degree to which the United States and its allies recognize and take advantage of al-Qaeda's missteps. As was argued in chapter 4, terrorist groups commonly end either through group implosion or loss of popular support. Regarding the former, we examined four typical scenarios, including failing to navigate the transition between generations, succumbing to in-fighting among members, losing operational control, and accepting amnesties or other exit pathways offered by a government.

First, although there was a time when the *failure to transition to a new generation* might have been a viable finale for al-Qaeda, that time is long past. Al-Qaeda has transitioned to a second, third, and perhaps fourth generation. The reason relates especially to the second distinctive element of al-Qaeda: its radicalization of followers, both individuals and groups, many of whom in turn connect to existing local networks. Al-Qaeda's spread is compared to a virus or a bacterium, dispersing contagion to disparate sites.[61] Although that is a seductive analogy, it is also misleading: the perpetuation of al-Qaeda is a sentient process involving well-considered marketing strategies and deliberate tactical decisions, not a mindless process of "disease." Thinking of it as a disease shores up the unfortunate American tendency to avoid the hard work of analyzing the mentality of the enemy. Al-Qaeda is operating with a long-term strategy and is certainly not following the left-wing groups of the 1970s in their failure to articulate a coherent ideological vision, or the peripatetic right-wing groups of the twentieth century. It has transitioned beyond its original structure and now represents a multigenerational threat with staying power comparable to the enthonationalist groups of the twentieth century.

On the other hand, the *in-fighting and fractionalization* that was so apparent in the declining months of predecessors such as the Italian and German left-wing groups, the PIRA, the FLQ, Combat 18, the Abu Nidal Organization, and others examined in chapter 4, are endemic to this movement and have been from the outset. In the 1980s, tribal and national divisions among the mujahideen were an impediment in fighting the Soviets in Afghanistan. Some 35,000 Muslim radicals came from 43 different nations to fight.[62] Divided by different languages, nationalities, customs, habits, and to some degree beliefs, they seemed best able to align against a common foe. The Wahhabist practices of some of the Arab fighters also offended the Afghans, who saw them as unwelcome aliens. Bin Laden spoke despairingly of their *fitna*, or division and faction, which the Prophet Mohammed had expressly forbidden but which dogged the fighters continually. As soon as the atheist Soviets had gone, the mujahideen fell again into bickering factionalism, with Afghan tribes seeking control over the country and the "Arab-Afghans"—Egyptians, Algerians, Yemenis, Sudanese, Saudis, Tajiks, Uzbeks, and others—refocused on the priorities of their own homelands.[63] These divisions have not gone away, although they are now subsumed under al-Qaeda's global anti-West jihad rhetoric.

Doctrinal disputes between key jihadi thinkers reveal crucial differences of opinion between senior members, even those of the same nationality. In some groups these disagreements might be accommodated; however, the al-Qaeda movement has at its heart a firm belief in the clarity of a single Salafist interpretation of Islam, as well as a strong distaste for anything that smacks of democratic pluralism.[64] One long-standing source of dispute, for example, is the argument between those who adhere to the beliefs of revered Salafist and Hadith scholar Shaikh al-Albani, who argues that jihad should entail some elements of compromise, and those who, like Zawahiri, argue that anything less than killing the infidels is "appeasement."[65] Likewise, a divisive and passionate element of discord is the issue of whether or not it is acceptable to kill Muslims, particularly women, children, and the elderly. This theme appears over and over again, typically in the form of criticism of specific operations. The usual response is that the violence is religiously sanctioned and necessary, and can really be laid at the feet of Israel and the West.[66] But the regular and repeated defensiveness by al-Qaeda strategists about these actions demonstrates a vulnerability. Other long-standing flash points include whether or not it is right to call other Muslims apostates, to attack the economy of Muslim states (especially the tourism and oil industries), or to create political and social disorder.[67] Sectarian disputes are likewise common, not just in Iraq: in captured training videotapes, Abu Musab Al Suri, architect of the flat hierarchical structure and "individual terrorism" of al-Qaeda's post-9/11 periphery, spurns any form of cooperation between Shia and Sunni, arguing that Shia groups like Hezbollah have had a negative influence on the Palestinians.[68]

These debates are openly and easily accessible, especially on the Internet but also in other media. Some very fine work is being done in accessing and analyzing them, notably at the Counterterrorism Center at West Point, New York, which has, for example, tapped al-Qaeda's library of over 3,000 books and articles written by major jihadist authors, translated and analyzed them, and made them available to Western researchers.[69] We are just scratching the surface here. But it is clear that this movement is full of deeply held divisions and ideological inconsistencies that could easily undermine it.

Third, *loss of operational control*, the element that promoted the implosion of terrorist groups as disparate as the Ulster Volunteer Force and the Red Brigades, is another serious threat to an organization's viability. In this respect, al–Qaeda's remarkable tripartite structure, which has allowed it to survive and rebuild itself in the wake of devastating military attacks, is also its vulnerability. Those in the first realm, the core, are of course responsive to its agenda and control; however, leaders do not have operational control over all elements in the nebula calling themselves "al-Qaeda." The network of new and established groups now has a potpourri of local organizations, some of which act without direction or even permission from the center. Admittedly, al-Qaeda from its origins never aspired to have full operational control over its elements; it arose from a desire to mobilize the masses in a widespread, self-generating uprising that would, in al-Qaeda's terms, "protect the *umma* from oppression." It was meant to be a resource and catalyst, not a military hierarchy. Yet the actions taken in its name do not always advance its agenda. Many elements that are attached to al-Qaeda, especially in the periphery of its reach, oppose important elements of its political agenda and attack targets that the center does not approve. Paradoxically, the ubiquity of its reputation and influence can make the movement responsible for the range of actions taken in its name, whether it approves of them or not. The lessons of how terrorism ends indicate that it is in the interests of those who oppose al-Qaeda to take advantage of the movement's direct and indirect responsibility for attacks that offend and hurt Muslims.

Senior members of the movement worry greatly about the implications of attacks carried out in al-Qaeda's name that are not initiated or controlled by the center. In his popular 2004 book, *The Management of Barbarism* (available in Arabic in al-Qaeda's electronic library),[70] strategist Abu Bakr Naji asserts that medium- and low-level attacks that happen spontaneously are acceptable; however, major attacks that are not approved by what he calls the High Command might turn the masses against them.[71] As for smaller attacks, Naji suggests that if jihadis are arrested in their aftermath, then a local cell in different country should launch an attack to reverse the perceptual impact of their arrest and to perpetuate the impression of a worldwide movement.[72] One notable example of a loss of operational control unfolded in the war in Iraq. Beginning in 2005, the tide began to turn against groups acting in al-Qaeda's name.[73] Their brutal methods, such as assassinations of opponents, enforced suicide bombings, forced marriages, and imposition of sharia law, repelled Iraqi Sunnis. The al-Qaeda faction in Baqubah, for example, deeply alienated the local population through kidnappings, killings, and the requisitioning of houses, and by declaring Baqubah the capital of al-Qaeda's "Islamic State of Iraq" (ISI).[74] Harith Dhahir Khamis al-Dariwas, the leader of the violent Sunni insurgent group, the 1920 Revolution Brigades, was killed by al-Qaeda in March 2007, reportedly because he refused to pledge allegiance to the emir of the ISI, Abu Omar al-Baghdadi.[75] Likewise, the leader of a Ba'ath Party insurgent group, the Iraqi Armed Forces, began to fight al-Qaeda in Iraq after it killed two of its members in Ramadi. Yet another group, Al-Jaysh Al-Islami, one of the largest Sunni Iraqi jihad groups, issued a communiqué refusing to declare its loyalty to the Islamic State of Iraq, and accusing al-Qaeda in Iraq of numerous violations of sharia law.[76]

These examples of backlash and division are an embarrassment to al-Qaeda and a blot on its vaunted image. The extent to which localized al-Qaeda groups in Iraq accurately responded to or reflected the wishes of the center is not clear: certainly, the well-publicized July 2005 letter from Zawahiri to Zarqawi, urging the latter to cease his attacks on Shiites, stop the brutal beheadings, and give some attention to building popular support for the good of the movement overall, revealed a lack of central control. Indeed, there have been many other vigorous criticisms of the indiscriminate killings of innocent Muslims in Iraq, as they "distort the true Jihad."[77]

Fourth, the lessons of the implosion of previous groups indicate that *offering an exit* to peripheral members of al-Qaeda may help to undermine the movement. Although amnesties for the core leadership and its most closely aligned groups are obviously impossible, providing a way out for individuals who do not support all of the movement's more rigid tenets would be prudent.[78] Given an alternative to death, disgruntled individuals might choose to move against other members of the movement, leading to better intelligence and the undermining of some local cells, as was the case with the *pentiti* of the Italian Red Brigades and the "supergrasses" of the PIRA. Alternatively, groups that are more interested in nationalist objectives than in al-Qaeda's transnational, nihilist ideology might shift their allegiances and tactics. Even if specific historical examples are unrealistic for al-Qaeda (whose ideology is admittedly more extreme), merely devising and announcing a potential avenue for escape will sow distrust among members, especially in al-Qaeda's periphery, and increase the resources necessary for vetting new participants.[79] Treating captured operatives extraordinarily *well*, for example, publicizing their handling and perhaps even releasing them back to their cells, might be an effective way to undermine trust within the group.[80] As was the case with the Second of June Movement, other members of the movement might then turn upon them and engage in fratricide. There are many other ways to promote implosion. By learning more about al-Qaeda and exploiting the ample lessons of its historical predecessors, the United States and its allies could help to pry open the natural fault lines that are proliferating in the movement.

Failure through Diminishment of Popular Support

Reducing popular support, both active and passive, is an effective means of hastening the demise of some terrorist groups. The case studies examined earlier in this book revealed three common scenarios for the marginalization of a terrorist group: the ideology becomes irrelevant, the group loses contact with "the people," and mistakes in targeting lead to a backlash by the group's constituency. As its key leaders regularly admit in their writings, all three of these are dangers for the al-Qaeda movement.

As is obvious in the bitter doctrinal disputes among jihadists that are accessible on the web, this is a complex movement packed with ideological discord. Therefore calling al-Qaeda itself "an ideology," as some in the West are wont to do, is unhelpful for counterterrorism; there are many crucial differences of opinion among the groups that, formally or informally, call themselves "al-Qaeda."[81] In his 2001 book, *Knights under the Prophet's Banner*, Ayman Zawahiri calls the fight with the West a "battle of ideologies, a struggle for survival, and a war with no truce."[82] In a sense he is correct, as there is of course a huge difference between Western liberalism and the ideas represented by the al-Qaeda movement. But the real fault lines of this fight lie within Islam. Although Zawahiri would like this to be a "battle of ideologies," the characterization is not accurate: this is, and always has been, primarily a battle *within* Islam over the ideology that will prevail among Muslims; and it is by no means the first such battle that has occurred within the faith. Al-Qaeda is one in a long line of radical splinter groups that have appeared in Islam.[83] Many of those who believe in what is loosely referred to as a "global jihad," for example, differ in what they mean by that, whom they are willing to target, what their overall aims are in pursuing it, and what the world will look like after they are finished. There is ample evidence of disagreement in the fractious debates that occur among them, often with more accord about what they are *against* than about what they are *for*.

Even though they may be loosely aligned, many groups are far more interested in local political aims than they are in the rhetoric of al-Qaeda. There are vast differences in the motivations, worldviews, tactics, and aims of groups such as the Bangladeshi Jihad Movement, the Philippine Abu Sayyaf, the Eastern Turkistan Islamist Movement (in the Xinjiang-Uighur autonomous region of China), the Libyan Islamic Fighting Group, and the Pakistan-based Lashkar-e-Taiba, for example—all of whom have some association with al-Qaeda. Even those who have most recently openly professed their loyalty to bin Laden, including Allah's Brigade (Palestine), Al-Qaeda Maghreb Commandment (Morocco), and the Brigades of Kurdistan (Iraq), differ in their specific local aims.[84] And yet it is in the interests of local groups to align themselves, at least in their public pronouncements, with the vaunted al-Qaeda logo. Since the war in Iraq, local networks with "al-Qaeda" appended to their names have surfaced in at least 12 countries. By calling themselves al-Qaeda, affiliates can use the war in Iraq and the appearance of global coordination to strengthen their own fund-raising and recruitment. The degree to which there is actual central direction, or even contact, with the core of al-Qaeda varies; but in its effects, that question is almost irrelevant. The core acts as a kind of facilitator, source of advice, sometimes a resource for practical training in bomb-making, explosives techniques, targeting, and so on; but most powerful of all, it is a rallying point.

We do ourselves no favors in glossing over these differences and simply referring to all of these groups as "al-Qaeda" or for that matter implying that *all* groups that use terrorism are al-Qaeda. There is a strong argument to be made for avoiding the name in many circumstances. It evokes an image that serves the movement, making it appear unified when it is not. As we have seen, the name evolved serendipitously, as even those within the movement point out. ʿAbd Allah b. Nasir al-Rashid, an important jihadist ideologue, strategist, and operations planner, wrote in a 2003 online article that the name *al-Qaeda* was imposed upon the organization by the West and is not the chosen name. He considers it too restrictive, as it refers to the former regime in Afghanistan and specifically to Osama bin Laden; whereas *mujahideen* appears in the Quran, evokes sacred Islamic history, and encompasses more Islamic activists.[85] Al-Rashid thus advocates the broader term. The fact that al-Rashid is moved to argue for a more inclusive, universalist name reflects the unease among some participants about the mythology of bin Laden and his cronies, especially the efforts of the center to project an element of ideological and operational deference to al-Qaeda.[86] Again, unity is *not* what this movement represents.

How we refer to this threat matters, because it suggests a narrative that guides and describes our efforts. Calling the al-Qaeda movement "jihadi international," as the Israeli intelligence services do, for example, again encourages a grouping together of disparate threats that undermines our best counterterrorism.[87] It is exactly the mistake we made when we lumped the Chinese and the Soviets together in the 1950s and early 1960s, calling them "international Communists." It was only after we began to understand the crucial differences between them, including the divisive doctrinal disputes, nationalist interests, competitions in the third world, and competing ambitions, that we were able to begin to build an effective response that took advantage of those points of leverage. Our worst mistakes grew out of our unwillingness to study their history and cultures, and to move beyond oversimplified ideological tenets. If we do the same thing with this Qutbist faction of "Islamists," then we will fail to respond effectively to them as well, and will give other factions every incentive to draw together more closely against us, in a reality that becomes a self-fulfilling prophecy.

Al-Qaeda's popular support has been tested by many of its operations. It has made a large number of serious targeting errors, errors that were decried by many in its own constituency, yet the West has not sufficiently capitalized on them. In Anbar Province of Iraq, the United States did effectively exploit al-Qaeda's excesses to recruit Sunni allies against al-Qaeda in Iraq; but much more must be done to exploit this kind of vulnerability on a global scale. The United States tends to act as if al-Qaeda is essentially a static enemy that will react to its actions, but then fails to react effectively and strategically to the movement's missteps. But as the Real IRA and the PFLP-GC demonstrate, the al-Qaeda movement can undermine itself, if it is enabled to.

A prominent example of mistaken targeting that Zawahiri himself recounts in his book, *Knights under the Banner of the Prophet*, is the fate of a little girl named Shayma Abdel-Halim, killed in a 1993 attack on the motorcade of Egyptian prime minister Atif Sidqi by his group, Islamic Jihad.[88] The minister was only slightly injured, but 12-year-old Shayma, who was standing nearby in her schoolyard, was crushed by a door blown off his car by the explosion. As Lawrence Wright describes, Shayma's death so outraged the Egyptian population, who had experienced more than 240 people killed by terrorist attacks during the previous two years, that they took to the streets in revulsion, shouting "Terrorism is the enemy of God!" The crackdown and arrests that followed gutted almost the entire structure of Zawahiri's group.[89] Virtually the entire operation in Egypt was destroyed.

It is no wonder that Zawahiri is keenly aware of the dangers of poor targeting and popular backlash. In a captured letter that was widely reported, Zawahiri sharply criticized the late Abu Musab al-Zarqawi for his brutal attacks on Shias and his videotaped beheadings, because they would cause disgust and potential backlash among common Muslims. "[M]any of your Muslim admirers among the common folk are wondering about your attacks on the Shia. The sharpness of this questioning increases when the attacks are on one of their mosques, and it increases more when the attacks are on the mausoleum of Imam Ali Bin Abi Talik, may God honor him. My opinion is that this matter won't be acceptable to the Muslim populace however much you have tried to explain it, and aversion to this will continue." He added, "Among the things which the feelings of the Muslim populace who love and support you will never find palatable—also—are the scenes of slaughtering the hostages. You shouldn't be deceived by the praise of some of the zealous young men and their description of you as the shaykh of the slaughterers, etc. They do not express the general view of the admirer and the supporter of the resistance in Iraq."[90] Zawahiri's main concern is, again, the mobilization of the Muslim masses. He concludes by stressing that he and his allies must avoid "exposing ourselves to the questions and answering to doubts. We don't need this."[91] And as events played out, Zawahiri was right: while Zarqawi's carefully orchestrated strategy of inciting sectarian civil war initially succeeded, his tactics provoked a backlash that ultimately turned both Shia and Sunnis against al-Qaeda in Iraq—precisely what Zawahiri had warned him against.

Numerous al-Qaeda attacks have resulted in the deaths of large numbers of Muslims, including women and children. The attacks of October 2002 in Bali,[92] of May 2003 in Saudi Arabia,[93] of November 2003 in Istanbul,[94] of March 11, 2004, in Madrid,[95] of July 7, 2005, in London—all resulted in large numbers of Muslim casualties. Similarly, the majority of the casualties of the five simultaneous Casablanca attacks of May 2003 were Muslims, as were *all* of the casualties of the November 8, 2003, attacks in Riyadh.[96] The Amman Jordan hotel bombings orchestrated by al-Qaeda in Iraq on November 9, 2005, killed 38 members of a Muslim wedding party, including parents of the bride and the groom, as well as Jordanians, Palestinians, and Iraqis.[97] The total number of Muslim casualties of al-Qaeda-sponsored terrorist attacks is difficult to determine precisely, but it is large. In attacks where al-Qaeda claimed responsibility, the proportion of Muslims killed is at least a third—and this in operations that were specifically designed to be a symbolic protest against Muslim oppression.[98]

In short, there is a growing commonality in the attitudes of Muslim and Western publics; yet the West focuses on itself and does little to nurture cooperation. There is a growing sense of outrage about killing innocent civilians—on vacation, on their way to work and school, many of whom are deeply religious and many of whom also happen to be Muslim. If the West fails to grasp this concept, to work with local cultures and local people to build upon common goals and increase their alienation from this movement, then it will have missed a long-established and promising technique for ending al-Qaeda.

Repression: Crushing Al-Qaeda with Force

Little can be said about the sixth scenario of decline, the use of overwhelming military force, in ending al-Qaeda. Even though the military and intelligence services have made important progress in tracking down and killing senior operatives, the resulting evolution in the movement has demonstrated the limits of such action, especially when poorly coordinated with other approaches and engaged in by a democracy. The invasion of Afghanistan removed a dangerous regime; however, the reconstitution of al-Qaeda in the mountains of North Waziristan just over the border in Pakistan is a discouraging development. The invasion of Iraq, sold as the centerpiece of the Bush administration's military response to al-Qaeda, defied available intelligence, diverted every type of resource from the stabilization of Afghanistan (intelligence, military, diplomatic and aid personnel, reconstruction funds, etc.), and failed to reduce the threat of al-Qaeda overall. Although apparently effective, the Turkish government's repression of the PKK within its borders, the Russian approach to Chechnya, and the Peruvian government's suppression of Sendero Luminoso, for example, yield few desirable parallels for the current campaign. There is no reason to believe that the application of even *more* overwhelming military force, even if it were available, would end the al-Qaeda movement.

Reorientation: Transitioning to Other Means

Transitioning out of terrorism and toward either criminality or full insurgency is the final, worrisome historical precedent for al-Qaeda. In a sense, the network is already doing both. Efforts to cut off funding through the formal banking system have ironically increased the incentive and necessity to engage in illicit activities, especially narcotics trafficking. With the increasing amount of poppy seed production in Afghanistan, al-Qaeda has a natural route to riches. This process is well under way.[99] As for al-Qaeda becoming a full insurgency, some analysts believe that it has already done so.[100]

Certainly in Iraq that reorientation is well developed, although the extent to which al-Qaeda itself is currently behaving as an effective "insurgency" there should not be overstated. The alliance negotiated in 2005 between bin Laden–Zawahiri and Zarqawi's organization in Iraq was an effective strategic and public relations move for both parties, breathing new life into the al-Qaeda movement at a time when its leaders were on the run, and providing legitimacy and fresh recruits for the insurgency in Iraq, with its opportunity to kill Americans and learn effective techniques to counter them. As many commentators observed, Iraq became an ideal focal point and training ground for this putative global insurgency. However, the limits of this approach have also been demonstrated. The Arab foreigners who entered Iraq (mainly Syrians, Jordanians, Saudi Arabians, and Egyptians) to fight in al-Qaeda's cause were not tied to the territory of Iraq in the sense that its native local population was. Even as the internal situation in Iraq became increasingly grim, with sectarian violence, tribal clashes, criminality, power grabs, and attacks against Western "occupiers," parts of the Sunni population turned against the outside influence of al-Qaeda. Al-Qaeda's efforts to bring the Sunni insurgents under its control and to establish a religio-totalitarian Islamic state in Iraq confronted Sunni insurgents with two, stark alternatives: either work with the Americans to counter al-Qaeda, or work with al-Qaeda and give up the hope of a unified Iraq. The longer-term outcome for Iraq is uncertain, particularly given the worrisome enhanced leverage acquired by Iran; but at this point it is clear what a future Iraq will *not* be: either a stable Western-style democracy or an al-Qaeda-aligned Islamist state.

The effective counter to this movement in Iraq, as in other areas of the world with local al-Qaeda affiliates, was to tap into the long-standing and deep association between peoples, their tribes, and their territory, and to work with the inevitable resentment toward alien agendas imposed on them from elsewhere, while attempting to ensure that the United States' was not perceived to be one of those agendas. Nationalism has been the most easily mobilized cause in the modern world, because it is grounded in the current international order of nation-states and takes advantage of the intersection between concepts of identity and territory. This is why (as we saw in chapter 3) terrorism that taps into the same source of inspiration as nationalism has been the most potent and long-lasting, the most able to mobilize support and successfully transition into insurgency, or occasionally even leadership of the state. After World War II, other causes have jockeyed with nationalism, including socialism and communism; but often the key to undermining those causes—to reversing their ability to mobilize and inspire—was to find the intersection between the ideology and the forces of nationalism, and then sever it.

Islamism, a potent source of inspiration and mobilization, aims to eclipse nationalism as the foundation of the state in the Muslim world, the successor to the nation-state. This is the source of its threat. Bin Laden and Zawahiri have focused on exploiting and displacing the local concerns of the Chechens, the Uighurs, the Islamic Movement of Uzbekistan, the Salafist Group for Call and Combat in Algeria, and many others, and sought to replace them with an international agenda.[101] Given the failure of Arab nationalism in the twentieth century, Islamism provides an alternative vision; but that does not mean that it satisfies and replaces local concerns. Whether or not Islamism is able to mobilize support in the twenty-first century in the way that nationalism once did will be a reflection of two variables: first, the degree to which Islamists can paper over the deep divisions within the 1.3 million members of the Muslim community with a vision labeled "Islam is the solution" that avoids explaining what exactly that solution would really mean; and second, the degree to which the actions and policies of the Western powers enhance and accelerate their ability to do so.

There is much scope to exploit the differences among these groups. The smart way to respond to this threat is to again sever the connection between Islamism and individualized local contexts for political violence, and then address them separately. The answer may not be to turn to what we know as nationalism per se; the concept has been an abject failure in the Arab region, and the twenty-first-century state is evolving beyond the classic nation-state anyway. Neither is it necessarily democratization, the term that has become a mantra in the United States and is increasingly seen elsewhere as a proxy for "Americanization." The answer is to stop looking for a one-size-fits-all answer, tolerate complexity and different hybrid political systems within their individual cultural contexts, and disaggregate this threat into its constituent parts by depriving it of an enemy.[102] We are witnessing the birth of a new entity that is the modern Islamic state; and as long as it does not destabilize the international system, attack us, or slaughter its own people, it is not up to outsiders to determine what form (or forms) it will take. On its current trajectory, al-Qaeda will find itself increasingly irrelevant to that process, especially if it is forced to describe what it would do after seizing power. Like many terrorist groups, al-Qaeda can kill and destroy with great effectiveness; but it has yet to construct a viable political entity *anywhere*.

AL-QAEDA'S DECLINE AND DEMISE

In facing the threat of al-Qaeda, the United States and its allies have allowed themselves to be trapped in a narrow dichotomy, where inaction invites attack and action exacerbates al-Qaeda's threat. To extricate ourselves from this paradox, we must take a broader, more strategic approach to the physical and psychological challenge that this terrorism represents. Al-Qaeda currently derives its strength from leveraging the policies of the West. To dissipate that strength, U.S. and allied policies must be smarter. Historically proven ways to end terrorism can be adapted to the novel circumstances that we face with the al-Qaeda movement.

Al-Qaeda is not exactly the same as its predecessors, and we would be foolish to slavishly follow a script written for an earlier age. It is unusually deadly, having killed thousands of people, exceeding the total of any predecessor group in a single attack. It is driven by an extreme ideology that can mobilize support among robust, existing networks, making it a focal point for simmering anger and activism. It has a resilient structure that could only exist in the twenty-first century, with web-based communications and cyberlinked operatives participating anonymously, at the tap of a few keys. After a decade spent perfecting it, al-Qaeda also has a media strategy that is appealing, ubiquitous, effective, and mature.

No previous organization has demonstrated the same fluid organization, sources of funding, exploitation of new communications, and carefully tailored methods of radicalization. Al-Qaeda's narrative draws enemies and followers alike to its Manichaean view of the world, by exploiting the full implications of the Internet, an invention that was, after all, designed to ensure the survivability and anonymity of a military organization in the wake of a nuclear attack. What an irony that the innovators who first thoroughly comprehended and tested the practical implications of the web for modern conflict were members of a two-bit Islamist faction, initially consisting of only a couple hundred fighters operating in the caves of Afghanistan.

But we must move beyond our surprise at this odd turn of events, calm our hysteria, and recover our awareness of history, comparing that which is new about al-Qaeda with echoes of earlier revolutionary groups. Al-Qaeda is indeed a serious threat, and it is almost certainly going to launch new, painful attacks against us; however, it is also a movement with many of the classic vulnerabilities of terrorist groups. Yet as things currently stand, the debate over al-Qaeda's nature mirrors the dysfunctional dichotomy of action and inaction in our policy. On the one hand, analysts and policymakers who argue that al-Qaeda is unique have Americans terrified and ready to embark on a decades-long struggle against Islamism that will become a self-fulfilling prophecy, because it includes reacting in ways that miss the classic pitfalls and commonalities of revolutionary violence. On the other hand, those who see al-Qaeda as just like earlier threats, who sanguinely look at it from the narrow perspective of "terrorology" (as Gilles Kepel puts it), miss the distinctive aspects of this fight, its unusual historical and cultural origins, and propose irrelevant counterterrorism models. We can marry up the constructive aspects of these two approaches and reach a new synthesis by considering how we reach al-Qaeda's end.

Three scenarios in our historical framework offer little hope for ending al-Qaeda: success, repression, and decapitation. First, al-Qaeda will not succeed in achieving its objectives, because it does not have limited aims that might be reached within the current international context. It is a "process" oriented group whose outcome goals have opportunistically shifted over time.[103] It is not a modern-day Irgun or EOKA. Second, even if Western democracies could muster the staying power to sustain such a campaign, crushing the movement with even more brute force than has already been employed will not finish it off. As with the Egyptian Muslim Brotherhood, the threat will merely evolve and reappear elsewhere. We have tested the effectiveness of military force and come up short. Third, although important tactical benefits have been achieved, al-Qaeda's end will not be reached through a policy of decapitation. Our obsession with bringing justice to individuals, silencing their taunts and ceasing their threatening activities, has also found its natural limit. Al-Qaeda's propagandists, especially Ayman Zawahiri but also Osama bin Laden, have catalyzed a movement that is larger than either. The ideological arguments that are at the heart of it rage apart from their involvement. This is not a cult of personality comparable to Guzmán's Sendero Luminoso or Öcalan's PKK. As for middle-level managers, they have been killed by the dozen; yet others are taking their place. The energy of this movement has gone beyond the drive of individuals, and we must now shift some of our assets to operations that will yield more results overall in driving toward its end.

The other three elements in the framework are more innovative in this case, and offer more promise for ending al-Qaeda. First, negotiations, not by any means with the core leadership but with some of the disparate entities on the periphery of this movement, hold potential. Our goal must be to differentiate the elements of what we call "al-Qaeda," to hive off local groups and individuals that have recently claimed an association but in the past have been more interested in classic, ethnonationalist-separatist aims. The United States and its allies can analyze and exploit the internal inconsistencies in this movement by using traditional tools, sometimes including talks, considered on a case-by-case basis. Second, and related, taking advantage of the serious mistakes that are endemic to al-Qaeda will help us nudge it toward failure. Al-Qaeda is a fractionated movement full of internal contradictions, in-fighting, ideological arguments, and discord that might easily lead to its end. Its connection to its own popular support is also highly vulnerable, because of clear evidence of loss of operational control and repeated, serious mistakes in targeting—mistakes that are decried by other Muslims. These activities have a long track record of leading to the demise of groups—even well-established movements like this one. Finally, there is potential for this movement to end its terrorism by reorienting toward activities that are worse, including insurgency, conventional war, or even catalyzing systemic war between major powers. Disaggregating the threat is likewise the answer to this specter—to stop overreacting to the myth of a ubiquitous threat, force al-Qaeda to describe the outlines of its political solutions to real-world grievances, and tap into the deep connection between local peoples and their territory. Whether or not al-Qaeda's terrorism ends in this way depends upon the behavior of states, including the United States and its allies, who must tolerate some level of risk and resist being provoked into ill-considered policies that accelerate the movement and are destabilizing.

If the United States continues to treat al-Qaeda as if it were utterly unprecedented, as if the decades-long experience with fighting modern terrorism were irrelevant, then it will continue to make predictable and avoidable mistakes, as well as miss important strategic opportunities. That experience points particularly toward dividing new local affiliates from al-Qaeda by understanding and exploiting their differences with the movement, rather than treating the movement as a monolith. It is also crucial to more effectively break the political and logistical connections between the movement and its supporters, reinvigorating time-honored counterterrorism tactics targeted at al-Qaeda's unique characteristics, including the perpetuation of its message, its process of radicalization, and its communications. Al-Qaeda continues to exploit what is essentially a civil war within the Muslim world, including alienated Muslims in a vast diaspora around the globe in its rage-filled movement. Al-Qaeda will end when the West removes itself from the heart of this fight, shores up international norms against terrorism, undermines al-Qaeda's ties with its followers, and effectively turns its own abundant missteps against it.

Conclusion

[W]hile the horizon of strategy is bounded by the war, grand
strategy looks beyond the war to the subsequent peace.
                                             —*B. H. Liddell Hart*[1]

UNDERSTANDING HOW terrorism ends is the necessary first step to fashioning an effective grand strategy against *any* terrorist campaign. We are learning at our peril that analyzing war termination is at least as important as dissecting the causes of war. Likewise, processes of ending for terrorist groups hold within them the best insights into which strategies succeed, which fail, and why. So the important question with respect to the current terrorist campaign and its counterterrorist response is not "How are we doing?" but "How will it end?" And, with classic strategies of leverage in mind, the second most important question is not "When will the next attack be?" but "What will we do after that?"

Thinking about how terrorism ends does not diminish the seriousness of the threat of terrorism. The United States and its allies may be attacked again at any time, conceivably even with weapons of mass destruction such as nuclear or biological weapons. But appreciating how terrorist campaigns *actually* end offers the best chance to remove ourselves from the strategic myopia that currently grips much of Western counterterrorism efforts, to avoid under- or overreacting when horrific events happen, and to steer clear of responding with passion-driven policies that are tactically gratifying but strategically unwise. Thinking through an endgame is the best way to inoculate ourselves against the strategies of terrorism, to avoid a dysfunctional action/reaction dynamic, gain the upper hand, and most important of all, to *win*—that is, to return the threat to a manageable nuisance. The United States and its allies cannot devise a more effective strategy for meeting the threat presented by the al-Qaeda movement unless we remove ourselves from the psychological framework of attack and counterattack and envision the end.

The historical record of how terrorist groups have met their demise has hardly been plumbed for patterns and insights for today. This book has sought to address this oversight with a conceptual structure on which future scholars and practitioners can build. Its purpose has been to fill a yawning intellectual gap, complementing the rich literature available on specific groups, regional analyses, ideological motivations, and other aspects of terrorism such as causes, weapons, tactics, technologies, and targets. It is hoped that the book lays the groundwork for a broader intellectual foundation on which to build counterterrorism strategy. In the process, it has necessarily reduced complex histories into lean analytical cases so as to facilitate comparative analysis of patterns of decline, uncovering questions as well as answers. But it has also laid out a logical framework for analyzing pathways toward the end, one that moves beyond the scores of exhaustive individual counterterrorism case studies or collections currently available (and usually unread) toward a broader synthesis of what they all mean for U.S. and allied strategy. Analyzing lessons from the terminal phases of scores of terrorist campaigns throughout history strengthens our ability to think objectively and to construct policies that minimize terrorism's effectiveness in the future. Focusing on how terrorism ends is the best way to avoid being manipulated by it.

Momentum requires energy. Terrorist campaigns siphon energy from their strong opponents. Any strategy must be predicated on an understanding of one's adversary, but in the case of terrorism it must be equally centered on an understanding of how terrorist campaigns derive their strength, momentum, and legitimacy. The crucial mistake after 9/11, as after countless other terror attacks throughout history, was in overreacting and treating a terrorist campaign as though it were part of a traditional military campaign in which the application of brute force would compel the enemy into submission. As we have seen, the classic strategies of leverage used throughout history draw their power from the actions of the state, using force indirectly against its user. Overly repressive law enforcement campaigns can likewise be tapped for momentum: treating this challenge as if it were a question of finding the right balance between law enforcement and military force says more about our anachronistic bureaucratic structures and intellectual models than it does about effective twenty-first-century counterterrorism. The nation-state's internal (legal) and external (strategic) realms of authority are evolving. It is hardly surprising that the means of manipulating the nation-state are evolving as well. The key question is where the locus of power and authority lies as we move forward.

Terrorism is a tactic of the weak aimed at exploiting chinks in the armor of the more powerful. Terrorists maximize their influence vis-à-vis the power of the state, by finding ways to wedge open the flaws, cracks, imperfections, and vulnerabilities of its current form and break them wide open. This is the hazard of terrorism today, and it exhibits a historical pattern that offers insights into what we are likely to face tomorrow.

Terrorism is inseparable from its historical, political, and societal context, a context that has both a local and a global dimension. There has always been a direct relationship between the strategies used by terrorist groups and the evolving nature of war, the state, and the international system. But at a time of Western dominance, that relationship is gradually shifting relative advantages to rogue nonstate actors. In the twenty-first century, terrorism threatens the integrity and value of the state by attempting to delegitimize it, either destroying the domestic contract of the state by undermining its ability to protect its people, or damaging the strategic capacity of the state by undermining its ability to prosecute war effectively. Unwise, self-destructive responses only accelerate the process. It therefore behooves us to examine more dispassionately the long-established strategies that groups are using to dismantle state authority and accomplish their ends.

Modern terrorism has always tested the legitimacy of the state and always will do so. Nineteenth-century terrorist attacks embraced strategies of provocation, daring aging autocratic regimes to test their popular legitimacy in the face of momentous societal changes. Transformations under way included the sweeping power of national self-determination and individual suffrage. In provoking overreactions, terrorist groups like Narodnaya Volya and their successors played an important role in helping to delegitimize those regimes. Compellence best fit the mid-twentieth century, because it aligned well with nationalist movements whose aims could be expressed in terms of territory. European states that responded to terrorism in the framework of compellence withdrew from colonies on which their hold and influence were already slipping, and groups evolved from terrorism to insurgency to independence as the legitimacy of European colonial empires faded away. Polarization was at the core of Marxist movements in the early years of the century, and it reappeared at the end of the century with terrorist attacks designed to polarize along racial, religious, tribal, linguistic, or ethnic lines. Polarization worked well against nation-states that were struggling to form or maintain an identity, and it delegitimized their hold on disparate communities by rotting their strength and influence from within. Civil wars have replaced the classic struggles between communism, fascism, and capitalism that played out throughout the twentieth century. States that reflect or serve nations become more immune to polarization, which is one reason why the strategy is most often seen now in developing countries that are not yet consolidated nation-states.

Contemporary terrorism tends to spring from a strategy of mobilization. Today states are struggling to keep pace with globalization, with its vast sweeping changes in communications and economic ties, porous borders, and dramatic cultural and political developments. A global environment of democratized communications, an increase in public access, a sharp reduction in cost, a growth in frequency of messages, and an exploitation of images presents groups like al-Qaeda an enhanced opportunity to leverage the effects of terrorist attacks in a way that is unprecedented. If a group is truly successful in mobilizing large numbers in disparate territorial locations, this strategy can prolong the fight and may enable the transition to other forms, including insurgency, broader conventional conflict, and even hegemonic war—especially if a nation-state responds to the threat in a foolish way. Mobilization of disparate audiences provides the best opportunity for terrorism to delegitimize the most advanced nation-states; and by doing that, potentially to destabilize the entire international system. A well-mobilized group, supported by a broader population scattered throughout the world, could carry out attacks using nuclear or biological weapons from which a nation-state could not provide effective protection to its citizens. The threat would go well beyond the direct casualties of the attack, as tragic as those would be; even if they numbered in the tens or hundreds of thousands, they would not necessarily bring down the state. The key danger would be the absence of good choices available for what a wounded giant like the United States would do *next*, and the cascade of actions and reactions among multiple states that would likely follow. That is why terrorism is a potent tactic today—and it is also why we must use the lessons of history to determine *in advance* how we would end it.

Most important, today's terrorism highlights the need to transition from linear, two-dimensional strategic concepts to dynamic, multidimensional concepts. Strategies of leverage are not new; but the degree to which they resonate within the evolving historical context, the degree to which they confound the classic twentieth-century dichotomous strategic framework so favored by Western policymakers *is* new. We are accustomed to thinking about the intricate relationship between modern states and war, with war shaping the state and the state shaping war. But the irony is that the same relationship appears, in more modest form, in the connection between actors that use terrorism and the governments that react to them: both of them affect their actual and potential constituencies in ways that, while initially invisible, can be just as formative over time, especially in an age when the state's ability to mobilize appears increasingly under assault.

In dealing with terrorism in the twenty-first century, states no longer have the luxury of a learning curve. To reduce the potential for a catastrophic and disruptive event involving terrorism, to develop a clear plan for what to do and what not to do in response, the United States and its allies must reexamine the common patterns of how terrorism ends and focus their energies on that long-term strategic aim.

Understanding How Terrorism Ends

The six-part framework presented in this book for how terrorism ends—decapitation, negotiation, success, failure, repression, and reorientation—incorporates the full range of options available, from states crushing terrorist campaigns to groups single-handedly gutting themselves, and every combination in between. In the six chapters that discuss these modes of demise, we can also discern a menu of consistent, often interlocking patterns that yield lessons for dealing with current and future threats, driving them toward the end.

Governments naturally respond to terrorism by trying to capture or kill the ringleader. But as we have seen, arresting a leader tends to be more effective than killing him because neutralizing leaders matters to the degree that it halts momentum. Crucial factors in any effort to "decapitate" a group and end it are not just the nature and structure of the group or even the imminent threat of attack (both vital tactical concerns), but also the likely effects of the leader's removal on those who actively or passively support the campaign. A clear finding from the first chapter was that, on the whole, arresting a leader damages a campaign more than does killing him, probably because the jailing of a leader demystifies him and demonstrates the power of the legal edifice of the state. The cases of Abimael Guzmán and Sendero Luminoso, Mickey McKevitt and the Real IRA, and Shoko Asahara and Aum Shinrikyo all demonstrated this effect. An issue associated with killing leaders is whether or not the act reduces or magnifies the threat, as it can result in martyrdom and inspire new recruits. For example, the Chechen Islamists and Palestinian groups suffered devastating attrition of their leaders yet continued to pose a serious threat. The second- and third-order effects of killing the leader may be unpredictable. As important as it has been to understand the relationship between the leader and his subordinates, therefore, if the goal is to drive a group toward its end, it is perhaps even more important as we move forward to understand the relationship between the leader and his likely constituents.

Negotiations rarely end terrorism by themselves, but adroit diplomacy can be a great strategic tool for managing the decline of a campaign. Most negotiations drag on inconclusively, hardly ever providing a quick resolution to the problem. Indeed, the statistical analysis at the foundation of this study reveals that fewer than one in five groups enters negotiations. However, once a group decides to negotiate (and a government also agrees to engage), the probability of outright failure for either side is less than 10 percent. The predominant scenario has been for negotiations to drag on, with interruptions and setbacks, and often a continuation of the violence at a lower level, but without obvious resolution. For this reason, negotiations may be best thought of as an alternative avenue of interaction for both the group and the government—one where civilians will almost certainly continue to be targeted and to suffer, but probably not as much as they would have done in the absence of talks.

But for states, the good news is that negotiations most often stimulate or complement other processes of ending terrorist campaigns. The Northern Ireland case shows the role of negotiations in a slow, drawn-out process, the Israeli-Palestinian process has been famously inconclusive, and the LTTE–Sri Lankan peace process has shown both promise and setback. These cases, as well as the broader statistical analyses, reveal seven key conditions that determine whether talks will be promising or unpromising. First, both sides must be in a situation where additional violence is counterproductive—groups may be losing ground to competitors, failing to recruit new members, or losing constituents because of their own targeting mistakes, for example. This type of "stalemate" reflects a group's determination that whether or not it is making tactical advances, the *political* situation is turning sour. Second, there must be strong leadership on both the challenger and the government side. Without strong leaders, talks do not yield progress and may even worsen the situation. Third, committed sponsors are required—whether mediators, outside guarantors, or other external actors who are willing to push the talks along. The corollary is that the most intractable terrorist campaigns tend to be in neighborhoods where states are unwilling to play a constructive role. Fourth, suicide tactics make terrorist campaigns particularly problematic, as they erode trust and reduce the ability of communities to live side-by-side. Building barriers to separate populations improves the tactical problem but can only be a short-term solution, as it fails to consolidate a state's governance (which is, after all, the point). Fifth, negotiations that cause a movement to splinter into smaller factions may increase violence in the short term, but they also disaggregate the threat, often revealing the most radical elements and supplying useful intelligence. They can be advantageous over the long run. Sixth, contrary to recent scholarship, the presence of spoilers does not necessarily derail negotiations. The outcome depends not on those who use violent attacks to destroy talks but on those who *react* to them: the key variable is whether or not negotiating parties and their sponsors collectively and publicly label the attacks illegitimate. Finally, the international context matters. Real or imagined relationships between terrorist groups that share sources of inspiration across regions are crucial. Talks will not succeed if the cause espoused is on the ascendancy on the international stage. Local concerns still trump international ideologies, but terrorist campaigns gain momentum from global narratives. Especially in a world of globalized communications, the connections between the local and the international are vital—even at the bargaining table.

Negotiations rarely end terrorism quickly or single-handedly. But they provide a means to manage the violence and facilitate the longer-term decline of a group. The key question for both the group and for the government is how negotiations play into an overall mobilization strategy, and they should be approached with this perspective in mind.

Success for terrorist campaigns is rare, but some groups do end in this way. Most campaigns have a difficult time merely surviving: the average life-span of a group is eight years, and that only includes groups that have achieved a level of staying power through multiple attacks. Terrorist groups, like other organizations, often have survival as a cardinal aim, and use the achievement of tactical or "process" goals to keep a campaign going. Yet that is a far cry from gaining political aims. Achieving strategic or "outcome" goals is far less common, but it does happen: Irgun played a role in the birth of Israel, and Umkhonto helped produce postapartheid South Africa. Whether these outcomes might have occurred in the *absence* of that kind of violence is an open question: we have reason to believe that the tactic of terrorism might even have been counterproductive. Regardless, the evidence examined here indicates that success is more likely when the goals are clear and attainable (such as territory or support for one's kin), terrorist tactics are supplanted by more legitimate uses of force (such as insurgency), and campaigns comport with larger trends (such as decolonization or national self-determination)—which again returns us to the essential ability to mobilize supporters for one's cause.

Terrorist campaigns have an uphill battle in trying to maintain momentum: most terrorist groups disintegrate, falling under the weight of their own unpopular tactics. They can gain a new lease on life when a state hands them derivative power or when a group acquires sufficient popular strength to transition to another form of violence. But over the long history of modern terrorism, these scenarios are the exceptions, not the rule. Implosion of groups emanates from mistakes, burnout, and collapse, sometimes nudged along by intelligent, carefully targeted pressure from the police or military. The key thing is to understand long-established processes of implosion and *work* with them for specific groups, avoiding classic mistakes that can hand over the energy that keeps campaigns alive in the eyes of their constituents.

Marginalization from their constituency is the death-knell for modern groups. Even groups that are small, clandestine, and peripatetic find it difficult to survive if they have neither active nor passive support from a surrounding population. Loss of support may occur if the driving narrative is overtaken by events, contact with ordinary people is lost, or above all if groups target potential members of their own constituencies and provoke a backlash. As discussed in chapter 4, this was the case with the Real IRA, the Egyptian GAI, and the Italian Red Brigades, for example. But comprehending this tendency is not an excuse for sanguinity. It certainly does *not* imply that governments can passively wait for movements to end. Groups can and do cause a huge amount of damage as they hobble along, killing innocents and eroding the legitimacy of a regime through its inability to prevent attacks. In the long run terrorism ends; but in the long run a lot of people also die. The point here is that counterterrorism policies that are synergistic with the tendency for people to be repulsed by terrorist violence are the best bets to marginalize operatives and maximize the odds that they will fail or be killed first.

Terrorism is so repulsive and outrageous that those responsible for order and the protection of civilians have a natural propensity to try to crush groups through overwhelming oppression, either domestically with police and security forces or externally with military force. The basic instinct to fight fire with fire, to meet treacherous force with a devastating counterpunch, is as long-standing as the Old Testament and Machiavelli's *The Prince*. What a shame that the modern historical record fails to support such a noble impulse. Sadly, the militarization of counterterrorism strategy can be counterproductive, even if every strategy for countering terrorism requires a military and coercive component. In chapter 5, case studies on Russia and Narodnaya Volya, Peru and the Shining Path, Turkey and the PKK, Uruguay and the Tupamaros, and Russian and Chechnya all demonstrated the limits of this approach. Even domestic repression is increasingly inadequate for ending campaigns, because in a globalized world the effects of government clampdowns on the regional neighborhood, or even on noncontiguous states, are blurring borders and testing state capacity. Legitimacy is central to mobilization, which today takes on new levels of complexity as audiences become both more fractionated and more powerful in their role in the nature, course, and outcomes of these conflicts.

Repression has difficulty ending terrorism because terrorist groups resort to strategies of leverage to turn a state's strength against itself. As the U.S. military likes to say, the adversary has a vote in how it fights. The strategies of provocation, polarization, and mobilization are at odds with the impulse to use force to pound the enemy into the ground. Indeed, that pounding may be just what a terrorist campaign needs to regain the initiative with its constituents.

The good news for states, however, is that winning strategies for ending terrorism tend to evolve. Successful governments are learning organizations, usually beginning with indiscriminate retaliation and then adapting to the setbacks that these campaigns can dish out, eventually gaining the experience to minimize their own mistakes and craft more fine-tuned responses. Even as they use force, twenty-first-century states must reach out to multiple audiences—not just their own territorial populations but increasingly others beyond their borders. As long as governments do not lose their bearings along the way, sound counterterrorism strategy can gain ascendancy over emotion-laden responses. In other words, in ending terrorism through the use of repressive force, the secret is to mobilize the rightful forces of the state effectively against violent perpetrators (and their supporters) within a community, without either catalyzing a larger countermobilization by that community or demobilizing the government's own support.

The last scenario for terrorism's end is the reorientation of campaigns to other forms, including criminal behavior, insurgency, or even conventional war. Naturally the concepts overlap: they have always been ambiguous in relation to one another and are only becoming more so with the changing paradigms of the twenty-first century. It would be knavish to argue that they are totally separable, as groups that use terrorism often fund their operations with criminal activities, for example. But sometimes organizations divert their core energies from the pursuit of altruistic ends (as they see them) to the pursuit of personal gain as an end in itself. Transition into criminality is not good news, but at least it is manageable within the current international system and represents one potential pathway to the end of terrorist attacks.

Groups that transition into insurgencies or even conventional wars are another matter, however. When groups become strong enough to transition out of reliance on terrorism (an inherently weak tactic) toward the use of more effective types of violence, they gain legitimacy and increase their ability to take control of states themselves. Unlike terrorist groups, insurgencies operate as military units, target military forces, seize and hold territory, and generally mimic the power and behavior of states, a development that may be either good or bad (depending on what one thinks about the cause behind an insurgency and the targeted government—the underdog can be right, after all). But whatever the viewpoint, these transitions do not serve the interests of the status quo. Transition of a group toward conventional war is an even more daunting prospect, as it holds the possibility of destabilizing escalation that draws states in and potentially spins out of control into a systemic war. The variable at the heart of this process of reorientation is again the degree to which nonstate actors are able to mobilize people and resources to support the use of force against the state. Only through popular mobilization is a terrorist campaign able to gain resources, support, numbers, and the military capacity that is inherent in the shift to more "regular" uses of force. At the core it is always a struggle for legitimacy. Apart from the self-destructive acts of states that can be set off in response to an attack (a serious danger, as we have discussed), terrorism is only a fundamental threat to the nation-state to the extent that it successfully mobilizes the hopes, dreams, energies, and resources of the people—while the government does not.

Terrorist campaigns end when they are denied leadership, when negotiations redirect energies, when they implode, when they are repressed, when they descend to selfish ends, or when they transmogrify into the strategic mainstream. These patterns regularly reappear, and we can use the weight of history to formulate a strategy that leads to the end. The good news is that terrorism virtually always fails, as long as policymakers are wise enough to avoid ceding power to this treacherous use of force. The lessons of the past must be considered, comprehended, and then carefully calibrated for the particular circumstances and the particular strategy of a particular group, directing its energies at the vulnerabilities of a particular kind of state. At the core of a successful counterterrorism strategy is understanding the nature of the appeal of a campaign in the evolving international context. In today's globalizing world, the focus must be on the countermobilization of the popular will, using strategies of leverage rather than compellence to prevent a campaign from drawing energy from the state's response and to lay bare the effects of this indiscriminate violence for those it claims to champion. Once we concentrate on how terrorism ends, forging a successful strategy for its defeat can begin.

Statistical Analysis of Terrorist Campaigns

A COMPREHENSIVE COMPARISON of terrorist organizations worldwide is a necessary complement to the case studies developed through this book in the effort for broader comparative perspective on the dynamics of terrorist group activity. The analysis developed here is a step toward an empirical exploration of common assumptions about the trajectories of terrorist organizations, examining basic dynamics of 457 terrorist organizations active since 1968. This statistical study provides information about the endings of groups, including how many engage in negotiations, the distribution of life spans of terrorist organizations, and to what extent groups achieve their strategic aims. But it is also a first step, uncovering questions as well as answers about the endings of campaigns; it is not meant to imply greater precision than can be offered by the imperfect information upon which it is based.

This discussion of broad patterns in the experiences of terrorist groups draws upon a unique database of terrorist organizations developed for this book from information available in the Memorial Institute for the Prevention of Terrorism (MIPT)'s Terrorism Knowledge Base. The MIPT database has been one of the most comprehensive databases on modern terrorism publicly available to the general researcher. However, the groups that it attempts to document and track provide by design an uncertain and changeable field of information, with name changes, aliases, splinter groups, and multiple or false claims of responsibility by different groups for single attacks. In addition to the repetition and incompleteness inherent in the study of terrorism, the MIPT database itself suffers from unevenness of detail across different groups, as well as consistent underreporting of incidents attributable to specific groups. Nevertheless, this database was the best and arguably most objective resource widely available online for the study of terrorism worldwide at the time this analysis was completed, particularly when cross-checked by other available journalistic sources. Following the completion of this study, the MIPT Terrorism Knowledge Base was transferred to the National Consortium for the Study of Terrorism and Responses to Terrorism (START) at the University of Maryland, at http://www.start.umd.edu/.

The specific database developed for this project is concerned with organizations rather than incidents, drawing on the information provided by the MIPT to create an index of 457 organizations that correspond as well as possible with the definition of terrorist groups developed in the introduction to this book. It is available at www.howterrorismends.com. Out of the 873 organizations listed by the MIPT as of December 2006, 457 organizations met the requirements of sustained (repeated) attacks harming civilians through physical injury or death. Most of the groups listed by the MIPT that were excluded from this database were excluded as either perpetrators of single or temporally limited incidents (e.g., a series of bombings that occurred on a single day), causing damage only to property without any indicated civilian casualties, or as believably limited to military targets. The inclusion of only durable groups that demonstrated some level of sustained activity was necessary for a meaningful discussion of organizational trends. Unfortunately, excluding groups that have not displayed durability across multiple attacks means that this database does not account for the widespread terrorist activity that arises from one-off attacks by groups who are subsequently repressed or disband. This may have resulted in some skewing of the data toward longer lifespans or stronger trends of negotiation or success, but we judged this approach the fairest and best available. We found no groups that engaged in a single attack and then achieved their aims, for example. This study therefore draws conclusions about the experiences of *durable* terrorist organizations.

Selection for inclusion in the database and subsequent coding of all variables (discussed in detail below) was based on a careful survey of all data available from the MIPT for each organization it lists, including descriptive and statistical group profiles, incident reports, and media reports. Given the limitations of the data, this can be only an imperfect survey of terrorist organizations since 1968; but it was the best available at the time of this study and should be considered a representative approximation of the patterns of terrorist organizations in this period.

SELECTION AND CODING

In building this database a number of criteria were used to select only those cases that fit the definitional requirements of a terrorist organization. The selection process proceeded generally as follows:

a. Eliminate any group indicated to have targeted only property or military targets, with no associated civilian injuries or fatalities.
b. Eliminate any group that did not display sustained organizational capabilities, that is, those groups with only one attack or a single series of coordinated attacks within several days of one another and with no subsequent evidence of activity or communication.

This rubric worked effectively in most cases but suffered from certain complications inherent in the MIPT data. One of the most common was inconsistencies within the MIPT reporting for a single group. In many cases, the MIPT incident statistics would indicate no civilian casualties as a result of the group's activities. In each of these cases, we carefully considered the group's descriptive profile, and if it suggested attacks in addition to those listed in the incident statistics, the group was included as a terrorist organization, unless the description explicitly indicated that there were no civilian casualties.

Another common complication was name changes and breakaway groups listed in the database. Again, for reasons of feasibility and consistency of interpretation, each listed group that met the requirements for terrorism was included as an individual group, regardless of any links to another group. The exception was the very few cases where a clearly and consistently defined "armed wing" and the general organization were both listed and made mutual reference to one another; in these cases only the "armed wing" was included to avoided double-counting the group (see the case of Resistenza Corsa and Accolta Nazinuale Corsa, for example). In general, splinter groups, aliases, and name changes, so long as terrorist attacks could be ascribed to the name, were all included.

A final note is necessary on the handling of kidnappings and hijackings. For consistency, hijackings and kidnappings were held to the same standards of civilian injury as other incidents. In the context of the construction of this database, both types of incident are only considered terrorist actions if civilians are injured or killed in the incident.

Groups that fit the selection criteria for inclusion as terrorist organizations were coded for life span, level of engagement in negotiations over the group's fundamental aims or strategies, and the extent to which the group achieved its strategic aims. In the very occasional cases where meaningful values of the variables in question could not be obtained from the MIPT data, the variables were coded as missing. As a result, the total number of observations for those variables (e.g., negotiations, achievement) was sometimes fewer than the 457 organizations that met our definition of terrorism. All other cases were coded as described in what follows.

Life Span

Precise numbers for organizational life-span are impossible to consistently obtain for terrorist groups, which often deliberately dissemble. Estimated life-span was obtained from information on the approximate years of the group's beginning and ending. For the purposes of obtaining a current life-span, ongoing groups were coded with an end year of 2006 (the year the data were compiled).

Start years were determined in the following way:

a. The founding year or period provided by MIPT is used (approximate periods such as early 1970s were coded by an approximate year such as 1972).
b. If a founding year is not provided, the start year is obtained by the year of the first attack or communication from the organization.

End years were determined in the following way:

a. The year or period the MIPT database states that the group ended, if available.
b. The year the group entered cease-fire, renounced violence, entered government, or otherwise indicated a halt to terrorist activities, *so long as that change occurred more than three years ago (2003 or earlier) and there has been no further violence under that group's name.*
c. The year of the last terrorist attack if the MIPT does not otherwise indicate that the group is still active and the attack occurred more than three years ago (2003 or earlier).

The life span is calculated by the difference between the end and start years. To adjust for the relative imprecision of the data on the founding and conclusion of terrorist organizations, the data on life spans is presented in five-year clusters. While the median organizational life-span is calculated as 8 years, that figure more accurately represents a life span between 5 and 9 years.

Negotiation

Organizations were coded as participating in negotiations if they engaged in any discussions with external agents, most commonly with the government of the state in which they were active, over the group's fundamental aims or strategies. Organizations solely engaged in tactical negotiations such as hostage negotiations were not coded as having negotiated (in accordance with the strategic focus of the book). In addition to coding for participation in negotiations, the extent of the impact of negotiations on the conflict was also covered. This data were obtained from the descriptive group profiles provided by the MIPT, sometimes double-checked by media reports.

The coding of negotiations was as follows:

0 No Negotiation: The organization has not engaged in any strategic negotiations

1 Negotiation, Resolved conflict: The organization has engaged in negotiations; negotiations have effectively resolved or diffused the conflict and group has either effectively disbanded or fully normalized activity.

2 Negotiation, Stable: The organization has engaged in negotiations; negotiations have led to a stable cessation of conflict, however without fundamental resolution to ensure that violence will not flare up again.

3 Negotiation, Unstable: The organization has engaged in negotiations; while not openly abandoned or broken, they have been disregarded or bypassed by one or both sides. This includes cases in which the state refuses to follow terms of an agreement, even if the terrorist organization has withheld violence; also includes cases of substantial split (not just splinter groups) in which part of the group attempts to maintain negotiations or the terms of the negotiations while a significant component carries on with the conflict.

4 Negotiation, Failed: The organization has engaged in negotiations; however, there has since been a clear, public breaking of any agreement or cease-fire or the full public breakdown and abandonment of talks prior to any conclusion.

The negotiation variable is coded according to the most current negotiation status. In other words, if an organization failed an early iteration of negotiations but more recent negotiations could be classified as stable, the group is coded as Negotiation, Stable (2).

Achievement

Achievement measures the extent to which a group was able to achieve its strategic objectives. Many of the groups listed by the MIPT are not indicated as having specific strategic goals beyond the expression of an ideal or ideology. While these groups could be understood to have "achieved" by virtue of having expressed themselves, they are nevertheless coded as having not achieved, as "expression" is qualitatively different from achieving specific strategic policy or political change that this variable is meant to measure. It is also important to note that achievement is indicated if the group's goals were wholly or partially achieved during the group's life span, *regardless of who directly achieved or negotiated that outcome*. Usually the strategic goal of a group is shared by various actors in a conflict, and this database does not attempt to claim which group enjoys primary responsibility for the outcome.

Achievement was coded as follows:

0 No Achievement: No indication that any of the group's strategic aims were achieved; no strategic aims were expressed by the group.
1 Achievement, Full: Full achievement of a group's stated strategic aims such as full independence of a territory, control of the government, or successful disruption of specified government action.
2 Achievement, Substantial: Achievement of a qualitatively substantial component of the group's strategic aims, such as establishment of regional autonomy without independent statehood.
3 Achievement, Limited: Minor compromise on elements of a group's strategic aims.

RESULTS

Life Span

Figure A.1 shows the distribution of life spans of terrorist groups across the 457 groups included in the database. Given the highly skewed distribution, the median is the most appropriate measure of the average terrorist group life-span. The median life-span is calculated as approximately 8 years, but given the sometimes inexact dates of origin and demise, it is better described as falling between 5 and 9 years.

Negotiation

Table A.1 shows that only 17.8 percent of terrorist groups enter into strategic negotiations. Table A.2 shows the distribution of the different extent of the impact of these negotiations across groups. This table demonstrates the high uncertainty of the outcomes of negotiations. It shows that most negotiations do not result in certain resolution or cessation of the conflict or certain failure, but rather occupy an uncertain middle ground ranging from stable cease-fire without full explicit resolution to high levels of violence and unstable noncompliance or breakaway groups. While nearly a third of negotiations resolve the conflict, most negotiations have not defused the conflict, although barely 10 percent of negotiations have actually failed outright.

A complication in this presentation of the data is that some of these distinctions also may reflect the timeline of negotiations—unstable negotiations may well be on their way to failure, and stable ones may well be one peaceful plebiscite away from resolution; it is not clear that there

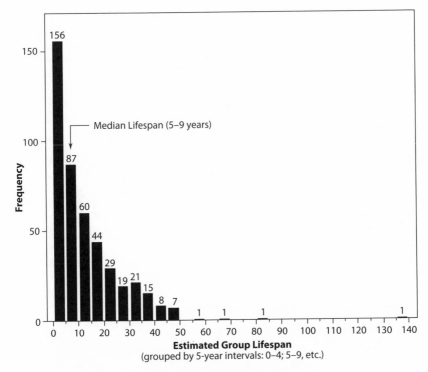

Figure A.1: Distribution of life spans of durable terrorist groups
Source: MIPT Terrorism Knowledge Base, December 2006. Figure 1, from "Ending Terrorism: Lessons for Defeating al-Qaeda," *Adelphi* (2008), p. 24. Taylor and Francis, Ltd., reprinted by permission of the publisher.

are any good ways to resolve this issue, as we cannot confidently make assumptions about the future. Most processes of negotiation do move through, and in spite of, continued violence; the issue is whether the negotiations *in the end* put a stop to the violence. Stable and resolved conflicts may well have experienced widespread violence during earlier stages of the negotiation process.

The relationship of negotiations to life span is also quite interesting. With a difference in means (significant with a *p*-value of 0.000) of approximately 11 years for nonnegotiating groups and approximately 22 for negotiating groups, there is a distinct relationship between negotiation and life spans, with negotiation associated with a longer life-span. Because of the skewed distribution, these means are somewhat higher that the more representative medians would be.

This effect can also be seen in figure A.2, which shows the increasing probability that negotiations will be observed for the longer-lived groups.

TABLE A.1
Engagement in Any Strategic Negotiations by Durable Terrorist Organizations

Engaged in negotiations	Observations	Percentage	Cumulative
No	374	82.2%	82.2%
Yes	81	17.8%	100.0%
Total	455	100.0%	

Source: MIPT database, December 2006.

TABLE A.2
Extent of Impact of Engagement in Negotiation by Durable Terrorist Organizations

Negotiation extent[a]	Observations	Percentage	Cumulative
Resolved conflict	24	29.6%	29.6%
Stable	22	27.2%	56.8%
Unstable	26	32.1%	88.9%
Failed	9	11.1%	100.0%
Total	81	100.0%	

Source: MIPT database, December 2006.

[a] Definitions of categories are as follows: resolved conflict: negotiations fully resolved conflict; stable: negotiations stabilized conflict, but no fundamental resolution reached; unstable: terms of negotiations disregarded or bypassed, but not openly abandoned, by one or more parties in negotiations; failed: negotiations fully broken down, or agreements openly abandoned.

It demonstrates the changing probability of negotiations having occurred as groups' life spans change. For example, in a group with a life span of 50 years we could expect a nearly 60 percent probability of negotiations involving that group. Alternatively, in a group with a life span of 10 years, we could expect negotiations to have occurred with a probability of about 17.5 percent (a figure that makes sense when considering a median life-span of 8 years and about 17.3 percent of the groups negotiating). These probabilities are generated from the results of a single variable logistic regression of life span on engagement in negotiations, which results in a highly statistically significant coefficient (p-value = 0.000; see table A.3). Much of this graph is not terribly interesting, however, as half the groups have a life span under 10 years, and very few go over 50.

It is necessary to keep in mind that this result does not indicate that negotiations become more likely as a group ages, as we did not have consistent information on the age of the group when it first entered into negotiations. This would be a significant element to incorporate in future research.

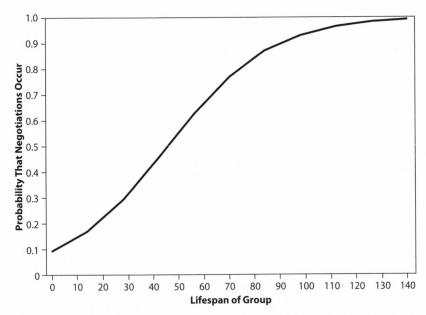

Figure A.2: Relationship of negotiations and life span for durable terrorist organizations
Source: MIPT Terrorism Knowledge Base. Calculated probabilities from logistic regression of life spans on engagement in negotiations (highly significant at *p*-value 0.000).

TABLE A.3
Relationship of Negotiations and Life Span of Durable Terrorist Organizations: Results of *t*-test

Engaged in negotiations	Mean approximate life span in years
No	10–15 (11)
Yes	20–25 (22)
Difference	11
p-value	0.000
Observations	449

Source: MIPT database.

Achievement

The overall results with regard to achievement of strategic aims (table A.4) show that the overwhelming majority of organizations have not done so, with only 29 organizations (or 6.4 percent) showing full or substantial achievement of their strategic aims.

Table A.4
Achievement of Strategic Aims of Durable Terrorist Organizations

Level of achievement[a]	Observations	Percentage	Cumulative
None	392	87.1%	87.1%
Full	20	4.4%	91.6%
Substantial	9	2.0%	93.6%
Limited	29	6.4%	100.0%
Total	450	100.0%	

Source: MIPT database, December 2006.

[a] Definitions of categories are as follows: *full*: full achievement of group's primary stated strategic aims; *substantial*: achievement of a qualitatively substantial component of group's strategic aims; *limited*: minor compromise to elements of group's strategic aims.

Table A.5
Association of Negotiation and Any Achievement of Strategic Aims of Durable Terrorist Organizations

Any achievement of objectives	None or failed negotiation	Any other negotiation	All groups
No	344	48	392
Row %	87.8	12.2	100.0
Column %	90.5	68.6	87.1
Yes	36	22	58
Row %	62.1	37.9	100.0
Column %	9.5	31.4	12.9
All groups	380	70	450
Row %	84.4	15.6	100.0
Column %	100.0	100.0	100.0

Source: MIPT database.
Note: Pearson $\chi^2 = 25.3771$; p-value = 0.000.

The relationship between nonfailed engagement in negotiation and strategic achievement is very interesting. As table A.5 demonstrates, a substantial and highly statistically significant relationship exists between engagement in negotiation and any level of achievement of strategic aims. Considering the difference of proportion between achievement of groups engaging in negotiations and those who have not engaged in negotiation or whose negotiations have failed, we can see a clear relationship between negotiation and success. Thirty-one percent of groups who engage in negotiations that have not clearly broken down have experienced some level of achievement of strategic objectives (from accommodation to their strategic goals to full achievement of strategic

TABLE A.6
Association of Negotiation and Full Strategic Achievement of Durable Terrorist
Organizations

Any achievement of objectives	None or failed negotiation	Any other negotiation	All groups
No	364	66	430
Row %	84.7	15.4	100.0
Column %	95.8	94.3	95.6
Yes	16	4	20
Row %	80.0	20.0	100.0
Column %	4.2	5.7	4.4
All groups	380	70	450
Row %	84.4	15.6	100.0
Column %	100.0	100.0	100.0

Source: MIPT database.
Note: Pearson χ^2 = 0.3147; p-value = 0.575.

objectives), as compared to under 10 percent of groups that have not maintained negotiations. An odds ratio of 4.38 suggests that the odds of a group achieving at least some part of its strategic goals are nearly four and a half times greater for a nonfailing negotiating group than a group that has not engaged in negotiations or for which negotiations have failed.

Interestingly, as table A.6 demonstrates, negotiations cannot be understood to be related to full achievement of strategic objectives, as there is no significant difference in proportions of achievement for negotiating groups versus nonnegotiating groups. This suggests that the increased likelihood of any level of achievement evident for negotiating groups is a result of successful compromise.

Table A.7 considers the relationship of nonfailing negotiation and different levels of strategic achievement. It demonstrates a significant relationship between the two, and makes evident where the effect of negotiations is strongest. The finding that negotiation is not related to a higher incidence of full achievement of objectives is reinforced, and the table shows that negotiation is associated with a higher rate of both partial achievement of objectives and limited achievement, such as limited and partial accommodation to a group's aims. Reflecting on the pattern across the population of groups as a whole, we can see that limited achievement is more likely than substantial achievement. Negotiation appears to have only a minor effect in increasing limited rather than partial achievement.

TABLE A.7
Associations of Negotiation and Different Levels of Strategic Achievement of Durable Terrorist Organizations

Any achievement of objectives	None or failed negotiation	Any other negotiation	All groups
No	344	48	392
Row %	87.8	12.2	100.0
Column %	90.5	68.6	87.1
Yes (full)	16	4	20
Row %	80.0	20.0	100.0
Column %	4.2	5.7	4.4
Yes (substantial)	5	4	9
Row %	55.6	44.4	100.0
Column %	1.3	5.7	2.0
Yes (limited)	15	14	29
Row %	51.7	48.3	100.0
Column %	4.0	20.0	6.4
All groups	380	70	450
Row %	84.4	15.6	100.0
Column %	100.0	100.0	100.0

Source: MIPT database.
Note: Pearson χ^2 = 32.9257; p-value = 0.000.

FTOs

Life Span

The U.S. Department of State regularly publishes a list of designated Foreign Terrorist Organizations (FTOs) that are subject to U.S. sanctions. This is one of a number of official lists of terrorist organizations, including those established by the UK and EU governments, and it is commonly used by political scientists for comparative or quantitative analysis.

Despite the importance of this list, which provides case studies for numerous analyses, these organizations do not fully reflect the overall population of terrorist organizations. The most notable difference is in the life span of FTOs. As figure A.3 shows, the approximate median life-span is 15–20 years, double that of the population of durable terrorist organizations as a whole. The FTO distribution is substantially skewed toward shorter life-spans.

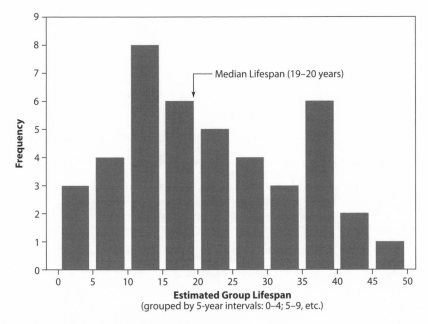

Figure A.3: Distribution of FTO life spans
Source: MIPT Terrorism Knowledge Base.

Negotiation

As demonstrated in table A.8, listed FTOs show a slightly higher rate of participation in negotiations than the population of organizations as a whole (with about 18 percent of all terrorist organizations engaging in negotiations), but the difference is not great enough to be of much significance.

Achievement

Similarly, there is no substantial difference in the proportion of FTOs that have achieved strategic aims. Among all durable terrorist organizations, 12.9 percent have seen some level of achievement, while 11.9 percent of FTOs have (table A.9). No FTOs have seen full or substantial achievement of their aims, but given the small size of the subset, this result should not be taken to mean that a listing as an FTO necessarily means the organization will not achieve its aims.

TABLE A.8
FTO Engagement in Strategic Negotiations

Engaged in Negotiations	Observations	Percentage	Cumulative
No	33	78.6%	78.6%
Yes[a]	9	21.4%	100.0%
Stable	3	33.3%	33.3%
Unstable	5	55.6%	88.9%
Failed	1	11.1%	100.0%
Total	42	100.0%	

Source: MIPT database, December 2006.

[a] Rows below demonstrate the breakdown of the impact of negotiations within the subset of negotiating FTOs. Stable: negotiations stabilized conflict, but no fundamental resolution reached. Unstable: terms of negotiations disregarded or bypassed, but not openly or permanently abandoned. Failed: negotiations fully broken down, or agreements openly abandoned.

TABLE A.9
FTO Achievement of Strategic Aims

Level of achievement	Observations	Percentage	Cumulative
None	37	88.1%	88.1%
Limited[a]	5	11.9%	100.0%
al-Aqsa Martyrs Brigades			
Hamas			
Hezbollah			
Palestine Liberation Front			
Popular Front for the Liberation of Palestine			
Total	42	100.0%	

Source: MIPT database, December 2006.

[a] Minor compromise to elements of group's strategic aims.

LONGEST-LIVED GROUPS

Another interesting subset of our database of durable terrorist organizations to consider is the set of longest-lived terrorist groups. In our database, 19 organizations had life spans greater than 40 years. These groups are listed in table A.10.

TABLE A.10
Longest-Lived Terrorist Organizations

Name	Approximate start year	Approximate life-span
Guerrilla Army of the Poor	1954	41
Islamic Action Organization	1961	42
National Liberation Army (Colombia)	1964	42
Palestine Liberation Organization (PLO)	1964	42
Revolutionary Armed Forces of Colombia (FARC)	1964	42
Barisan Revolusi Nasional Melayu Pattani (BRN)	1963	43
Front for the Liberation of the Cabinda Enclave	1963	43
Guatemalan Labor Party	1952	44
Free Papua Movement (OPM)	1961	45
Popular Movement for the Liberation of Angola	1956	46
Basque Fatherland and Freedom (ETA)	1959	47
Kayin National Union (KNU)	1959	47
Khmer Rouge	1951	47
Kurdish Democratic Party	1946	47
Chukakuha	1957	49
Syrian Social Nationalist Party	1931	58
Islami Chhatra Shibir (ICS)	1941	65
Irish Republican Army (IRA)	1922	84
Ku Klux Klan (KKK)	1866	140
Total observations	19	

Source: MIPT database, 2006.

Name and Life Span

NEGOTIATION

Reflecting the relationship of negotiation and life span discussed above, the longest-lived groups demonstrate a much higher rate of participation in negotiations, with nearly 50 percent of the groups engaging in them (table A.11). Of those who have engaged in negotiations, a much higher proportion (two-thirds) have also seen negotiations stabilize or resolve the conflict. This may be because negotiations are often a long and complicated process that may take a number of years to move toward stabilization or resolution.

ACHIEVEMENT

As shown in table A.12, the longest-lived groups have also seen higher rates of achievement, with four out of 18 groups (22.2 percent) experiencing some level of strategic achievement.

Table A.11
Long-Lived Group Engagement in Strategic Negotiations and Impact

Engaged in negotiations	*Observations*	*Percentage*	*Cumulative*
No	10.00	52.6%	52.6%
Yes[a]	9	47.4%	100.0%
Resolved conflict	3.00	33.3%	33.3%
Stable	3.00	33.3%	66.7%
Unstable	2.00	22.2%	88.9%
Failed	1.00	11.1%	100.0%
Total	19	100.0%	

Source: MIPT database, December 2006.

[a] Rows below demonstrate the breakdown of the impact of negotiations within the subset of the longest-lived organizations. *Resolved conflict*: fully resolved conflict. *Stable*: Negotiations have stabilized conflict, but no fundamental resolution has been reached. *Unstable*: Terms of negotiations disregarded or bypassed, but not openly or permanently abandoned. *Failed*: Negotiations fully broken down, or agreements openly abandoned.

Table A.12
Long-Lived Group Achievement of Strategic Aims

Level of Achievement	*Observations*	*Percentage*	*Cumulative*
None	14	77.8%	77.8%
Substantial[a]	1	5.6%	83.3%
Kurdish Democratic Party			
Limited[b]	3	16.7%	100.0%
Guatemalan Labor Party			
Guerrilla Army of the Poor			
Palestine Liberation Organization (PLO)			
Total	18	100.0%	

Source: MIPT database, December 2006.

[a] Achievement of a qualitatively substantial component of group's strategic aims.

[b] Minor compromise to elements of group's strategic aims.

Notes

INTRODUCTION

1. Alexis de Tocqueville, "Why Democratic Nations Naturally Desire Peace, and Democratic Armies, War," book 2, chap. 22, *Democracy in America*.

2. Exceptions include Martha Crenshaw, "How Terrorism Declines," *Terrorism and Political Violence* 3, no. 1 (1991): 69–87, and Jon B. Alterman, "How Terrorism Ends," Special Report No. 48, U.S. Institute of Peace, May 25, 1999, as well as a few comparative case studies such as Jeffrey Ian Ross and Ted Robert Gurr, "Why Terrorism Subsides: A Comparative Study of Canada and the United States," *Comparative Politics* 21, no. 4 (July 1989): 405–26; and Rogelio Alonso, "Pathways Out of Terrorism in Northern Ireland and the Basque Country: The Misrepresentation of the Irish Model," *Terrorism and Political Violence* 16, no. 4 (Winter 2004): 695–713.

3. A detailed discussion of the various forms and meanings of "al-Qaeda" is undertaken in chapter 7.

4. Authors who argue that this threat is fundamentally new include Daniel Benjamin and Steven Simon, *The Age of Sacred Terror: Radical Islam's War against America* (New York: Random House, 2003) and *The Next Attack: The Failure of the War on Terror and a Strategy for Getting It Right* (New York: Owl Books, 2006); Michael Scheuer, "The Plotters against America," *Washington Post Book World*, November 26, 2006, 4; Ian O. Lesser et al., *Countering the New Terrorism* (Santa Monica, Calif.: RAND, 1999); and L. Paul Bremer, "A New Strategy for the New Face of Terrorism" *National Interest*, November 2001, 23–30.

5. This position was brilliantly argued by Paul Johnson in "The Age of Terror," *New Statesman*, November 29, 1974, 763–64.

6. Caleb Carr, "Terrorism as Warfare: The Lessons of Military History," *World Policy Journal* 13, no. 4 (Winter 1996–97): 2.

7. Most attacks occurred in democratic states or targeted civilians of those states. For supporting data, see Audrey Kurth Cronin, "Rethinking Sovereignty: American Strategy in the Age of Terror," *Survival* 44, no. 2 (Summer 2002): 119–39.

8. Abu Daoud, quoted by Zeina Karam, "For Planner of Assault on Munich Olympics, No Regret Three Decades Later," Associated Press, February 23, 2006.

9. Robert A. Pape, *Dying to Win: The Strategic Logic of Suicide Terrorism* (New York: Random House, 2005); and Martha Crenshaw, "Coercive Diplomacy and the Response to Terrorism," chap. 8 of *The United States and Coercive Diplomacy*, ed. Robert J. Art and Patrick M. Cronin (Washington, D.C.: U.S. Institute of Peace Press, 2003), 305–357.

10. Internationally in the 1990s, the number averaged below 400 per year, whereas in the 1980s the number of incidents per year averaged well above 500. See Cronin, "Rethinking Sovereignty, 123–24 and 128.

11. Chris Quillen, "A Historical Analysis of Mass Casualty Bombers," *Studies in Conflict and Terrorism* 25, no. 5 (September–October 2002): 279–92; and Quillen, "Mass Casualty Bombings Chronology," *Studies in Conflict and Terrorism* 25, no. 5 (September–October 2002): 293–302. Quillen defines mass casualty attacks as those that kill more than 25 people.

12. On the difficulty of defining terrorism, see Omar Malik, *Enough of the Definition of Terrorism!* (London: Royal Institute of International Affairs, 2001); and Alex P. Schmid, *Political Terrorism: A Research Guide* (New Brunswick, N.J.: Transaction Books, 1984). Schmid spends more than 100 pages grappling with a definition only to conclude that none is universally accepted.

13. Saying that terrorism is a political act is not the same as arguing that the political ends toward which it is directed are negotiable. If violent acts do not have a political aim, then they are criminal acts, as will be discussed in chapter 6.

14. These concepts were introduced by E. V. Walter, *Terror and Resistance* (New York: Oxford University Press, 1969).

15. There are various lists of designated terrorist groups, including the U.S. Foreign Terrorist Organizations list and the European Union's designated terrorist list. All the groups on those lists are included in this book, but not all groups here are designated on such lists. See Audrey Kurth Cronin, *The "FTO List" and Congress: Sanctioning Designated Foreign Terrorist Organizations*, CRS Report for Congress, No. RL32120 (Washington, D.C.: Congressional Research Service, October 2003), available at http://www.fas.org/irp/crs/rl32120.pdf.

16. See Alexander L. George and Andrew Bennett, *Case Studies and Theory Development in the Social Sciences* (Cambridge: MIT Press, 2005), esp. chap. 1, "Case Study and Theory Development," 3–36.

17. Ibid.

18. The MIPT database is a merging of information from the RAND Terrorism Chronology (1968–97), which covers international terrorist incidents, the RAND-MIPT Terrorism Incident database (1998–present), which covers both domestic and international terrorist incidents; and the Terrorism Indictment Database (from 1988). RAND compiled the incident data, and the group profiles were written by a consulting firm, DFI international (which merged with Detica in 2007 to become DeticaDFI). The database is not perfect (see appendix); but it has been the best resource publicly available. As this book goes to press, MIPT has incorporated its database into the START program at the University of Maryland (www.start.umd.edu), apparently for funding reasons.

CHAPTER ONE: DECAPITATION

1. James Macgregor Burns, *Leadership* (New York: Harper Collins, 1982), 237. Burns explains the core tenets of the leadership philosophy of Mao Tse-tung in these terms. The statement is not actually a direct quote but a famous summation by Burns of leadership concepts from Mao's "Little Red Book," *Quotations from Chairman Mao Tse-Tung* (New York: Bantam Books, 1967).

2. In some notable cases, such as the Red Army Faction's Andreas Baader and the Red Brigades' Renato Curcio, the leaders were captured early on but the group

endured. Decapitation does not *always* lead to the near-term end of a group. The goal here is to determine the conditions under which it has done so.

3. This is not to imply that counterterrorist forces always control this outcome. Sometimes leaders die in combat. For the purposes of this discussion, they are included here as killings.

4. A statistical analysis on decapitation across groups is attempted by Aaron Mannes, "Testing the Snake Head Strategy: Does Killing or Capturing Its Leaders Reduce a Terrorist Group's Activity?" *Journal of International Policy Solutions* 9, no. 40 (Spring 2008): 40–49. Admitting that his results are statistically insignificant, Mannes concludes that a decapitation strategy has little effect on the reduction of terrorist activity, except in the case of Islamist groups, where it may actually increase the number of terrorist attack fatalities.

5. See, for example, "Ba'asyir Release: Implications for Islamist Militancy in Indonesia," IDSS Commentaries, June 13, 2006, accessed at www.idss.edu.sg, July 25, 2006. They can also die in prison: Sam Melville of the leftist New York Collective (linked to the Weather Underground) was sentenced to prison and died in the 1971 Attica prison uprising, thereby becoming one of the New Left's most beloved martyrs.

6. See Jeremy Varon, *Bringing the War Home: The Weather Underground, the Red Army Faction, and Revolutionary Violence in the Sixties and Seventies* (Berkeley and Los Angeles: University of California Press, 2004). This group transitioned to a second generation whose purpose was retribution and the release of its leaders from jail. See chapter 4.

7. MIPT database, http://www.tkb.org/Incident.jsp?incID=1057, accessed on January 15, 2007. The Red Army Faction is also known as the Baader-Meinhof group.

8. Simon Reeve, *One Day in September: The Story of the 1972 Munich Olympics Massacre, a Government Cover-up, and a Covert Revenge Mission* (London: Faber, 2000), 178.

9. Brian Michael Jenkins, "Should Our Arsenal against Terrorism Include Assassination?" RAND Paper No. P-7303, January 1987, 4–5.

10. Ibid., and MIPT Terrorism database. Abdallah was a member of the Lebanese Armed Revolutionary Faction.

11. This according to the Peruvian Truth and Reconciliation Commission. An unknown proportion of these victims suffered at the hands of the military. Comision de la Verdad y Reconciliacion Peru, *Informe Final*, vol. 1, part 1: *El proceso, los hechos, las victimas* (Lima: Navarrete, 2003).

12. An excellent overview is David Scott Palmer, "'Terror in the Name of Mao': Revolution and Response in Peru," in *Democracy and Counterterrorism: Lessons from the Past*, ed. Robert J. Art and Louise Richardson (Washington, D.C.: U.S. Institute of Peace Press, 2007), 195–220.

13. Gustavo Gorriti, "The War of the Philosopher-King," *New Republic*, June 18, 1990, 15–22; and Gorriti, *The Shining Path: A History of the Millenarian War in Peru* (Chapel Hill: University of North Carolina Press, 1999).

14. Guzmán's 17 years spent laying the groundwork for Sendero was unusually long. According to Martha Crenshaw the average is two years. Crenshaw, "Theories of Terrorism: Instrumental and Organization Approaches," in *Inside*

Terrorist Organizations, ed. Dave C. Rapoport, 2nd ed. (London: Frank Cass, 2001), 13–31; and Palmer, "Name of Mao," 198.

15. David Scott Palmer, "Conclusion: The View from the Windows," in *Shining Path of Peru*, ed. Palmer, 2nd. ed. (New York: St. Martin's Press, 1994), 265–66.

16. See, for example, Gabriela Tarazona-Sevillano with John B. Reuter, *Sendero Luminoso and the Threat of Narcoterrorism* (Washington, D.C.: Center for Strategic and International Studies, 1990), 23. Others disagreed. Palmer in *Shining Path of Peru* correctly predicts the effects of Guzmán's capture.

17. Gordon McCormick, *The Shining Path and the Future of Peru* (Santa Monica, Calif.: RAND, March 1990), 74 and figure 6, p. 68.

18. Gustavo Gorriti, "What Happens When the Queen Bee Falls?" *IPI Report* 41, no. 10 (October 1991): 3, 6.

19. Guzmán was captured through old-fashioned police work. He had psoriasis, a chronic skin condition requiring medication, and was traced through prescription records. See Charles Lane, "Superman Meets Shining Path: Story of a CIA Success," *Washington Post*, December 7, 2000.

20. Palmer, "Conclusion," 261. In early 1993, supporters were also offered an amnesty under a "repentance law," in effect until November 1994.

21. Duran was captured in July 1999, apparently marking the demise of the group. Following attacks in 2002–3, some feared the group was resurging. Preceding President Bush's visit in March 2002, a car bomb exploded near the U.S. Embassy in Lima, killing nine people and wounding 30. See Audrey Kurth Cronin, Huda Aden, Adam Frost, and Benjamin Jones, *Foreign Terrorist Organizations*, CRS Report for Congress, No. RL32223, February 6, 2004, 103; accessible at http://www.fas.org/irp/crs/RL32223.pdf. A resurgence (or reinvention) of SL remains possible but unlikely.

22. See, for example, William F. Buckley, "Execute Guzman," *National Review*, November 2, 1992, 70–71.

23. See, for example, Monte Hayes, "Shining Path on the Rise Again," Associated Press, May 30, 2008.

24. This terminology gradually changed following the collapse of the Soviet Union.

25. Roger Cohen, "Arrest Uniting Europe's Kurds in Indignation," *New York Times*, February 19, 1999.

26. Öcalan personally ordered the targeting of civilians, notably including teachers, and the destruction of 137 schools. Chris Kutschera, "Mad Dreams of Independence: The Kurds of Turkey and the PKK," *Middle East Report*, No. 189, The Kurdish Experience, July–August 1994, 12–15.

27. "U.S. Welcomes Ocalan Capture," Agence France-Presse, February 16, 1999. Öcalan was apparently being harbored in the Greek Embassy in Nairobi. The role of Greek diplomats led to the resignation of three senior ministers.

28. U.S. Department of State, *Patterns of Global Terrorism*, 43, http://www.terrorisminfo.mipt.org/pdf/2000pogt.pdf, accessed on January 12, 2007.

29. See James Brandon, "Mount Qandil: A Safe Haven for Kurdish Militants—Part 1," *Terrorism Monitor* (Jamestown Foundation) 4, no. 17 (September 8, 2006), accessed at http://www.jamestown.org on September 20, 2006.

30. Cronin et al., *Foreign Terrorist Organizations*, 88–89; and U.S. Department of State, *Patterns of Global Terrorism 2003*, DoS Publication 11124, Office of the Coordinator for Counterterrorism (Washington, D.C.: U.S. Government Printing Office, April 2004), 133. Attempts have included a 1,200 pound fertilizer bomb, targeted at a police station in Londonderry in June 2003, which was found and defused.

31. Dissident republicans are also suspected of car bombs in London and Birmingham in August and November 2001, each of which caused injuries but no fatalities.

32. Government of Japan, Public Security Intelligence Agency, "Review and Prospect of Internal and External Situations," January 2006, 51–54; and U.S. Department of State, *Country Reports on Terrorism, 2005*, U.S. Department of State Publications 11324, April 2006, 190–91. Although it is a cult, the group also engaged in very high profile terrorist attacks, which is why Aum is included here. The group has since split into factions. One faction unsuccessfully planned to set off bombs near the Imperial Palace in Tokyo, free Asahara, and smuggle him to Russia.

33. On these questions, see Elizabeth B. Bazan, *Assassination Ban and E.O. 12333: A Brief Summary*, CRS Report for Congress, No. RS21037, January 4, 2002, accessible at http://www.fas.org/irp/crs/RS21037.pdf.

34. For example, the United States ambushed and shot down a plane carrying Admiral Yamamoto in World War II, although the decision to do so went all the way to President Franklin Roosevelt.

35. Michael L. Gross, "Fighting by Other Means in the Mideast: A Critical Analysis of Israel's Assassination Policy," *Political Studies* 51 (2003): 350–68.

36. Former Indian prime minister Rajiv Gandhi (May 21, 1991) and Sri Lankan president Ranasinghe Premadasa (May 1, 1993) were killed by LTTE suicide attacks, and Sri Lankan president Chandrika Kumaratunga lost an eye to a suicide attack that also killed 26 people (December 1999).

37. On targeting and operation of the units, see Thomas Marks, *Maoist Insurgency since Vietnam* (London: Frank Cass, 1996), 166–69.

38. Jenkins, "Arsenal against Terrorism," 1–2.

39. Jenkins, "Arsenal against Terrorism," 8.

40. This may be for a number of reasons. Some conclude that Palestinians respond only when organizations are threatened. Or it could be that when civilians are killed, terrorist organizations reduce activities to allow the media to focus on the tragedy. Edward H. Kaplan, Alex Mintz, Shaul Mishal, and Claudio Samban, "What Happened to Suicide Bombings in Israel?" *Studies in Conflict and Terrorism* 28, no. 3 (May–June 2005): 232.

41. Israeli assassinated Fathi Shqaqi, leader of the Palestinian Islamic Jihad in 1995, resulting in reduced activity immediately thereafter, then heightened organizational effectiveness when he was replaced by Ramadan Abdullah Shallah. See Mannes, "Snake Head Strategy"; and Daniel Byman, "Do Targeted Killings Work?" *Foreign Affairs* 85, no. 2 (March–April 2006): 103.

42. Also killed was Janjalani's deputy, Edwin Angeles. Alfredo L. Filler, "The Abu Sayyaf Group: A Growing Menace to Civil Society," *Terrorism and Political Violence* 14, no. 4 (Winter 2002): 132.

43. The elder Jajalani reportedly had a close relationship with bin Laden's brother-in-law, Mahamed Jamal Khalifa, receiving training and funding through Khalifa's network of charities.

44. Steven Rogers, "Beyond the Abu Sayyaf: The Lessons of Failure in the Philippines," *Foreign Affairs* 83, no.1 (January–February 2004): 17.

45. For more on this case, particularly its translation to a criminal organization, see chapter 6.

46. U.S. Department of State, *Country Reports on Terrorism, 2005*, 185, and 252–53. See also Alastair McIndoe, "Tip-off on Terrorist: Two Get $800,000," *Straits Times*, June 1, 2006, 15.

47. IISS Armed Conflict Database, "Abu Sayyaf Group: Latest Developments," January–March 2006.

48. C. S. Kuppuswamy, "Abu Sayyaf: The Cause for the Return of U.S. Troops to Philippines?" South Asia Analysis Group, No. 417 (February 2002), accessed at http://www.saag.org/papers5/paper417.html on April 14, 2007.

49. For more in-depth analysis, see Audrey Kurth Cronin, "Russia and Chechnya," chap. 12 in Art and Richardson, *Democracy and Counterterrorism*, 383–424.

50. The date of Khattab's death is not agreed on. Jim Nichol reports that he was killed during a clandestine Russian operation using biological toxins in March 2002. See *Russia's Chechnya Conflict: An Update*, CRS Report for Congress, No. RL31620, April 16, 2003, 20.

51. Peter Baker, "Russia Moving to Eliminate Chechen Rebel Leaders; Separatists Defiant after Series of Setbacks," *Washington Post*, April 20, 2004, A13.

52. "Chechen Leader Maskhadov Killed," BBC News, March 8, 2005, http://news.bbc.co.uk/2/hi/europe/4330039.

53. Ariel Cohen, "After Maskhadov: Islamist Terrorism Threatens North Caucasus and Russia," Backgrounder, Heritage Foundation, No. 1838, April 1, 2005, at www.heritage.org/research/russiaandeurasie/bg1838.cfm. The media described Basayev as "Putin's Osama bin laden."

54. Steven Lee Myers, "Chechnya Bomb Kills President, a Blow to Putin," *New York Times*, May 10, 2004, 1; and Susan B. Glasser and Peter Baker, "Chechen President Killed in Bomb Blast," *Washington Post*, May 10, 2004, 1.

55. Doku Umarov also appeared in the video, posted on a rebel website. Steven Lee Myers, "Russian Troops Kill Leader of Chechen Separatists," *New York Times*, June 18, 2006.

56. Andrew McGregor, "Russia Threatens Hit-Squads after Murder of Its Diplomats in Iraq," *Terrorism Monitor* (Jamestown Foundation) 4, no. 14 (July 13, 2006): 6–8.

57. "Assassination" is difficult to define. An interpretation under customary international law is "the selected killing of an individual enemy by treacherous means." That is how the word is used here. See Jami Melissa Jackson, "The Legality of Assassination of Independent Terrorist Leaders: An Examination of National and International Implications," *North Carolina Journal of International Law and Commercial Regulation* 24 (1999): 687. On defining the term, see Daniel B. Pickard, "Legalizing Assassination? Terrorism, the Central Intelligence

Agency, and International Law," *Georgia Journal of International and Comparative Law* 30, no. 1 (2001): 8–10.

58. Jamal Al-Gashey, Adnan Al-Gashey, and Mohammed Safady flew to Libya, where they were greeted as heroes. Reeve, *One Day in September*, 155–59.

59. Innocent civilians were also killed and injured in the operations, notably Ahmed Bouchiki, a Moroccan waiter mistaken for a Black September leader.

60. Two analysts studied the reaction of the Tel Aviv Stock Exchange to assassinations and found that a positive response depended on two factors: the rank of the operative killed (with low-ranking members causing no reaction and high-ranking members a favorable reaction); and wing membership (with military leaders engendering a positive response and political leaders a negative response.) Asaf Zussman and Noam Zussman, "Assassinations: Evaluating the Effectiveness of a Counterterrorism Policy Using Stock Market Data," *Journal of Economic Perspectives* 20, no. 2 (2006): 193–206; and Byman, "Do Targeted Killings Work?" 95–111.

61. For example, the Israelis reportedly killed Wadi Haddad, leader of the PFLP-EO, by giving him a poisoned box of chocolates. The result was a long hiatus in operations carried out by his group, but also arguably the establishment of the breakaway groups May 15 Organization and the PFLP-SC.

62. There is dispute over when the policy of targeting began. Although military sources denied that there was an assassination policy during the first intifada, B'tselem claims that roughly 90 Palestinians were killed in secret operations where they might have been captured. See B'Tselem, *Special Units Activities in the Occupied Territories*, May 1992.

63. According to B'Tselem, some 1,378 Palestinians living in the occupied territories were killed by Israeli security forces in the first intifada, from December 9, 1987, to September 13, 1993. During the second ("al-Aqsa") intifada, the comparable number was 3,441. http://www.btselem.org/english/statistics/first_intifada_tables.asp, accessed December 6, 2008.

64. Kaplan et al., "Suicide Bombings in Israel," 232.

65. The number of Palestinians killed through targeted killings in the second intifada is tallied at http://www.btselem.org/english/Statistics/Casualties_Data.asp?Category=19.

66. Amos Guiora, "Targeted Killing as Active Self-Defense," *Case Western Reserve Journal of International Law* 36, nos. 2–3 (2004): 319–35.

67. For more on this issue see David Kretzmer, "Targeted Killing of Suspected Terrorists: Extra-judicial Executions or Legitimate Means of Defence?" *European Journal of International Law* 16, no. 2 (2005): 171–212; Gross, "Fighting by Other Means"; and the lengthy exchanges between Steven R. David and Yael Stein in *Ethics and International Affairs* 17, no. 3 (2003): 111–40. See also Molly Moore, "Israel's Lethal Weapon of Choice: Assassinations of Militants Increase, Citizens' Uneasiness Grows," *Washington Post*, June 29, 2004, A1, A20.

68. According to one anonymous Israeli official, "The liquidation of wanted persons is proving itself useful. . . . This activity paralyzes and frightens entire villages and as a result, there are areas where people are afraid to carry out hostile action." Eldar Akiva, "Liquidation Sale for the Peace Process," *Ha'aretz*, January 4,

2001, cited in Michael L. Gross, "Killing Civilians Intentionally: Double Effect, Reprisal, and Necessity in the Middle East," *Political Science Quarterly* 120, no. 4 (2005–6): 564.

69. Kaplan et al., "Suicide Bombings in Israel," 233–34.

70. Mannes, "Snake Head Strategy."

71. Yael Stein, "By Any Name Illegal and Immoral: Response to Israel's Policy of Targeted Killing," *Ethics and International Affairs* 17, no. 3 (2003): 127–37.

72. Gross, "Fighting by Other Means." In Gross's words: "In this morally symmetrical conflict, confined to a tiny geographical area that must eventually accommodate two peoples, there is little room for assassination, the damage it inflicts, and the outrage it provokes" (365).

73. Mohammed M. Hafez and Joseph M. Hatfield, "Do Targeted Assassinations Work? A Multivariate Analysis of Israel's Controversial Tactic during Al-Aqsa Uprising," *Studies in Conflict and Terrorism* 29, no. 4 (June 2006): 359–82.

74. Action Directe's four principal leaders, Nathalie Menigon, Jean-Marc Rouillan, Joelle Aubron, and Georges Cipriani, were arrested in Febuary 1987, followed shortly thereafter by Max Frerot, effectively putting an end to its activities. The Chilean group Manuel Rodriguez Patriotic Front Dissidents (FPMR-D) essentially ceased to exist following the arrest of key leaders in the 1990s. After a four-day siege of their compound in April 1985, eight leaders of the U.S. group The Covenant, the Sword and the Arm of the Lord were arrested and imprisoned, effectively ending the group. There are many other examples.

75. Che Guevara was captured and killed by the Bolivian army in October 1967. His death marked the end of a revolt that was already failing, Che subsequently became a legendary figure, inspirational to leftist and separatist groups in South America and elsewhere. Leila Ali Khaled of the PFLP carried the book *My Friend Che* with her when she hijacked TWA flight 840 in August 1969. The Weathermen organized massive protests over the second anniversary of Che Guevara's death, October 8–11, 1969. Harvey Kushner, *Encyclopedia of Terrorism* (Thousand Oaks, Calif.: Sage, 2003), 155–56, 372, and 406.

76. Sheikh Omar is leader of the Egyptian Al Gamma'a Islamiya (also closely tied with Egyptian Islamic Jihad) and known as "the Blind Sheikh." He is imprisoned for life in the United States, but has continued to call on his followers to engage in violence, especially against Jews. He was convicted for conspiracy in the 1993 World Trade Center bombing and plots to bomb the Holland and Lincoln Tunnels and the United Nations building, and to assassinate Senator Alfonse D'Amato and U.N. Secretary General Boutros Boutros-Ghali.

77. Hayes, "Shining Path."

CHAPTER TWO: NEGOTIATIONS

1. It was revealed a few weeks later, on November 29, that British government officials (though not ministers) were in negotiations with Sinn Féin and the IRA.

2. Paul Wilkinson argues that a firm maxim of refusing terrorist demands should be followed without exception. *Terrorism and the Liberal State*, 2nd ed. (London:

Macmillan, 1986), 301. The opposing case is put by Martin Hughes, "Terror and Negotiation," *Terrorism and Political Violence* 2, no. 1 (Spring 1990): 72–82.

3. This chapter does not deal with negotiations with states that sponsor terrorists. Some officials use the term *terrorist* where the violence is not targeted against civilians, so as to avoid negotiating with substate groups. Such abuse of the term is one reason why terrorism is both difficult to study and difficult to eliminate. The chapter also does not deal with talks that occur in the final moments of campaigns that are winding down primarily because of other factors.

4. A long list of states have made claims about never negotiating with terrorists and then been forced to make exceptions, including the Israeli government, well known for its no-negotiations policy during the 1970s. For a list of the exceptions made in hostage negotiations see Harvey E. Lapan and Todd Sandler, "To Bargain or Not to Bargain: That Is the Question," *American Economic Review* 78, no. 2 (May 1988): 16–21.

5. Charles King, *Ending Civil Wars*, Adelphi Paper No. 308 (Oxford: Oxford University Press for the International Institute for Strategic Studies, 1997), 66–67; Ann Hironaka, *Neverending Wars: The International Community, Weak States, and the Perpetuation of Civil War* (Cambridge: Harvard University Press, 2005), 78–79.

6. This chapter covers negotiations over a group's fundamental goals or strategy. It does not analyze talks to resolve events such as hostage takings and airline hijackings. See, for example, Richard L. Clutterbuck, *Kidnap, Hijack, and Extortion: The Response* (New York: St. Martin's Press, 1987), Brian M. Jenkins, "Talking to Terrorists," RAND Paper No. P-6750, 1982; Abraham H. Miller, *Terrorism and Hostage Negotiations* (Boulder, Colo.: Westview Press, 1980); and Todd Sandler and John L. Scott, "Terrorist Success in Hostage-Taking Incidents: An Empirical Study," *Journal of Conflict Resolution* 31, no. 1 (March 1987), 35–53.

7. The U.S. government asked the *Washington Post* and the *New York Times* to publish the Unabomber's 35,000-word manifesto. The publication led to the arrest and conviction of Theodore Kaczynski when Kaczynski's brother recognized his ideas and language and contacted the FBI. His bombing campaign had included 16 attacks in 17 years, killing three people and injuring 23. David Tucker, *Skirimishes at the Edge of Empire: The United States and International Terrorism* (Westport, Conn.: Praeger, 1997), 78–79.

8. And example is Margaret Thatcher's and John Major's public refusal to talk to terrorists, with later revelations of their governments' indirect contacts with Irish republicans in the 1980s. Of course in hindsight it is a good thing that the Major government did talk; but best of all would have been not to comment publicly on the matter at all. See Brendan O'Leary, "The Conservative Stewardship of Northern Ireland, 1979–97: Sound-Bottomed Contradictions or Slow Learning?" *Political Studies* 45 (1997): 671–73.

9. The powerful Association of Victims of Terrorism has been instrumental in the ETA case, for example. See Gorka Espiau Idoiaga, "The Basque Conflict: New Ideas and Prospects for Peace," Special Report No. 161, U.S. Institute of Peace, April 2006, available at www.usip.org.

10. Adam Roberts, "The 'War on Terror' in Historical Perspective," *Survival* 47, no. 2 (Summer 2005): 109. See also John Mueller, "Six Rather Unusual Propositions about Terrorism," and "Response," *Terrorism and Political Violence* 17, no. 4 (2005): 526.

11. Crenshaw, "How Terrorism Declines," 79; and Tucker, *Skirmishes*, 74.

12. For a broader discussion of distinctions between terrorism, insurgency, civil war, and conventional war, see chapter 6.

13. Compare the arguments of King in *Ending Civil Wars*, 72–82.

14. "The cause is not the cause." Jerrold M. Post, "Terrorist Psycho-Logic: Terrorist Behavior as a Product of Psychological Forces," in *Origins of Terrorism: Psychologies, Ideologies, Theologies, States of Mind*, ed. Walter Reich (Cambridge: Cambridge University Press, 1990), 35. See also Alexander L. George, foreword to *Leaders and Their Followers in a Dangerous World*, ed. Jerrold M. Post (Ithaca, N.Y.: Cornell University Press, 2004).

15. As explained in the introduction, the core characteristics were a fundamentally politically nature, the symbolic use of violence, purposeful targeting of the innocent, carried out by nonstate actors. We were deliberately conservative in calling a group's activity "terrorism" for the purposes of this analysis, so as to avoid skewing the data; however, this may have resulted in elongation of the average life-span of groups.

16. On the strengths and weaknesses of the MIPT database, see the appendix. After weeding out the entries in the database for groups that only had one attack, or only hit economic targets like pipelines and empty banks, we were able to reduce the size of the pool down to the activities and experiences of only those groups that have indisputably engaged in targeted violence against civilians—and thus meet our four fundamental characteristics of terrorism. The pool of groups that indisputably met each of these characteristics numbered 457.

17. This is not the same as arguing that all decolonization struggles were terrorist campaigns. Many that included terrorist tactics, notably those in Indochina, Algeria, and Kenya, became insurgencies or even conventional wars. See chapter 6.

18. The strength of the government is another factor to be considered. Governments may only have been strong enough to engage after groups were beyond a certain age.

19. Peter Neumann is insightful on this point. See "Negotiating with Terrorists," *Foreign Affairs* 86, no. 1 (January–February 2007): 128–38.

20. "Failed" refers to formal negotiations with conditions or accords that were clearly and substantially broken by main groups (not just breakaway elements), substantial negotiations that one party permanently pulled out of, or talks that broke down and were terminated. Likewise, "success" did not necessarily imply the immediate and complete cessation of violence. As will be discussed below, sometimes even if negotiations neutralize or reorient a group, there are violent splinter groups.

21. For example, both the declaration following the 1988 meeting of the Palestine National Council and the 1989 African National Congress Harare declaration were unilateral statements indicating that the organization's goals were no longer maximal. Daniel Lieberfeld, "Post-handshake Politics: Israel/Palestine and South Africa Compared," *Middle East Policy* 6, no. 3 (February 1999): 133.

22. There were two periods called the Troubles in Ireland in the twentieth century. The first was in association with the Irish War of Independence (also called the Anglo-Irish War) and the subsequent Irish Civil War, from 1919 to 1923. This analysis treats only the second, from the 1960s to the 1990s.

23. The "Official IRA" ended its armed campaign in June 1972, but the newer Provisional IRA (PIRA) continued. A key point of tension between the Old IRA and the PIRA was the transition from the failed border campaign to a new urban strategy, that carried with it greater risk of sectarian violence.

24. According to the University of Ulster CAIN (Conflict Archive on the Internet) website, during this period 1,981 people were detained; 1,874 were Catholic/Republican, while 107 were Protestant/Loyalist. See http://cain.ulst.ac.uk/events/intern/sum.htm, accessed on January 3, 2007.

25. Marie-Therese Fay, Mike Morrissey, and Marie Smyth, *Northern Ireland's Troubles: The Human Costs* (London: Pluto Press in association with the Cost of the Trouble Study, 1999), 136.

26. Support for the PIRA was particularly strong in the working-class Catholic areas of Belfast, Derry, and North and West Belfast. Rural areas with a strong republican tradition also provided support, including South Armagh, East Tyrone, and south county Londonderry.

27. http://cain.ulst.ac.uk/sutton/tables/Organisation_Responsible.html, viewed on January 5, 2007.

28. John Darby, "Northern Ireland: The Background to the Peace Process," available at CAIN Web Service, University of Ulster, http://cain.ulst.ac.uk/events/peace/darby03.htm, last accessed on January 2, 2007. See also Fay, Morrissey, and Smyth, *Northern Ireland's Troubles*; and Marie Smyth, "Lost Lives: Victims and the Construction of 'Victimhood' in Northern Ireland," chapter 1 of *A Farewell to Arms?* ed. Michael Cox, Adrian Guelke, and Fiona Stephen, 2nd ed. (Manchester: Manchester University Press, 2006), especially the chart on p. 9.

29. Darby, "Northern Ireland." See also John Horgan, *The Psychology of Terrorism* (London: Routledge, 2005), esp. 151; and Louise Richardson, *What Terrorists Want* (London: John Murray, 2006), 258–59.

30. For casualty figures see David McKittrick, Seamus Kelters, Brian Feeney, and Chris Thornton, *Lost Lives: The Stories of the Men, Women, and Children Who Died as a Result of the Northern Ireland Troubles* (Edinburgh: Mainstream Press, 2001).

31. On the links between unionists and South African arms, see Richard Dowden, "Guns, Missiles, Blueprints and the Ulster Connection," *The Independent*, July 15, 1992.

32. O'Leary, "Conservative Stewardship," 667–70. See also Margaret Thatcher, *The Downing Street Years* (London: HarperCollins, 1995), 406–7.

33. This chronology of the peace process is selective. A comprehensive description is at http://cain.ulst.ac.uk/events/peace/pp8893.htm, accessed on January 3, 2007.

34. Ibid. Also see "Going to the Edge," in Brian Rowan, *Behind the Lines: The Story of the IRA and Loyalist Ceasefires* (Belfast: Blackstaff Press, 1995).

35. Secret meetings between the British government and Sinn Féin were revealed in November 1993. See Anthony Bevins, Eamonn Malliem, and Mary

Holland, "Major's Secret Links with IRA Leadership Revealed," *The Observer*, November 28, 1993.

36. O'Leary, "Conservative Stewardship," 668–69. See also Brendan O'Brien, *The Long War: The IRA and Sinn Féin from Armed Struggle to Peace Talks* (Dublin: O'Brien Press, 1995) on the evolution of republican strategy.

37. Also called the Downing Street Declaration, issued on December 15, 1993. The full text is at http://cain.ulst.ac.uk/events/peace/docs/dsd151293.htm, accessed on January 3, 2007.

38. McKittrick et al., *Lost Lives*, 1307.

39. http://news.bbc.co.uk/1/hi/events/northern_ireland/latest_news/166668.stm, accessed January 5, 2007.

40. In response to the killing of Catholics, the IRA carried out the Shankill Road bombing in October 1993, targeting the UDA leadership but instead slaughtering nine Protestant civilians. The UDA retaliated with the Greysteel massacre, in which Johnny Adair's Loyalist Freedom Fighters murdered eight people (including two Protestants) in a bar in a Catholic area of Londonderry. Shortly thereafter the INLA murdered two UDF members at Shankill Road, and a few days after that the UVF shot six civilians in a Loughinisland pub. The PIRA killed four more senior loyalists, three from the UDA and one from the UVF. See http://cain.ulst.ac.uk/sutton/chron/1993.html, accessed on January 5, 2007.

41. http://news.bbc.co.uk/onthisday/hi/dates/stories/february/10/newsid_2539000/2539265.stm, accessed on January 5, 2007.

42. Gerry Adams finally met with British prime minister Tony Blair at Downing Street on January 18, 1998.

43. Intelligence operatives in the British Army's Force Research Unit allegedly provided information on PIRA operatives to unionist paramilitaries who then assassinated them. One operative, Brian Nelson, became the UDA's intelligence chief for the whole of the province. See Peter Taylor, "Dark Side of the War," BBC News, May 31, 2000, accessed at BBCNews.com on January 11, 2007. Matthew Teague analyzes the infiltration in "Double Blind," *Atlantic Monthly*, April 2006.

44. A series of inquiries led by the commissioner of the Metropolitan Police, John Stevens, concluded that there had been collusion leading to the murder of republicans. See "Army 'Colluded' with Loyalist Killers: Rogue Elements within the Police and Army in Northern Ireland Helped Loyalist Paramilitaries to Murder Catholics in the Late 1980s, the UK's Most Senior Police Officer Has Said," BBC News, April 17, 2003, accessed at BBCNews.com on January 11, 2007; and "RUC 'Colluded with Loyalist Killers,'" *The Times* (London), January 22, 2007, 12.

45. "Top IRA Informer Named: A Spy Who Penetrated the IRA Leadership on Behalf of the British Military Has Been Named as Freddie Scappaticci by Security Sources," BBC News, May 11, 2003, accessed at BBCNews.com on January 11, 2007. An autobiography about a British agent working for Special Branch in the PIRA is Martin McGartland, *Fifty Dead Men Walking* (London: Blake, 1997).

46. http://news.bbc.co.uk/onthisday/hi/dates/stories/june/15/newsid_2527000/2527009.stm, accessed on January 5, 2007.

47. Subsequent attacks are detailed at http://cain.ulst.ac.uk/events/peace/pp9398.htm, accessed on January 3, 2007.

48. Quoted in McKittrick et al., *Lost Lives*, 1402.

49. Also known as the Belfast Agreement or, rarely, the Stormont Agreement. The main provisions are a devolved, power-sharing government in Northern Ireland and cross-border agencies jointly run by the Northern Ireland Assembly and the Irish parliament. The United Kingdom retains sovereignty over the territory, unless a majority of the inhabitants vote to alter the arrangement. Notably the failed Sunningdale Agreement of December 1973 had the same basic contours. See Michael Mansergh, "The Background to the Irish Peace Process," in Guelke, Cox, and Stephen, *Farewell to Arms*. The full text is at http://cain.ulst.ac.uk/events/peace/docs/agreement.htm, accessed on January 5, 2007.

50. An excellent analysis of the behavioral transition during the peace process is John Darby and Roger MacGinty, eds., *The Management of Peace Processes* (Basingstoke: Macmillan, 2000).

51. The Omagh bombing claimed the largest number of lives in a single bombing since the start of the Troubles (29 killed, 220 injured). Sectarian violence was particularly strong in North Belfast during summer 2001, and many feared that the unionist cease-fire, in place since at least 1994, was unraveling.

52. Michael McDowell, Irish justice minister, speaking in the Dáil, June 24, 2005. http://news.bbc.co.uk/1/hi/northern_ireland/4617943.stm, accessed on January 5, 2007.

53. The Sinn Féin party has 24 members of the Northern Ireland Assembly out of 108, five Westminster MPs out of the 18 from Northern Ireland, and five Republic of Ireland representatives out of 166. Election results available at http://cain.ulst.ac.uk/issues/politics/election/ra1998.htm and http://cain.ulst.ac.uk/issues/politics/election/ra2003.htm, accessed on January 5, 2007. Support for Sinn Féin increased substantially after the Good Friday Agreement.

54. John Darby, "A Truce Rather Than a Treaty? The Effect of Violence on the Irish Peace Process," chap. 14 of Guelke, Cox, and Stephen, *Farewell to Arms*, 219–21.

55. Jane's Intelligence Review reports that in 2005 the PIRA decommissioned 1,000 rifles, three tonnes of Semtex, 30 heavy machine guns, and over 100 grenades. MI5 claims that not all of this matériel has been destroyed. See http://news.bbc.co.uk/1/hi/northern_ireland/4284048.stm, accessed on January 5, 2007. According to the Independent Monitoring Commission's eighth report (published February 2006), elements of the PIRA continue to be involved in organized criminal activity.

56. Support for local police continues to be a sticking point between Sinn Féin and the Democratic Unionist Party. See "'Positive' Replies to Blair Views," BBC News, January 4, 2007, at http://news.bbc.co.uk/1/hi/northern_ireland/6230971.stm, accessed on January 10, 2007; and Owen Bowcott, "Blair Returns Home to Warn Sinn Féin over Devolution," *Guardian Unlimited*, January 4, 2007, at http://politics.guardian.co.uk/northernirelandassembly/story/0,,1982943,00.html, accessed on January 10, 2007.

57. Adrian Guelke, Michael Cox, and Fiona Stephen, "Conclusion: Peace beyond the Good Friday Agreement?" in *A Farewell to Arms*, 450.

58. Darby, "Truce Rather Than Treaty?" 223.

59. Roger MacGinty, "Irish Republicanism and the Peace Process: From Revolution to Reform," in Guelke, Cox, and Stephen, *A Farewell to Arms*, 126.

60. Adrian Guelke, "Political Comparisons: From Johannesburg to Jerusalem," in Guelke, Cox, and Stephen, *A Farewell to Arms*, 367–74.

61. For more elaboration, see Audrey Kurth Cronin, "Behind the Curve: Globalization and International Terrorism," *International Security*, 27, no. 3 (Winter 2002–3), 30–58; and David Rapoport, "The Four Waves of Modern Terrorism," chap. 2 of *Attacking Terrorism: Elements of a Grand Strategy*, ed. Audrey Kurth Cronin and James M. Ludes (Washington, D.C.: Georgetown University Press, 2004), 46–73.

62. Guelke, "Political Comparisons."

63. Francesco Letamendia and John Loughlin, "Learning from Other Places: Northern Ireland, the Basque Country and Corsica," in Guelke, Cox, and Stephen, *A Farewell to Arms*, 378.

64. *Intifada*, usually translated as "uprising," is actually closer to the English phrase "shaking off," as in a dog shaking off a flea. Benny Morris, *Righteous Victims: A History of the Zionist-Arab Conflict, 1881–2001* (New York: Alfred A. Knopf, 1999), 561.

65. Fatalities in the first intifada are listed by the human rights organization B'Tselem at http://www.btselem.org/english/Statistics/First_Intifada_Tables.asp.

66. Aryeh Shalev, *The Intifada: Causes and Effects* (Oxford: Westview Press, 1999), 125. See also Morris, *Righteous Victims*, 591.

67. T. G. Fraser, *The Arab-Israeli Conflict*, 2nd ed. (Basingstoke: Palgrave Macmillan, 2004), 133.

68. Fraser, *The Arab-Israeli Conflict*, 32.

69. Mark A. Tessler, *A History of the Israeli-Palestinian Conflict* (Bloomington: Indiana University Press, 1994), 747. The killing of collaborators began on a small scale in 1989, but increased after the Gulf War. Tessler argues that such killings resulted less from political differences than from personal rivalries and old scores.

70. Daniel Lieberfeld, *Talking with the Enemy: Negotiation and Threat Perception in South Africa and Israel/Palestine* (Westport, Conn.: Praeger, 1999), 62.

71. According to www.btselem.org, casualties in the first intifada (November 1987 to September 1993) included 1,162 Palestinians (241 of whom were children, though some in an active military role). In the first 13 months, 332 Palestinians and 12 Israelis were killed.

72. Asked, "So your starting point for Oslo was the weakness of Mr Arafat?" Shimon Peres replied, "Yes, the weakness of Arafat and the danger that he would disappear. I mean, his disappearance was in my opinion a greater danger than his existence." Shimon Peres and Robert Littell, *For the Future of Israel* (Baltimore: Johns Hopkins University Press, 1998), 75. Ironically, Israel had sought to undermine the PLO in the 1980s by covertly supporting radical religious groups.

73. The case study does not include the Camp David accords signed in September 1978 between Israel and Egypt, brokered by the United States, as this agreement occurred between states.

74. The Knesset (website of the Israeli government), "The Main Events and Issues During the Thirteenth Knesset," accessed at http://www.knesset.gov.il/history/eng/eng_hist13.htm. on December 29, 2008.

75. The Palestinian Islamic Jihad was not technically a "splinter" group, although it did vigorously oppose the peace process engaged in by the PLO. It is a

violent offshoot of the Muslim Brotherhood and was founded in Egypt in 1970. The leadership of the organization was exiled to the Gaza Strip following the assassination of Egyptian president Anwar Sadat. PIJ leader Fathi Shaqaqi was assassinated in Malta in 1995.

76. MIPT database http://www.tkb.org/Group.jsp?groupID=82, accessed on January 25, 2007; see also John King, *Handshake in Washington: The Beginning of Middle East Peace?* (Reading, UK: Ithaca Press, 1994), 44–47.

77. On the Khudaybiyya armistice, see *al-Quds*, May 10, 1998: Arafat was asked if Oslo was a mistake: "No . . . Allah's messenger Muhammad accepted the al-Khudaybiyya peace treaty." On Jihad, see *Ha'aretz*, November 22, 1994: "The Palestinian people are maintaining their Jihad, but the process will continue until one of the Fatah youths or a Palestinian boy will raise the flag over the walls of Jerusalem." On the right of return, see *Ma'ariv*, September 7, 1995: "O Gaza, your sons are returning. O Jaffa, O Lod, O Haifa, O Jerusalem, you are returning" (all except Gaza are in Israel proper).

78. Three Palestinian suicide bombers attacked Israelis in 1994, killing 28 and injuring over 100. Four suicide attacks occurred in 1995, killing 40 and injuring over 128. Four attacks occurred in 1996, killing 57 and injuring over 213. In comparison, one suicide attack occurred in 1993, killing only the bomber. Anthony H. Cordesman, *The Israeli-Palestinian War: Escalating to Nowhere* (Westport, Conn.: Praeger Security International, 2005), 22–25. See also Mohammed Hafez, *Manufacturing Human Bombs: The Making of Palestinian Suicide Bombers* (Washington, D.C.: U.S. Institute of Peace, 2006).

79. Pape, *Dying to Win*, 66–73.

80. Morris, *Righteous Victims*, 596. For example, on March 20, 1995, a Hamas truck was found in southern Israel with 400 lbs of explosives on board. Six activists were arrested a few days later. On August 12, 1995, heavily armed infiltrators were apprehended while crossing the Jordanian border. MIPT Terrorism Knowledge Base, www.tkb.org, accessed on February 6, 2006. At this point, Islamic Jihad targeted soldiers as they were heading to or from leave; but Hamas did not distinguish between soldiers and civilians. Morris, *Righteous Victims*, 626.

81. Goldstein was an activist in Kach, an extremist Jewish religious movement. The Israeli government disbanded it; however, Yigal Amir, Itzhak Rabin's assassin, was also associated with Kach.

82. Carol Migdalovitz, *Israeli-Arab Negotiations: Background, Conflicts, and U.S. Policy*, CRS Report for Congress, No. RL 33530, updated December 12, 2006, 27. Full texts of all of the agreements in the Israeli-Palestinian peace process are available at http://www.state.gov/p/nea/rls/c9646.htm.

83. The level of support among the Israeli public for employing "illegal" (including violent) means of protest was very high during the period immediately preceding the Rabin assassination. This according to polls carried out by Ephraim Yaar and Tamar Hermann. See the Tami Steinmetz Center for Peace Research—Peace Index; available at http://www.tau.ac.il/peace/, accessed January 21, 2007.

84. "A Landslide for Arafat," January 21, 2006, CNN, http://www.cnn.com/WORLD/9601/palestine_elex/01-21/12am/index.html, accessed on February 6, 2006. See also Mark August, "Shifting Sands and Arafat's Popularity," *Tampa Tribune*, November 28, 1994, 4.

85. Andrew Kydd and Barbara Walter, "Sabotaging the Peace: The Politics of Extremist Violence," *International Organization* 56, no. 2 (Spring 2002): 263–96.

86. Dennis Ross, *The Missing Peace: The Inside Story of the Fight for Middle East Peace* (New York: Farrar, Straus and Giroux, 2004). Hamas's attacks begun in 1992, thus before the Oslo agreement was signed. The attacks harmed the peace process, not least because the Syrians refused to condemn them. Ross said to the Syrian negotiator, "This is bullshit. How do you expect the Israeli public to believe they have partners for peace when something as human as expressing outrage or even sadness over the killing of innocents is not possible?" (244).

87. Following his defeat, Peres said "I believe we lost it [the election] basically because of the attacks by the Hamas." Anat Cygielman, "Peres Blames Himself for Not Pressing Arafat," *Ha'Aretz*, January 5, 1999. See also Lieberfeld, "Post-handshake Politics," 140. Such claims must be treated with care. To argue that one variable drives either Palestinian or Israeli actions is to oversimplify overlapping and intertwined motivations at the expense of a complex reality. See Kydd and Walter, "Sabotaging the Peace," 285 and n. 32.

88. Ross, *The Missing Peace*, 244.

89. In a May 1996 poll undertaken by the Tami Steinmetz Center for Peace Research, more than half of those interviewed (56.8 percent) believed that the signing of the Oslo Accord adversely affected citizen safety, but nearly half of the respondents (48.4 percent) voted for Likud because they believed the party would demand stricter Palestinian compliance with the agreement. See http://www.tau.ac.il/peace/, accessed on January 20, 2007.

90. Cordesman, *The Israeli-Palestinian War*, 22–28.

91. Ephraim Yaar and Tamar Hermann, "Peace Index, October 1998," available at http://www.tau.ac.il/peace/, accessed on January 20, 2007.

92. The Israeli polls conducted shortly after the election of Barak indicated that most respondents preferred the establishment of a broad coalition government (69 percent) to the installation of a narrower government that would advance the peace process (19.5 percent). See Ephraim Yaar and Tamar Herman, "Peace Index, May 1999," available at http://www.tau.ac.il/peace/, accessed on January 20, 2007.

93. The concessions offered by Barak at the Camp David summit were overwhelmingly condemned by the Israeli public as too conciliatory (74 percent opposed strongly; 60 percent opposed). Yaar and Hermann, "Peace Index, July 2000," available at http://www.tau.ac.il/peace/, accessed on January 20, 2007.

94. On September 28, 2000, Sharon and other members of the Likud Party visited the Temple Mount. The Palestinians saw the trip as provocative. Many people believe that this catalyzed the second intifada. Others argue that the killing of Israeli sergeant David Biri the day before (September 27, 2000) actually started the violence. Arafat explicitly supported the uprising: probably to avoid being preempted by Hamas, Fatah's armed wing, Tanzim, led it. Some analysts even assert that Arafat deliberately orchestrated the al-Aqsa intifada to gain additional Israeli concessions and international support for the Palestinian cause. See Nadav Morag, "Measuring Success in Coping with Terrorism: The Israeli Case," *Studies in Conflict and Terrorism* 28, no. 4 (July–August 2005): 316.

95. On the early events of the al-Aqsa intifada, see the Mitchell Report, May 4, 2001, available at http://www.jewishvirtuallibrary.org/jsource/Peace/Mitchellrep .html, accessed January 22, 2007.

96. Cordesman, *The Israeli-Palestinian War*, 32.

97. Ibid., 9.

98. *JMCC Public Opinion Polls 2000–3*, Jerusalem Media and Communication Centre, http://www.jmcc.org/publicpoll/results.html, accessed on February 6, 2006.

99. See Luca Ricolfi, "Palestinians, 1981–2003," chap. 3 of *Making Sense of Suicide Missions*, ed. Diego Gambetta (Oxford: Oxford University Press, 2005), especially figure 3.2, p. 84; and 92–97.

100. According to the "Peace Index, July 2000," 65 percent held the Palestinians mainly or wholly responsible for the breakdown of the summit, 59 percent were against handing over most of the West Bank, 76 percent were against allowing the right of return to 100,000 refugees, and 58 percent opposed Palestinian sovereignty over the Arab neighborhoods in East Jerusalem. Tami Steinmetz Center for Peace Research, http://www.tau.ac.il/peace/, accessed on January 20, 2007.

101. Under this title at Palestinian Center for Policy and Survey Research, Ramallah http://www.pcpsr.org/survey/polls/2000/p1ejoint.html, accessed on February 6, 2006.

102. Although, of course, there are connections, I am not including the violence that occurred in the Lebanese area in the 1980s.

103. Kydd and Walter, "Sabotaging the Peace," 276–77. Polls are not at all clear on this point, however. The February 2001 Peace Index poll indicated that even during the second intifada, the Israeli public were split about the extent to which Arafat could control the violence, with 49 percent believing that he had partial or absolute control of anti-Israeli violence, and 47 percent believing that he had little or no control.

104. Ricolfi, "Palestinians, 1981–2003," 95.

105. Ibid., 96 and 99. This hypothesis was first put forward by Martin Kramer in reference to the first intifada. See Martin Kramer, "Sacrifice and Fratricide in Shiite Lebanon," *Terrorism and Political Violence* 3, no. 3 (1991): 30–47. For the al-Aqsa intifada, see Mia Bloom, *Dying to Kill: The Allure of Suicide Terror* (New York: Columbia University Press, 2005).

106. Related is the question of who the casualties were. The Israelis were paying the heaviest *relative* price for efforts at peace: clashes between the IDF and the Palestinians became less deadly for the Palestinians between 1995 and 2000, yet in 1998 the Israeli Foreign Ministry claimed that more Israelis had died during the five years following the Oslo Accords as a result of terrorist attacks than had died in the 15 years before the peace process began. The absolute number of Palestinian victims of clashes with the IDF (as well as killed during internal Palestinian violence) was always orders of magnitude higher, however. For statistics on casualties see B'Tselem, at http://www.btselem.org/english/statistics/First_ Intifada_Tables.asp, accessed on January 12, 2007.

107. Ricolfi, "Palestinians, 1981–2003," 93.

108. The LTTE have used suicide attacks more than 200 times since their founding, against both military and civilian targets. This case study was written in early 2007 and only reflects events to that time.

109. Sisira Edirippulige, *Sri Lanka's Twisted Path to Peace: Domestic and International Obstacles to the Peace Process* (Pilimathalawa: Resource Management Foundation, 2004), 10. The IISS puts the figure at 78,610 fatalities since 1983 and approximately 500,000 displaced. See IISS Armed Conflict Database, http://acd.iiss.org/armedconflict/MainPages/dsp_Conflict Summary.asp?ConflictID=174, accessed February 19, 2007. Stephen Hopgood provides a lower estimate of 65,000 fatalities. See Stephen Hopgood, "The Tamil Tigers," in Gambetta, *Making Sense*, 45.

110. Edirippulige, *Sri Lanka's Twisted Path*, 246.

111. Nira Wickramasinghe, *Sri Lanka in the Modern Age: A History of Contested Identities* (London: Hurst, 2006), 290.

112. There were also 200,000 Tamil refugees at the time of the Black July pogrom. Ibid., 286.

113. The five groups were the LTTE, the PLOTE (People's Liberation Organisation of Tamil Eelam), the TELO (Tamil Eelam Liberation Organisation), EROS (the Eelam Revolutionary Organisation), and the EPRLF (Eelam People's Liberation Front). Wickramasinghe, *Sri Lanka*, 286.

114. At this time the government was absorbed in cracking down on the Marxist Sinhalese JVP (Janatha Vimukthi Peramuna) in the South, so both parties appreciated the hiatus.

115. L. R. Reddy, *Sri Lanka: Past and Present* (New Delhi: APH Press, 2003), 351.

116. The incident was called the Batticaloa massacre. There were two subsequent commissions of inquiry, but no legal proceedings.

117. The United National Party had ruled Sri Lanka politics for 17 years.

118. Reddy, *Sri Lanka*, 352. An LTTE suicide attack took place on two naval boats in Trincomalee harbor, killing 12 naval personnel and wounding 21, followed in July by the government's Navaly Church massacre, where 125 Tamil refugees were killed and 150 injured in a bombing by the Sri Lankan Air Force. The church had been designated a refuge by the government, but the government denied having deliberately targeted it.

119. In September, there was a massacre of 40 in the Nagerkrovil school (34 of them children), with 150 others injured. In October 1995, the government launched Operation Riviresa to recapture Jaffna, which drove out the LTTE; but the LTTE moved to control the entire eastern region except Batticaloa, Amparai, and part of Trincomalee town. Later that month, the LTTE burned two oil installations in Colombo, and ethnic cleansing took place in Sinhalese villages on the borders of the North Eastern province.

120. Walter Nubin, ed., *Sri Lanka: Current Issues and Historical Background* (New York: Nova Science, 2002), 5.

121. A key figure in moving Prabhakaran toward this cease-fire and the subsequent peace process was Erik Solheim, special adviser to Norway's foreign minister and previously the leader of the Norwegian Socialist Left Party. Rajat Ganguly, "Sri Lanka's Ethnic Conflict: At a Crossroad between Peace and War," *Third World Quarterly* 25, no. 5 (2004): 904.

122. Norway was selected to arbitrate because it has historically been a neutral country, without a colonial legacy. There is also a large Tamil diaspora in Nor-

way, giving the country an interest in resolving the conflict. Unfortunately, this connection has led to Sri Lankan charges of pro-Tamil bias. Japan also played a crucial, though low-profile, role, providing financial resources in support of Norwegian diplomatic measures. See Edirippulige, *Sri Lanka's Twisted Path*, 246.

123. Another notable development as a result of these elections was the Tamil National Alliance (TNA), formed from a group of four Tamil parties that had in the past been targeted by the LTTE, but now supported negotiations with the government. Ganguly, "Sri Lanka's Ethnic Conflict," 906.

124. International Crisis Group, "Sri Lanka: The Failure of the Peace Process," Asia Report No. 124, November 28, 2006, 8.

125. Ganguly, "Sri Lanka's Ethnic Conflict," 906; and Alisa Stack-O'Connor, "Lions, Tigers, and Freedom Birds: How and Why the Liberation Tigers of Tamil Eelam Employs Women," *Terrorism and Political Violence* 19, no. 1 (2007): 43–63.

126. International Crisis Group, "Sri Lanka," 5.

127. Ganguly, "Sri Lanka's Ethnic Conflict," 906.

128. For example, Lieberfeld points out that both the declaration following the 1988 meeting of the Palestine National Council and the 1989 African National Congress Harare declaration were unilateral statements signaling that the organization's goals were no longer maximal. Lieberfeld, "Post-Handshake Politics,"133. See also his *Talking with the Enemy: Negotiation and Threat Perception in South Africa and Israel/Palestine* (Westport, Conn.: Praeger, 1999).

129. I. William Zartman, *Ripe for Resolution: Conflict and Intervention in Africa* (New York: Oxford University Press, 1985).

130. See I. William Zartman, "Dynamics and Constraints in Negotiations in Internal Conflicts," chap. 1 of *Elusive Peace: Negotiating an End to Civil Wars*, ed. Zartman (Washington, D.C.: Brookings Institution, 1995), 13–16. When groups successfully transition to other types of behavior, the conditions for negotiation may improve but other types of problems ensue, as explained in chapter 6.

131. Zartman, "Dynamics and Constraints," 3.

132. I. William Zartman, ed., *The 50 Percent Solution* (New Haven: Yale University Press, 1983), 120–21. The caveat I would add is that terrorists' targeting of civilians and potential access to chemical, biological, or nuclear weapons increase their leverage and cast doubt on the usual assumptions about power relationships with the state.

133. Daniel Kahneman and Amos Tversky, "Prospect Theory: An Analysis of Decision under Risk," *Econometrica* 47, no. 2 (March 1979): 263–91.

134. Kevin Myers, "The Terrorist as Statesman," *National Interest* 75 (Spring 2004): 142.

135. Paul Wilkinson, "Politics, Diplomacy and Peace Processes: Pathways out of Terrorism?" *Terrorism and Political Violence* 11, no. 4 (Winter 1999): 78. See also Daniel Byman, "The Decision to Begin Talks with Terrorists," *Studies in Conflict and Terrorism*, 29, no. 5 (July–August 2006): 408.

136. King, *Ending Civil Wars*, 62.

137 . A discussion of the relationship between the concepts of war, civil war, insurgency and terrorism is undertaken in chapter 6.

138. When populations are largely mobilized, individual leadership is less crucial—but negotiations are also less likely to succeed. This is a very bad outcome (see chapter 7).

139. On this point, see Martha Crenshaw, "Pathways Out of Terrorism: A Conceptual Framework," in *Pathways Out of Terrorism and Insurgency: The Dynamics of Terrorist Violence and Peace Processes*, ed. L. Sergio Germani and D. R. Kaarthikeyan (New Delhi: Sterling, 2005), 7.

140. Wilkinson, "Politics, Diplomacy," 79.

141. Lieberfeld, "Post-Handshake Politics," 134.

142. Byman, "Decision to Begin Talks," 404.

143. During the peace process, Solheim was joined by Yassushi Akashi, Tokyo's special envoy, and Norwegian deputy foreign minister Vidar Helgesen. Ganguly, "Sri Lanka's Ethnic Conflict," 911.

144. For a discussion of such contacts in advance of the Oslo Accords, see Peter Demand, "Unofficial Contacts and Peacemaking: Israeli-Palestinian Dialogue, 1967–1993," in *Israel in the Nineties: Development and Conflict* (Gainesville: University Press of Florida, 1996), 73–104.

145. Suicide attacks are generally believed to be more deadly, involving a higher number of casualties per attack; however, their efficacy is a complex question. Suicide attacks involving the largest numbers of casualties are the result of vehicle bombs rather than individuals carrying bombs on their person. Numbers of casualties are therefore better correlated with the ability to construct and deliver big vehicle-borne bombs than with the readiness of the individual bomber to commit suicide. I am grateful to Brian Jenkins for this observation.

146. The so-called sacrifice trap derives from an analogy drawn with Aztec civilization, which used human sacrifices to ensure good harvests. If the subsequent harvest was bad, however, the interpretation was not that the sacrifices were a waste of time but that not enough people had been sacrificed. Stephen Ryan, "Conflict Management and Conflict Resolution," *Terrorism and Political Violence* 2, no. 1 (Spring 1990): 69.

147. About the Israeli-Palestinian case, Boaz Ganor argues, "Suicide bombing changed the face of peace forever." Quoted by Barbara Victor, *Army of Roses: Inside the World of Palestinian Women Suicide Bombers* (Emmaus, Pa.: Radale, 2003), 278.

148. This is not to imply that physical barriers are unique to suicide campaigns. Other examples include the "peace" line in Belfast and the Green Lines in Nicosia and Lebanon. See Ryan, "Conflict Management," 61.

149. Other splinter groups include the Continuity IRA and the Irish National Liberation Army.

150. Peter Sederberg argues that the opportunities to pursue disintegrative strategies increase as support for the terrorist group increases, since there are more layers of support and more potentially exploitable linkages among them. "Conciliation as Counter-terrorist Strategy," *Journal of Peace Research* 32, no. 3 (August 1995): 306–7.

151. For a discussion of this problem, see Fred Charles Iklé, "The Struggle Within: The Search for an Exit," in *Every War Must End*, 2nd ed. (New York: Columbia University Press, 2005), 84–105.

152. These right-wing groups grew out of groups of gunmen hired by ranchers to protect them from proliferating ransom kidnappings, but they became politicized movements with the signing of the 1984 accords. The EPL signed a truce with the Columbian government in 1991 and essentially disbanded, although a breakaway faction continues to operate today. The effects of the peace accord on the government's relationship with the FARC and M-19 are, of course, another story.

153. In very complex situations, coming to an agreement with one faction can benefit another faction. For example, the demobilization of 32,000 right-wing militiamen in Columbia resulted in moves by the FARC to fill the power vacuum. See Tom Regan, "Columbia's FARC Rebels Still Undermine Peace Effort," *Christian Science Monitor*, Terrorism & Security Daily Update, posted July 25, 2006.

154. Kydd and Walter, "Sabotaging the Peace," 264; using data from the International Policy Institute for Counter-Terrorism database, the Interdisciplinary Center, Herzliya; and Barbara Walter, *Committing to Peace: The Successful Settlement of Civil Wars* (Princeton: Princeton University Press, 2002).

155. Stephen Stedman refers to involved outside parties as "custodians for peace" that must "judge what is right or wrong, just or unjust, and fair or unfair in peace processes. . . . The research presented here strongly suggests that international consensus about norms, coordination behind a strategy of aggressive management of spoilers, and unambiguous signals to peace supporters and spoilers provide the difference between successful and failed implementation of peace agreements." Stedman, "Spoiler Problems in Peace Processes," *International Security*, 22, no. 2 (Autumn, 1997): 5–53.

156. These also include, for example, the Cypriot EOKA, the Algerian FLN, and the Kenyan Mau Mau.

157. On this point, see Myers, "The Terrorist as Statesman," 139–43.

158. For more on the effect of the international context on negotiations with terrorists, see Fred Halliday, "Peace Processes in the Late-Twentieth Century and Beyond: A Mixed Record," and Michael Cox, "Rethinking the International and Northern Ireland: A Defence," in Cox, Guelke, and Stephen, *A Farewell to Arms*.

CHAPTER THREE: SUCCESS

1. Serge Stepniak-Kravchinski, *Underground Russia: Revolutionary Profiles and Sketches from Life*, translation of *Podpol'naia Rossiia* (New York: Scribner, 1883; rpt. Westport, Conn.: Hyperion Press, 1973); also quoted in Walter Laqueur, ed., *The Terrorism Reader: A Historical Anthology* (Philadelphia: Temple University Press, 1978), 89.

2. Menachem Begin argued that in running the Jewish organization Irgun Zvai Le'umi, one of his top priorities was to avoid the mistakes of his ancient predecessors, the Zealots. Begin, *The Revolt*, 2nd ed. (New York: Nash, 1997), 47.

3. James Boswell, *The Life of Samuel Johnson* (London: Alfred A. Knopf, 1992), 396.

4. Examples of effective terrorist information campaigns are legion, from Irgun to al-Qaeda. For insight into the information operations of Irgun see Zadka,

Blood in Zion: How the Jewish Guerrillas Drove the British Out of Palestine (London: Brassey's, 1995).

5. Max Abrahms, "Are Terrorists Really Rational? The Palestinian Example," *Orbis* 48, no. 3 (Summer 2004): 546; and Abrahms, "Why Terrorism Does Not Work," *International Security* 31, no. 2 (Fall 2006): 42–78. See also Martha Crenshaw, "The Psychology of Terrorism: An Agenda for the 21st Century," *Political Psychology* 21, no. 2 (June 2000): 415.

6. I can think of no campaigns that carried out an attack and immediately "won."

7. According to David Rapoport, 90 percent of terrorist organizations in the late twentieth century lasted less than a year, and of those that made it to the one-year point, more than half disappeared within a decade. Rapoport may have counted groups that we did not include here, such as those with one attack. See Rapoport, "Terrorism," in *Routledge Encyclopedia of Government and Politics*, ed. Mary Hawkesworth and Maurice Kogan, vol. 2 (London: Routledge, 1992), 1067. Brian Jackson argues that the short life-span of groups explains why most are noninnovative, using proven technologies. See Brian A. Jackson, "Technology Acquisition by Terrorist Groups: Threat Assessment Informed by Lessons from Private Sector Technology Adoption," *Studies in Conflict and Terrorism* 24, no. 3 (January–February 2001): 202.

8. See Andrew H. Kydd and Barbara F. Walter, "The Strategies of Terrorism," *International Security* 31, no. 1 (Summer 2006): 49–80.

9. On the U.S. listing process see Cronin, *FTO List*.

10. Using the groups on the U.S. Foreign Terrorist Organizations list to draw conclusions about terrorism's effectiveness is akin to using the FBI's Most Wanted list to judge the efficacy of crime.

11. See Crenshaw, "How Terrorism Declines."

12. There are many examples, especially among the leftist groups of the 1970s and 1980s such as the Red Army Faction (or Baader-Meinhof group) and the June 2nd Movement.

13. Good sources on the "new" religious terrorism include Mark Juergensmeyer, *Terror in the Mind of God: The Global Rise of Religious Violence* (Berkeley and Los Angeles: University of California Press, 2000); Lesser et al., *Countering the New Terrorism*; and Robert Jay Lifton, *Destroying the World to Save It: Aum Shinrokyo, Apocalyptic Violence, and the New Global Terrorism* (New York: Henry Holt, 1999). Also see David Tucker, "What Is New about the New Terrorism and How Dangerous Is It?" *Political Violence and Terrorism* 13, no. 3 (Summer 2001): 1–14.

14. David C. Rapoport, "Fear and Trembling: Terrorism in Three Religious Traditions," *American Political Science Review* 78 (1984): 658–77. Rapoport asserts that before the nineteenth century, religion was the *only* acceptable cause for terrorism.

15. Examples include Hamas in Palestine, the PIRA in Northern Ireland, the East Turkestan Islamic Movement in China, the Pattani Islamic Mujahideen Movement in Thailand, and Chechen rebels. Michael Scheuer argues that al-Qaeda has nationalist motives, and in *The Looming Tower: Al-Qaeda and the Road to 9/11* (New York: Vintage, 2006), Lawrence Wright demonstrates that Ayman Zawahiri borrows from earlier discourses of national liberation.

16. Crenshaw, "The Psychology of Terrorism," 415.

17. See Richardson, *What Terrorists Want*, 98ff.; Christopher Harmon, *Terrorism Today* (London: Frank Cass, 2000); and Abrahms, "Are Terrorists Really Rational?" 544. Richardson argues that all terrorist organizations have two kinds of objectives: short-term organizational objectives and long-term political objectives. Abrams calls them "process" and "outcome" goals.

18. See Herbert A. Simon, "From Substantive to Procedural Rationality," in *Method and Appraisal in Economics*, ed. Spiro J. Latsis (Cambridge: Cambridge University Press, 1976), 129–48. Louise Richardson calls them "secondary" and "primary" goals, or "short-term organizational objectives and long-term political objectives requiring significant political change." Richardson, *What Terrorists Want*, 98–100. Like states in a conflict, terrorist groups may change their "war aims" over the course of a campaign; indeed, doing so may be the only way to perpetuate their existence. As Martha Crenshaw points out, terrorist organizations (or their leaders) tend to describe such changes as "tactical" but successful operations as "strategic." See "How Terrorism Declines," 85.

19. For arguments that use state-centric logic in dissecting the strategies of terrorist groups, see Kydd and Walter, "The Strategies of Terrorism," esp. 56–59; and Ivan Arreguín-Toft, "How the Weak Win Wars: A Theory of Asymmetric Conflict," *International Security* 26, no. 1 (Summer 2001): 93–128.

20. On signaling, see Kydd and Walter, "The Strategies of Terrorism," 58. See also Andrew H. Kydd, *Trust and Mistrust in International Relations* (Princeton: Princeton University Press, 2005).

21. In the short term there is no necessary correlation between frequency of attacks and success, as some groups increase their attacks when they are losing ground.

22. One source defines the five terrorist strategies as attrition, intimidation, outbidding, provocation, and spoiling. While this is an interesting framework, it is too narrowly focused on the target state and does not reflect the range of organizational, individual, and ideological reasons why some groups use violence. See Kydd and Walter, "The Strategies of Terrorism." For an alternative viewpoint, see Richardson, "The Three Rs: Revenge, Renown, Reaction," chap. 4 of *What Terrorists Want*, 95–132.

23. On this topic, see Ronald H. Jones, "Terrorist Beheadings: Cultural and Strategic Implications," Carlisle Paper, Strategic Studies Institute, U.S. Army War College, available at http://www.carlisle.army.mil/ssi.

24. Mia Bloom, "Palestinian Suicide Bombing: Public Support, Market Share and Outbidding," *Political Science Quarterly* 119, no. 1 (Summer 2004): 61–88.

25. See Gabriel Sheffer, "Ethno-National Diasporas and Security," *Survival* 36, no. 1 (Spring 1994): 60–79.

26. See Daniel Byman, "Syria and Palestinian Radical Groups," chap. 5 of *Deadly Connections* (Cambridge: Cambridge University Press, 2005), 117–53.

27. Post, "Terrorist Psycho-logic," 25–40.

28. Michael Walzer thinks that Arafat may not have wanted to tackle the problems of state-building. See *Arguing about War* (New Haven: Yale University Press, 2005), 117.

29. Christopher Harmon argues that in using terrorism, all groups achieve their initial aim, which is wrecking normality and political order. See Harmon, *Terrorism Today*, 74–75.

30. Different motivations sometimes led to different styles and modes of behavior; understanding the long-term outcome sought by a group was vital to constructing a counterterrorist campaign against it. See Cronin, "Behind the Curve," especially 39–42.

31. We did not include all the groups in the database, as some attacked only economic targets, had only carried out one attack and then disappeared, etc. We were deliberately conservative and narrowed down the entries to only those that were clearly "terrorist" (meaning they displayed political aims, the surprise use of violence, purposeful targeting of civilians, and were nonstate actors) in order to avoid exaggerating the data. We also coded those few organizations for which there was no information as "missing." Our results indicated that of the 450 groups observed, only 4.4 percent (20 groups) achieved their full strategic objectives, and an additional 9 groups, or 2.0 percent, achieved substantial aspects of their strategic aims. For a fuller explanation, see the statistical appendix.

32. Christopher Harmon calls these situations, where governments are smashed but militants may not be strong enough to take power, "partial strategic successes." See *Terrorism Today*, 74–75. See also Crenshaw, "How Terrorism Declines," 79–80.

33. Crenshaw, "How Terrorism Declines," 79–80.

34. Success through insurgencies and "asymmetric conflicts" has been examined by a wide range of authors, notably Austin Long, *On "Other War": Lessons from Five Decades of RAND Counterinsurgency Research* (Santa Monica, Calif.: RAND, 2006); Andrew J. Mack, "Why Big Nations Lose Small Wars: The Politics of Asymmetric Conflict," *World Politics* 27, no. 2 (January 1975): 175–200; and Arreguín-Toft, "How the Weak Win Wars." The latter defines attacks against noncombatants as "barbarism," and concludes that compared to other strategies it is ineffective.

35. Samuel Katz, *Days of Fire* (London: W. H. Allen, 1968), 44 and passim.

36. Hebrew acronym for Lohamei Herut Israel (Fighters for the Freedom of Israel)

37. This according to Begin himself. See *The Revolt*, 52–55.

38. Begin writes: "Our enemies called us terrorists. People who were neither friends nor enemies, like the correspondents of the New York Herald-Tribune, also used this Latin name, either under the influence of British propaganda or out of habit. Our friends, like the Irishman O'Reilly, preferred, as he wrote in his letter, to 'get ahead of history' and called us by a simpler, though also a Latin name: patriots. . . . And yet, we were not terrorists." Ibid., 59.

39. Begin took over Irgun after the death of David Raziel, who was killed carrying out a dangerous British mission in Iraq for which he had volunteered. His task was to organize guerrilla activities behind Arab lines. Katz, *Days of Fire*, 54.

40. J. Bowyer Bell, *Terror Out of Zion: Irgun Zvai Leumi, Lehi, and the Palestine Underground, 1929–1949* (New York: Avon, 1977), 172.

41. Zadka, *Blood in Zion*, 70–72.

42. Ibid., 78–85. The killing of the two sergeants had been carried out in retribution for the hanging by a British military court of three members of IZL captured during the Acre prison break-in. According to Zadka, the sergeant's

body was suspended over a hidden landmine; the mine exploded when the body fell on it.

43. The dissolution of Irgun coincided with the sinking of the ship *Altalena*, which was filled with Irgun fighters and arms. Irgun were given an ultimatum to lay down its arms and did so rather than engage in a civil war against the new Israeli regime.

44. Truth and Reconciliation Commission of South Africa Report, vol. 3, chap. 6, October 1998.

45. Howard Barrell, *The ANC's Armed Struggle* (London: Penguin, 1990), 14.

46. The December 16, 1961, MK manifesto specified the following aims: "the overthrow of the Nationalist government, the abolition of white supremacy and the winning of liberty, democracy and full national rights of equality for all the people of this country." As translated by Barrell, *The ANC's Armed Struggle*, 2.

47. A transcript of Mandela's statement for the 1964 Rivonia trial, entitled "I Am Prepared to Die," is available at http://www.anc.org.za/ancdocs/history/mandela/1960s/rivonia.html. See also Sheridan Johns and R. Hunt Davis Jr., *Mandela, Tambo, and the African National Congress: A Documentary Survey* (Oxford: Oxford University Press, 1991), 115–33.

48. Following the ending of apartheid, Mandela established and cooperated with the Truth and Reconciliation Commission, accepting its criticisms of both the ANC and MK when the latter's actions failed to live up to ANC commitments under the Geneva Conventions.

49. Biko died in police custody in 1977.

50. D. T. McKinley, *The ANC and the Liberation Struggle: A Critical Political Biography* (London: Pluto Press, 1997), 28. McKinley also cites the influence of the South African Communist Party, to which many ANC leaders were linked. In addition, the involvement of a number of prominent white Jewish activists in the activities of the MK lends credence to the view that Umkhonto was modeled on Irgun.

51. Mandela mentioned a link between Irgun and the ANC in his courtroom speech for the 1964 Rivonia trial, He said that "the terms High Command and Regional Command were an importation from the Jewish national underground organization Irgun Zvai Leumi, which operated in Israel between 1944 and 1948." Mandela, "Prepared to Die."

52. Barrell, *The ANC's Armed Struggle*, 4; and McKinley, *ANC and Liberation Struggle*, 158. The ANC had white members, notably Denis Goldberg, Jewish South African social campaigner who was a member of MK and convicted in the Rivonia trials along with Mandela. Goldberg spent twenty-two years in jail.

53. Barrell, *The ANC's Armed Struggle*, 32.

54. In fact, MK units acting within South African before 1976 were instructed to have nothing at all to do with the local population, for fear of state infiltration. A midranking MK member interviewed by Barrell described an argument he had with his commander: "Wait, wait, wait, we can't do it like this. We can't just go in and hit. What are we doing it for? We've got to get the people to help us. We've got to get them involved. Because only then can we be protected." Ibid., 33, 40.

55. Ibid., 42.

56. R. Harvey, *The Fall of Apartheid: The Inside Story from Smuts to Mbeki* (Basingstoke: Palgrave, 2001), 89.

57. Barrell, *The ANC's Armed Struggle*, 60–61.

58. Harvey, *The Fall of Apartheid*, 233.

59. William Beinart, *Twentieth Century South Africa* (Oxford: Oxford University Press, 2001), 276.

60. MK's activities did change the political shape of what followed apartheid. Barrell has a more favorable view of MK's activities in the late 1960s, arguing that it created an "old guard" of veterans with militant credentials who were able to assume political leadership in the 1980s and facilitate the organization's transition to a moderate and peaceful party of government. But Adrian Guelke seems to share skepticism of MK's overall role, arguing that in the end "De Klerk recognized that the days of white minority rule in South Africa were numbered. The campaign of the ANC's military wing, *Umkhonto we Sizwe*, had played an insignificant role in the failure of apartheid." Guelke, *Terrorism and Global Disorder* (London: Tauris, 2006), 105.

61. Rapoport, "Fear and Trembling," 672.

62. Walter Laqueur, *Terrorism*, 2nd ed. (New York: Weidenfeld and Nicolson, 1977), 118.

63. Harmon argues that terrorism in Colombia worked. See *Terrorism Today*, xviii.

64. Martha Crenshaw, "Terrorism in the Algerian War," in *Terrorism in Context*, ed. Crenshaw (University Park: Pennsylvania State University Press, 1995), 512–13.

65. The remaining 2 percent were Armenians, Maronites, and others. Farid Mirbagheri, *Cyprus and International Peacemaking* (London: Hurst, 1998), 13.

66. In response to its activities, the Turkish Cypriots formed the TMT, Turk Mughavemat Tashkilat (Turkish Defence Organisation) which also killed civilians and received military supplies from Turkey. Ibid., 39; and Christopher Hitchens, *Hostage to History: Cyprus from the Ottomans to Kissinger* (London: Verso, 1977), 52–54.

67. Under the agreement, the British retained military bases on the island.

68. The EOKA-B was supported by the right-wing Greek military junta. The group engaged in assassinations and killings of civilians, eventually carrying out a coup that led to military invasion by Turkey and partition of the island. On the first campaign, see Laqueur, *Terrorism*, 119.

69. See Alan Dershowitz, *Why Terrorism Works: Understanding the Threat, Responding to the Challenge* (New Haven: Yale University Press, 2002); Kydd and Walter, "Sabotaging the Peace"; and Abrahms, "Are Terrorists Really Rational?" 534–37. On the success of Israeli counterterrorism, see Morag, "Measuring Success."

70. Walter Laqueur, *No End to War: Terrorism in the Twentieth Century* (New York: Continuum, 2003), 229–30.

71. Walter Laqueur divides terrorist groups that attained their objectives into three groups: (1) those with narrow, clearly defined aims that were realistically attainable; (2) those with powerful outside protectors; and (3) those facing impe-

rial powers that were no longer able or willing to hold on to their colonies or protectorates. See *Terrorism* (1977), 116–19.

72. Ibid., 221.

CHAPTER FOUR: FAILURE

1. Frantz Fanon, *Black Skin, White Masks*, trans. Charles Lamm Markmann (New York: Grove, 1967), 12.

2. Ehud Sprinzak argued that left-wing groups evolve through three stages: crisis of confidence, conflict of legitimacy, and crisis of legitimacy. See "The Psychopolitical Formation of Extreme Left Terrorism in a Democracy: The Case of the Weatherman," in Reich, *Origins of Terrorism*, 65–85. For another argument about psychological phases see Albert Bandura, "Mechanisms of Moral Disengagement," in Reich, *Origins of Terrorism*, 161–91.

3. Leonard Weinberg and Louise Richardson, "Conflict Theory and the Trajectory of Terrorist Campaigns in Western Europe," in *Research on Terrorism: Trends, Achievements, and Failures*, ed. Andrew Silke (London: Frank Cass, 2004), 138–60. There were monumental government projects launched in both Italy and Germany to study the terrorist movements of the New Left. These yielded massive information about these relatively narrow case studies—valuable, but perhaps exerting a disproportionate influence on the field.

4. Ehud Sprinzak, "Right-Wing Terrorism in Comparative Perspective: The Case of Split Delegitimization," in *Terror from the Extreme Right*, ed. Tore Bjørgo (London: Frank Cass, 1995), 17–43. See also Sprinzak, "The Process of Delegitimation: Towards a Linkage Theory of Political Terrorism," *Terrorism and Political Violence* 3, no. 1 (Spring 1991): 50–68.

5. Ted Robert Gurr, *Why Men Rebel* (Princeton: Princeton University Press, 1970). There is a rich literature from the 1960 and 1970s on political violence, of which terrorism is arguably a subset. Gurr defines political violence as "all collective attacks within a political community against the political regime, its actor—including competing political groups as well as incumbents—or its policies" (3–4).

6. Crenshaw, "How Terrorism Declines," 82, and Donatella Della Porta, *Social Movements, Political Violence, and the State* (Cambridge: Cambridge University Press, 1995). See also John O. Voll, "Bin Laden and the New Age of Global Terrorism," *Middle East Policy* 8, no. 4 (December 2001): 1–5; and Quintan Wiktorowicz, "Framing Jihad: Intramovement Framing Contests and al-Qaeda's Struggle for Sacred Authority," *International Review of Social History* 29 (2004): 159–77.

7. Rapoport, "Four Waves."

8. The New Left movement had already begun to slow down by the 1980s; however, breakup of the Soviet Union accelerated the delegitimation of its ideology. According to Peter Chalk, only three of the Western European groups active in the 1980s were still operating in the late 1990s: the Spanish October 1st Anti-Fascist Organisation (GRAPO); the Turkish Devrimci Sol (Dev Sol), and the Greek group 17 November Revolutionary Organization. Chalk, "The Evolving Dynamic of Terrorism in the 1990s," *Australian Journal of International Affairs* 53, no. 2

(1999): 151–52 n. 2. Notably, the Italian Red Brigades did recruit succeeding cohorts; but each generation was less ideologically motivated than its predecessors. The so-called third generation brigatisti were nothing more than thugs.

9. Left-wing groups tended to define "generations" as those militants in prison and those outside. Della Porta, *Social Movements*, 119. One of the key problems for the Red Army Faction was communications between prisoners and their successors. See Hans Josef Horchem, "The Decline of the Red Army Faction," *Terrorism and Political Violence* 3, no. 2 (Summer 1991): 61–75.

10. For reasons that have never been fully understood, Meinhof hanged herself in her cell in 1976. Some argue that she was mentally ill, others that the state played a role in her death. Jillian Becker, *Hitler's Children: The Story of the Baader-Meinhof Terrorist Gang* (London: Pickwick, 1989); and Stefan Aust, *The Baader-Meinhof Group: The Inside Story of a Phenomenon* (London: Anthea Bell, 1987).

11. The RAF's 1992 communiqué admits that none of its current members predated 1984. Dennis A. Pluchinsky, "Germany's Red Army Faction: An Obituary," *Studies in Conflict and Terrorism* 16, no. 2 (April–June 1993): 142.

12. On the RAF, see ibid., 135–57. Other groups that had operated in Italy included the proletarian Armed Nucleus (NAP), the Fighting Communist Units, the Prima Linea (Front Line), the Proletarian Armies for Communism, and the Revolutionary Communist Movement, most of which had extremely short lifespans. The Red Brigades were by far the most durable. Xavier Raufer, "The Red Brigades: Farewell to Arms," *Studies in Conflict and Terrorism* 16, no. 4 (October–December 1993): 316, 322.

13. On activities 1977–87, see Jillian Becker, *Terrorism in West Germany: The Struggle for What?* (London: Institute for the Study of Terrorism, 1988). For the closing statement see Clare Murphy, "Who Were the Baader-Meinhof Group," BBC News, February 12, 2007, http://www.bbcnews.co.uk, accessed on May 16, 2007.

14. Crenshaw, "How Terrorism Declines," 78. On right-wing groups, see Cronin, "Behind the Curve," 39–42.

15. These include the Christian Patriots, the Aryan Nations, the Ku Klux Klan, The Order (a short-lived faction of Aryan Nations), and the Hammerskin Nation in the United States; the Anti-Zionist Movement, Combat 18, the German People's Union, and the National Front in Europe; and the National Warriors of South Africa. Recent demographic shifts may affect the viability of neo-Nazi groups in eastern Germany: many more women than men are going west for work, leaving a large proportion of frustrated, underemployed men reportedly ripe for recruitment by the German neo-Nazis. In 2006, there were only 90 women for every 100 men in eastern Germany. See Steffen Kroehnert, Franziska Medicus, and Reiner Klingholz, "Shortage of Women in the East," in *The Demographic State of the Nation* (Berlin: Berlin Institute for Population and Development, March 2006); and *Foreign Policy* magazine blog, http://blog.foreignpolicy.com/node/4971?fpsrc+ealert070605, accessed on June 8, 2007.

16. The Ku Klux Klan is an example.

17. Some groups, such as The Order (active between 1982 and 1984), have been idolized by their admirers and continue to exercise influence.

18. Col. Ulius Louis Amoss apparently originated the phrase in an 1962 essay of that title. It was later popularized by Louis R. Beam Jr., Aryan Nations leader and former Texas Ku Klux Klan Grand Dragon. See Louis R. Beam, "Leaderless Resistance," *The Seditionist* 12 (February 1991), cited by Jeffrey Kaplan, "'Leaderless Resistance,'" in Rapoport, *Inside Terrorist Organizations*, 260–73.

19. The name refers to Adolph Hitler's initials—the first and eighth letters of the alphabet.

20. Rajeev Syal and Andrew Gilligan, "MI5 Swoops on Army Neo-Nazis," *Telegraph*, March 7, 1999, www.telegraph.co.uk, accessed May 20, 2007.

21. Fifty people were injured in the Brixton blast; 13 were injured in the Brick Lane blast; three were killed, 83 injured (some of them very seriously) in the Soho pub bombing. Nick Hopkins and Sarah Hall, "Festering Hate That Turned Quiet Son into a Murderer," *Guardian*, July 1, 2000, http://www.guardian.co.uk, accessed May 20, 2007.

22. Stuart Millar, "We're at war and if that means more bombs, so be it . . . ," *Guardian Unlimited*, April 27, 1999, accessed at http://www.guardian.co.uk/bombs/Story/0,,204779,00.html, May 28, 2007. See also Paul Harris, "Far Right Plot to Provoke Race Riots," *Observer*, June 2, 2001, http://www.guardian.co.uk, accessed May 20, 2007.

23. "Ex-Combat-18 Man Speaks Out," Panorama, BBC News, http://news.bbc.co.uk/1/hi/programmes/panorama/1672100.stm, accessed May 20, 2007. This is not to imply that all right-wing groups fit the same profile: notably, right-wing extremists in Sweden are more deeply embedded in society, enjoying larger numbers of supporters than in neighboring countries. This may be because Swedish National Socialists were not considered traitors during World War II. See Heléne Loow, "Racist Violence and Criminal Behavior in Sweden: Myths and Reality," in Bjørgo, *Terror from Extreme Right*, 119–61.

24. Extrapolating from groups in the United States and Canada, Ross and Gurr argue that groups decline for four reasons: preemption, deterrence, burnout, and backlash. Like most traditional approaches, this set of four only encompasses a dichotomous interaction between group and government, however. See Ross and Gurr, "Why Terrorism Subsides," 108–9.

25. Della Porta, *Social Movements*, 104–12, 129–35.

26. Sean O'Callaghan, *The Informer: The Real Life Story of One Man's War against Terrorism* (New York: Bantam, 1998). See also Eamon Collins with Mick McGovern, *Killing Rage* (London: Granta, 1997).

27. Personal ambition played an important role in the formation of the Algerian GIA, for example. In the first half of 1992, Mansour Meliani withdrew from the MIA in disgust, following bitter rivalry for its leadership with Abdelkader Chebouti. Meliani proceeded to unite three small groups under his leadership—the first incarnation of the GIA. Meliani was arrested soon after, but the group's next leader, Abdelhak Layada, had also been a rival of Chebouti's. See Michael Willis, *The Islamist Challenge in Algeria* (London: Ithaca Press, 1996).

28. Donatella Della Porta, "Left-Wing Terrorism in Italy," in *Terrorism in Context*, 153.

29. Becker, *Hitler's Children*, 198–99.

30. Nick Hopkins, "Splinter Group That Found the BNP Too Soft," April 20, 1999, *Guardian Unlimited*, accessed at http://www.guardian.co.uk on May 20, 2007.

31. For the full story, see Ronald D. Crelinsten, "The Internal Dynamics of the FLQ during the October Crisis of 1970," in Rapoport, *Inside Terrorist Organizations*, 59–89.

32. Horgan, *The Psychology of Terrorism*, 144.

33. Pluchinsky, "German's Red Army Faction," 137.

34. Sidney Tarrow, "Violence and Institutionalisation after the Italian Protest Cycles," chap. 2 of *The Red Brigades and Left-Wing Terrorism in Italy*, ed. Raimondo Catanzaro (London: Pinter, 1991), 41–69.

35. According to a former senior member, "Membership in the RB was voluntary. Anyone could leave the RB at any time, on the basis of mutual assurances." Raufer, "The Red Brigades," 322. One member who was an excessive drinker was taken over the border into Switzerland, given "liquidation pay," and ejected. Alison Jamieson, "Entry, Discipline and Exit in the Italian Red Brigades," *Terrorism and Political Violence* 2, no. 1 (Spring 1990): 9.

36. For more, see Lifton, *Destroying the World*, 8–39, and 147–48.

37. For this reason, Brian Hayes has argued that telephone call graphs may be used to identify cliques and track patterns in the communications between potential terrorist operatives. Hayes, "Connecting the Dots," *American Scientist* 94 (2006): 400–404.

38. Andrew Silke, "In Defense of the Realm: Financing Loyalist Terrorism in Northern Ireland—Part One: Extortion and Blackmail," *Studies in Conflict and Terrorism* 21, no. 4 (October–December 1998): 331–61; and Silke, "Drink, Drugs, and Rock 'n Roll: Financing Loyalist Terrorism in Northern Ireland—Part Two," *Studies in Conflict and Terrorism* 23, no. 2 (April–June 2000): 107–27.

39. Their sense of purpose frittered away over the 1970s; their top priority was to stay out of jail. Varon, *Bringing the War Home*, 172–73, 180. A large number of groups have lost members to accidents, including the IRA, Hamas, the Red Brigades, and the Nuclei Armati Proletari (NAP). Accidents have likewise resulted in the exposure of operations, notoriously Ramzi Yousef's plot to destroy multiple airliners in flight. See Brian A. Jackson, "Organizational Learning and Terrorist Groups," Working Paper WR-133-NIJ, RAND Public Safety and Justice Program, February 2004.

40. The most famous *pentito* was Patrizio Peci, who wrote a book *Il L'Iinfame* (I, the Vile One) which explained his reasons for accepting the amnesty. See also Robert C. Meade Jr., *The Red Brigades: The Story of Italian Terrorism* (Basingstoke: Macmillan, 1990); Leonard Weinberg and William L. Eubank, *The Rise and Fall of Italian Terrorism* (Boulder, Colo.: Westview Press, 1987). The second generation of terrorists found it easier to exit than did the founding members. See Franco Ferracuti, "Ideology and Repentance: Terrorism in Italy," chap. 4 of Reich, *Origins of Terrorism*, 63.

41. In the 1980s, this group was the second largest in Colombia after the FARC. M-19 is best known for its siege of the embassy of the Dominican Republic, taking 18 ambassadors hostage (including the U.S. ambassador), all of whom were eventually released.

42. For more on this, see Mark Urban, *Big Boys' Rules: The SAS and the Secret Struggle against the IRA* (London: Faber and Faber, 1992) and Steven Greer, *Supergrasses: A Study in Anti-terrorist Law Enforcement in Northern Ireland* (Oxford: Clarendon Press, 1995).

43. Amnesties also occur in the context of broader negotiations (discussed in chapter 2). All conflict-related prisoners in the United Kingdom and Republic of Ireland were released in the Belfast Agreement of 1998, though the release was on license and was not a general amnesty. Re-offenders have since been sent back to prison to serve their original sentences. For example, on June 22, 1999, Patrick Magee, the Brighton bomber, was freed. A Downing Street spokesman said, "It is hard to swallow. In the end though, we have to keep the process moving forward." Michael Von Tangen Page, "'A Most Difficult and Unpalatable Part': The Release of Politically Motivated Violent Offenders," chap. 13 in Guelke, Cox, and Stephen, *Farewell to Arms*, 208.

44. Cyrus Ernesto Zirakzadeh, "From Revolutionary Dreams to Organizational Fragmentation: Disputes over Violence within ETA and Sendero Luminoso," *Terrorism and Political Violence* 14, no. 4 (Winter 2002): 76.

45. Ibid., 76–77. In 1987, ETA gunmen began to kill local officials and party politicians who were cooperating with the regime in Madrid.

46. Renwick Maclean, "Madrid Sees Signs of ETA's Death Throes," *International Herald Tribune*, December 20, 2004, accessed at http://www.iht.com/articles/2004/12/20/basque_ed3_.php.

47. Individuals may simply develop new and stronger networks, as we will see with the Muslim Brotherhood. Or prison can be a means to break the cycle of activism without undermining the ideology, as is common with members of right-wing groups. Recent research among Muslim prisoners in Britain and France demonstrates that extremism is often *facilitated* by incarceration. See James A. Beckford, Daniele Joly, and Farhad Khosrokhavar, eds., *Muslims in Prison: Challenge and Change in Britain and France* (London: Palgrave Macmillan, 2006).

48. An excellent review of these factors, with particular emphasis on the PIRA, is John Horgan's "Disengaging," chap. 6 of *The Psychology of Terrorism*, 140–57.

49. Peter A. Lupsha, "Explanation of Political Violence: Some Psychological Theories versus Indignation," *Politics and Society* 2, no. 1 (Fall 1971): 89–104; and Luigi Bonanate, "Some Unanticipated Consequences of Terrorism," *Journal of Peace Research* 16, no. 3 (1979): 197–211. Specifically with respect to Muslims in the West, see Quintan Wiktorowicz, *Radical Islam Rising: Muslim Extremism in the West* (New York: Rowman and Littlefield, 2005).

50. Ross and Gurr, "Why Terrorism Subsides," 418–20.

51. A Soviet document dated May 16, 1975, published by Boris Yeltsin in 1992, officially records the Central Committee's decision. Tucker, *Skirmishes*, 25–26. "For example, according to some of the German Red Army Faction terrorists who participated, the government of what was then called South Yemen provided training facilities and safe haven for a variety of terrorist groups in the 1970s, including the Irish Republican Army (IRA) and Basque separatists. Through the Stasi, the East Germans support this work, in part by training South Yemen's 'fraternal' intelligence service." Tucker cites *Der Spiegel*, "The Desperadoes' Camp,"

January 16, 1995, 72, in Foreign Broadcast Information Service (FBIS), March 10, 1995, 47, to support this contention. Tucker may not be precisely correct on the IRA, however: the Provisional IRA was explicitly anti-Communist in its outlook and gave left-wing influence as a reason for its break with the existing leadership of the Republican movement. The Soviet Union supported the Official IRA, a much less important part of the movement that was largely inactive after 1972. I am grateful to an anonymous reviewer for this clarification.

52. According to Daniel Byman, the Abu Nidal Organization (ANO), the ETA, Al-Gama'a al-Islamiyya (Islamic Group), Al-Jihad (Egyptian Islamic Jihad), Armed Islamic Group, Liberation Tigers of Tamil Elam (LTTE), National Liberation Army (ELN), Kurdistan Workers' Party (PKK), Mujahedin-e Khalq (MEK), al-Qaeda, and the FARC all lost their direct state support over the course of the decade. Many adapted, including by building up criminal enterprises, combining with other groups, and transitioning to other forms of behavior (see chapter 6). For more on state sponsorship, see Byman, *Deadly Connections*, 3–4 and n. 5.

53. Coral M. Davenport, "Elusive Terrorist Group Takes a Hit—Finally," *Christian Science Monitor*, July 5, 2002; see also MIPT Terrorism Knowledge Base 17 November entry, accessed May 14, 2007.

54. They had ratified 10 of them. On the killing of Stephen Saunders and its aftermath, see "Justice: A Greek Tragedy," BBC News, March 12, 2001, http://news.bbc.co.uk/1/hi/programmes/correspondent/1205893.stm, accessed May 14, 2007; and "Gun Used to Kill Brigadier Found," BBC News, July 17, 2002, http://news.bbc.co.uk/1/hi/uk/2133623.stm, accessed May 14, 2007.

55. Police found a rucksack near the explosion site that contained two hand grenades and a .38 handgun stolen from a police officer killed by 17 November in 1984. The same Smith and Wessen had been used in a number of subsequent operations. George Kassimeris, "Last Act in a Violent Drama? The Trial of Greece's Revolutionary Organization 17 November," *Terrorism and Political Violence* 18, no. 1 (Spring 2006): 137–38.

56. Ibid., 138–39.

57. The upcoming 2004 Athens Olympics contributed to the government's desire to disable the group so as to demonstrate that Greece was safe for tourists. Alan Abrahamson, "Athens Makes Security 'Priority No. 1,'" *Los Angeles Times*, August 13, 2003.

58. Donatella Della Porta has studied this phenomenon in depth among Italian and German groups. See Della Porta, "The Logic of Underground Organizations," chap. 5 of *Social Movements*, 113–35.

59. Ibid., 115.

60. Meade, *The Red Brigades*, 50–51.

61. Donatella Della Porta and Gian Carlo Caselli, "The History of the Red Brigades: Organisational Structures and Strategies of Action, 1970–1982," in Catanzaro, *Red Brigades*, 73.

62. William R. Farrell, *Blood and Rage: The Story of the Japanese Red Army* (Lexington, Ky.: Lexington Books, 1990), 197.

63. The capture of Mickey McKevitt also contributed to the group's decline. (See chapter one.) James Dingley, "The Bombing of Omagh, 15 August 1998: The Bombers, Their Tactics, Strategy and Purpose behind the Incident," *Studies in Conflict and*

Terrorism 24, no. 6 (November–December 2001): 451–65; and Sean Boyne, "The Real IRA: After Omagh, What Now?" *Jane's Intelligence Review*, October 1998, accessed at http://www.janes.com/regional_news/europe/news/jir/jir980824_1_n .shtml on June 17, 2005. The Omagh bombing was the first attack carried out by republicans that was condemned by Gerry Adams. Earlier PIRA atrocities that had resulted in the loss of a large number of civilians included the 1972 Belfast bombs (11 dead, more than 100 injured); the 1974 Birmingham pub bombings (21 killed, more than 100 injured); the 1987 Enniskillen cenotaph bomb (11 killed), and the 1993 Shankill Road bomb (10 killed). See also Rogelio Alonso, "The Modernization in Irish Republican Thinking toward the Utility of Violence," *Studies in Conflict and Terrorism* 24, no. 2 (March–April 2001): 131–44.

64. The deal was to have resulted in the release of 39 RIRA prisoners held in jails in the Irish Republic. See Jonathan Tonge, "'They Haven't Gone Away, You Know': Irish Republican 'Dissidents' and 'Armed Struggle,'" *Terrorism and Political Violence* 16, no. 3 (Autumn 2004): 683.

65. See Ross and Gurr, "Why Terrorism Subsides," 413–14.

66. Sikh separatism aimed at establishing an independent state of Khalistan killed tens of thousands between 1981 and 1995, including Indian prime minister Indira Gandhi on October 31, 1984.

67. After Beslan, Western officials and diplomats were no longer willing to meet with Chechen rebels.

68. Zirakzadeh, "Revolutionary Dreams," 76.

69. In the beginning, ETA targets were mainly symbols of the Spanish government, such as public buildings and the police. However, their targeting evolved to become increasingly indiscriminate and counterproductive to the cause: between 1994 and 2004, 70 percent of the victims were civilians, and most were Basques. Maclean, "Madrid Sees Signs."

70. The precise poll figure was 47 percent. Ludger Mees, "The Basque Peace Process, National and Political Violence," in Darby and MacGinty, *Management of Peace Processes*, 169.

71. "Italy Mourns Murdered Statesman," BBC News, May 10, 1978, bbc.co .uk, accessed May 12, 2007.

72. Numerous Red Brigades members have written memoirs, including the man who actually killed Moro. See Mario Moretti, *Brigate Rosse: Una storia italiana* (Milan: Baldini & Castoldi, 2000). Also see Enrico Fenzi, *Armi e bagagli: Un diario dalle Brigate Rosse* (Milan: Costa & Nolan, 2006).

73. Senato della Repubblica/Camera dei Deputati, *Senato della Repubblica/ Camera dei Deputati parlamentare d'inchiesta sulla strage di Via Fani* (Rome: Senato della Repubblica, 1983), 131–32, cited by Leonard Weinberg, "The Red Brigades," chap. 2 of Art and Richardson, *Democracy and Counterterrorism*, 35–36 n. 15.

74. The BR had demanded that the Italian government release 13 jailed companions, but the government refused to negotiate. After his body was found, the interior minister Francesco Cossiga identified Mr. Moro, and then resigned. "Italy Mourns Murdered Statesman," BBC News.

75. Jamieson, "Entry, Discipline and Exit," 12–15; and Weinberg, "The Red Brigades," 36.

76. The release of the letter spawned two new offspring, the New Red Brigades/Communist Combatant Party (BR/PCC) and the Red Brigades/Union of Combatant Communists (BR/UCC). The former assassinated two government economic advisers (Professor Marco Biagi in 2002 and Professor Massimo D'Antona in 1999) and claimed the original Red Brigades legacy. Following the capture and trial of 17 members of the BR/PCC, however, police believed that they had likewise crippled its ability to operate. See "Red Brigades Suspects to Be Tried," BBC News, October 20, 2004, and David Willey, "Ghosts Return to Haunt Italy," BBC News, March 20, 2002, both accessed at http://news.bbc.co.uk on May 12, 2007.

77. This account is drawn from Wright, *The Looming Tower*, 290–93. See also Montasser al-Zayyat, *The Road to Al-Qaeda: The Story of Bin Laden's Right-Hand Man*, trans. Ahmen Fekry (New York: Pluto Press, 2004).

78. Lawrence Wright claims that they committed ritual suicide, but this seems to be a minority view. *The Looming Tower*, 257–58. See also MIPT Terrorism Knowledge Base, http://www.tkb.org/Incident.jsp?incID=8303, accessed June 6, 2007.

79. For an overview of the relationship between the foreign-based Islamists and indigenous Egyptian groups see Diaa Rashwan, "'Two Targets, One Enemy,'" *Al-Ahram Weekly Online*, Issue No. 746, June 9–15, 2005, http://weekly.ahram.org.eg/2005/746/focus.htm.

80. Wright, *The Looming Tower*, 258. See also Gilles Kepel, *Jihad: The Trail of Political Islam*, 4th ed. (London: I. B. Taurus, 2006), 288–89.

81. Millar, "We're at War."

82. According to Bruce Hoffman, state-sponsored attacks during the 1980s were eight times more lethal than those carried out by groups acting on their own. *Inside Terrorism* (London: Victor Gollancz, 1998), 189.

CHAPTER FIVE: REPRESSION

1. Ivanov was speaking at the Munich Conference on Security Policy. C. J. Chivers, "Russian Aide Says Problem of Chechnya Is 'Solved,'" *International Herald Tribune*, February 13, 2007, 3.

2. On intervention, see Roberts, "War on Terror," 115–21.

3. This process of state formation is brilliantly explained and described by Phillip Bobbitt, *The Shield of Achilles: War, Peace, and the Course of History* (London: Penguin, 2003).

4. Much of political science focuses only on domestic repression. An excellent research review is Christian Davenport, "State Repression and Political Order," *Annual Review of Political Science* 10 (June 2007): 85–101.

5. According to Walter Laqueur, the meaning of terrorism was given in the 1798 supplement of the *Dictionnaire* of the Académie Française as *système, regime de la terreur*. *Dictionnaire, Supplément* (Paris, [1798]), 775, cited by Laqueur, *Terrorism*, 6 and n. 1.

6. Examples include Argentina, Britain, China, Egypt, France, Germany, Mexico, Pakistan, Peru, the Philippines, Russia, Saudi Arabia, Turkey, and Uruguay.

7. Between 1983 and 2000, the United States used military responses to terrorist attacks in three instances: the El Dorado canyon strikes against Libya, fol-

lowing the La Belle discotheque bombing in 1986; cruise missile strikes on Iraq's intelligence agencies in 1993, in response to an assassination attempt on President George H. W. Bush; and cruise missile strikes against al-Qaeda sites in Afghanistan, following the 1998 bombing of the U.S. embassies in Tanzania and Kenya. See Michelle L. Malvesti, "Explaining the United States' Decision to Strike Back at Terrorists," *Terrorism and Political Violence* 13, no. 2 (Summer 2001): 85–106; Martha Crenshaw, "Coercive Diplomacy and the Response to Terrorism," in Art and Cronin, *Coercive Diplomacy*; and Timothy Hoyt, "Military Force," in Cronin and Ludes, *Attacking Terrorism*, 162–85.

8. For an argument that terrorism is a form of war, see Everett L. Wheeler, "Terrorism and Military Theory: An Historical Perspective," in *Terrorism Research and Public Policy* (Abingdon: Frank Cass, 1991), 6–33. For an eloquent rejoinder, see Michael Howard, "What's in a Name? How to Fight Terrorism," *Foreign Affairs* 81, no. 1 (January–February 2002): 8–13.

9. According to Walter Laqueur, horse thieves in Latin American used to claim political motives in order to avoid being hanged. See *Terrorism*, 4.

10. See note 6.

11. I have written at greater length about strategies of leverage in *Ending Terrorism: Lessons for Defeating al-Qaeda*, Adelphi Paper No. 394 (London: Routledge for the International Institute for Strategic Studies, 2008).

12. The strategic concept of "coercion" is the use of force or threatened use of force, but it can be mixed with diplomacy to provide positive inducements, too. Compellence is a subset of coercion and better describes what state leaders usually think terrorist groups are trying to do.

13. An argument about the effectiveness of terrorism as a strategy of attrition, particularly forcing states to withdraw from territory, is provided by Kydd and Walter, "The Strategies of Terrorism." In addition to the strategies mentioned here, Kydd and Walter include spoiling and outbidding; but spoiling applies only to narrow situations such as negotiations, and outbidding refers only to competitions between rival terrorist groups. Both are tactics (or process goals); neither directly addresses a campaign's overall purpose (or outcome goals). See chapter 3.

14. States may also respond by redoubling their efforts, as the Russians in Chechnya and the Indians in Kashmir.

15. This kind of thinking also removes the imperative to grapple with the divergent strategic thinking and worldview of the attacker. A Western economic model of two "rational" actors is enough.

16. This argument builds on the excellent overview of terrorism's strategies provided by Martha Crenshaw in "Terrorism and Global Security," chap. 5 of *Leashing the Dogs of War: Conflict Management in a Divided World* (Washington, D.C.: U.S. Institute of Peace Press, 2007), 73–75.

17. One of the best-known twentieth-century theorists of provoking the state to repression is Carlos Marighella, in his *Minimanual of the Urban Guerrilla* (Harmondsworth: Penguin, 1971).

18. Robert Gerwarth, presentation to the Changing Character of War seminar, "White Terror: Paramilitary Violence in Germany, Austria and Hungary after the Great War," February 13, 2007.

258 • Notes to Chapter Five

19. Rami Khouri, "Algeria's Terrifying but Unsurprising Agony," *Middle East Review of International Affairs*, March 1998; and Kydd and Walter, "The Strategies of Terrorism," 67.

20. This is one reason why they occur in the immediate aftermath of attacks, "while the situation is hot," in former national security advisor Brent Scowcroft's words. See Malvesti, "Explaining the Decision," 95.

21. Research on U.S. opinion polls in the wake of attacks from 1979 to 2003 indicates that support for the president varies according to the costs in human and material terms, the types of people targeted, and the types of weapons used. See William Josiger and George Shaumbaugh, "Public Prudence, the Policy Salience of Terrorism and Presidential Approval following Terrorist Incidents," unpublished paper, September 2005. Specifically regarding 9/11, one U.S. poll found 71 percent in favor of military retaliation. See "Poll: Shock Gives Way to Anger," CBS News, September 13, 2001, http://www.cbsnews.com/stories/2001/09/13/archive/main311139.shtml. On September 17, the Gallup Poll quoted a figure closer to 90 percent. See "Support for Military Action against Terrorist Attackers," CNN.com/Community, September 17, 2001, http://archives.cnn.com/2001/COMMUNITY/09/17/newport/index.html. A similar media poll in the UK weeks later found 70 percent supported military retaliation. See "The Observer Poll Results," *The Observer*, October 7, 2001, http://politics.guardian.co.uk/conservatives2001/story/0,,564832,00.html. The figures in France and Italy were 68 percent and 88 percent respectively. See "EU Leaders to Hold Emergency Summit on Security," *Daily Telegraph*, September 18, 2001, http://www.telegraph.co.uk/news/main.jhtml?xml=/news/2001/09/18/wdip18.xml (all websites viewed on March 22, 2007).

22. Jack Levy famously wrote, "The absence of war between democracies comes as close as anything we have to an empirical law in international relations." "Domestic Politics and War," *Journal of Interdisciplinary History* 18, no. 4 (Spring 1988): 662.

23. For example, the 2002 U.S. National Security Strategy says: "Traditional concepts of deterrence will not work against a terrorist enemy." George W. Bush, *The National Security Strategy of the United States of America* (Washington, D.C.: GPO, 2002), 46. A sophisticated argument about deterrence and terrorism is Paul K. Davis and Brian Michael Jenkins, *Deterrence and Influence in Counterterrorism: A Component in the War on al Qaeda* (Santa Monica, Calif.: RAND, 2002). For critics' arguments and a much fuller discussion of the efficacy of deterrence than can be presented here see Patrick M. Cronin and Audrey Kurth Cronin, *Challenging Deterrence: Strategic Stability in the 21st Century*, IISS/CCW Joint Report, February 2007, accessed at http://ccw.politics.ox.lac.uk on June 13, 2008.

24. Robert F. Trager and Dessislava P. Zagorcheva also argue that deterrence worked against the MILF. See "Deterring Terrorism: It Can Be Done," *International Security* 30, no. 2 (Winter 2005–6): 87–123.

25. But it is not just a state's prestige that may appear to be at stake: brazen defiance by leaders who sponsor terrorist attacks has been seen as personal provocation for military counterattack, as in U.S. retaliations against Mu'ammar Gadhafi, Saddam Hussein, and Osama bin Laden. Malvesti, "Explaining the Decision," 96.

26. An excellent argument about using military force against terrorism is Caleb Carr's "Terrorism as Warfare," 1–12.

27. *Preemption* and *prevention* are often used interchangeably, leading to confusion. Preemption requires knowledge of an impending attack. See Lawrence Freedman, "Prevention, not Preemption," *Washington Quarterly* 26, no. 2 (Spring 2003): 105–14; and Martha Crenshaw, "Terrorism, Strategies, and Grand Strategies," chap. 3 of *Attacking Terrorism*, 93 n. 43.

28. For an interesting discussion of how democracies learn in counterterrorism, see Art and Richardson, "Conclusion," in *Democracy and Counterterrorism*, 563–601.

29. I am grateful to Brian Jenkins for this observation.

30. The word *volya* means both "will" and "liberty" in Russian. The name is sometimes translated as People's Liberty.

31. German idealism was expressed, for example, in the ideas of Hegel and Schelling, and positivism was drawn from the writings of Buchner and Moleschott.

32. Material on the ideas and evolution of the social revolutionaries in Russia is drawn from Richard Pipes, "The Intelligentsia," chap. 10 of *Russia under the Old Regime*, 2nd ed. (London: Penguin, 1993), 249–80. Other important sources on Narodnaya Volya (in addition to those specifically cited below) are Hans Rogger, *Russia in the Age of Modernisation and Revolution, 1881–1917* (London: Longman, 1983); David Saunders, *Russia in the Age of Reaction and Reform, 1801–1881* (London: Longman, 1992), esp. chap. 11; and Philip Pomper, "Russian Revolutionary Terrorism" chap. 3 of Crenshaw, *Terrorism in Context*, 63–101.

33. Adam Ulam, *Russia's Failed Revolutions: From the Decembrists to the Dissidents* (London: Weidenfeld and Nicolson, 1981), 127–28.

34. For detailed descriptions of all attempts on the tsar's life see David Footman, *Red Prelude: A Life of A. I. Zhelyabov*, 2nd ed. (London: Cresset Press, 1968), esp. chap. 8.

35. In spring 1880, two members of the Executive Committee (Kviatkovski and Presnyakov) went on trial and were hanged. Sofia Lvovna Perovskaya was the first female in Russia to be hanged for a political crime.

36. Ironically, Perovskaya's father had lost his job because of an earlier attempt on Alexander II carried out by nihilist Dmitri Karakozov in 1866.

37. According to Yarmolinsky, he was an errand boy for the butcher. Avrahm Yarmolisky, *Road to Revolution: A Century of Russian Radicalism* (New York: Macmillan, 1959), 279.

38. In all, four bombers were deployed by Perovskaya to kill the tsar. In addition to Ryasakov and Grinevitski were Timothy Mihailov, a factory hand, aged 21, and Ivan Emilianov, a student, aged 19. Mikhailov was hanged with the others in April 1881, and Emilianov was sentenced to a life of hard labor in Siberia. Footman, *Red Prelude*. See also Walter G. Moss, *Alexander II and His Times: A Narrative History of Russia in the Age of Alexander II, Tolstoy, and Dostoevsky* (London: Anthem Press, 2002); and Edvard Radzinsky, *Alexander II: The Last Great Tsar* (New York: Free Press, 2005); and Hugh Seton-Watson, *The Decline of Imperial Russia, 1855–1914* (London: Methuen, 1952).

39. On the fate of populism see Isaiah Berlin, *Russian Thinkers* (London: Hogarth Press, 1978), esp. 210–37. For a detailed explanation of the changes instituted after the murder of the tsar, see Pipes, "Towards the Police State," chap. 11 of *Russia under Old Regime*, 281–318.

40. An excellent description of the changes instituted in the assassination's aftermath is given by Seton-Watson, *Decline of Imperial Russia*, esp. part 2, "Reaction, 1881–1904," 109–217.

41. Ronald Seth, *The Russian Terrorists: The Story of the Narodniki* (London: Barrie and Rockliff, 1966), 168–71.

42. Ronald H. Berg, "Peasant Responses to Shining Path in Andahuaylas," chap. 5 of Palmer, *Shining Path of Peru*, 102; Ton de Wit and Vera Gianotten, "The Origins and Logic of the Shining Path: Two Views; The Center's Multiple Failures," chap. 3 of Palmer, *Shining Path of Peru*, 68. Palmer argues that although there was astonishing violence, Sendero Luminoso did not engage in indiscriminate violence, as the Khmer Rouge did. See "Conclusion," 265.

43. Of the approximately 69,000 people who died or "disappeared" as a result of the campaign of Shining Path, about half were killed by the group, about a third at the hands of the military, and the remainder were either unaccounted for or killed by smaller militia forces. "Final Report," *Truth and Reconciliation Commission of Peru (English translation by International Center for Transitional Justice)*, 2003, 2–3. http://216.70.99.144/images/uploads/peru_trc_conclusions .pdf, viewed on March 22, 2007.

44. By comparison, Argentina's notorious "dirty war" of the 1980s killed fewer than half that many (about 30,000), Turkey's campaign against the PKK also killed about 30,000 (as we shall discuss shortly), and Pinochet's Chile killed about 3,000. See "Truth and Reconciliation in Peru—World Notes," *Catholic New Times*, November 16, 2003.

45. In both 1959 and 1965, the government had sent the military to answer peasant rebellions; but in the latter case, the military had then taken over in a coup. President Belaúnde Terry feared that the pattern might repeat itself.

46. The Truth and Reconciliation Commission, Final Report, vol. 6, *The Periods of Violence*, 53, cited by Amnesty International, "The Truth and Reconciliation Commission: A First Step towards a Country without Injustice," available at http:// web.amnesty.org/library/index/engamr460032004, accessed on March 19, 2007.

47. David Scott Palmer, "The Revolutionary Terrorism of Peru's Shining Path," chap. 7 of Crenshaw, *Terrorism in Context*, 295 and table 7.1 on p. 271.

48. Amnesty International, "Peru: Summary of Amnesty International's Concerns 1980–1995," http://web.amnesty.org, accessed on March 19, 2007.

49. See David Scott Palmer, "Appendix: Political Violence in Peru—Analysis of Data, 1980–1992," in Crenshaw, *Terrorism in Context*, 307.

50. An excellent commentary on Peru's counterterrorist operation is Palmer, "Name of Mao," 195–220.

51. "We have reconstructed history and we have reached the conclusion that it would not have been so grave if it were not for the indifference, passivity, and simple ineptness of those who held the highest political office at the time," said Salomon Lerner, president of the Truth and Reconciliation Commission of Peru. Lucien Chauvin, "Peru: Truth, but No Reconciliation," *World Press Review* 50,

no. 11 (November 2003), http://www.worldpress.org/Americas/1595.cfm, accessed on March 20, 2007.

52. *The Military Balance, 1993–4* (London: International Institute for Strategic Studies), 62. Sources used for background on the PKK are Henri J. Barkey, "Turkey and the PKK," in Art and Richardson, *Democracy and Counterterrorism,* 343–81; Michael M. Gunter, *The Kurds and the Future of Turkey* (London: Macmillan, 1997); Ismet G. Imset, *The PKK: A Report on Separatist Violence in Turkey (1973–1992)* (Istanbul: Turkish Daily News Publications, 1992); Kemal Kirisci and Gareth M. Winrow, *The Kurdish Question and Turkey: An Example of a Transstate Ethnic Conflict* (London: Frank Cass, 1997); Andrew Mango, "Ataturk and the Kurds," in *Seventy-Five Years of the Turkish Republic,* ed. Sylvia Kedourie (London: Frank Cass, 2000), 1–25; and Philip Robins, *Suits and Uniforms: Turkish Foreign Policy since the Cold War* (London: Hurst, 2003), esp. chaps. 5 and 9.

53. Human Rights Watch, "Ocalan Trial Monitor: Backgrounder on Repression of Kurds in Turkey," 1999, http://www.hrw.org/backgrounder/eca/turkey/kurd.htm, accessed on March 20, 2007; and Michael Radu, "The Land of Many Crossroads: The Rise and Fall of the PKK," *Orbis* 45, no. 1 (Winter 2001): 57.

54. The casualty figures are broken down by the head of the antiterrorist department of the Turkish police as 5,121 members of the security forces killed, 4,049 civilians, and 17,248 persons described as terrorists. *Milliyet,* June 30, 1998, 8, cited by Mango, "Ataturk and the Kurds," 1. See also Barkey, "Turkey and the PKK," 344.

55. The antiterrorism law went into effect in April 1991. The U.S. State Department's 1996 report on human rights singled it out for condemnation, claiming that almost 6,000 people were in jail as a result. U.S. Department of State, *Turkey Country Report on Human Rights Practices,* Bureau of Democracy, Human Rights and Labor, January 30, 1997.

56. The connection with Syria was important. In the early 1980s, the PKK reportedly got its first real training alongside various Palestinian groups and with the help of Syrian intelligence. When Öcalan was in Damascus, he functioned under the protection of Syrian secret service goons, a fact officially denied by the Syrian government even as it dispatched them. Henri Barkey and Graham Fuller, *Turkey's Kurdish Question* (Oxford: Rowman and Littlefield, 1998).

57. The Turkish government carried out cross-border operations against the PKK in Iraq, both during the war (tolerated by Saddam Hussein's government) and during the 1990s (tolerated by Washington). At the end of the 1990s, Turkey had between 1,000 and 10,000 men in northern Iraq at any one time. Robins, *Suits and Uniforms,* 318. It did so again in 2008.

58. Barkey, "Turkey and the PKK," 372–73.

59. Jeffrey Cason, "Electoral Reform and Stability in Uruguay," *Journal of Democracy* 11, no. 2 (April 2000): 86–87.

60. Fernando Lopez-Alves, "Political Crises, Strategic Choices and Terrorism: The Rise and Fall of the Uruguayan Tupamaros," *Terrorism and Political Violence* 1, no. 2 (April 1989): 225. Hostages included U.S. public safety officer Daniel Mitrione, whose release was made contingent on the freeing of some 150 jailed Tupamaros. The Uruguayan government refused to negotiate and police cordoned off the entire city, but he was killed after 10 days.

61. Jennifer S. Holmes, *Terrorism and Democratic Stability* (Manchester: Manchester University Press, 2001). On the effects of military repression see "Uruguay," U.S. Library of Congress Country Studies, Federal Research Division, available at http://lcweb2.loc.gov/frd/cs/uytoc.html.

62. Lopez-Alves, "Political Crises," 225. Uruguay established a Peace Commission 30 years later, in August 2000. Because of the elapsed time, as well as popular ambivalence about uncovering the past, clear casualty figures have been elusive. See Eugenia Allier, "The Peace Commission: A Consensus on the Recent Past in Uruguay?" *European Review of Latin American and Caribbean Studies* 81 (October 2006): 87–96. On the use of torture in Uruguay, see Lawrence Weschler, "Reporter at Large: The Great Exception," *New Yorker*, April 10, 1989; and *A Miracle, a Universe: Settling Accounts with Torturers* (Chicago: University of Chicago Press, 1998).

63. For much more depth on this case, see my "Russia and Chechnya," in Art and Richardson, *Democracy and Counterterrorism*, 383–424.

64. Matthew Evangelista, *The Chechen Wars: Will Russia Go the Way of the Soviet Union?* (Washington, D.C.: Brookings Institution, 2002), 19–20.

65. See Anatol Lieven, *Chechnya: Tombstone of Russian Power* (New Haven: Yale University Press, 1998), 86. For an opposing viewpoint, see Evangelista, *The Chechen Wars*, 30–31. Dmitri V. Trenin argues the hijackers were criminals who sought profit, not independence. See Trenin, "The Forgotten War: Chechnya and Russia's Future," Policy Brief No. 28, Carnegie Endowment for International Peace, 2. A Moscow-backed faction had tried a fortnight earlier to overthrow Dudayev's government.

66. The evidence for this viewpoint is indirect. Olga Oliker cites an email exchange with BG John Reppert (ret.), December 10, 2000, based on General Reppert's personal conversations with General Grachev. Nonetheless, given how events transpired, it seems a plausible explanation. See Olga Oliker, *Russia's Chechen Wars, 1994–2000: Lessons from Urban Combat* (Santa Monica, Calif.: RAND, 2001), 9 n. 13, downloaded from http://www.rand.org/publications/MR/MR1289/ on December 12, 2003. See also John R. Pilloni, "Burning Corpses in the Streets: Russia's Doctrinal Flaws in the 1995 Fight for Grozny," *Journal of Slavic Military Studies* 13, no. 2 (June 2000), 62 n. 45.

67. For much more on this see Oliker, *Russia's Chechen Wars*, 12–16.

68. "Casualty Figures," *Chechnya Weekly* (Jamestown Foundation) 4, no. 5 (February 20, 2003). The 5,500 figure is the official Russian government number, and 14,000 is the estimate of the Soldiers' Mothers of Russia organization.

69. It is difficult to get reliable casualty statistics. The Russian Interior Ministry claimed that 20,000 civilians had been killed. Sergey Kovalyov, a prominent human rights activist, estimated more than 50,000 had died. Chechen authorities have claimed about 100,000 deaths. See Human Rights Violations in Chechnya, at http://www.hrvc.net; and "Casualty Figures."

70. Carlotta Gaal and Thomas de Waal, *Chechnya: Calamity in the Caucasus* (New York: New York University Press, 1998), 244.

71. Pilloni, "Burning Corpses," 54. See also "The 'Dirty War' in Chechnya: Forced Disappearances, Torture, and Summary Executions," *Human Rights*

Watch 13, no. 1 (D) (March 2001), available at http://www.hrw.org/reports/2001/chechnya/, accessed on April 24, 2004.

72. Oliker, *Russia's Chechen Wars*, 9–12.

73. Gaal and de Waal, *Chechnya*, 275. The Russian Al'fa commando force had been deployed against the Chechens in the Budennovsk hospital siege but was forced to disengage under fire when the government decided to negotiate. See Mark Galeotti, "Elite Squad Hoping to Share Expertise," www.janes.com, accessed at http://www.janes.com/security/law_enforcement/news/ipi/ipi0313.shtml, on December 12, 2003.

74. The Budennovsk incident was followed in January 1996 by a raid by 200 Chechen rebels led by Salman Raduyev on a Russian military airfield and the taking of thousands of hostages at a hospital in the town of Kizlyar, in Dagestan. Like Basayev's raid, the Chechens demanded that Russian troops leave Chechnya. Most of the hostages were released the next day; however, more than 2,400 Russian military, security, and police troops lay siege to the rebels, disregarding the fate of the remaining hostages and vowing to deal a "decisive blow" to terrorism. See Jim Nichol, *Chechnya Conflict: Recent Developments and Implications for U.S. Interests*, CRS Report for Congress, No. 96-193, March 1, 1996, 2.

75. Dennis A. Pluchinsky, "Terrorism in the Former Soviet Union: A Primer, a Puzzle, a Prognosis," *Studies in Conflict and Terrorism* 21 (1998): 126.

76. Fiona Hill, Statement to the Helsinki Commission Hearing, "The Chechen Crisis and Its Implications for Russian Democracy," November 3, 1999, 2–3, accessed at http://www.eurasia.org/publications/news/view.aspx?ID=80 on December 30, 2008.

77. Some argue that the Chechens may not have been responsible for the bombings. See Michael Wines, "A Film Clip, and Charges of a Kremlin Plot," *New York Times*, March 6, 2002, A8; and Stephen J. Blank, "An Ambivalent War: Russia's War on Terrorism," *Small Wars and Insurgencies* 14, no. 1 (Spring 2003): 134.

78. "Putin's Chechen Remark Causes Stir," BBC News, November 13, 2002, accessed at http://news.bbc.co.uk/2/hi/europe/2460305.stm on February 16, 2004.

79. *Izvestia*, October 1, 1999, cited by James Hughes, "Chechnya: The Causes of a Protracted Post-Soviet Conflict," *Civil Wars* 4, no. 4 (Winter 2001): 37.

80. Hill, 1999 Statement to the Helsinki Commission, 3.

81. According to RAND, these included Alos Abudzhafar, a camp focused on partisan tactics and marksmanship; Yakub, a camp specializing in heavy weapons; Abubakar, a camp devoted to terrorist tactics, and Davlat, a camp teaching psychological and ideological warfare. These reports are not confirmed. Oliker, *Russia's Chechen Wars*, 39–40.

82. Ibid., 39–50.

83. Four days after the event, the Russian government announced that the drug was derived from fentanyl, but this claim is questioned. See Martin Enserink and Richard Stone, "Questions Swirl over Knockout Gas Used in Hostage Crisis," *Science* 298, no. 5596 (November 8, 2002): 1150–51.

84. Nichol, *Russia's Chechnya Conflict* (RL31620), 11. The *Washington Post* reported on June 10, 2002: "Though Russian military forces are no closer to winning the war than they were when Putin launched it in the fall of 1999, Mr.

Putin has succeeded in squelching almost all critical discussion of the conflict in the Russian media." "Chechnya's Refugees," A20.

85. Hughes, "Chechnya," 37; and Oliker, *Russia's Chechen Wars*, 62–65.

86. Oliker, *Russia's Chechen Wars*, 297–98. Putin won 71 percent of the vote and faced no serious opposition. See Stuart D. Goldman, *Russia*, Issue Brief for Congress, No. IB 92089, April 9, 2004.

87. This was followed in October 2006 by the murder of journalist Anna Politkovskaya, one of few remaining reporters covering the Chechen conflict, shot dead in the elevator of her Moscow flat.

88. C. J. Chivers, "Signs of Renewal Emerge from Chechnya's Ruins," *New York Times*, May 4, 2006; and Chivers, "Problem of Chechnya Solved," 3.

89. In February 2007, Putin personally elevated Ramzan Kadyrov, son of the assassinated president, to the presidency. In bringing prosperity and stability to Chechnya, Kadyrov seemed to enjoy a degree of genuine local support. Tom Parfitt, "Putin Hands Chechnya Control to Militia Leader," *Guardian*, February 17, 2007, http://www.guardian.co.uk, accessed March 17, 2007.

90. Gangs reportedly regrouped in the North Caucasus, where the ratio of Russian federal military services to operatives killed is 1.5 to 1, worse than in the final stages of operations in Chechnya (where operatives were consistently at a disadvantage). Mkhail Lukanin, "Terrorism Changes Addresses, Meeting Places," *Nezavisimoye Voyennoye Obozreniye*, March 16, 2007; in Johnson's Russia List, "Russia Battles Fewer, More Dispersed, Committed Insurgents in North Caucasus," 2007, no. 65, March 18, 2007, item no. 23.

91. Julia Latynina, "Open Season: Life in Putin's Russia," *Washington Post*, June 22, 2008, B1, B4.

92. The organization is given many names, including Muslim Brotherhood, Society of Muslim Brothers, Muslim Brothers, Brothers, the Society, Ikhwan al-Muslimin, and Ikhwan (Brothers).

93. Notably Ayman Zawahiri, Osama bin Laden's partner in leadership of al-Qaeda, in 1991 wrote a well-known book harshly condemning the Muslim Brotherhood, entitled *The Muslim Brotherhood's Bitter Harvest in Sixty Years* (Al-Hisad al-Murr lil Al-Ikhwan al-Muslimin fi Sittin Aman), better known as *Bitter Harvest*.

94. Richard P. Mitchell, *The Society of the Muslim Brothers*, 2nd ed. (Oxford: Oxford University Press, 1993), preface, xxvi. Much of the following account is drawn from this well-respected history. Other sources used include Gilles Kepel, *The Prophet and Pharaoh: Muslim Extremism in Egypt* (London: Al Saqi Books, 1985); and Barry Rubin, *Islamic Fundamentalism in Egyptian Politics* (London: Palgrave Macmillan, 1990).

95. There is disagreement about the year of founding, but the most reliable is the Arabic date Dhu al-Qi'ida, 1347, or March 1928, as Banna himself recorded it. Mitchell, 8.

96. This was a situation Banna described as British military and foreign "economic occupation."

97. Goals are taken from Mitchell, *Society of Muslim Brothers*, 234–41.

98. By 1949, there were 500,000 members in 2,000 branches. After 1949, the number dropped sharply; there were 1,500 branches with 200,000–300,000

members. Mitchell, 328. Mitchell's original source is Muhammad Shawqi Zaki, *The Muslim Brothers and the Egyptian Society,* 33 (adapted from a University of Cairo thesis supervised by Muslim Brother Kamal Khalifa; no date given). This assessment is confirmed by Ishak Musa Husseini, who wrote that the membership may have declined to 200,000–300,000 members after 1949 due to repression by the 'Abd al-Hadi government. Ishak Musa Husseini, *The Moslem Brothers* (Beirut: Khayat's 1956, 18, cited by Kirk J. Beattie, *Egypt during the Nasser Years: Ideology, Politics, and Civil Society* (Oxford: Westview Press, 1994), 34 n. 34.

99. Mitchell, *Society of Muslim Brothers,* 68.

100. Ibid., 69–70. Original source is al-Mabahith, 12, December 19, 1950.

101. See Yvonne Yazbeck Haddad, "The Qur'anic Justification for an Islamic Revolution: The View of Sayyid Qutb," *Middle East Journal* 37, no. 1 (Winter 1983): 14–29. On the trip to Mecca, see Derek Hopwood, *Egypt: Politics and Society, 1945–1984* (London: Allen and Unwin, 1985), 95.

102. Interview with Sha'arawi Gumai, Minister of Interior, in *al-Ahram,* December 12, 1967. Cited by John Waterbury, *The Egypt of Nasser and Sadat* (Princeton: Princeton University Press, 1983), 34.

103. Mitchell, *Society of Muslim Brothers,* 148–49.

104. The exact date is unknown. See William E. Shepard, *Sayyid Qutb and Islamic Activism: A Translation and Critical Analysis of Social Justice in Islam* (New York: E. J. Brill, 1996), especially the introduction, ix–xvii.

105. The three books published after 1957 are *Khasais al-Tasawwur al-Islami wa Muqawamatuhu* (The Characteristics and Values of Islamic Conduct), 1960; *Al-Islam was Mushkilat al-Hadara* (Islam and the Problems of Civilization), n.d. (after 1954); and *Ma'alim fi'l-Taria* (Signposts on the Road), 1964. See the list of writings given by Kepel, *The Prophet and Pharaoh,* 68–69.

106. After the 1950s and 1960s, the Brothers carefully promoted a reputation as a nonviolent movement, although riots have occurred that may have been encouraged by them, and there has been terrorist activity by other groups that may be related to them. See Hesham Al-Awadi, *In Pursuit of Legitimacy: The Muslim Brothers and Mubarak, 1982–2000* (London: Tauris, 2004), 117–18 and 178–80.

107. Robert L. Leiken and Steven Brooke, "The Moderate Muslim Brotherhood," *Foreign Affairs* 86, no. 2 (March–April 2007): 107–21. This is an excellent summary of the history of the movement and the debate over its current status. See also John Walsh, "Egypt's Muslim Brotherhood: Understanding Centrist Islam," *Harvard International Review* 24, no. 4 (Winter 2003): 32–36; and Abd al-Monein Said Aly and Manfred W. Wenner, "Modern Islamic Reform Movements: The Muslim Brotherhood in Contemporary Egypt," *Middle East Journal* 36, no. 3 (Summer 1982): 336–61.

108. A well-reasoned argument about the fundamentally radical viewpoints of all Islamists is offered by Martin Kramer, "Ballots and Bullets: Islamists and the Relentless drive for Power," *Harvard International Review* 19, no. 2 (Spring 1997): 16–19, 61.

109. Walsh, "Egypt's Muslim Brotherhood."

110. Kepel, *Jihad,* 50–52.

111. Al-Suri is a Syrian now in U.S. custody. In captured documents he examines the failings of the campaign in Syria and proposes an alternative strategy for

waging jihad successfully. See Harmony document no. AFGP-2002-600080; and "Al-Qa'ida: Back to the Future: The Vanguard and Muslim Brotherhood Operations in Syria," both published in Combating Terrorism Center, *Harmony and Disharmony: Exploiting Al-Qa'ida's Organizational Vulnerabilities*, February 2006, available at http://www.ctc.usma.edu. See also Paul Cruickshank and Mohannad Hage Ali, "Abu Musab Al Suri: Architect of the new Al Qaeda," *Studies in Conflict and Terrorism* 30, no. 1 (January–February 2007): 1–14. Al-Suri's analysis of the Syrian campaign is discussed in more depth in chapter 7.

112. Al-Jihad was responsible for the 1981 assassination of Anwar Sadat. In 2001 al-Jihad merged with al-Qaida; Ayman Zawahiri was its leader and has been the intellectual force behind al-Qaeda. Egyptian al-Gama'a al-Islamiyya (EIG) violently opposed the Camp David Accords of 1978. Its spiritual leader, Sheikh Omar Abdel al-Rahman, is currently serving a life sentence for conspiring in the 1993 World Trade Center bombing. EIG's merger with al-Qaeda was announced by Zawahiri on August 5, 2006. See the article by Andrew Black, "The Reconstituted al-Qaeda Threat in the Maghreb," *Terrorism Monitor* (Jamestown Foundation) 5, no. 2 (February 1, 2007), available at http://www.jamestown.org.

113. Gilles Kepel, *The War for Muslim Minds: Islam and the West* (Cambridge: Belknap Press of Harvard University Press, 2004), 79.

CHAPTER SIX: REORIENTATION

1. Augustine, *City of God*, book 4, chap. 4 (London: Oxford University Press, 1963), 72.

2. See the *Seventh Report of the Independent Monitoring Commission* (London: Stationery Office, October 19, 2005), particularly 33–39. Available at http://www.independentmonitoringcommission.org/documents/uploads/7th%20%20IMC%20%20Report.pdf, accessed on May 5, 2007. The PIRA had long been involved in criminal activities; however, those activities increased markedly following the 1998 agreement.

3. As Bruce Hoffman points out, nearly a third of the groups listed as Foreign Terrorist Organizations by the U.S. State Departments might also be called insurgencies. Hoffman, *Inside Terrorism*, 2nd ed. (New York: Columbia University Press, 2006), 35.

4. These would include the Revolutionary Armed Forces of Colombia (FARC), the National Liberation Army (ELN), and the United Self-Defense Forces of Colombia (AUC).

5. See Ratko Parezanin, *Mlada Bosna I prvi svetski rat* (Young Bosnia and the First World War) (Munich: Iskra, 1974), cited by Roberts, "War on Terror," 107 n. 15.

6. Sari Horwitz, "Cigarette Smuggling Linked to Terrorism," *Washington Post*, June 8, 2004. This is just a notable example. Hezbollah has a broad base of financial support, including funds from wealthy patrons, a sympathetic diaspora, its own criminal activities, and a cut of profits from wealthy criminals.

7. Criminal activities may harm the reputation of a terrorist group with its potential constituency, making its commitment to an ideology seem shallow. This has occurred with the FARC, the PIRA, and with left-wing groups in Italy.

8. Malik, *Enough of the Definition*, 54.

9. Individuals who start out in criminal gangs may also become radicalized, as was the case with those who carried out the 2005 Madrid train attacks. The transition can go both ways.

10. Terrorist expertise itself can even become a kind of commodity, with groups selling their services to each other. Technical expertise in such things as explosives, weaponry, suicide techniques, and targeting tips have been shared among groups as disparate as Hezbollah, the Tamil Tigers, the PIRA, and the FARC. On criminality in Northern Ireland, see Marie Smyth, "The Process of Demilitarization and the Reversibility of the Peace Process in Northern Ireland," *Terrorism and Political Violence* 16, no. 3 (August 2004): 544.

11. Criminal behavior and political ideology might be thought of as being at different ends of a spectrum. See Svante E. Cornell, "Narcotics and Armed Conflict: Interaction and Implications," *Studies in Conflict and Terrorism* 30, no. 3 (March 2007): 207–27.

12. The relationship between drugs, crime, and violence is extremely complex and will not be fully parsed here. Good overviews on criminal behavior and terrorism include Phil Williams, "Transnational Criminal Organizations and International Security," *Survival* 36, no. 1 (1994): 96–113; Thomas M. Sanderson, "Transnational Terror and Organized Crime: Blurring the Lines," *SAIS Review* 24, no. 1 (Winter–Spring 2004): 49–61; and Chris Dishman, "Terrorism, Crime, and Transformation," *Studies in Conflict and Terrorism* 24, no. 1 (2001): 43–58.

13. Allison Jamieson, "Mafia and Institutional Power in Italy," *International Relations* 12, no. 1 (April 1994): 1–24. Jamieson describes the "Colombianization" of the Mafia, 22–23.

14. Colombia, Military Developments 2006, IISS Armed Conflict Database. Available at http://acd.iiss.org/armedconflict/MainPages/dsp_ConflictWeapons .asp?ConflictID=169&YearID=1020, accessed on May 5, 2007.

15. Juan Forero, "U.S. Indicts 50 Colombians for Drug Trafficking," *New York Times*, March 23, 2006, A6.

16. Waldman estimates 25 percent are political. Peter Waldmann, "Colombia and the FARC: Failed Attempts to Stop Violence and Terrorism in a Weak State," chap. 8 of Art and Richardson, *Democracy and Counterterrorism*, 227. Thomas Fischer places the total at only about 12–15 percent. See Fischer, "War and Peace in Colombia," in *Civil Wars: Consequences and Possibilities of Regulation*, ed. Heinrich-W. Krumwided and Peter Waldmann (Baden-Baden: Nomos, 2000), 291.

17. There are alleged connections between the PIRA and the FARC. In 2001 three PIRA members were accused of training members of the FARC in the use of explosives. Tried in 2003, they were acquitted of the explosives charge but convicted of traveling into Colombia on false passports. Connie Veillette, *Colombia: Issues for Congress*, CRS Report for Congress, No. RL32250, January 19, 2005, 4.

18. For an interesting analysis of the transition from left-wing Marxist group to a credible alternative for "good government" see Román D. Ortiz, "Insurgent

268 • Notes to Chapter Six

Strategies in the Post–Cold War: The Case of the Revolutionary Armed Forces of Colombia," *Studies in Conflict and Terrorism* 25, no. 2 (March–April 2002): 127–43. Also see Chalk, "Evolving Dynamic," 151–52.

19. Veillette, *Colombia*, 3.

20. Periodically the group has negotiated with the Colombian government and achieved concessions. In 1999, for example, the FARC was granted autonomy over a Switzerland-size zone in southern Colombia (the *Zona de Despeje*, or Area of Distension). When the group's military activity continued, including the kidnapping of a Colombian senator, the Colombian government launched an operation to retake the territory.

21. The FARC is the largest of the substate actors, along with the ELN (Ejercito de Liberación Nacional), and the AUC (Autodefensas Unidas de Colombia). Four smaller groups, the M-19, the EPL (Ejército Popular de Liberación), the Quintin Lame Armed Movement (Movimiento Armado Quintin Lame), and the Revolutionary Worker's Party (Partido Revolucionario de los Trabajadores de Colombia) gave up the struggle in the early 1990s following negotiations.

22. The FARC was first designated a terrorist organization by the United States in 1997. Most of the aid went to the Colombian police. For an approving U.S. discussion of Colombian military action, see Thomas A. Marks, "A Model Counterinsurgency: Uribe's Colombia (2002–2006) vs. FARC," *Military Review*, March–April 2007, 41–56. Opposing viewpoints are described in Gary Fields, "Move to Link Drug, Terror Wars Draws Flak; Critics Say Effort Could Invite Colombian Human-Rights Abuses," *Wall Street Journal*, April 1, 2002, A14.

23. The status would have given the group increased legal standing under international law and would also have made it explicitly subject to a wide range of obligations—e.g., not targeting civilians. Andres Cala, "The Enigmatic Guerrilla: FARC's Manuel Marulanda," *Current History* 99, no. 634 (February 2000): 59; and Michael Shifter, "The United States and Colombia: Partners in Ambiguity," *Current History* 99, no. 634 (February 2000): 52.

24. A careful analysis of claims and available evidence see Chris Zambelis, "Al-Qaeda in the Andes: Spotlight on Colombia," *Terrorism Monitor* (Jamestown Foundation) 4, no. 7 (April 6, 2006): 6–8.

25. Most notably, the documents allegedly confirmed years of coordination between the FARC and the Venezuelan army, as well as offers of $300 million from Venezuelan president Hugo Chávez. "The FARC Files: Colombia and Venezuela," *The Economist* (U.S. ed.), May 24, 2008.

26. Juan Forero, "Millions Rally for Colombian Hostages: Protests Condemn Kidnappings by FARC Rebels," *Washington Post*, July 21, 2008, A01. According to the Free Country Foundation in Bogota, nearly 700 hostages remain under FARC control.

27. Patrick J. McDonnell and Chris Kraul, "Colombian Rebels Splintering," *Los Angeles Times*, July 5, 2008; Gray Miles and Kathryn Jezer-Morton, "Rescue Puts Guerrillas Closer to the History Books," *Globe and Mail* (Canada), July 4, 2008. Marulanda died of a heart attack in March 2008.

28. Abu Sayyaf also draws members from its successor, the Moro Islamic Liberation Front (MILF), with which government negotiations continue. Some argue that it has restored ties with the MILF in Mondanao and is pressuring

them not to come to an accord. Simon Elegant, "The Return of Abu Sayyaf," *Time*, August 23, 2004, accessed at www.time.com/time/magazine/article/0,9171,501040830-686107,00.html on April 7, 2007.

29. Membership figures taken from the IISS Armed Conflict Database.

30. Other successors were also killed: Khadaffy Janjalani (September 2006) and Abu Sulaiman (January 2007). Romeo Ricardo, chief of the Intelligence Group of the Philippine police, claims that these two provided the connection to Middle East donors. See Council on Foreign Relations, Backgrounder on the Abu Sayyaf Group, accessed at http://www.cfr.org/publication/9235/ on June 7, 2008.

31. Before 9/11, the FBI tried to ransom the Burnhams and lost $300,000 in the process, reportedly to elements within the Philippine police. Mark Bowden, "Jihadists in Paradise," *The Atlantic*, March 2007, 54–60.

32. BBC News Online, June 1, 2001, accessed at http://news.bbc.co.uk on April 14, 2007.

33. This according to the Philippine National Bureau of Investigation (NBI). See IISS Armed Conflict Database, "Abu Sayyaf Group (ASG): Annual Update 2006," January–March 2006, available online at http://acd.iiss.org/armedconflict/MainPages/dsp_AnnualUpdate.asp?ConflictID=207&YearID=1048, accessed on May 5, 2007.

34. For a strong argument that Abu Sayyaf has returned to its Islamist roots, see Zachary Abuza, *Balik-Terrorism: The Return of the Abu Sayyaf*, Strategic Studies Institute Monograph (Carlisle: U.S. Army War College, September 2005), accessible athttp://www.carlisle.army.mil/ssi. See also Filler, "The Abu Sayyaf Group."

35. Bowden, "Jihadists in Paradise," 60. Brian Jenkins observed in private correspondence that this "adolescent understanding of Islam" is true of the majority of the jihadists. It also makes them comparable to many members of the RAF, Revolutionary Cells, Red Brigades, etc., who had only a superficial understanding of Marxism. Jenkins believes that the appeal is therefore emotional and psychological, not ideological.

36. *Guerrillas* is another term referring to a numerically larger group of armed individuals who operate as a military unit, attack enemy military forces, and seize and hold territory, at least temporarily. Bruce Hoffman distinguishes between guerrillas and insurgents, saying that only the latter have "coordinated informational (e.g., propaganda) and psychological warfare efforts designed to mobilize popular support in a struggle against an established national government, imperialist power, or foreign occupying force" (Hoffman, *Inside Terrorism* [2006], 35). I do not think that, in the twenty-first century, there is a meaningful distinction between the terms *guerrilla* and *insurgent*—though the former has more often been used to refer to rural campaigns and the latter to urban.

37. Small, weak organizations that target the military and police tend to be crushed by them. Brazil's Carlos Marighella, in his *Minimanual of the Urban Guerrilla* advocates targeting military and police targets in order to keep them in a state of fear and undermine confidence in the state's authority. But as his own experience demonstrated (he was shot by police in an ambush), such an approach is foolish without the numbers and military assets to back it up. This is one reason that terrorism targets noncombatants. See *Minimanual*, chap. 16, "Objectives of the Guerrilla's Actions."

38. Hoffman, *Inside Terrorism* (2006), 41. Some scholars have defined *all* terrorist behavior as a subset of insurgency; one defines seven types of insurgent movements, including anarchist, egalitarian, traditionalist, pluralist, secessionist, reformist, and preservationist, for example. See Bard E. O'Neill, *Insurgency and Terrorism: Inside Modern Revolutionary Warfare* (Washington, D.C.: Brassey's, 1990), esp. chap. 2, pp. 13–30. While recognizing areas of overlap between the two terms, I argue that they can and should be distinguished because the distinctions carry important psychological and even operational implications.

39. The best arguments for the use of the term *insurgency* to describe the al-Qaeda movement are offered by David J. Kilcullen, "Countering Global Insurgency," *Journal of Strategic Studies* 28, no. 4 (August 2005): 597–617.

40. For an interesting analysis of the regime, see William Quandt, *Between Ballots and Bullets: Algeria's Transition from Authoritarianism* (Washington, D.C.: Brookings Institution, 1998), esp. chap. 3, "Pressures for Change," 30–41.

41. Martin Stone, *The Agony of Algeria* (London: Hurst, 1997), 63–64.

42. Ibid.

43. Arun Kapil, "Algeria's Elections Show Islamist Strength," *Middle East Report*, No. 166, September–October 1990, 32.

44. Willis, *Islamist Challenge in Algeria*, 110.

45. There were 14 other Islamist parties, including HAMAS and MNI, which were the major competitors; but the FIS was easily the most dominant. See Mohammed M. Hafez, "From Marginalization to Massacres: A Political Process Explanation of GIA Violence in Algeria," chap. 1 of *Islamic Activism: A Social Movement Theory Approach*, ed. Quintan Wiktorowicz (Bloomington: Indiana University Press, 2004), 45–46 and n. 5.

46. Figures are from the *Journal Officiel de la République Algérienne*, January 4, 1992, annex 2, cited by Hugh Roberts, "Algeria's Ruinous Impasse and the Honourable Way Out," *International Affairs* (Royal Institute of International Affairs) 71, no. 2 (April 1995): 257. Fashioned after the French, it was a two-part, winner-take-all electoral process, and the military intervened after the first round. One reason that the FIS won such a large proportion of the votes was that the system had been deliberately skewed in favor of the major party, which everyone expected would be the FLN. See Quandt, *Between Ballots and Bullets*, 59.

47. The new president, Mohammed Boudiaf, was killed by his own security guard only six months later, in June 1992.

48. The founders of the FIS were Abbassi Madani, a professor who avowed commitment to democratic principles merged with moderate Islam, and Ali Ben Hadj, an extremist Islamist who called democracy *kufr* (unbelief) and argued for conservative Islamic social practices. See Kapil, "Algeria's Elections," 34.

49. FIS Communiqué no. 21, May 3, 1992, quoted in Willis, *Islamist Challenge in Algeria*, 267.

50. Hafez, "From Marginalization to Massacres," 46–47.

51. Willis, *Islamist Challenge in Algeria*, 281–82.

52. Ibid., 366–69.

53. Andrew J. Pierre and William B. Quandt, "Algeria's War on Itself," *Foreign Policy* 99 (Summer 1995): 137. There was also extensive GIA terrorist activity in France. For an excellent analysis, see Jeremy Shapiro, "France and the GIA,"

chap. 5 of Art and Richardson, *Democracy and Counterterrorism*, 133–66. To escape the Algerian government's crackdown, members of the GIA and the AIS used the Iberian peninsula as a stopover on their way to safe haven in Britain and Canada. The GIA also set up several cells in Belgium. Kepel, *War for Muslim Minds*, 242.

54. Bruno Callies de Salies, "Algeria in the Grip of Terror," *Le Monde diplomatique*, October 1997, accessed at http://mondediplo.com/1997/10/alger1 on April 18, 2007.

55. Human Rights Watch World Report 1999: Algeria, accessed at http://www .hrw.org/worldreport99/mideast/algeria.html on April 18, 2007.

56. Muriel Mirak-Weissbach, "The Case of the GIA," *Executive Intelligence Review*, October 13, 1995.

57. Human Rights Watch, "Algeria: New Amnesty Law Will Ensure Atrocities Go Unpunished," Joint Statement by Amnesty International, Human Rights Watch, the International Center for Transitional Justice, and the International Federation for Human Rights, March 1, 2006, accessed at http://hrw.org/english/docs/2006/03/01/algeri12743.htm on April 19, 2007.

58. In January 2007 the group renamed itself the Al-Qaeda Organization in the Islamic Maghreb and was officially welcomed into union with the al-Qaeda "consortium" by Ayman Zawahiri. Kidnappings and attacks on military, police, and civilians have continued, although the Algerian government does not publish official statistics and experts disagree over whether the violence is increasing.

59. There is much written about this issue. See Graham T. Allison, *Nuclear Terrorism: The Risks and Consequences of the Ultimate Disaster* (London: Robinson, 2006); Michael A. Levi and Michael O'Hanlon, *The Future of Arms Control* (New York: Brookings Institution, 2005); Joseph Cirincione and Kathleen Newland, *Repairing the Regime: Preventing the Spread of Weapons of Mass Destruction* (London: Routledge, 2000); Daryl G. Kimball, "The Future of the Nuclear Non-proliferation Regime," Arms Control Association website, 2005, http://www.armscontrol.org/events/20050219_AAAS.asp, accessed May 5, 2007; Jacob Blackford, "Multilateral Nuclear Export Controls after the A.Q. Khan Network," *Institute for Science and International Security Website*, 2005, http://www .isis-online.org/publications/expcontrol/multilateralexportcontrols.pdf, accessed May 5, 2007; John Simpson, "The Nuclear Non-proliferation Regime: Back to the Future?" *Disarmament Forum*, 2004, http://www.unidir.org/pdf/articles/pdf-art2015.pdf, viewed on May 7, 2007.

60. Vladimir Dedijer, *The Road to Sarajevo* (London: MacGibbon and Kee, 1967). Princip had not wanted to set off a major war. The goal of at least some of those who plotted the assassination was to *defer* an Austro-Serbian war that Serbia, weakened by the Balkan Wars, would clearly lose. It did the opposite. See David MacKenzie, *Apis: The Congenial Conspirator; the Life of Colonel Dragutin R. Dimitrijevic* (New York: Columbia University Press, 1989), 137.

61. For excellent analyses of Austria-Hungary's role in the origins of the war, see Samuel R. Williamson Jr., *Austria-Hungary and the Origins of the First World War* (London: Palgrave Macmillan, 1991), esp. chap. 10, "Vienna and the July Crisis," 190–216; and Hew Strachan, *The First World War* (London: Penguin, 2003), esp. chap. 1, "To Arms," 1–32.

62. Although connections to officials such as Dragutin Dimitrijevic (known as "Apis"), head of Serbian military intelligence, emerged only after the war had begun, a clear link with Belgrade had been established within four days of the assassination. Gavril Princip, the 19-year-old who fired the pistol, was one of seven conspirators who called themselves the "Young Bosnians" and had been equipped by members of the Serbian group "Black Hand." The others were Trifko Gravez, Nedeljkio Cabrinovic, Mehmed Memedbasic, Basa Cubrilovic, and Cvetko Popovic, all assisted by Danilo Ilic. C. Popovic, "Rad organizacije," *Nova Evropa* (Zagreb) 16, nos. 10–11 (1927): 321; Ljubibratic, *Mlada Bosna*, 37, cited by David MacKenzie, *The "Black Hand" on Trial: Salonika, 1917* (New York: Columbia University Press, 1995), 49 n. 44. See also Williamson, *Austria-Hungary*, 188–89; and MacKenzie, *Apis*, esp. chap. 12, "Murder in Sarajevo (June 1914)," 123–37.

63. For much more information and analysis of the outbreak of the war, see Keith Wilson, ed., *Decisions for War, 1914* (London: University College London Press, 1995).

64. The Line of Control is mainly along the cease-fire line arranged by the United Nations in 1949, then adjusted by the 1972 Simla Accord following the 1971 conflict. See Michael Quinlan, "How Robust Is India-Pakistan Deterrence?" *Survival* 42, no. 4 (Winter 2000–2001): 145–46; and Howard B. Schaffer and Teresita C. Schaffer, "Kashmir: Fifty Years of Running in Place," chap. 12 of *Grasping the Nettle: Analyzing Cases of Intractable Conflict*, ed. Chester A. Crocker, Fen Osler Hampson, and Pamela Aall (Washington, D.C.: U.S. Institute of Peace Press, 2005), 295–98.

65. The largest of these is Hizb-ul Mujahideen, which, according to Indian government estimates, has about 1230 members. See Praveen Swami, "Beating the Retreat," *Frontline*, October 26–November 8, 2002.

66. Between 1989 and 1995, the Indian government captured Afghan weapons including 13,427 AK-47s, 750 rocket launchers, 1,682 rockets, and 789 machine guns. On average, the government claims to recover 4,000 weapons per year, of varying sophistication. Quoted in Victoria Schofield, *Kashmir in Conflict: India, Pakistan, and the Unending War* (London: Tauris, 2003), 176.

67. Quinlan, "How Robust Is India-Pakistan Deterrence?" 146.

68. There is dispute about the initial date of the action; it was either May 4, 5, or 6, 1999. Rahul Roy-Chaudhury, "India and Pakistan: Nuclear Weapons and the Use of Force," Lecture for the Changing Character of War Programme, Oxford University, April 24, 2007.

69. Sumantra Bose, "Kashmir: Sources of Conflict, Dimensions of Peace," *Survival* 41, no. 3 (Autumn 1999): 149–50. Victoria Schofield claims 30,000 civilians were displaced. *Kashmir in Conflict*, 219.

70. Jaish-e-Mohammed initially claimed credit for the bombing on the state assembly building and then denied involvement.

71. S. Paul Kapur, "India and Pakistan's Unstable Peace: Why Nuclear South Asia Is Not Like Cold War Europe," *International Security* 30, no. 2 (Fall 2005): 148–49.

72. Swami, "Beating the Retreat."

73. Ihtasham ul Haque, "Pakistan Forces Put on High Alert: Storming of Parliament," *Dawn*, December 15, 2001.

74. Statement of Director of Central Intelligence George Tenet before the Senate Armed Services Committee, Hearing on "Worldwide Threat: Converging Dangers in a Post-9/11 World," March 19, 2002. See also K. Alan Kronstadt, *Terrorism in South Asia*, CRS Report for Congress, No. RL32259, December 13, 2004, 29.

75. Sumit Ganguly, "Will Kashmir Stop India's Rise?" *Foreign Affairs* 85, no. 4 (July–August 2006): 49.

76. Ibid., 50. A series of attacks occurred in Mumbai, India, in November 2008 (after this book had gone to press) and once again nearly resulted in war.

77. On Pakistan's history and complex domestic politics, see Stephen Philip Cohen, *The Idea of Pakistan* (Washington, D.C.: Brookings Institution Press, 2004).

78. Some confidence-building measures go back to the 1980s. See Michael Quinlan, "India-Pakistan Deterrence Revisited," *Survival* 47, no. 3 (Autumn 2005): 103–15. See also "Nuclear Safety and Security in South Asia—an Agenda for Risk Reduction," *Strategic Comments* (IISS, London) 11, no. 3 (March 2005).

79. Of course, states also relied on countervalue targeting as a means of deterrence, especially during the early nuclear era—a challenging ethical practice that will not be debated here. See Michael Quinlan, "A British Political Perspective," in *The Price of Peace: Just War in the Twenty-first Century*, ed. Charles Reed and David Ryall (Cambridge: Cambridge University Press, 2007), 286–94.

80. It is no wonder that our soldiers are sometimes confused, even badly misguided, in carrying out their duties. There are scores of examples of practical dilemmas and mistakes made by U.S. soldiers in Iraq. These include a young boy whose backpack was mistaken for a bomb, a pair of fishermen who leaned over to turn off the boat engine and were shot, and a man and his sister who were killed because they approached a checkpoint too quickly. See Paul von Zielbauer, "Civilian Claims on U.S. Suggest the Toll of War," *New York Times*, April 12, 2007, http://www.nytimes.com.

81. Others assert that the source of legitimacy for this new state is religion; still others argue that it is the ability of the state to provide welfare and opportunities for its people. But for elites to make such assertions is not enough. This debate over sources of legitimacy is being carried out on the ground, both through the use of force and through the power of new communications media. The "winner" of this "war" will be the popular entity that gains the greatest legitimacy as the successor to the nineteenth-century nation-state.

82. Kilcullen, "Countering Global Insurgency."

83. I have written about the relationship between twenty-first-century communications and the state's capacity to mobilize in my "Cyber-mobilization: The New Levée en Masse," *Parameters* 36, no. 2 (Summer 2006): 77–87.

CHAPTER SEVEN: HOW AL-QAEDA ENDS

1. Al Jazeera, November 2, 2004, http://english.aljazeera.net/English/archive/ archive?ArchiveId=7403, accessed July 16, 2007.

2. "The Terrorism Index," *Foreign Policy* and the Center for American Progress, July–August 2006. According to a poll of experts in both Democratic and Republican parties, 84 percent believed that the United States was not winning

the so-called war on terror. Accessed at http://www.foreignpolicy.com/issue_july aug_2006/TI-index/index.html on July 16, 2007.

3. This 75 percent figure was given by President Bush on at least four occasions during the 2004 presidential campaign, including at the Republican convention and in three presidential debates. See Anne Cherbonnier, "The 75% Solution," *Baltimore Chronicle and Sentinel*, October 26, 2004.

4 Some of the following discussion builds on my "How al-Qaida Ends: The Decline and Demise of Terrorist Groups," *International Security* 31, No. 1 (Summer 2006): 7–48.

5. See, for example, David Cook, *Paradigmatic Jihadi Movements*, CTC's Jihadi After Action Report series, ed. Jarret Brachman and Chris Heffelfinger, Combating Terrorism Center, United States Military Academy, West Point, 2006; and Abu Mus'ab al-Suri, *Observations Concerning the Jihadi Experience in Syria*, date unknown, 6–7, quoted and cited by Jarret M. Brachman and William F. McCants, "Stealing Al-Qa'ida's Playbook," CTC Report; both accessed at http://www.ctc .usma.edu on June 11, 2007.

6. *Qaeda* can mean base of operation, vanguard, foundation, or method. It also had a prosaic meaning: during the late 1980s, bin Laden set up a database of fighters in the Afghan war against the Soviets. The computer file on which their names appeared was called al-Qaeda (the [Data]base). Kepel, *Jihad*, 315; and Jason Burke, "Think Again: Al Qaeda," *Foreign Policy* 142 (May–June 2004): 18. See also Jason Burke, "What Is Al-Qaeda," Chap. 1 of *Al-Qaeda: Casting a Shadow of Terror* (London: Tauris, 2003), 7–22.

7. Wright, *The Looming Tower*, 259.

8. Burke, "Think Again," 18.

9. Burke, "What Is al-Qaeda?" 13–17. Bruce Hoffman divides the organization into four elements: al-Qaeda central; al-Qaeda affiliates and associates; al-Qaeda locals; and the al-Qaeda homegrown network. See Hoffman, "Challenges for the U.S. Special Operations Command Posed by the Global Terrorist Threat: Al Qaeda on the Run or on the March?" written testimony submitted to the House Armed Services Subcommittee on Terrorism, Unconventional Threats and Capabilities of the U.S. Congress, February 14, 2007.

10. An article that discusses the process of formal alignment is Rita Katz and Josh Deven, "Franchising Al Qaeda," *Boston Globe*, June 22, 2007, accessed at http://www.boston.com/news/globe/editorial_opinion/oped/articles/2007/06/22/franchising_al_qaeda?mode=PF on June 29, 2007.

11. "If a Muslim is in Britain and doesn't want to leave his job or university and go and fight Jihad on the front, what he can do is call the press agency and tell them, 'I'm from the global Islamic resistance' and claim responsibility for whatever action is being done around the world." August 2000 training video; captured in 2006. Cited by Cruickshank and Ali, "Abu Musab Al Suri," 8.

<comp.: apostrophe in '05, next note>

12. Senior al-Qaeda leaders who have been captured or killed include Haitham al-Yemeni, Abu Atef, Khalid Sheikh Mohammed, Hambali (Riduan Isamuddin), Abu Faran al-Libi and Abu Hamza Rabia. A failed airstrike was launched against Ayman Zawahiri in January 2006. Mark Mazzetti, "U.S. Aborted Raid on Qaeda

Chiefs in '05," *New York Times*, July 8, 2007; and Hoffman, "Challenges for Special Operations," 4.

13. For more information on this phenomenon, see Steve Coll and Susan B. Glasser, "Terrorists Turn to the Web as Base of Operations," *Washington Post*, August 7, 2005, A01.

14. For an early analysis, see Audrey Kurth Cronin, *Al-Qaeda after the Iraq Conflict*, CRS Report for Congress, No. RS21529, May 23, 2003, available at http://www.fas.org/irp/crs/RS21529.pdf.

15. For a comprehensive list of groups alleged to have ties with al-Qaeda, including some who have merged with it, see the al-Qaeda entry in the MIPT terrorism knowledge database, at http://www.tkb.org/; accessed June 2007.

16. Conversation with Ahmed Rashid, Pakistani author and journalist, Oslo, Norway, June 24, 2007; and Katherine Shrader and Matthew Lee, "U.S. Intel Warns al-Qaida Has Rebuilt," Associated Press, July 12, 2007, accessed at http://www .breitbart.com/article.php?id=D8QAROG00&show_article=1%3Cp on July 12, 2007.

17. Conversation with Rashid, June 26, 2007; and Mark Mazzetti, David Rohde, and Margot Williams, "Al-Qaeda Chiefs Are Seen to Regain Power," *New York Times*, February 19, 2007, A1.

18. Possible exceptions include the international anarchist movement, though it was active only in Russia, Europe, and the United States.

19. According to Sageman's analysis, operatives have gathered in regional clusters, including the central staff of al-Qaeda, the Southeast Asian cluster, the Maghreb cluster, and the core Arab cluster. Marc Sageman, *Understanding Terror Networks* (Philadelphia: University of Pennsylvania Press, 2004).

20. Ibid., 119. Sageman's book analyzes the patterns of growth of cells involved in past attacks, including vigorous refutation of the thesis that exposure to ideology alone explains the growth of al-Qaeda.

21. Ibid., 178.

22. See Diane Singerman, "The Networked World of Islamist Social Movements," chap. 5 of Wiktorowicz, *Islamic Activism*, 143–63.

23. See Quintain Wiktorowicz, "The New Global Threat: Transnational Salafis and Jihad," *Middle East Policy* 8, no. 4 (December 2001): 18–38.

24. Doug McAdam and Ronnell Paulsen, "Specifying the Relationship between Social Ties and Activitism," in *Social Movements: Readings on Their Emergence, Mobilization, and Dynamics*, ed. Doug McAdam and David A. Snow (Los Angeles: Roxbury, 1997), 146, cited by Singerman, "Networked World," 153.

25. Bruce Hoffman strongly disagrees, seeing the hand of al-Qaeda directly involved in almost all of the significant terrorist attacks since 2001. See Hoffman, "The Myth of Grass-Roots Terrorism: Why Osama bin Laden Still Matters," *Foreign Affairs* 87, no. 3 (May–June 2008): 133–38.

26. Marc Sageman points to a "third wave" of operatives that "had no or very faint connection to al Qaeda Central." While the core remains dangerous, he argues, "Beginning in 2004, the clear operational links (command, control, training, personnel, or financing) of the second-wave operations gradually disappeared." See Sageman, *Leaderless Jihad: Terror Networks in the Twenty-first Century*

(Philadelphia: University of Pennsylvania Press, 2008), 139; and Sageman, "The Reality of Grass-Roots Terrorism," *Foreign Affairs* 87, no. 4 (July–August 2008): 165–66. See also Jack Kalpakian, "Building the Human Bomb: The Case of the 16 May 2003 Attacks in Casablanca," *Studies in Conflict and Terrorism* 28, no. 2 (March–April 2005): 113–27.

27. Paul Pillar, "Counterterrorism after Al-Qaeda," *Washington Quarterly* 27, no. 3 (Summer 2004): 101–13.

28. Paul Reynolds, "Bomber Video 'Points to al-Qaeda,'" *BBC News*, September 2, 2005.

29. Michael Moss and Souad Mekhennet, "Militants Widen Reach as Terror Seeps Out of Iraq," *New York Times*, May 28, 2007. The Ansar al Islam plot to attack the 2004 NATO summit in Turkey was, according to Turkish sources, developed in part by operatives who had fought in Iraq. See also Jeffrey Cozzens, "Islamist Groups Develop New Recruiting Strategies," Terrorism and Insurgency Centre, *Jane's Intelligence Review*, February 1, 2005.

30. Sageman, *Understanding Terrorist Networks,* esp. 92.

31. On this point, see Bruce Hoffman, "The Changing Face of Al-Qaeda and the Global War on Terrorism," *Studies in Conflict and Terrorism* 27, no. 6 (December 2004): 556. See also the 2008 *Foreign Affairs* dispute between Hoffman and Sageman cited in notes 24 and 25. Both were right.

32. On this subject see Laqueur, *Terrorism*, 3–20; and James Joll, *The Second International, 1889–1914* (London: Weidenfeld and Nicolson, 1955).

33. See Douglas Farah and Peter Finn, "Terrorism, Inc.: Al-Qaeda Franchises Brand of Violence to Groups across World," *Washington Post*, November 21, 2003; Daniel Benjamin, "Are the Sparks Catching?" *Washington Post*, November 23, 2003; and Sebastian Rotella and Richard C. Paddock, "Experts See Major Shift in Al-Qaeda's Strategy," *Los Angeles Times*, November 19, 2003.

34. As the IISS points out, the 2002 Bali bombing cost less than $35,000, the 2000 *USS Cole* operations about $50,000, and the September 11, 2001, attacks less than $500,000. IISS, *Strategic Survey*, 2003–4 (Oxford: Oxford University Press, 2004), 8. Estimates indicate that more recent attacks were also inexpensive: 2004 Madrid bombings, $10,000 (Gordon Corera, "Al Qaeda Undimmed By Sanctions," BBC Online, August 27, 2004, http://news.bbc.co.uk/1/hi/world/americas/3606384.stm, accessed July 16, 2007); the 2003 Istanbul bombings, $40,000 (BBC, "Al Qaeda Sanctions "Ineffective," BBC Online, August 27, 2004, http://news.bbc.co.uk/1/hi/world/americas/3603862.stm, accessed July 16, 2007); 2003 Jakarta bombings $30,000 (Joshua Prober, "Accounting for Terror: Debunking the Paradigm of Inexpensive Terrorism." *Policywatch*, No. 1041, November 1 2005, Washington Institute for Near East Policy, http://www.washingtoninstitute.org/templateC05.php?CID=2389, accessed July 16, 2007); and the 2005 London bombings, £8,000 (Home Office Narrative, cited by BBC, "At a Glance: July 7 Reports," BBC Online, May 12, 2006, http://news.bbc.co.uk/1/hi/uk/4764427.stm, accessed July 16, 2007).

35. "U.S.: Terror Funding Stymied," CBS News, January 11, 2005, http://www.cbsnews.com/stories/2005/01/11/terror/main666168.shtml.

36. On the pervasiveness of these channels, see Moises Naim, "It's the Illicit Economy, Stupid," *Foreign Policy* 151 (November–December 2005): 96; and

Naim, *Illicit: How Smugglers, Traffickers, and Copycats Are Hijacking the Global Economy* (New York: Doubleday, 2005).

37. On informal financing mechanisms, see testimony of Juan Carlos Zarate, Assistant Secretary, Terrorist Financing and Financial Crimes, U.S. Department of the Treasury, before the House Financial Services Committee Subcommittee on Oversight and Investigations, 109th Congress, lst Session, February 16, 2005, http://www.ustreas.gov/press/releases/js2256.htm. See also Rensselaer Lee, *Terrorist Financing: The U.S. and International Response*, CRS Report for Congress, No. RL31658, December 6, 2002, 11–13.

38. For more on illegal and legal globalized networks of financing, see *Terrorist Financing*, Report of an Independent Task Sponsored by the Council on Foreign Relations (New York: Council on Foreign Relations Press, October 2002); *Update on the Global Campaign against Terrorist Financing*, Second Report of an Independent Task Force on Terrorist Financing Sponsored by the Council on Foreign Relations (New York: Council on Foreign Relations Press, June 15, 2004); Loretta Napoleoni, *Modern Jihad: Tracing the Dollars behind the Terror Networks* (London: Pluto Press, 2003); and Douglas Farah, *Blood from Stones: The Secret Financial Network of Terror* (New York: Broadway Books, 2004).

39. Greg Miller, "Influx of Al-Qaeda Money into Pakistan Is Seen," *Los Angeles Times*, May 20, 2007.

40. For more on this phenomenon, see Cronin, "Behind the Curve," 30–58.

41. Harmony document no. AFGP-2002-600321, 2, quoted in Combating Terrorism Center, *Harmony and Disharmony*, 53.

42. On terrorist use of the Internet, see Gabriel Weimann, "www.terror.net: How Modern Terrorism Uses the Internet," Special Report No. 116, U.S. Institute of Peace, March 2004; and Weimann, *Terror on the Internet: The New Arena, the New Challenges* (Washington, D.C.: U.S. Institute of Peace Press, 2006).

43. Popular historical reference points are the reconstruction of the spread of Islam in the seventh century, and the defeat of the Crusaders in the eleventh century.

44. Statement by U.S. secretary of defense Donald Rumsfeld, January 15, 2003, cited by Weimann, "www.terror.net," 7.

45. The SITE Institute (Search for International Terrorists) monitors al-Qaeda's Internet communications, at http://siteinstitute.org. See also the book by its founder, Rita Katz, *Terrorist Hunter* (New York: Ecco, 2003).

46. I have written more on this phenomenon elsewhere. See Audrey Kurth Cronin, "Cyber-mobilization: The New *Levée en Masse*," *Parameters* 36, no. 2 (Summer 2006): 77–87.

47. Arrest is simply not possible, not least because bin Laden is surrounded by body guards who are instructed to kill him before he could be taken alive. There have been regular rumors that he has already died. See for example "Officials, Friends Can't Confirm Bin Laden Death Report," CNN.com, September 24, 2006. These reports are unlikely to be true. See also Amir Taheri, "Is Bin Laden Dead or Alive?" *Gulf News*, March 14, 2007.

48. For a compelling presentation of this argument, see Wright, *The Looming Tower*.

49. Comparable cell-based "immortal" terrorist networks have included the socialist-anarchist movements of the late nineteenth century and the Party of Social Revolutionaries in Russia in the early 1900s.

50. For further information see, for example, Mark Mazzetti, "New Generation of Qaeda Chiefs Is Seen on Rise," *New York Times*, April 2, 2007, A1.

51. Bruce Reidel, "Al Qaeda Strikes Back," *Foreign Affairs* 86, no. 3 (May–June 2007): 24–40.

52. Mark Mazzetti, "Qaeda Leaders Losing Sway over Militants, Study Finds," *New York Times*, November 15, 2006, A1. The authors of the study argue that a group of Saudi and Jordanian clerics is having a greater intellectual impact upon the next generation of militants than is bin Laden or Zawahiri. See William McCants and Jarret Brachman, eds., *Militant Ideology Atlas: Executive Summary* (West Point, N.Y.: Combating Terrorism Center, November 2006).

53. The effort against the al-Qaeda movement has involved both a law enforcement paradigm and a war paradigm. Arrests have been made of key terrorist planners like Khalid Sheikh Mohammed and Hambali, and al-Qaeda leaders have been killed in the Pakistan border region. These have had important tactical effects but have not ended the movement. See also Mark Mazzetti, "U.S. Aborted Raid," *New York Times*, July 8, 2007, A1. Killings by armed aerial drones have also enraged many in Pakistan.

54. Mazzetti, Rohde, and Williams, "Al-Qaeda Chiefs," A1; and Ahmed Rashid, *Descent into Chaos: The United States and the Failure of Nation Building in Pakistan, Afghanistan, and Central Asia* (New York: Viking, 2008).

55. Mazzetti, " New Generation," A1.

56. Burke, *Al-Qaeda*, 39, and chap. 8, "Seekers," 106–23. See also Angel Rabasa, Peter Chalk, Kim Cragin, Sara A. Daly, Heather S. Gregg, Theodore W. Karasik, Kevin A. O'Brien, and William Rosenau, *Beyond al-Qaeda, Part One: The Global Jihadist Movement* (Santa Monica, Calif.: RAND, 2006), chap. 2, "Al-Qaeda's Ideology and Propaganda," 7–22.

57. Zawahiri himself realizes the danger of negotiations for the movement. "If I fall as a martyr in the defense of Islam, my son Muhammad will avenge me, but if I am finished politically and I spend my time arguing with governments about some partial solutions, what will motivate my son to take up my weapons after I have sold these weapons in the bargains' market?" Laura Mansfield, *His Own Words: A Translation of the Writings of Dr. Ayman al Zawahiri*, Part I: *Knights under the Prophet's Banner* ([Old Tappan, N.J.]: TLG Publications, 2006), 128.

58. This is a discourse that is regrettably advanced by those in the West who speak of a "clash of civilizations."

59. For an interesting argument about negotiations with the core or periphery, see Ram Manikkalingam and Pablo Policzer, "Engaging Al-Qaeda? Armed Groups, Information and Coercion," unpublished paper presented at the Canadian Political Science Association Conference, Saskatoon, Saskatchewan, May 29–June 1, 2007.

60. See Souad Mekhennet and Michael Moss, "A New Face of Jihad Vows Attacks on U.S.," *New York Times*, March 16, 2007; and Craig Whitlock, "From Iraq to Algeria, Al-Qaeda's Long Reach," *Washington Post*, May 30, 2007.

61. See, for example, Corine Hegland, "Global Jihad," *National Journal,* May 8, 2004, 1396–1402.

62. Ahmed Rashid, *Taliban: Militant Islam, Oil, and Fundamentalism in Central Asia* (New Haven: Yale University Press, 2001), 130.

63. Many of the so-called Afghan Arabs were neither Afghani nor Arab. According to Jason Burke, one of bin Laden's contributions to the cause during the war against the Soviets was to pay rent for a building at 38 Syed Jamal al-Din road in Pashawar, used as neutral ground for talks between bickering factions. Burke, citing interview with former Hizb-e-Islami activist, Peshawar, October 2001, in *Al-Qaeda*, 76 and n. 32. See also Rashid, *Taliban*, chap. 10, "Global Jihad: The Arab-Afghans and Osama Bin Laden," 128–49.

64. McCants and Brachman, *Militant Ideology Atlas: Executive Summary*, 9. This is a summary of the recurring themes and divisive issues in jihadist thinking, an excellent insight into its ideological vulnerabilities.

65. This debate occurs between Salafi Sheikhs in the so-called Awakening Movement, including Shaikh Al-Albani, Abd al-Aziz Bin Baz, Salim al-Hilali, and Rabee Madkhalee, among others, on the one hand, and Zawahiri and other followers of Qutb ("Qutubis") on the other. See Harmony document AFGP-2002-601041, quoted and translated in Combating Terrorism Center, *Harmony and Disharmony*, 53–54.

66. McCants and Brachman, *Militant Ideology Atlas: Executive Summary*, 9.

67. All of these points have been translated and analyzed in McCants and Brachman, *Militant Ideology Atlas: Executive Summary*.

68. Al-Suri's real name is Mustafa Setmariam Nasar; he is sometimes called Setmariam for short. The videotapes were recovered from Afghanistan in 2006, dated August 2000. See the introduction; and Cruickshank and Ali, "Abu Musab Al Suri."

69. This analysis is available at http://www.ctc.usma.edu/atlas.asp. See also Statement of Jarret Brachman before the House Armed Services Committee, Subcommittee on Terrorism, Unconventional Threats and Capabilities, Hearing on Challenges Posed to the Special Operations command by the Global Terrorist Threat, February 14, 2007.

70. http://www.tawhed.ws. This site is no longer accessible from North American IP addresses.

71. Abu Bakr Naji, *The Management of Savagery: The Most Critical Stage Through Which the Umma Will Pass*, trans. William McCants (Cambridge: John M. Olin Institute for Strategic Studies, 2006), 17, 25, http://www.ctc.usma.edu/Management_of_Savagery.pdf.

72. Naji, *The Management of Savagery*, 33.

73. Joe Klein, "Operation Last Chance," *Time*, July 9, 2007, 26–27.

74. Michael R. Gordon, "A New Alliance Tackles Insurgents in Iraq," *International Herald Tribune*, July 6, 2007, 8.

75. Lilia Khalil, "Leader of 1920 Revolution Brigades Killed by Al-Qaeda," *Terrorism Focus* (Jamestown Foundation) 4, no. 9 (April 10, 2007), accessed at http://jamestown.org/terrorism/news/article.php?articleid=2373310 on July 9, 2007.

76. MEMRI, "Large Sunni Iraqi Jihad Group Comes Out against Al-Qaeda," *Islamist Websites Monitor*, no. 85 (April 11, 2007), in *MEMRI Special Dispatch*

Series, no. 1543 (April 13, 2007), http://memri.org/bin/articles.cgi?Page=subjects &Area=jihad&ID=SP154307, accessed July 17, 2007.

77. This according to an online interview with Jordanian-Palestinian Islamist scholar and spiritual guide of Al-Tawhid wal-Jihad in Jordan and Iraq, Abu Muhammad al-Maqdesi. See Gabriel Weimann, "Virtual Disputes: The Use of the Internet for Terrorist Debates," *Studies in Conflict and Terrorism* 2 No. 7 (November 2006): 627.

78. This is wisely recommended in the Combating Terrorism Center's *Harmony and Disharmony*, 43.

79. Ibid.

80. Rightly or wrongly, public perception in many parts of the Muslim world was united as a result of the narrative of the Abu Ghraib and Guantánamo Bay prison debacles. Any benefit gained from interrogation of those prisoners has been dwarfed many times over by the propaganda coup handed to al-Qaeda.

81. There is benefit in fighting the ideas at the core of this violent movement, but our clumsy efforts to "empower moderates" often result in getting them killed. A more subtle approach of demystifying al-Qaeda, drawing attention to its ample mistakes, becoming much more familiar with internal schisms, and pointing out inconsistencies in the debates among its associates would be more effective. Compare Rabasa et al., *Beyond al-Qaeda*, especially the section "Attack the Ideology," 160–61. See also Fred Burton, "The Quiet Campaign against al Qaeda's Local Nodes," STRATFOR, June 20, 2007, who writes "It is important to remember that this is not so much a war against a group of individuals as it is a war against an ideology. The problem is, ideologies are harder to kill than people. Consider, for example, how the revolutionary ideas of Karl Marz, Vladimir Lenin and Che Guevara have outlived the men themselves." Accessed at http://www.stratfor.com/quiet_campaign_against_al_qaedas_local_nodes on 30 December 2008.

82. Zawahiri, *Knights*, 111. Zawahiri is referring to the Islamist movement in Egypt.

83. Radical splinter groups have been common in Islam, beginning with the Kharijites who assassinated Ali, the fourth caliph, in Iraq during the seventh century. There is a long tradition of messianic young men giving their lives for the sake of a more pure Islam. Robert F. Worth, "Al-Qaeda's Inner Circle," *New York Review of Books*, October 19, 2006, http://nybooks.com/articles/19433?email, accessed June 13, 2007.

84. Michael Scheuer provides a useful list of 40 groups that have announced their formation and pledged allegiance to bin Laden, al-Qaeda, and al-Qaeda's strategic objectives since January 2005. See "Al-Qaeda and Algeria's GSPC: Part of a Much Bigger Picture, *Terrorism Focus* (Jamestown Foundation) 4, no. 8 (April 3, 2007).

85. He was born 'Abd al-'Aziz b. Rashid b. Hamdan al-'Anzi, but better known as 'Abd allah b. Nasir al-Rashid. Currently in prison in Saudi Arabia, al-Rashid has been called "a central shaper of contemporary jihadi discourse." See William McCants and Jarret Brachman, *Militant Ideology Atlas: Research Compendium* (West Point, N.Y.: Combating Terrorism Center, November 2006), 54–56.

86. See Katz and Deven, "Franchising Al Qaeda."

87. Burke, "Think Again."

88. Zawahiri, *Knights*, 102–5.

89. Lawrence Wright, "The Man behind Bin Laden," *New Yorker*, September 16, 2002. See also Jarret M. Brachman and William F. McCants, "Stealing Al-Qaeda's Playbook," *Studies in Conflict and Terrorism* 29, no. 4 (June 2006): 309–21.

90. Letter from Zawahiri to Zarqawi, October 11, 2005, *His Own Words*, 268 and 271–72.

91. Ibid., 273.

92. The October 12, 2002, attacks in the entertainment district of Kuta Beach killed 202 and injured more than 300, virtually all tourists. They were orchestrated by Jemaah Islamiya, a group that is linked to al-Qaeda. A spokesman for al-Qaeda also claimed credit. See MIPT Terrorism Knowledge Base entry, at http://www.tkb.org/Incident.jsp?incID=13504, accessed June 25, 2007.

93. The Riyadh, Saudi Arabia, attacks of May 12, 2003, were four simultaneous bombings, carried out by al-Qaeda. The majority of casualties were Westerners, although there were also a large number of Arab Muslims. See MIPT Terrorism Knowledge Base entry at http://www.tkb.org/Incident.jsp?incID=20353, accessed June 25, 2007.

94. Two simultaneous bombings in were carried out by a Turkish al-Qaeda cell; 28 people were killed and 450 injured. See MIPT Terrorism Knowledge Base entry at http://www.tkb.org/Incident.jsp?incID=17488.

95. 191 were killed and more than 600 others were injured in the attacks on the Madrid transportation system. The Abu Hafs al-Masri Brigade claimed responsibility on behalf of al-Qaeda. See MIPT Terrorism Knowledge Base entry at http://www.tkb.org/Incident.jsp?incID=18518, accessed June 25, 2007.

96. See MIPT Terrorism Knowledge Base entries at http://www.tkb.org/Incident .jsp?incID=16033; and http://www.tkb.org/Incident.jsp?incID=17375, accessed June 25, 2007.

97. Those attacks also resulted in mass marches and shouts of "Burn in hell Abu Musab al-Zarqawi!" Al-Qaeda in Iraq was forced to admit that the Muslim deaths were accidental, and claimed that the group would never target innocent Muslims Their third communiqué read as follows: "As for the Muslims who were killed in this operation, we beseech Allah to have mercy on them and forgive them, and swear that they were not the [intended] target of the operation. We did not intend, and would never have intended for a moment, to harm them, even had they been infidels. This, assuming they were [really] in the area of the attack. The brothers who carried out the martyrdom operation meant to target the halls which served as meeting places for intelligence officers of several infidel Crusader countries and countries allied with them. The people [at the wedding feast] were killed because part of the ceiling collapsed from the intensity of the blast, and it is no secret that this was not intended; it was an unintended accident, which had not been taken into account." See http://www.memri.org/bin/articles.cgi?Page= subjects&Area=jihad&ID=SP104305, viewed December 16, 2008.

98. The proportion is drawn from information gathered in newspaper reports, government press statements, and other open sources. It is imprecise because we were sometimes forced to make assumptions based on a victim's home country. Most government and media organizations define victims according to their nationalities, reflecting our state-centric view of the world. But nationalities may

be less meaningful to a potential al-Qaeda constituent than a description of the number of Muslims or coreligionists dying would be. If Western governments are to develop a more effective countermobilization strategy in the Muslim world, they must take the perspective of the audience into better account. Keeping track of the number of Muslim victims could be a good place to start.

99. The battle lines on drugs in Central Asia are complex and always have been. The Northern Alliance, with which the United States allied in the fight against the Taliban after September 11, was deeply involved in the heroin trade across the 800-mile border with Tajikistan and onward to Europe. Alan Cullison and James M. Dorsey, "In Targeting Terrorists' Drug Money, U.S. Faces Dilemma—Analysts Say Taliban Foes, Likely Allies of Bush, Use Opium for Funds," *Wall Street Journal,* October 2, 2001, A16.

100. Among them is Michael Scheuer, author of the anonymous *Imperial Hubris: Why the West Is Losing the War on Terror* (Washington, D.C.: Brassey's, 2004).

101. For example, the Islamic Movement of Uzbekistan engaged in fierce fighting with the pro-Taliban tribesmen in South Waziristan, an engagement that resulted in at least 58 dead. The Uzbeks killed an Arab reportedly linked to al-Qaeda. See Arthur Bright, "Pro-Taliban Tribesmen Battle al-Qaeda-linked Militants in Pakistan," *Christian Science Monitor,* March 21, 2007.

102. According to Zawahiri, "The new crusader onslaught will not be pleased with them until they join the faith of the infidels . . . all the tricks of politics and pacification will not work. It is better for the youth of Islam to carry arms and defend their religion with pride and dignity instead of living in humiliation in the empire of the New World order." Zawahiri, *Knights,* 168.

103. As Brian Jenkins writes, "The jihadist idea of warfare emphasized process and prowess—not progress." Brian Michael Jenkins, *Unconquerable Nation: Knowing Our Enemy, Strengthening Ourselves* (Santa Monica, Calif.: RAND, 2006), 84. On pp. 74–84 he gives a detailed analysis of why al-Qaeda is process-oriented rather than progress-oriented.

CONCLUSION

1. B. H. Liddell Hart, *Strategy* (London: Faber and Faber, 1954; reprinted by Penguin Books, 1991), 322.

Selected Bibliography

Abrahms, Max. "Are Terrorists Really Rational? The Palestinian Example." *Orbis* 48, no. 3 (Summer 2004): 533–49.

———. "Al Qaeda's Scorecard: A Progress Report on Al Qaeda's Objectives." *Studies in Conflict and Terrorism* 29, no.5 (July–August 2006): 509–29.

Abuza, Zachary. "Balik-Terrorism: The Return of the Abu Sayyaf." *Strategic Studies Institute Monograph*. Carlisle: U.S. Army War College, September 2005.

Al-Awadi, Hesham. *In Pursuit of Legitimacy: The Muslim Brothers and Mubarak, 1982–2000*. London: Tauris, 2004.

Alexander, Yonah, and Dennis Pluchinsky, eds. *Europe's Red Terrorists: The Fighting Communist Organizations*. London: Frank Cass, 1992.

Allison, Graham T. *Nuclear Terrorism: The Risks and Consequences of the Ultimate Disaster*. London: Robinson, 2006.

Al-Monein Said Aly, Abd, and Manfred W. Wenner. "Modern Islamic Reform Movements: The Muslim Brotherhood in Contemporary Egypt." *Middle East Journal* 36, no. 3 (Summer 1982): 336–61.

Alonso, Rogelio. "The Modernization in Irish Republican Thinking toward the Utility of Violence." *Studies in Conflict and Terrorism* 24, no. 2 (March–April 2001): 131–44.

———. "Pathways Out of Terrorism in Northern Ireland and the Basque Country: The Misrepresentation of the Irish Model." *Terrorism and Political Violence* 16, no. 4 (Winter 2004): 695–713.

Alterman, Jon B. "How Terrorism Ends." Special Report No. 48, U.S. Institute of Peace, May 25, 1999.

Anonymous. *Through Our Enemies' Eyes: Osama bin laden, Radical Islam, and the Future of America*. Washington, D.C.: Brassey's, 2002.

Arreguín-Toft, Ivan. "How the Weak Win Wars: A Theory of Asymmetric Conflict." *International Security* 26, no. 1 (Summer 2001): 93–128.

Art, Robert J., and Louise Richardson, eds. *Democracy and Counterterrorism: Lessons from the Past*. Washington, D.C.: U.S. Institute of Peace Press, 2007.

Aust, Stefan. *The Baader-Meinhof Group: The Inside Story of a Phenomenon*. London: Anthea Bell, 1987.

Barkey, Henri, and Graham Fuller. *Turkey's Kurdish Question*. Oxford: Rowman and Littlefield , 1998.

Barrell, Howard. *The ANC's Armed Struggle*. London: Penguin, 1990.

Bazan, Elizabeth B. *Assassination Ban and E.O. 12333: A Brief Summary*. CRS Report for Congress, No. RS21037, January 4, 2002.

Beattie, Kirk J. *Egypt during the Nasser Years: Ideology, Politics, and Civil Society*. Oxford: Westview Press, 1994.

Becker, Jillian. *Hitler's Children: The Story of the Baader-Meinhof Terrorist Gang*. London: Pickwick, 1989.

Beckford, James A., Daniele Joly, and Farhad Khosrokhavar, eds. *Muslims in Prison: Challenge and Change in Britain and France*. London: Palgrave Macmillan, 2006.

Begin, Menachem. *The Revolt*. New York: Nash, 1997.

Bell, J. Bowyer, *The Dynamics of the Armed Struggle*. London: Frank Cass, 1998.

———. "Revolutionary Dynamics: The Inherent Inefficiency of the Underground." *Terrorism and Political Violence* 2, no. 2 (Summer 1990): 193–211.

———. *Terror Out of Zion: Irgun Zvai Leumi, Lehi, and the Palestine Underground, 1929–1949*. New York: Avon, 1977.

Berlin, Isaiah. *Russian Thinkers*. London: Hogarth Press, 1978.

Bjørgo, Tore, ed. *Terror from the Extreme Right*. London: Frank Cass, 1995.

Bloom, Mia. *Dying to Kill: The Allure of Suicide Terror*. New York: Columbia University Press, 2005.

———. "Palestinian Suicide Bombing: Public Support, Market Share and Outbidding." *Political Science Quarterly* 119, no. 1 (Summer 2004): 61–88.

Bobbitt, Philip. *The Shield of Achilles: War, Peace, and the Course of History*. London: Penguin, 2003.

———. *Terror and Consent*. New York: Alfred A. Knopf, 2008.

Bonanate, Luigi. "Some Unanticipated Consequences of Terrorism." *Journal of Peace Research* 16, no. 3 (1979): 197–211.

Bose, Sumantra. "Kashmir: Sources of Conflict, Dimensions of Peace." *Survival* 41, no. 3 (Autumn 1999): 149–71.

Bowden, Mark. "Jihadists in Paradise." *The Atlantic*, March 2007, 54–60.

Byman, Daniel. *Deadly Connections: States That Sponsor Terrorism*. Cambridge: Cambridge University Press, 2005.

———. "Do Targeted Killings Work?" *Foreign Affairs* 85, no. 2 (March–April 2006): 95–111.

Carr, Caleb. "Terrorism as Warfare: The Lessons of Military History." *World Policy Journal* 13, no. 4 (Winter 1996–97): 1–12.

Cirincione, Joseph, and Kathleen Newland. *Repairing the Regime: Preventing the Spread of Weapons of Mass Destruction*. London: Routledge, 2000.

Cohen, Stephen Philip. *The Idea of Pakistan*. Washington, D.C.: Brookings Institution Press, 2004.

Cordesman, Anthony H. *The Israeli-Palestinian War: Escalating to Nowhere*. Westport, Conn.: Praeger Security International, 2005.

Cornell, Svante E. "Narcotics and Armed Conflict: Interaction and Implications." *Studies in Conflict and Terrorism* 30, no. 3 (March 2007): 207–27.

Cox, Michael, Adrian Guelke, and Fiona Stephen, eds. *A Farewell to Arms?* Manchester: Manchester University Press, 2006.

Crenshaw, Martha. "How Terrorism Declines." *Terrorism and Political Violence* 3, no. 1 (Spring 1991): 69–87.

———. "The Psychology of Terrorism: An Agenda for the Twenty-first Century." *Political Psychology* 21, no. 2 (June 2000): 405–20.

———. "Terrorism and Global Security". In *Leashing the Dogs of War: Conflict Management in a Divided World*, ed. Chester A. Crocker, Fen Osler Hampson, and Pamela Aall. Washington, D.C.: U.S. Institute of Peace Press, 2007.

————. *Terrorism in Context.* University Park: Pennsylvania State University Press, 1995.

Crocker, Chester A., Fen Osler Hampson, and Pamela Aall, eds. *Grasping the Nettle: Analyzing Cases of Intractable Conflict.* Washington, D.C.: U.S. Institute of Peace Press, 2005.

Cronin, Audrey Kurth. "Behind the Curve: Globalization and International Terrorism." *International Security* 27, no. 3 (Winter 2002–3): 30–58.

————. "Cyber-mobilization: The New Levée en Masse." *Parameters* 36, no. 2 (Summer 2006): 77–87.

————. *Ending Terrorism: Lessons for Defeating al-Qaeda.* Adelphi Paper No. 394. London: Routledge for the International Institute for Strategic Studies, 2008.

————. *The "FTO List" and Congress: Sanctioning Designated Foreign Terrorist Organizations.* CRS Report for Congress, No. RL32120, October 21, 2003.

Cronin, Audrey Kurth, and James M. Ludes, eds. *Attacking Terrorism: Elements of a Grand Strategy.* Washington, D.C.: Georgetown University Press, 2004.

Darby, John, and Roger Mac Ginty, eds. *The Management of Peace Processes.* Basingstoke: Macmillan, 2000.

Davis, Paul K., and Brian Michael Jenkins. *Deterrence and Influence in Counterterrorism: A Component in the War on al Qaeda.* Santa Monica, Calif.: RAND, 2002.

Dedijer, Vladimir. *The Road to Sarajevo.* London: MacGibbon and Kee, 1967.

Della Porta, Donatella. *Social Movements, Political Violence, and the State: A Comparative Analysis of Italy and Germany.* Cambridge: Cambridge University Press, 1995.

Della Porta, Donatella, and Gian Carlo Caselli. "The History of the Red Brigades: Organisational Structures and Strategies of Action, 1970–1982." In *The Red Brigades and Left-Wing Terrorism in Italy,* ed. Raimondo Catanzaro. London: Pinter, 1991.

Demant, Peter. "Unofficial Contacts and Peacemaking: Israeli-Palestinian Dialogue, 1967–1993." In *Israel in the Nineties: Development and Conflict,* ed. Gregory S. Mahler and Frederick A. Lazin. Gainesville: University Press of Florida, 1996.

Dershowitz, Alan. *The Case for Peace: How the Arab-Israeli Conflict Can Be Resolved.* Hoboken: John Wiley, 2005.

————. *Why Terrorism Works.* New Haven: Yale University Press, 2002.

Dingley, James. "The Bombing of Omagh, 15 August 1998: The Bombers, Their Tactics, Strategy and Purpose behind the Incident." *Studies in Conflict and Terrorism* 24, no. 6 (November–December 2001): 451–65.

Dishman, Chris. "Terrorism, Crime, and Transformation." *Studies in Conflict and Terrorism* 24, no. 1 (2001): 43–58.

Edirippulige, Sisira. *Sri Lanka's Twisted Path to Peace: Domestic and International Obstacles to the Peace Process.* Pilimathalawa: Resource Manage Foundation, 2004.

Eubank, William Lee. *The Rise and Fall of Italian Terrorism.* Boulder, Colo.: Westview Press, 1987.

Evangelista, Matthew. *The Chechen Wars: Will Russia Go the Way of the Soviet Union?* Washington, D.C.: Brookings Institution, 2002.

286 • Selected Bibliography

Fair, C. Christine. "Diaspora Involvement in Insurgencies: Insights from the Khalistan and Tamil Eelam Movements." *Nationalism and Ethnic Politics* 11, no. 1 (Spring 2005): 125–56.

Farrell, William R. *Blood and Rage: The Story of the Japanese Red Army*. Lexington, Ky.: Lexington Books, 1990.

Fay, Marie-Therese, Mike Morrissey, and Marie Smyth. *Northern Ireland's Troubles: The Human Costs*. London: Pluto Press in association with The Cost of the Troubles Study, 1999.

Fenzi, Enrico. *Armi e bagagli: Un diario dalle Brigate Rosse*. Milan: Costa & Nolan, 2006.

Filler, Alfredo L. "The Abu Sayyaf Group: A Growing Menace to Civil Society." *Terrorism and Political Violence* 14, no. 4 (Winter 2002): 131–62.

Footman, David. *Red Prelude: A Life of A. I. Zhelyabov*. 2nd ed. London: Cresset Press, 1968.

Fraser, T. G. *The Arab-Israeli Conflict*. 2nd ed. Basingstoke: Palgrave Macmillan, 2004.

Freedman, Lawrence. "Prevention, not Preemption." *Washington Quarterly* 26, no. 2 (Spring 2006): 105–14.

Gambetta, Diego, ed. *Making Sense of Suicide Missions*. Oxford: Oxford University Press, 2005.

Ganguly, Rajat. "Sri Lanka's Ethnic Conflict: At a Crossroad between Peace and War." *Third World Quarterly* 25, no. 5 (2004): 903–18.

Ganguly, Sumit. "Will Kashmir Stop India's Rise?" *Foreign Affairs* 85, no. 4 (July–August 2006): 45–57.

Gerges, Fawaz A. "The Decline of Revolutionary Islam in Algeria and Egypt." *Survival* 41, no. 1 (Spring 1999): 113–25.

———. *The Far Enemy: Why Jihad Went Global*. Cambridge: Cambridge University Press, 2005.

———. *Journey of the Jihadist: Inside Muslim Militancy*. New York: Harcourt, 2006.

Germani, L. Sergio, and D. R. Kaarthikeyan, eds. *Pathways out of Terrorism and Insurgency: the Dynamics of Terrorist Violence and Peace Processes*. New Dehli: New Dawn Press Group, 2005.

Gorriti, Gustavo. "The War of the Philosopher-King." *New Republic*, June 18, 1990.

———. "What Happens When the Queen Bee Falls?" *IPI Report* 41, no. 10 (October 1991).

Greer, Steven. *Supergrasses: A Study in Anti-terrorist Law Enforcement in Northern Ireland*. Oxford: Clarendon Press, 1995.

Grob-Fitzgibbon, Benjamin. "From the Dagger to the Bomb: Karl Heinzen and the Evolution of Political Terror." *Terrorism and Political Violence* 16, no. 1 (Spring 2004): 97–115.

Gross, Michael G. "Fighting by Other Means in the Mideast: A Critical Analysis of Israel's Assassination Policy." *Political Studies* 51 (2003): 350–68.

———. "Killing Civilians Intentionally: Double Effect, Reprisal, and Necessity in the Middle East." *Political Science Quarterly* 120, no. 4 (2005–6): 555–79.

Guelke, Adrian. *The Age of Terrorism and the International Political System.* London: Tauris Academic Studies, 1995.

Guiora, Amos. "Targeted Killing as Active Self-Defense." *Case Western Reserve Journal of International Law* 36, nos. 2–3 (2004): 319–35.

Gunter, Michael M. *The Kurds and the Future of Turkey.* London: Macmillan, 1997.

Gurr, Ted Robert. *Why Men Rebel.* Princeton: Princeton University Press, 1970.

Hacker, Frederick J. *Crusaders, Criminals, Crazies: Terror and Terrorism in Our Time.* New York: Norton, 1976.

Haddad, Yvonne Yazbeck. "The Qur'anic Justification for an Islamic Revolution: The View of Sayyid Qutb." *Middle East Journal* 37, no. 1 (Winter 1983): 14–29.

Harmon, Christopher. *Terrorism Today.* London: Frank Cass, 2000.

Harvey, R. *The Fall of Apartheid: The Inside Story from Smuts to Mbeki.* Basingstoke: Palgrave, 2001.

Hayes, Bernadette C., and Ian McAllister. "Public Support for Political Violence and Paramilitarism in Northern Ireland and the Republic of Ireland." *Terrorism and Political Violence* 17, no. 4 (Autumn 2005): 599–617.

United States Congress, House, Committee on Foreign Affairs, Subcommittee on Western Hemisphere Affairs, *The Shining Path after Guzman: The Threat and the International Response.* 102nd Congress, 2nd Session, September 23, 1992. Washington, D.C.: Government Printing Office, 1992.

Hironaka, Ann. *Neverending Wars: The International Community, Weak States, and the Perpetuation of Civil War.* Cambridge: Harvard University Press, 2005.

Hitchens, Christopher. *Hostage to History: Cyprus from the Ottomans to Kissinger.* London: Verso, 1977.

Hoffman, Bruce. *Inside Terrorism.* London: Victor Gollancz, 1998
———. *Inside Terrorism.* 2nd ed. New York: Columbia University Press, 2006.

Holmes, Jennifer S. *Terrorism and Democratic Stability.* Manchester: Manchester University Press, 2001.

Hopwood, Derek. *Egypt: Politics and Society, 1945–1984.* London: Allen and Unwin, 1984.

Horchem, Hans Josef. "The Decline of the Red Army Faction." *Terrorism and Political Violence* 3, no. 2 (Summer 1991): 61–75.

Horgan, John. *The Psychology of Terrorism.* New York: Routledge, 2005.

Howard, Michael. "What's in a Name?: How to Fight Terrorism." *Foreign Affairs* 81, no. 1 (January–February 2002): 8–13.

Hughes, James. "Chechnya: The Causes of a Protracted Post-Soviet Conflict." *Civil Wars* 4, no. 4 (Winter 2001): 11–48.

Hughes, Martin. "Terror and Negotiation." *Terrorism and Political Violence* 2, no. 1 (Spring 1990): 72–82.

Idoiaga, Gorka Espiau. "The Basque Conflict: New Ideas and Prospects for Peace." Special Report No. 161, U.S. Institute of Peace, April 2006.

Iklé, Fred Charles. *Every War Must End.* 2nd ed. New York: Columbia University Press, 2005.

Imset, Ismet G. *The PKK: A Report on Separatist Violence in Turkey (1973–1992).* Istanbul: Turkish Daily News Publications, 1992.

IISS. "The Good Friday Agreement." *IISS Strategic Comment* 7, no 8 (October 2001).

Jackson, Brian A. "Technology Acquisition by Terrorist Groups: Threat Assessment Informed by Lessons from Private Sector Technology Adoption." *Studies in Conflict and Terrorism* 24, no. 3 (May 2001): 183–213.

Jackson, Jami Melissa. "The Legality of Assassination of Independent Terrorist Leaders: An Examination of National and International Implications." *North Carolina Journal of International Law and Commercial Regulation* 24 (1999): 669–97.

Jamieson, Alison. "Entry, Discipline and Exit in the Italian Red Brigades." *Terrorism and Political Violence* 2, no. 1 (Spring 1990): 1–21.

———. "Mafia and Institutional Power in Italy." *International Relations* 12, no. 1 (April 1994): 1–24.

Jenkins, Brian Michael. "Should Our Arsenal against Terrorism Include Assassination?" RAND Paper No. P-7303, January 1987.

———. *Unconquerable Nation: Knowing Our Enemy, Strengthening Ourselves.* Santa Monica, Calif.: RAND, 2006.

Jenson, Richard Bach. "Daggers, Rifles and Dynamite: Anarchist Terrorism in Nineteenth Century Europe." *Terrorism and Political Violence* 16, no. 1 (Spring 2004): 116–53.

Johns, Sheridan, and R. Hunt Davis Jr. *Mandela, Tambo, and the African National Congress: A Documentary Survey.* Oxford: Oxford University Press, 1991.

Jones, Ronald H. "Terrorist Beheadings: Cultural and Strategic Implications." Carlisle Paper, Strategic Studies Institute, U.S. Army War College, June 2005.

Juergensmeyer, Mark. *Terror in the Mind of God: The Global Rise of Religious Violence.* Berkeley and Los Angeles: University of California Press, 2000.

Kahneman, Daniel, and Amos Tversky. "Prospect Theory: An Analysis of Decision under Risk." *Econometrica* 47, no. 2 (March 1979): 263–91.

Kapil, Arun. "Algeria's Elections Show Islamist Strength." *Middle East Report*, No. 166, September–October 1990, 31–36.

Kaplan, Edward H., Alex Mintz, Shaul Mishal, and Claudio Samban. "What Happened to Suicide Bombings in Israel?" *Studies in Conflict and Terrorism* 28, no. 3 (May–June 2005): 225–35.

Kapur, S. Paul. "India and Pakistan's Unstable Peace: Why Nuclear South Asia Is Not Like Cold War Europe." *International Security* 30, no. 2 (Fall 2005): 127–52.

Kassimeris, George. "Last Act in a Violent Drama? The Trial of Greece's Revolutionary Organization 17 November." *Terrorism and Political Violence* 18, no. 1 (Spring 2006): 137–57.

Katz, Daniel. *Days of Fire.* London: W. H. Allen, 1968.

Katzman, Kenneth. *The PLO and Its Factions.* CRS Report for Congress, No. RS21235, June 10, 2002.

Kedourie, Sylvia, ed. *Seventy-five Years of the Turkish Republic.* London: Frank Cass, 2000.

Kepel, Gilles. *The Prophet and Pharaoh: Muslim Extremism in Egypt.* London: Al Saqi Books, 1985.

Kilcullen, David J. "Countering Global Insurgency." *Journal of Strategic Studies* 28, no. 4 (August 2005): 597–617.

King, Charles. *Ending Civil Wars*. Adelphi Paper No. 308. Oxford: Oxford University Press for the International Institute for Strategic Studies, 1997.

King, John. *Handshake in Washington: The Beginning of Middle East Peace?* Reading, UK: Ithaca Press, 1994.

Kirisci, Kemal, and Gareth M. Winrow. *The Kurdish Question and Turkey: An Example of a Trans-state Ethnic Conflict*. London: Frank Cass, 1997.

Kramer, Martin. "Ballots and Bullets: Islamists and the Relentless Drive for Power." *Harvard International Review* 19, no. 2 (Spring 1997): 16–19.

———. "Sacrifice and Fratricide in Shiite Lebanon." *Terrorism and Political Violence* 3, no. 3 (Autumn 1991): 30–47.

Kretzmer, David. "Targeted Killing of Suspected Terrorists: Extra-judicial Executions or Legitimate Means of Defence?" *European Journal of International Law* 16, no. 2 (2005): 171–212.

Kronstadt, K. Alan. "Pakistan-U.S. Relations." CRS Issue Brief for Congress, No. RL33498, 6 June 2007.

———. *Terrorism in South Asia*. CRS Report for Congress, No. RL32259, December 13, 2004.

Krumwiede, Heinrich W., and Peter Waldmann. *Civil Wars: Consequences and Possibilities of Regulation*. Baden-Baden: Nomos, 2000.

Kushner, Harvey. *Encyclopedia of Terrorism*. Thousand Oaks, Calif.: Sage, 2003.

Kutschera, Chris. "Mad Dreams of Independence: The Kurds of Turkey and the PKK." *Middle East Report*, No. 189, The Kurdish Experience, July–August 1994.

Kydd, Andrew H. *Trust and Mistrust in International Relations*. Princeton: Princeton University Press, 2005.

Kydd, Andrew H., and Barbara F. Walter. "Sabotaging the Peace: The Politics of Extremist Violence." *International Organization* 56, no. 2 (Spring 2002): 263–96.

———. "The Strategies of Terrorism." *International Security* 31, no. 1 (Summer 2006): 49–80.

Lane, Charles. "Superman Meets Shining Path: Story of a CIA Success." *Washington Post*, December 7, 2000.

Lapan, Harvey E., and Todd Sandler. "To Bargain or Not to Bargain: That Is the Question." *American Economic Review* 78, no. 2, (May 1988): 16–21.

Laqueur, Walter. *No End to War: Terrorism in the Twentieth Century*. New York: Continuum, 2003.

———. "Postmodern Terrorism." *Foreign Affairs* 75, no. 5 (September–October 1996): 24–36.

———. *Terrorism*. London: Weidenfeld and Nicolson, 1977.

Lesser, Ian, Bruce Hoffman, John Arquilla, David Ronfeldt, Michele Zanini, and Brian Michael Jenkins. *Countering the New Terrorism*. Santa Monica, Calif.: Rand Corporation, 1999.

Levi, Michael A., and Michael O'Hanlon. *The Future of Arms Control*. New York: Brookings Institution, 2005.

Levy, Jack S. "Domestic Politics and War." *Journal of Interdisciplinary History* 18, no. 4 (Spring 1988): 653–73.

Licklider, Roy, ed. *Stopping the Killing: How Civil Wars End*. New York: New York University Press, 1993.

Lieberfeld, Daniel. "Post-handshake Politics: Israel/Palestine and South Africa Compared." *Middle East Policy* 6, no. 3 (February 1999): 131–40.

———. *Talking with the Enemy: Negotiation and Threat Perception in South Africa and Israel/Palestine*. Westport: Praeger, 1999.

Lieven, Anatol. *Chechnya: Tombstone of Russian* Power. New Haven: Yale University Press, 1998.

Lifton, Robert Jay. *Destroying the World to Save It: Aum Shinrikyo, Apocalyptic Violence, and the New Global Terrorism*. New York: Henry Holt, 1999.

Lopez-Alves, Fernando. "Political Crises, Strategic Choices and Terrorism: The Rise and Fall of the Uruguayan Tupamaros." *Terrorism and Political Violence* 1, no. 2 (April 1989): 202–41.

Lupsha, Peter A. "Explanation of Political Violence: Some Psychological Theories versus Indignation." *Politics and Society* 2, no. 1 (Fall 1971): 89–104.

MacDonald, Scott B., and Jonathan Lemco. "Political Islam in Southeast Asia." *Current History* 100, no. 658 (November 2002): 388–92.

Malik, Omar. *Enough of the Definition of Terrorism*. London: Royal Institute of International Affairs, 2001.

Malvesti, Michelle L. "Explaining the United States' Decision to Strike Back at Terrorists." *Terrorism and Political Violence* 13, no. 2 (Summer 2001): 85–106.

Marighella, Carlos. *Minimanual of the Urban Guerrilla*. Harmondsworth: Penguin, 1971.

Marks, Thomas A. *Maoist Insurgency since Vietnam*. London: Frank Cass, 1996.

———. "A Model Counterinsurgency: Uribe's Colombia (2002–2006) vs. FARC." *Military Review* 87 (March–April 2007): 41–56.

McCormick, Gordon. *The Shining Path and the Future of Peru*. Santa Monica, Calif.: RAND, March 1990.

McGartland, Martin. *Fifty Dead Men Walking*. London: Blake, 1997.

McGregor, Andrew. "Russia Threatens Hit-Squads after Murder of Its Diplomats in Iraq." *Terrorism Monitor* 4, no. 14 (July 13, 2006): 6–8.

McKinley, D. T. *The ANC and the Liberation Struggle: A Critical Political Biography*. London: Pluto Press, 1997.

McKittrick, David, Seamus Kelters, Brian Feeney, and Chris Thornton. *Lost Lives: The Stories of the Men, Women, and Children Who Died as a Result of the Northern Ireland Troubles*. Edinburgh: Mainstream Press, 2001.

Meade, Robert C. *The Red Brigades: The Story of Italian Terrorism*. Basingstoke: Macmillan, 1990.

Migdalovitz, Carol. *Israeli-Arab Negotiations: Background, Conflicts, and U.S. Policy*. CRS Report for Congress, No. RL 33530, April 10, 2007.

Miller, Abraham H. *Terrorism and Hostage Negotiations*. Boulder, Colo.: Westview Press, 1980.

Mirbagheri, Farid. *Cyprus and International Peacemaking*. London: Hurst and Company, 1998.

Mitchell, Richard P. *The Society of the Muslim Brothers*. Oxford: Oxford University Press, 1993.

Morag, Nadav. "Measuring Success in Coping with Terrorism: The Israeli Case." *Studies in Conflict and Terrorism* 28, no. 4 (July–August 2005): 307–20.

Moretti, Mario. *Brigate Rosse: Una storia italiana*. Milan: Baldini & Castoldi, 2000.

Morris, Benny. *Righteous Victims: A History of the Zionist-Arab Conflict, 1881–2001*. New York: Alfred A. Knopf, 1999.

Moss, Walter G. *Alexander II and His Times: A Narrative History of Russia in the Age of Alexander II, Tolstoy, and Dostoevsky*. London: Anthem Press, 2002.

Mueller, John. "Six Rather Unusual Propositions about Terrorism" and "Response." *Terrorism and Political Violence* 17, no. 4 (Autumn 2005): 487–505.

Myers, Kevin. "The Terrorist as Statesman." *National Interest* 75 (Spring 2004): 139–43.

Neumann, Peter. "Negotiating with Terrorists." *Foreign Affairs* 86, no. 1 (January–February 2007): 128–38.

Nichol, Jim. *Chechnya Conflict: Recent Developments*. CRS Report for Congress, No. RL30389, March 1, 1996.

———. *Russia's Chechnya Conflict: An Update*. CRS Report for Congress, No. RL31620, April 16, 2003.

Niksch, Larry. *Abu Sayyaf: Target of Philippine-U.S. Antiterrorism Cooperation*. CRS Report for Congress, No. RL31265, April 8, 2003.

Nubin, Walter, ed. *Sri Lanka: Current Issues and Historical Background*. New York: Nova Science Publishers, 2002.

O'Brien, Brendan. *The Long War: The IRA and Sinn Féin from Armed Struggle to Peace Talks*. Dublin: O'Brien Press, 1995.

O'Callaghan, Sean. *The Informer: The Real Life Story of One Man's War against Terrorism*. New York: Bantam Press, 1998.

O'Cleary, Conor. "Washington's Green House." *Prospect*, no. 2., November 1995.

O'Leary, Brendan. "The Conservative Stewardship of Northern Ireland, 1979–97: Sound-Bottomed Contradictions or Slow Learning?" *Political Studies* 45 (1997): 671–73.

O'Neill, Bard E. *Insurgency and Terrorism: Inside Modern Revolutionary Warfare*. Washington, D.C.: Brassey's, 1990.

Oliker, Olga. *Russia's Chechen Wars 1994–2000: Lessons from Urban Combat*. Santa Monica, Calif.: RAND, 2001.

Ortiz, Román D. "Insurgent Strategies in the Post–Cold War: The Case of the Revolutionary Armed Forces of Colombia." *Studies in Conflict and Terrorism* 25, no. 2, (March–April 2002): 127–43.

Palmer, David Scott, ed. *Shining Path of Peru*. 2nd ed. New York: St. Martin's Press, 1994.

Pape, Robert A. *Dying to Win: The Strategic Logic of Suicide Terrorism*. New York: Random House, 2005.

Parezanin, Ratko. *Mlada Bosna I prvi svetski rat* (Young Bosnia and the First World War). Munich: Iskra, 1974.

Peres, Shimon, and Robert Littell. *For the Future of Israel*. Baltimore: Johns Hopkins University Press, 1998.

Pickard, Daniel B. "Legalizing Assassination? Terrorism, the Central Intelligence Agency, and International Law." *Georgia Journal of International and Comparative Law* 30, no. 1 (2001): 1–35.

Pillar, Paul R. *Terrorism and U.S. Foreign Policy*. Washington, D.C.: Brookings Institution, 2001.

Pilloni, John R. "Burning Corpses in the Streets: Russia's Doctrinal Flaws in the 1995 Fight for Grozny." *Journal of Slavic Military Studies* 13, no. 2 (June 2000): 39–66.

Pipes, Richard. *Russia under the Old Regime*. 2nd ed. London: Penguin, 1993.

Pluchinsky, Dennis A. "Germany's Red Army Faction: An Obituary." *Studies in Conflict and Terrorism* 16, no. 2 (April–June 1993): 135–57.

———. "Terrorism in the Former Soviet Union: A Primer, a Puzzle, a Prognosis." *Studies in Conflict and Terrorism* 21 (1998): 119–47.

Post, Jerrold M., ed. *Leaders and Their Followers in a Dangerous World*. Ithaca, N.Y.: Cornell University Press, 2004.

Quandt, William. *Between Ballots and Bullets: Algeria's Transition from Authoritarianism*. Washington, D.C.: Brookings Institution, 1998.

Quinlan, Michael. "How Robust Is India-Pakistan Deterrence?" *Survival* 42, no. 4 (Winter 2000–2001): 141–54.

———. "India-Pakistan Deterrence Revisited." *Survival* 47, no. 3 (Autumn 2005): 109–19.

Radu, Michael. "The Land of Many Crossroads: The Rise and Fall of the PKK." *Orbis* 45, no. 1 (Winter 2001): 47–64.

Radzinsky, Edvard. *Alexander II: The Last Great Tsar*. New York: Free Press, 2005.

Rapoport, David C. "Fear and Trembling: Terrorism in Three Religious Traditions." *American Political Science Review* 78 (April 1984): 658–77.

———. "The Fourth Wave: September 11 in the History of Terrorism." *Current History* 100, no. 650 (December 2001): 419–24.

———, ed. *Inside Terrorist Organizations*. London: Frank Cass, 2001.

Rashid, Ahmed. *Descent into Chaos: The United States and the Failure of Nation Building in Pakistan, Afghanistan, and Central Asia*. New York: Viking, 2008.

Raufer, Xavier. "The Red Brigades: Farewell to Arms." *Studies in Conflict and Terrorism* 16, no. 4 (October–December 1993).

Record, Jeffrey. "Why the Strong Lose." *Parameters* 35 (Winter 2005–6): 16–31.

Reddy, L. R. *Sri Lanka: Past and Present*. New Delhi: APH Press, 2003.

Reed, Charles, and David Ryall, eds. *The Price of Peace: Just War in the Twenty-first Century*. Cambridge: Cambridge University Press, 2007.

Reeve, Simon. *One Day in September: The Story of the 1972 Munich Olympics Massacre, a Government Cover-up, and a Covert Revenge Mission*. London: Faber, 2000.

Reich, Walter, ed. *Origins of Terrorism: Psychologies, Ideologies, Theologies, States of Mind*. Washington, D.C.: Woodrow Wilson Center Press, 1990.

Richardson, Louise. *What Terrorists Want*. London: John Murray, 2006.

Ritchken, Edwin. *"The Meaning of Rural Political Violence."* Seminar paper, University of the Witwatersrand, Johannesburg, June 29, 1989.

Roberts, Adam. "The 'War on Terror' in Historical Perspective." *Survival* 47, no. 2 (Summer 2005): 101–30.

Roberts, Hugh. "Algeria's Ruinous Impasse and the Honourable Way Out." *International Affairs* 71, no. 2 (April 1995): 247–67.

Robins, Philip. *Suits and Uniforms: Turkish Foreign Policy since the Cold War.* London: Hurst, 2003.

Rogers, Steven. "Beyond the Abu Sayyaf: The Lessons of Failure in the Philippines." *Foreign Affairs* 83, no.1 (January–February 2004): 14–20.

Rogger, Hans. *Russia in the Age of Modernisation and Revolution, 1881–1917.* London: Longman, 1983.

Ross, Dennis. *The Missing Peace: The Inside Story of the Fight for Middle East Peace.* New York: Farrar, Straus and Giroux, 2004.

Ross, Jeffrey Ian, and Ted Robert Gurr. "Why Terrorism Subsides: A Comparative Study of Canada and the United States." *Comparative Politics* 21, no. 4 (July 1989): 405–26.

Rowan, Brian. *Behind the Lines: The Story of the IRA and Loyalist Ceasefires.* Belfast: Blackstaff Press, 1995.

Rubin, Barry. *Islamic Fundamentalism in Egyptian Politics.* London: Palgrave Macmillan, 1990.

Ryan, Stephen. "Conflict Management and Conflict Resolution." *Terrorism and Political Violence* 2, no. 1 (Spring 1990): 54–71.

Sageman, Marc. *Understanding Terror Networks.* Philadelphia: University of Pennsylvania, 2004.

Sanderson, Thomas M. "Transnational Terror and Organized Crime: Blurring the Lines." *SAIS Review* 24, no. 1 (Winter–Spring 2004): 49–61.

Sandler, Todd, and John L. Scott. "Terrorist Success in Hostage-Taking Incidents: An Empirical Study." *Journal of Conflict Resolution* 31, no. 1 (March 1987): 35–53.

Saunders, David. *Russia in the Age of Reaction and Reform, 1801–1881.* London: Longman, 1992.

Scheuer, Michael. "Toronto, London and the Jihadi Spring: Bin Laden as a Successful Instigator." *Terrorism Focus* 3, no. 22 (June 6, 2006): 6–8.

Schofield, Victoria. *Kashmir in Conflict: India, Pakistan, and the Unending War.* London: Tauris, 2003.

Sederberg, Peter. "Conciliation as Counter-terrorist Strategy." *Journal of Peace Research* 32, no. 3 (August 1995): 295–312.

Sedgwick, Mark. *Against the Modern World: Traditionalism and the Secret Intellectual History of the Twentieth Century.* Oxford: Oxford University Press, 2004.

Seth, Ronald. *The Russian Terrorists: The Story of the Narodniki.* London: Barrie and Rockliff, 1966.

Seton-Watson, Hugh. *The Decline of Imperial Russia, 1855–1914.* London: Methuen, 1952.

Shalev, Aryeh. *The Intifada: Causes and Effects.* Oxford: Westview Press, 1999.

Sheffer, Gabriel. "Ethno-National Diasporas and Security." *Survival* 36, no. 1 (Spring 1994): 60–79.

Shepard, William E. *Sayyid Qutb and Islamic Activism: A Translation and Critical Analysis of Social Justice in Islam.* New York: E. J. Brill, 1996.

Shifter, Michael. "The United States and Colombia: Partners in Ambiguity." *Current History* 99, no. 634 (February 2000): 51–55.

Smyth, Marie. "The Process of Demilitarization and the Reversibility of the Peace Process in Northern Ireland." *Terrorism and Political Violence* 16, no. 3 (August 2004): 544–66.

Sprinzak, Ehud. "The Process of Delegitimation: Towards a Linkage Theory of Political Terrorism." *Terrorism and Political Violence* 3, no. 1 (Spring 1991): 50–68.

———. "Right-Wing Terrorism in a Comparative Perspective: The Case of Split Delegitimization." *Terrorism and Political Violence* 7, no. 1 (March 1995): 96–118.

Stack-O'Connor, Alisa. "Lions, Tigers, and Freedom Birds: How and Why the Liberation Tigers of Tamil Eelam Employs Women." *Terrorism and Political Violence* 19, no.1 (March 2007) p. 43–63.

Stedman, Stephen John. "Spoiler Problems in Peace Processes." *International Security* 22, no. 2 (Autumn, 1997): 5–53.

Stein, Yael. "By Any Name Illegal and Immoral: Response to Israel's Policy of Targeted Killing." *Ethics and International Affairs* 17, no. 1 (Spring 2003): 127–37.

Steinhoff, Patricia G. "Kidnapped Japanese in North Korea: The New Left Connection." *Journal of Japanese Studies* 30, no. 1 (Winter 2004): 123–42.

Stepniak-Kravchinski, Serge. *Underground Russia: Revolutionary Profiles and Sketches from Life*. London: Smith, Elder, 1883.

Stern, Peter A. *Sendero Luminoso: An Annotated Bibliography of the Shining Path Guerrilla Movement, 1980–1993*. N.p.: SALALM Secretariat, General Library, University of New Mexico, 1995.

Stone, Martin. *The Agony of Algeria*. London: Hurst, 1997.

Strachan, Hew. *The First World War*. London: Penguin, 2003.

Sullivan, Mark P. *Latin America: Terrorism Issues*. CRS Report for Congress, No. RS21049, September 16, 2006.

Tarazona-Sevillano, Gabriela, with John B. Reuter. *Sendero Luminoso and the Threat of Narcoterrorism*. Washington, D.C.: Center for Strategic and International Studies, 1990.

Tessler, Mark A. *A History of the Israeli-Palestinian Conflict*. Bloomington: Indiana University Press, 1994.

Thatcher, Margaret. *The Downing Street Years*. London: HarperCollins, 1995.

Tonge, Jonathan. "'They Haven't Gone Away, You Know': Irish Republican 'Dissidents' and 'Armed Struggle.'" *Terrorism and Political Violence* 16, no. 3 (Autumn 2004): 671–93.

Trenin, Dmitri V. "The Forgotten War: Chechnya and Russia's Future." Policy Brief No. 28, Carnegie Endowment for International Peace, November 2003, 1–7.

Truth and Reconciliation Commission of Peru. *Final Report: General Conclusions*. English translation by International Center for Transitional Justice, 2003, http://216.70.99.144/images/uploads/peru_trc_conclusions.pdf, accessed July 12, 2007.

Tucker, David. *Skirmishes at the Edge of Empire: The United States and International Terrorism*. Westport, Conn.: Praeger, 1997.

———. "What Is New about the New Terrorism and How Dangerous Is It?" *Political Violence and Terrorism* 13, no. 3 (Summer 2001): 1–14.

Ulam, Adam. *Russia's Failed Revolutions: From the Decembrists to the Dissidents*. London: Weidenfeld and Nicolson, 1981.

Varon, Jeremy. *Bringing the War Home: The Weather Underground, the Red Army Faction, and Revolutionary Violence in the Sixties and Seventies*. Berkeley and Los Angeles: University of California Press, 2004.

Veillette, Connie. *Colombia: Issues for Congress*. CRS Report for Congress, No. RL32250, January 19, 2005.

Victor, Barbara. *Army of Roses: Inside the World of Palestinian Women Suicide Bombers*. Emmaus, Pa.: Radale, 2003.

Voll, John O. "Bin Laden and the New Age of Global Terrorism." *Middle East Policy* 8, no. 4 (December 2001): 1–5.

Walsh, John. "Egypt's Muslim Brotherhood: Understanding Centrist Islam." *Harvard International Review* 24, no. 4 (Winter 2003): 32–36.

Walter, Barbara. *Committing to Peace: The Successful Settlement of Civil Wars*. Princeton: Princeton University Press, 2002.

Waltzer, Michael. *Arguing about War*. New Haven: Yale University Press, 2004.

Waterbury, John. *The Egypt of Nasser and Sadat*. Princeton: Princeton University Press, 1983.

Wheeler, Everett L. "Terrorism and Military Theory: An Historical Perspective." In *Terrorism Research and Public Policy*, ed. Clark McCauley. Abingdon: Frank Cass, 1991.

Wickham, Carrie Rosefsky. *Mobilizing Islam: Religion, Activism, and Political Change in Egypt*. New York: Colombia University Press, 2002.

Wickramasinghe, Nira. *Sri Lanka in the Modern Age: A History of Contested Identities*. London: Hurst, 2006.

Wiktorowicz, Quintan. "Framing Jihad: Intramovement Framing Contests and al-Qaeda's Struggle for Sacred Authority." *International Review of Social History* 49, Supplement 12 (December 2004): 159–77.

———. *Islamic Activism: A Social Movement Theory Approach*. Bloomington: Indiana University Press, 2003.

———. *Radical Islam Rising: Muslim Extremism in the West*. New York: Rowman and Littlefield, 2005.

Wilkinson, Paul. "Politics, Diplomacy and Peace Processes: Pathways out of Terrorism?" *Terrorism and Political Violence* 11, no. 4 (Winter 1999): 66–82.

———. *Terrorism and the Liberal State*. 2nd ed. London: Macmillan, 1986.

———. *Terrorism versus Democracy: The Liberal State Response*. London: Frank Cass, 2001.

Williams, Phil. "Transnational Criminal Organizations and International Security." *Survival* 36, no. 1 (1994): 96–113.

Williamson, Samuel R. *Austria-Hungary and the Origins of the First World War*. London: Palgrave Macmillan, 1991.

Willis, Michael. *The Islamist Challenge in Algeria*. London: Ithaca Press, 1996.

Worden, N. *A Concise Dictionary of South African History*. Cape Town: Francolin, 1998.

Wright, Lawrence. *The Looming Tower: Al-Qaeda and the Road to 9/11*. New York: Knopf, 2006.

Yarmolisky, Avrahm. *Road to Revolution: A Century of Russian Radicalism*. New York: Macmillan, 1959.

Zadka, Saul. *Blood in Zion: How the Jewish Guerrillas Drove the British out of Palestine*. London: Brassey's, 1995.

Zartman, I. William. *Ripe for Resolution: Conflict and Intervention in Africa*. New York: Oxford University Press, 1985.

———, ed. *Elusive Peace: Negotiating an End to Civil Wars*. Washington, D.C.: Brookings Institution, 1995.

———, ed. *The 50 Percent Solution*. New Haven: Yale University Press, 1983.

Zirakzadeh, Cyrus Ernesto. "From Revolutionary Dreams to Organizational Fragmentation: Disputes over Violence within ETA and Sendero Luminoso." *Terrorism and Political Violence* 14, no. 4 (Winter 2002): 66–92.

Zussman, Asaf, and Noam Zussman. "Assassinations: Evaluating the Effectiveness of a Counterterrorism Policy Using Stock Market Data." *Journal of Economic Perspectives* 20, no. 2 (Spring 2006): 193–206.

Index

'Abd al-Hadi, Ibrahim, 138–39
Abdallah, Georges Ibrahim, 18
Abdel-Halim, Shayma, 189
Abrahms, Max, 245n.17
Abu Daoud, 4
Abu Ghraib, 280n.80
Abu Hafs al-Masri Brigade, 281n.95
Abu Nidal Organization (ANO), 106, 111, 254n.52
Abu Nidal (Sabri al-Banna), 100
Abu Sayyaf ("Bearer of the Sword"): al-Qaeda, connection to, 153, 170, 187; criminality, shift to, 146, 152–53; decapitation, impact of, 27–28, 33; Moro Islamic Liberation Front, ties with, 268–69n.28; step-up in violence after a setback, 79
Action Directe, 31, 81, 98, 108, 230n.74
Adair, Johnny, 234n.40
Adams, Gerry, 44–46, 234n.42, 255n.63
African National Congress (ANC): Harare declaration of 1989, 232n.21, 241n.128; Irgun Zvai Leumi, links to, 247n.50–51; Irish republicanism, parallels to, 48; South African Communist Party, links to, 86, 91, 247n.50; successful terrorism by, 85–89, 92
Ahmad as-Salim, Muhammad bin, 173
Akashi, Yassushi, 242n.143
al-Albani, Shaikh, 184, 279n.65
Aleph. See Aum Shinrikyo
Alexander II (tsar of Russia), 123–24, 158, 259n.36
Alexander III (tsar of Russia), 124–25
Al-Gashey, Adnan, 229n.58
Al-Gashey, Jamal, 229n.58
Algeria: brutal crackdown by new post-colonial regime in, 116; democratic institutions undermined by terrorism in, 81; Front de Libération Nationale in, 15, 81, 89, 118, 155–56; Front Islamique de Salut in, 155–57, 270n.45–46, 270n.48; Groupe Islamique Armé (Armed Islamic Group; GIA) in, 100, 119, 156–57, 251n.27, 254n.52, 270–71n.53; Groupe

Salafiste pour la Prédication et le Combat in, 157, 170; guerrilla warfare against the French in, 92
Al-Jaysh Al-Islami, 186
Allah's Brigade, 187
al-Qaeda, 12–13, 167–68; Abu Sayyaf and, 153, 170, 187; Colombia, claims regarding infiltration of, 151; decapitation as a strategy against, 177–79, 274–75n.12; decline and demise of, 193–96; failure through diminishing popular support, potential for, 187–90; failure through implosion, potential for, 183–86; financial resources of, 174–75, 254n.52; Groupe Salafiste pour la Prédication et le Combat, alliance with, 157; the history of terrorism and the end of, 1–3; labeling, significance of, 148; longevity of, Western expectations regarding, 76; means of communication of, 175–77; mobilization strategy of, religious militants and, 119; the Muslim Brotherhood and, 137, 141; nationalist motives of, 244n.15; negotiations with, 179–82, 278n.57; "qaeda," meaning of, 274n.6; radicalization and recruitment, methods of, 171–74; reorientation of, 191–93; repression as a strategy against, 190–91; resilient structure of, 169–71; success of, potential for, 182; uniqueness of, question of, 168–69. See also Islamist terrorist groups
al-Qaeda in Iraq, 186, 189–90, 281n.97
Al-Qaeda Maghreb Commandment, 187
Al-Qaeda Organization in the Islamic Maghreb, 271n.58
Al-Suri, Abu Musab (Mustafa Setmariam Nasar), 141, 184, 265–66n.111, 279n.68
Amir, Yigal, 25, 52, 237n.81
amnesties, 103–4, 186, 253n.43
Amnesty International, 131
Amoss, Ulius Louis, 251n.18
ANC. See African National Congress
Andang, Ghalib, 27
Andersontown News, 46